CREATIVE INDUSTRIES IN CANADA

CREATIVE INDUSTRIES IN CANADA

Edited by Cheryl Thompson and Miranda Campbell

CANADIAN SCHOLARS

Toronto | Vancouver

Creative Industries in Canada
Edited by Cheryl Thompson and Miranda Campbell

First published in 2022 by
Canadian Scholars, an imprint of CSP Books Inc.
425 Adelaide Street West, Suite 200
Toronto, Ontario
M5V 3C1

www.canadianscholars.ca

Library and Archives Canada Cataloguing in Publication

Title: Creative industries in Canada / edited by Cheryl Thompson and Miranda Campbell.
Names: Thompson, Cheryl, 1977- editor. | Campbell, Miranda, 1981- editor.
Description: Includes bibliographical references.
Identifiers: Canadiana (print) 20220232032 | Canadiana (ebook) 20220232075 |
    ISBN 9781773383132 (softcover) | ISBN 9781773383149 (PDF) |
    ISBN 9781773383156 (EPUB)
Subjects: LCSH: Cultural industries—Canada.
Classification: LCC HD9999.C9473 C3 2022 | DDC 338.4/770971—dc23

Page layout by S4Carlisle Publishing Services
Cover design by Rafael Chimicatti
Cover art by Adobe Stock/garrykillian

21   22   23   24   25   5   4   3   2   1

Printed and bound in Ontario, Canada

Canadä

Contents

PART I   PRODUCTION: MEANING MAKING IN THE CREATIVE INDUSTRIES

PART II   PARTICIPATION: WORKING AND COMMUNITY BUILDING IN THE CREATIVE INDUSTRIES

PART III PEDAGOGIES: TEACHING AND LEARNING THROUGH THE CREATIVE INDUSTRIES

Acknowledgements

We would like to thank our fellow faculty and staff at The Creative School at Toronto Metropolitan University. This book reflects our shared pursuit to broaden and expand the field of creative industries in Canada. We would also like to acknowledge our students, who inspired us to write this book.

INTRODUCTION

Cheryl Thompson and Miranda Campbell

DEFINING THE CREATIVE INDUSTRIES

This book grew out of our teaching and research in the School of Creative Industries (CI) at Toronto Metropolitan University, the first undergraduate program in Canada to explicitly focus on the creative industries. Even though the school is named "creative industries," we both had to evolve in our understanding of its numerous meanings. When Cheryl was faculty in CI, with her background in communication and culture, the term *cultural* industries was familiar but *creative* industries was not. Investigating the question of "why do the cultural industries matter?," cultural industries scholar David Hesmondhalgh asserts that "[they] are involved in the making and circulating of products that, more than the products of any other kind of industry, have an influence on our understanding and knowledge of the world" (7). The cultural/creative industries are embedded in and produce particular economic, social, and political relations, impacting structural dynamics of race, gender, sexuality, and power, including what is visible and valorized in society. These industries also impact modes of participation in the workforce and in communities, influencing how we labour and how we form belonging and connection. The creative industries have implications for what we teach and learn—both in the classroom, as the creative industries increasingly become a field of post-secondary study and training, and through the media, as the creative industries reflect and shape views of ourselves and the world. With this expansive definition of production, participation, and pedagogies in mind, it was not until Cheryl was teaching the introductory course in the program, CRI100: Creative Industries Overview, that the concept of the creative industries became clearer, though it remains a loosely defined field of study.

For four years, the textbook *Key Concepts in Creative Industries*, written by John Hartley, Jason Potts, Stuart Cunningham, Terry Flew, Michael Keane, and John Banks (hereinafter Hartley et al.), was required reading in the course. For over 20 years, these scholars, who are based in the United Kingdom and Australia, have been at the forefront of not only defining creative industries scholarship but also making sense of its productions, practices, and pedagogies. Hartley et al. pinpoint the 1990s as the starting point for the term *creative industries* being used in policy and industry forums. Specifically, in 1997, the new United Kingdom Labour government, through minister Chris Smith and the Department of Culture, Media and Sport (DCMS), launched the Creative Industries Taskforce, which published the *Creative Industries Mapping Document* that was used to establish what they call a foundational definition. This document defined the creative industries as "those industries which have their origin in individual creativity, skill and talent which have a potential for job and wealth creation through the generation and exploitation of intellectual property." Hartley et al. state further that the term "brings together in a provisional convergence a range of sectors which have not typically been linked with each other" (59). These sectors include the visual and performing arts, traditional broadcast media, new media, architecture and design, as well as information and communication technologies (ICTs). Advertising, fashion, marketing, and graphic design are sometimes also included in this definition.

While there is nothing inherently problematic with defining the creative industries this way—in that this conceptualization acknowledges that the field has, from the start, reflected some combination of locally based, non-commercial, culturally specific creative production and globally circulated, commercially driven (and often content-based) products—in writing this book, we felt it would answer a gap in the literature not only related to non-commercial, culturally specific cases studies but also Canada-specific policy and industry analyses. Our examination of Canada's creative industries reflects both the commercial and non-commercial; locally based and globally circulated; culturally specific and generically creative (i.e., mass produced versus craft produced). Much of the research literature and discussions in the creative industries have emphasized large-scale, corporate players in the field. In our book, we expand this overarching economic focus and reposition the field to better capture a more diverse array of art forms and cultural producers in the creative industries ecosystem. Across the chapters in this book, we explore major Canadian cultural and creative industries institutions, such as the Royal Ontario Museum, the Just for Laughs Festival, Rogers Media, the CBC, Ubisoft, BIPOC TV & Film, the Canada Media Fund, and the Truth and Reconciliation Commission's call to action to educate media professionals on

Indigenous history and rights. We also unpack how these industries, spaces, and festivals are experienced by workers and participants, as well as what other cultural forms exist alongside the larger-scale players. As such, in *Creative Industries in Canada*, we examine the articulation of economic, social, and cultural values in the Canadian creative industries.

Importantly, Cheryl's moment of reflection happened almost immediately after adopting the Hartley et al. text for CRI100. How can you teach an introductory course in Canada to majority Canadian students while relying almost exclusively on course content from British, Australian, and American scholars? This realization put into clear focus the need to write a book about Canada's creative industries. Miranda has also had teaching experiences engaging with undergraduate students about what the creative industries are, how they are defined, and having this understanding "click." One class that Miranda teaches in creative industries is called the "Creative Industries International Lab," taking students abroad to Berlin, Germany to learn about social inclusion and societal betterment through the creative industries. The course is run through two weeks of site visits, taking students to grassroots organizations and institutions to talk with founders and managers about how they pursue socially engaged creative industries work, creating inclusive spaces for more people to engage in culture, alongside making a living and employing themselves and others. In Berlin, available space and infrastructure for socially engaged creative industries pursuits has been shaped by a particular history and context, including World War II, the Cold War, and the fall of the Berlin Wall. However, this course seeks to inspire students to undertake creative industries pursuits that span social, economic, and cultural values in their local environments, in their own communities, contexts, and histories, rather than suggest this is only possible in one time or place, like post–Cold War Berlin.

Responding to the course, one student wrote that "it opened my mind to so many more career possibilities and opportunities and made me more excited to one day work in creative fields. There seemed to be less barriers between various creative industries and more creative and cultural overlap. This also inspired me in a different way than I have been in the past and taught me to think differently and more openly about my own creative pursuits." How can we also foster this knowledge and awareness about the potentials of the creative industries, in our local places and spaces, without the need to travel abroad? These forms of socially engaged creative industries pursuits, geared to social change and expanding the participation of creators and participants, also exist in local Canadian contexts, but they are often less visible in a neoliberal environment where economic values dominate and where global products often take centre stage. From podcasting to screendance, stand-up comedy, creative hubs, and more, *Creative Industries in Canada* responds to this question, shining a light on Canadian creative industries that offer inroads for social inclusion and engagement, exploring both challenges and opportunities.

The history of Canadian cultural policy has been well traced, often identifying the landmark role of the Royal Commission on National Development in the Arts, Letters and Sciences, commonly known as the Massey-Lévesque Commission. This large-scale inventory, which began in 1949 and released its report in 1951, sought to protect, nurture, and sustain Canadian culture from the influence and expansion of American creative industries, and it gave birth to some of Canada's foremost national cultural institutions, like the National Library of Canada (1953), the Canada Council (1957), the Canadian Film Development Corporation (1968), the Department of Communications (1969), and the Canadian Radio and Television Commission (1969).[1] More than 70 years later, we need a major refresh and reset on which institutions are galvanizing the Canadian creative industries. We can turn to and include the role of digital spaces for cultural production, without casting the digital landscape as a utopia or barrier-free economic launchpad. Though Canada's existing arts and culture funding is sometimes favourably compared to that in other countries', particularly to that in the United States, continued challenges and gaps exist, especially for supporting diverse, emerging, interdisciplinary creative work that pushes and expands traditional silos and funding categories of art and culture.

While Cheryl's first book, *Beauty in a Box: Detangling the Roots of Canada's Black Beauty Culture*, established a historical timeline for the growth and development of Black beauty culture in Canada, it validated the contributions of Black Canadians to local media and performance industries, such as through newspapers, television, and theatre. It also pinpointed how legislative changes beginning in the 1960s provided an apparatus for Black and other racialized Canadians to challenge racism and/or acts of exclusion. Ontario's Human Rights Code (1962) came first; it was followed by the Nova Scotia Human Rights Act (1963), and then other human rights legislation passed across the country—in Alberta (1966), New Brunswick (1967), Prince Edward Island (1968), British Columbia (1969), Newfoundland (1969), Manitoba (1970), and Quebec (1975). These legislative gains are often celebrated, alongside the *Multiculturalism Act* (1988); however, the growing fields of Black Canadian studies, Indigenous studies, disability studies, women's and gender studies, among others, remind us of the need to have new conversations about dominant narratives in Canada related not singularly to race, gender, disability, or sexuality but also to how we think of, and establish, communities.[2]

With this context in mind, *Creative Industries in Canada* offers a broad snapshot of contemporary cultural production in Canada from a creative industries perspective, but it is beyond our scope to cover all creative industries disciplines or to encompass the range of locations that would be representative of Canadian experiences from coast to coast to coast. As such, we encourage further exploration of creative industries in Canada with expanded locations, disciplines, and communities. For example, we are keen to hear how spaces and places have incubated economic, social, and cultural values for decades, like the Dorset Fine Arts cooperative in Kinngait, Nunavut; the Royal Art Lodge in Winnipeg, Manitoba; the Dawson City Music Festival in Yukon; or the Ceilidh Trail in Cape Breton. And what about contemporary collectives like the Black Artists Union, Bricks and Glitter, the Lotus Collective, BIPOC TV & Film, Tea Base, and so many more? With *Creative Industries in Canada*, we aim to spark conversations that shift what is visible *as* Canadian creative industries and galvanize further research and writing. We take a broad approach to research and analysis, allowing for an expansion of hegemonic norms that have marginalized creators and cultural production from underrepresented communities. This expanded focus of what constitutes the creative industries in Canada allows for a wider, more equitable, and ultimately more vibrant and visionary picture of the creative industries landscape.

EXPANDING WHAT IS POSSIBLE IN THE CREATIVE INDUSTRIES

The old adage "If a tree falls in a forest and no one is around to hear it, does it make a sound?" is a simple question that asks us to think about the difference between observation and perception. Similarly, if a creative industry is not fostering wealth creation, does it still count as a creative industry? The creative industries are significant not only as a growing sector of the Canadian economy but also as a sector that produces and circulates meaning that impacts discourses, identities, belonging, and livelihoods. In Canada, however, the creative industries are often referenced only to celebrate their impact on economic growth and the gross domestic product (GDP). The 2021 figures from Canada's Creative Export Strategy state that the creative industries accounted for $56.1 billion, 2.7 percent of Canada's overall GDP, and more than 655,000 direct jobs. These figures are of course important to think about as the creative industries expand in Canada, but what is missing from these facts and figures is the qualitative nature of the sector.

What is absent are the stories about Canada's creative industries that speak to the creative process—including co-creation, community building, and collaboration. In this book, we suggest a shift away from studying either the impact of the creative industries' symbolic messages or the outputs of creatives or the generation and protection of intellectual property. Instead, we suggest a both/and framework to include the critical discourses that challenge not only the aforementioned aspects but also the economic frameworks that have tended to ignore or undervalue the non-commercial sectors of the creative industries. We believe that in the 21st century, it is vitally important that conversations about diversity, equity, and inclusion move beyond prioritizing histories of trauma and equity-based language, which can have the adverse effect of retraumatizing historically marginalized groups, to embracing discourses of active resistance that decentre dominant narratives about creativity and the creative industries.

For example, Linda Leung, an honorary associate professor in Arts, Cultural and Digital Creative Industries at the University of Technology Sydney, writes, "there are different dynamics of marginalization taking place: of the creative industries themselves as well as within them. At one level, there is a hierarchy within the creative industries whereby those engaged in cultural production receive more prominence and attention on their own terms and in academic studies but constitute a minority" (202). At the same time, Leung writes further that "'Other' people are left with two options: either enter the game or be excluded ... either integrate/assimilate or remain an outsider.... This ensures that the position of the non-white in a white-dominated world ... is always necessarily and inescapably an 'impure' position, always dependent on and defined in relation to the white/Western dominant" (204). *Creative Industries in Canada* aims to challenge this dominant position not only in terms of race but also gender, sexuality, disability, and power. Who are the decision makers? How are gatekeepers chosen and maintained? How are Canadian scholars defining Canada's creative industries, and what sets us apart from our counterparts in the United Kingdom and Australia?

Across disciplines, the creative industries tell stories and communicate meaning about dominant norms, alongside enabling space for critique, alternatives, and contestation. The chapters in this book collectively represent an attempt to apply an anti-oppressive lens to defining the field. This approach aims to disrupt purely economic frameworks while encouraging readers to think about other approaches, such as ethics of care and accountability, practices of naming and representation, as well as critiques of creative cities and gaming.

OUTLINE OF THE BOOK

In Part I of this book, "Production: Meaning Making in the Creative Industries," we examine the influence of and the tensions between dominant and alternative meanings in the creative industries, opening up a space of critical engagement with regard to the role of creative industries in shaping narratives, histories, and city landscapes. Here we explore the history of creative industries policy, its dominant focuses, and how definitions and policy programs have impacted what counts as culture and creative expression. In "Creativity Policies and Districts: The Ambiguous Meaning of Creativity as a Source of Local Tensions in Montreal," Joëlle Gélinas and Anouk Bélanger examine the tensions between policy hype and working realities in the creative industries through a case study of the development of creative districts in Montreal. The expansion from "cultural" to "creative" industries has been celebrated to open up economic opportunities and entrepreneurial benefits, but these opportunities and benefits are often inequitable. Gélinas and Bélanger identify that the labour and products of artists and small-scale cultural producers drew attention to the creativity of Montreal, but the subsequent creative district development displaced artists through top-down policy development rather than bottom-up support for working artists. To this end, the authors call for critical engagement with and recognition of tensions between artists, policy development, creative industries, and real estate developers, rather than assuming that these stakeholders have common goals or interests or that creative industries policy development is necessarily beneficial for individuals working in the sector.

Jeff Donison's chapter, "Race and Representation in Canadian Public Podcasting: A CBC Study," probes how podcasting, a highly popular form of mass communication, has become an outlet for racial and ethnic minorities to digitally self-represent while also carving out space for critiquing the dominant narratives about "Canadian" identity and culture. Donison uses multiple public podcasts—the CBC's *The Secret Life of Canada* and *New Fire*—to explore how CBC's mandate to represent Canadian audiences, exchange cultural expression, contribute to national identity, be widely accessible, and reflect "the multicultural nature of Canada" is (or, in some cases, is not) being fulfilled through these podcasts. Donison's discussion asks readers to think about the impact public podcasting has on marginalized voices and the ways in which these voices not only challenge what being "Canadian" means but also enables the general Canadian viewer to cross cultural contexts and geographic boundaries that are often not possible via mainstream public television and radio platforms.

The final chapter in this part, Susan L. T. Ashley's "Institutional Production of Heritage within the Culture Sector in Canada," unpacks the cultural production of "heritage" within Canadian policy and institutions, exploring the effect that cultural policies, organizations, and practices have on valuing the past as "our heritage." Using the Royal Ontario Museum (ROM), Canada's largest institution of "heritage," and the federal Community Historical Recognition Program (CHRP), specifically community exhibitions and memorials developed by Italian-Canadians, as case studies, Ashley probes how heritage is employed as a resource for public policy and for economic generation. Ultimately, Ashley examines heritage in Canada as a form of cultural production and analyzes the policy and institutional processes by which heritage has been used to both symbolize and perform Canadian identity.

The creative industries are shaped not only by economic, political, and social forces and policies. Policy objectives and symbolic meaning in the creative industries are also experienced and created in work and community life. Part II of this book, "Participation: Working and Community Building in the Creative Industries," engages with how the creative industries are experienced by people who participate in these industries, either as workers, audiences, performers, or community members. In "Laughter from the Sidelines: Precarious Work in the Canadian Comedy Industry," Madison Trusolino examines the problems of definition in arts and cultural policy through the lens of the comedy industry in Canada. Though comedy is a burgeoning sector that contributes to Canada's visibility in the global creative industries landscape, comedians are not considered artists in Canadian cultural policy and are ineligible for arts funding. These funding challenges are particularly acute given the low-to-no pay for entry-level stand-up comedians when they perform and the predominance and visibility of white, cisgender, straight men working in this industry. Trusolino's research centres women, BIPOC, and LGBTQ+ comedians and highlights their strategies for navigating participation in the comedy industry, including building community through formal and informal organizing and building inclusive spaces to foster opportunities for emerging comedians.

While Canadian film, especially Quebec films, are lauded internationally for their cultural specificity and storytelling, George Turnbull's "Film in Canada's Creative Industries: Old Barriers and New Opportunities" raises important questions about the two solitudes—English- and French-language films—and the ways in which the screendance genres offer new opportunities for thinking about Canadian filmmaking. Turnbull argues that Canadian film, like television, has had to compete in an American-dominated distribution network that has limited the exhibition of Canadian films. Given this, the chapter furthermore explores how innovative digital technologies are offering new ways to produce and exhibit films that will have potentially new benefits for Canada's filmmaking industry. Turnbull provides a historical timeline for the growth and development of Canada's film industry, the emergence of festivals such as the Toronto International Film Festival (TIFF), and the role of federal agencies such as the National Film Board (NFB) and the Canadian Film Development Corporation (CFDC; now known as Telefilm). Finally, the chapter outlines why screendance, which encourages and supports greater participation by diverse voices, stories, and perspectives, could be the future of Canadian film.

In "Inclusion, Access, and Equity: Diversity Initiatives in Canada's Game Industry," Matthew E. Perks and Jennifer R. Whitson provide an in-depth analysis of the game industries in Canada, specifically in "hub" cities, such as Vancouver, Toronto, and Montreal. The authors outline the economic impact of video game development in Canada's creative industries as well as its influence on the visual arts, culture, and technological innovation. They also probe the other side of the game industry: how it creates and reinforces barriers faced by women and historically marginalized groups. Perks and Whitson explore gender initiatives introduced by the Canada Media Fund (CMF) in 2017–2018 that sought to systematically count, promote, and increase the representation of women in Canada's media industries, and through interviews with game industries workers, they examine perceptions of diversity, reactions to and experiences with the CMF policy, and individual experiences with diversity and gender diversity policies. This chapter also considers the role of labour in the game industries, which is often exemplified by precarious and exploitative working conditions, long hours, and unpaid overtime.

Given the challenges associated with making a living in the creative industries, alternative spaces and places are vital for supporting creative work. In "Creative Hubs: Sites of Community and Creative Work," Mary Elizabeth Luka identifies the importance of creative hubs, which are spaces that can help to develop a cultural district; offer co-working or presentation spaces for professional creative workers to share skills, networks, or their current work; spark innovation; or involve citizens, clients, and users in the creative sector in more collaborative ways. Creative hubs are found across Canada, and Luka's research on creative hubs examines spaces like cSPACE (a co-working building) and the National accessArts Centre (a multidisciplinary disability arts organization) in Calgary, Alberta; BC Artscape (a social service and arts co-working building) in Vancouver, British Columbia; Yukonstruct (a social enterprise and business incubation centre) in Whitehorse,

Yukon Territory; and the New Dawn Centre for Social Innovation in rural Nova Scotia. This expansive array of creative hubs necessitates enlarged definitions and frameworks for understanding the importance of the creative industries. While the creative economy's entrepreneurial emphasis abounds with business and economic taxonomies for measuring "success," Luka suggests that arts, culture, and media-based creative hubs aspire to find measures that emphasize community inclusion, long-term social impact, artistic excellence, and creativity as well as financial measures. Luka suggests a framework of creative citizenship, which emphasizes developing shared objectives for cultural creation and distribution beyond economic objectives.

As the creative industries are increasingly recognized for their economic, social, and cultural significance, post-secondary institutions have responded by creating programs and courses to prepare students to work in this field. The rapidly changing creative industries landscape poses critical questions for creative industries educators about the best approaches to ready students to make a living in the creative industries and to act responsibly, for the social good. The term *pedagogies* evokes connotations of classroom learning but also, more broadly, public pedagogies, including teaching and learning through the creative industries. Pedagogically, the creative industries can impact inclusion and exclusion, who is marginalized and who is centred in the public eye by what is represented and celebrated. In Part III, "Pedagogies: Teaching and Learning through the Creative Industries," we explore both of these meanings of pedagogy, asking how classroom instruction might best prepare students to work and participate in the creative industries, while also investigating the potentials and limitations of the creative industries' pedagogical capacities more broadly.

In "Don Cherry's 'You People' Rant: A Critical Race Approach to Understanding Corporate Nationalism, Audience Commodification, and Cultural Citizenship," Ryan J. Phillips examines how profitable but problematic figures like Don Cherry have been enabled to promote harmful and racist views through public broadcasting. Through an analysis of *Hockey Night in Canada*, broadcast by the CBC and then Rogers Communications, Phillips traces how systemic racism has historically been interwoven through the fabric of Canadian hockey broadcasting. Similar to Luka, Phillips proposes an alternative through the framework of cultural citizenship, exploring the potential ways in which we might reconceptualize audiences as democratic citizens rather than commodities to be sold for advertising dollars. Through notions like cultural citizenship, the creative industries have the potential to foster critical engagement and learning in ways that transcend solely economic concerns.

After a motion in 1995 by the Honourable Jean Augustine, the first Black Canadian woman to be elected to Parliament, the House of Commons formally established February as Black History Month in Canada. Since then, every February, Black History Month is recognized in most provinces across the country. While it is an important celebration, it also serves a pedagogical function, as for many Canadians, it is the only time they are exposed to Black history in this country. Selina Linda Mudavanhu's "When Black History Month Media Posts Double as Pedagogical Tools: Appraising Existing BHM Coverage and Proposing Future Directions" considers the role Canada's media industries play in teaching and informing the public about Black Canadians. This chapter studies representations of Black History Month between 2018 and 2020 on news websites of broadcasters (CBC and CTV) and English-language newspapers (the *Globe & Mail* and *Toronto Star*), seeking to unpack what Canada's dominant English-language media industries prioritize during Black History Month and the implications of these choices.

In "Applying Critical Creativity: Navigating Tensions between Art and Business in the Creative City," Brandon McFarlane explores how policy directs and drives what is emphasized and celebrated in the creative industries. The so-called "creative turn" has most readily been taken up through creative cities discourse in Canada; McFarlane identifies a "creative script," the economic instrumentalization of creativity in this discourse that overemphasizes economic imperatives in attempts to brand places as global creative cities. In this context, creative industries education can crucially facilitate critical creativity and restore a balance of social and cultural values, so that economic values can be in tension and dialogue with these other values. Practical, skills-based development in creative industries education can and should also include critical thinking tools to navigate making a living in precarious industries alongside being a change maker, recognizing inequity and underrepresentation, and producing good creative work.

In "Transforming Industry Standards: Tensions between Social Change and Media Production Education," Ki Wight examines the tensions between technical skill and conceptual understanding that have long been debated in media education discussions. In the 21st century, these debates have taken on new salience, given the urgent challenges of diversity, equity, and inclusion in the creative industries. Wight suggests that prioritizing skills-based industry standards and bracketing social justice concerns as beyond the purview of post-secondary media production do a disservice to students, given the growing importance and impact of social movements in society and in the creative industries. This chapter provides an alternative framework for creative industries education that emphasizes critical media literacy, community engagement, and responsiveness. Wight suggests that critically rethinking media education can occur by re-engaging with social movements, both in media education and in the creative industries themselves.

Collectively, these chapters engage with questions of making a living and making a life, responding to systemic injustice and forging new paths, and unpacking the challenges and opportunities in the creative industries to engage with some of the most pressing issues of our time. We invite readers to further engage with these issues through the suggested activities at the end of each chapter, explore their own case studies and examples, and review the core concepts identified in the glossary. From their teaching experiences, Cheryl and Miranda have learned much from the questions, examples, and contexts that students bring to the classroom, and we hope to spark further learning and expansion in the field of creative industries through this collection.

NOTES

1. For further discussion of the history of the development of cultural policy and the creative industries in Canada, see Miranda Campbell, "Federal Cultural Policy in Canada: Past, Present, and Future" in *Out of the Basement: Youth Cultural Production in Practice and in Policy*. A comprehensive overview of ownership, cultural policy, and Canadian content regulation is beyond the scope of this book, but this overview has been detailed elsewhere (see, for example, Ira Wagman and Peter Urquhart, eds., *Cultural Industries.ca*). Instead, our purpose here is to add to this work by offering a more expansive and inclusive definition of the creative industries.

2. For more discussion on the tension between shifts in policy and Black community building in 1960s Canada, see Cheryl Thompson, "From *Ebony*'s 'Brownskin' to 'Black is Beautiful' in the *News Observer*, 1946–1969" in *Beauty in a Box: Detangling the Roots of Canada's Black Beauty Culture*.

REFERENCES

Campbell, Miranda. *Out of the Basement: Youth Cultural Production in Practice and in Policy*. McGill-Queen's University Press, 2013.

Canada. *Canada's Creative Export Strategy*. Government of Canada, 2021, https://www.canada.ca/en/canadian-heritage/services/exporting-creative-industries/creative-export-strategy.html. Accessed 1 March 2022.

Hartley, John, et al. *Key Concepts in Creative Industries*. Sage, 2012.

Hesmondhalgh, David. *The Cultural Industries*. 4th ed., Sage, 2019.

Leung, Linda. "The Creative Other: Marginalization of and from the Creative Industries." *The Journal of Arts Management, Law, and Society,* vol. 46, no. 4, 2016, pp. 200–211.

Thompson, Cheryl. *Beauty in a Box: Detangling the Roots of Canada's Black Beauty Culture.* Wilfrid Laurier University Press, 2019.

Wagman, Ira, and Peter Urquhart, editors. *Cultural Industries.ca: Making Sense of Canadian Media in the Digital Age.* Lorimer Press, 2012.

PART I

PRODUCTION: MEANING MAKING IN THE CREATIVE INDUSTRIES

CHAPTER 1

Creativity Policies and Districts: The Ambiguous Meaning of Creativity as a Source of Local Tensions in Montreal

Joëlle Gélinas and Anouk Bélanger

INTRODUCTION

The term *creative industries* first appeared as a new policy category in a very specific political context. It was part of an effort to reshape cultural policy in the United Kingdom that was led by Tony Blair's New Labour party in the late 1990s. *Creative industries* replaced the more specific term *cultural industries* in order to include industrial sectors that were not traditionally seen as "cultural," such as design, software, and fashion, but that still, it was argued, required creativity and talent. As Nicholas Garnham first showed, these cultural policy changes also aimed to create and promote new sectors on which to base the British economic future in a context of global capitalism. Creative industries quickly gained momentum and spread across many countries as international organizations such as UNESCO (the United Nations Educational, Scientific and Cultural Organization) endorsed the category and started producing studies, statistics, and recommendations. As analysts like Bouquillon have argued, it became a new societal paradigm, advancing a central discourse for understanding society and its future development as well as a dominant model to guide political action towards culture and economy. The name change from cultural to creative industries, far from being trivial, as many have pointed out (Garnham; Bouquillon; Tremblay), was meant to foster more profitable, technology-driven industries with cultural value. In doing so, it has established a rather ambiguous meaning for "creativity." The term has since been used in policy as much to refer to creative arts as to technological and economic innovation.

In this movement of profound cultural policy transformation, the city is established as a privileged site for strategic development and implementation. Indeed, municipal authorities, even before national governments, are most often the ones to initiate creativity policies. The development of so-called creative districts (quarters, clusters, or neighbourhoods) in city centres is a widespread intervention and an important part of these policies. This process particularly affects neighbourhoods that are already associated with artistic and cultural production and that function as a resource and organizational model for creative industries (Vivant, *Qu'est-ce que la ville créative?*). However, this phenomenon also raises the concern that creative industries, as they benefit from public support and become established in specific quarters, will push out (or push further underground) local artists and other bohemian cultural production. Thus, if the city has become a major site for creative policies and industries, it is also becoming significative for their contestation.

In this broader context, where creativity becomes central to urban economies and policies, this chapter presents and analyzes the tension it has created in the specific case of Montreal. Our objective is to understand the development of creative districts within the city, along with rising tensions between artists, public authorities, creative industries, and real estate developers. We do so in the specific milieu of the recent integration of creativity in municipal and provincial public policies.[1] The chapter is structured in three sections. First, we outline the history of cultural policy in Quebec and Montreal to show how culture, following a general trend in the Global North, was progressively thought of as a catalyst for Montreal's economic and territorial revitalization. We summarize some of the conflicts that arose from these policies due to a lack of attention to small-scale cultural production and its specific needs. Second, we analyze the integration of creative industries into local public policies and their implementation in the urban territory of Montreal. As mentioned, policymaking plays a powerful role in shaping creative industries and districts as well as what creativity comes to signify and how it becomes visible in and through city spaces. That said, it is not necessarily a straightforward process that imposes itself on social actors and spaces. As we show in the third section, recent support for the creative industries and the labelling of their dedicated spaces (creative districts, creative poles, creative hubs, etc.) is paradoxically reviving struggles associated with the preservation of artists' workshops within these areas. Local artist communities have a long history of battling against gentrification and its corollaries. Many old industrial buildings historically used by artists at affordable costs have been turned into condos or head offices for tech firms. Creative industries move into these post-industrial areas and revive local tensions and struggles. Their presence accelerates gentrification and increases rental costs, and, consequently, artist studios, workshops, and gallery spaces are no longer affordable for a large majority of the artist community. One aspect of the current development of a creative economy and culture, as demonstrated by using Montreal as a case study, is thus the ambivalent position of artists as they become key actors in building the symbolic value of creative districts.

Finally, our analysis of Montreal's recent developments brings us to argue for a critical understanding that grasps how creative arts and the relatively new creative economy are interacting together, rather than simply assuming the replacement of the former by the latter. The various ways in which the arts and economic aspects come together in this synergy form a complex field that is still "in the making." Our chapter aims to map and disentangle this complex synergy. Key to our critique of creative cities and districts is the articulation (economic, symbolic, and policy-related) between artistic communities and creative industries.

CULTURAL POLICIES AND URBAN RENEWAL: A PLACE FOR SMALL-SCALE CULTURAL PRODUCTION?

Culture has been closely associated with urbanity for quite some time now, if only because of cities' concentrated populations, which foster the emergence of cultural scenes and movements. However, in the last 40 years in North America and Western Europe, this association has been reinforced through urban policies that have been the subject of a "cultural turn." Culture has become an object of "conscious and deliberate manipulation" (Cochrane 104) by municipal governments, to whom nations have granted more power not only for the implementation of cultural policies but also in terms of decision making regarding policies themselves.

In Quebec, political power over culture has been debated since the "Quiet Revolution" and the 1961 creation of the Ministère des Affaires culturelles. Because support for culture was primarily seen as way of promoting a French-speaking identity, the province laid the groundwork for cultural conceptualization and implementation. Until recently, the province oversaw the majority of cultural development, while municipalities assumed a secondary role (Saint-Pierre et al.) and were generally only responsible for public libraries and heritage buildings. However, the 1992 Quebec cultural policy *Notre culture, notre avenir* reversed this trend and made municipalities central partners in cultural development. Cities thus now have greater autonomy, which allows them to adapt services, financial support, and facilities to their specific cultural needs (Québec 130). The policy also encourages local governments to develop their own cultural policies, and this is particularly the case for Montreal, which occupies a notable place in Quebec's cultural scenes and more broadly in North America's. The policy emphasizes the importance of preserving and encouraging the centrality of Montreal's cultural activities for the city to assume both national and international responsibilities.

This greater weight on Montreal's cultural development is twofold. On the one hand, as noted previously, the decentralization of responsibility and decision-making power in the realm of culture underscores the Montreal municipal government's role in Quebec's broader cultural development. On the other hand, the policy emphasizes the importance of culture for the city's development. With this emphasis, the Quebec government is effectively making cultural development one of the axes of the city's economic growth and territorial development. As in other large post-industrial cities, some central Montreal neighbourhoods were abandoned as industrial wastelands after the 1970s because of the relocation of the manufacturing sector. Culture appears in this context as a tool for development—that is to say, a means of revitalizing these spaces and renewing their economic function.

In 2005, following a long consultation process, the City of Montreal adopted its first cultural development policy, *Montréal, métropole culturelle*. With this policy, the city took the decentralization of public cultural action one step further by recommending that each of the 19 boroughs establish at least one consultative body on cultural matters and, at best, with an arts and culture action plan in order to "make their respective territories even more distinctive and attractive" (52). It was also argued that culture would become a key dimension of Montreal's urban territorial development policies and planning. This new way of urban policymaking was based on "a vision of development that places the cultural dimension at the very genesis of projects" (Bachand et al. 22). Culture was no longer strictly a sector of activity but a dimension that had to be understood and integrated into all local public activities, including those aimed at economic and territorial development (Saint-Pierre). Moreover, the cultural plan was directly embedded in the city's Economic Development Strategy and Urban Revitalization Program, which were both being developed at about the same time.

One of the flagship projects of this new relationship between cultural, economic, and territorial development promoted by the policy and action plan is the Quartier des Spectacles—a large-scale urban renewal project in an area of downtown Montreal where many cultural institutions, theatres, and international festivals are located. As Martin Lussier has shown, the Quartier des Spectacles has had a considerable impact on how we think about the spaces and purposes of cultural action in Montreal. It is through this project that the neighbourhood emerged as a privileged space for culture (arts, events, and industries). However, as Lussier explains, the neighbourhood has not only become a new space for cultural planning, it has also become the object of it. In other words, the municipality's direction has turned the neighbourhood itself into a form of cultural production, since it is now represented as "a delimited and autonomous reality on which it is subsequently possible to intervene" (317). While not all cultural districts can exist on the same scale as the Quartier des Spectacles, the fact remains that it is their visibility and positioning that are emphasized. As described in city documents, the implementation of the cultural district plan aims to identify, develop, and show-case Montreal neighbourhoods through their respective "cultural experiences," which implies the development of planning tools, territorial strategies, flagship development projects, branding, and the like (Ville de Montréal 26).

Thus, the scale of the decentralization of cultural policy has become increasingly smaller. Yet this shift has not necessarily been accompanied by measures to support artistic creation and small-scale cultural production. The development of cultural districts puts the heaviest emphasis on spaces' visibility and cultural staging. It is based on the mapping and ranking of cultural institutions and places of cultural consumption, the development of brand identities for neighbourhoods (place marketing), and place-making practices. These measures intend to increase the attractiveness of neighbourhoods in order to renew their value and thus attract new actors with diverse and sometimes conflicting interests: new residents, new businesses, and real estate developers. Rather than supporting local creators, cultural policy at the neighbourhood level has contributed to placing them at the centre of a field of tensions, in which maintaining some of their practices has become a struggle.

Conflicts have emerged with various local authorities, including during the construction of the Quartier des Spectacles, highlighting the power dynamics that structure how cultural districts are organized. Several fringe venues, such as Café Cleopatra, one of the last burlesque halls of the former red light district, voiced their fear of being expelled by this major development project and the "cleaning" it entailed (Le Bel 203). But tensions were not limited to this area—one conflict concerned postering on city property and street furniture such as postal boxes, street lamps, utility poles, and building facades. In 2010, two newly created cultural organizations, APLAS (Association des petits lieux d'art et de spectacles) and COLLE (Coalition pour la liberté d'expression),[2] joined forces to challenge the City of Montreal's ban on postering and subsequent fines that had a "suffocating effect" on the small-scale arts and cultural scene, "prohibiting the very mechanisms through which this community survives and thrives"

(COLLE, cited in Grenier and Lussier 181). Construction worksites were the only designated areas where postering was still legal, but the process had to go through a private company, Publicité Sauvage, which had established a monopoly (Campbell, "Montreal, City of Strife?"). Invoking freedom of expression and arguing that paying for postering was out of reach for small-scale cultural producers, the movement had to go as far as presenting their case against the City of Montreal to the Quebec Superior Court to establish a legal space for DIY cultural advertising.

That same year, another conflict arose between the municipal government, residents, and small-scale cultural actors in the Plateau-Mont-Royal borough and the Mile End area, where a high concentration of artists' spaces and small venues can be found. After citizens complained about noise, the borough's administration put forward Project Noise, a resolution that significantly increased fines directed at bars and venues for noise complaints (Grenier and Lussier 183). As Miranda Campbell details, these situations place small venues in particularly vulnerable positions, as they have to come up with creative ways to survive despite changes that affect their districts and limit their activities. Le Divan Orange, a cornerstone of the city's emerging indie scene and of the "Montreal sound," was already struggling at the time and closed its doors in 2018. Finding solutions on their own is all the more difficult considering that, for the most part, small-scale cultural infrastructure operates in rented and precarious spaces. This precariousness makes investing in renovations such as soundproofing too costly and risky (Campbell, "Montreal, City of Strife?" 166–67).

The dependence on rented spaces became problematic for visual and craft artists as well, since most rely on studios for their practices. The Mile End industrial area is an emblematic case in this regard. Starting in the 1990s and increasingly at the beginning of the 2000s, Mile End followed a process of cultural regeneration as artists and cultural producers invested in cheap industrial spaces left empty by textile factories that had relocated to more affordable locations.[3] In their study on Mile End designers, Norma Rantisi and Deborah Leslie shed light on the feeling shared among them that "the landscape [was] emergent rather than given and that they ha[d] the potential to benefit from and contribute to its constitution through their presence and work" (Rantisi and Leslie, "Materiality and Creative Production" 2836). Despite their investment in building a network of art production and dissemination in the neighbourhood—which has undoubtedly contributed to the reshaping of its urban decay as *cool* and attractive—artists' presence has been gradually threatened. Companies and start-ups, especially ones from the tech industry, moved to the Mile End to benefit from its creative character. For example, French video game company Ubisoft did not set up shop *accidentally* in that specific neighbourhood:[4]

> Indeed, considered as one of the hippest urban areas in the city, the Mile End neighbourhood has greatly contributed to stimulate and inspire the employees, by giving them the opportunity to actively take part in the local creative communities … and frequently meet together in the different concert halls, bars, clubs, art galleries and trendy stores. (Cohendet et al. 102)

While Ubisoft initially occupied a small space when it settled in the area in 1997, it rapidly grew and later took over the whole building. Over the years, Ubisoft has come to occupy an important part of the neighbourhood, both in terms of space and in terms of decision making related to its activities and development. For example, the company financed the revival of a summer block party that used to be community-led and was intended as a celebration of the multi-ethnic spirit of the neighbourhood. A multinational corporation's involvement in such a community event got residents worried about being dispossessed of their space, both materially and symbolically (Roy-Valex 369). Ubisoft also started courting the Mile End creative arts underground crowd, establishing contacts and organizing activities in collaboration with art galleries to inspire their employees and to create, collaborate on, and exchange ideas and concepts (Cohendet).

Furthermore, in 2008, the borough's administration initiated a revitalization plan that, according to Rantisi and Leslie ("Creativity by Design?" 39), was inspired by Richard Florida's creative class thesis. Florida, who has been very influential among urban policymakers, defended[5] a direct link between the economic development of cities and their capacity to attract workers in technology and information, arts and culture, and educational and managerial activities (the creative class). He also designed a ranking system that allowed cities to assess and compare their level of attraction. Identified by many as state-led gentrification, this urban policy approach has been highly criticized (see, for example, Peck). In Mile End, the announcement of this investment plan sparked several mobilizations. Between 2009 and 2013, citizen and artist associations asked to be included in the planning and also made formal requests to see the plan. The Forum Citoyen Le Mile End en Chantier, an anti-gentrification movement, was the leading actor. Pied Carré, an organization set up specifically to protect artists' studios and interests, was also founded in the midst of this active deployment. As anticipated by the organization, the city's attention to the area and investment in its embellishment attracted real estate developers. In 2011, the two most-heavily occupied buildings by the artistic community were sold for over $30 million to Allied Properties, which planned to build luxury offices. After lengthy negotiations—which received a great deal of media attention—between Pied Carré, city and borough representatives, and the real estate developer, a moratorium was put in place on the construction of luxury offices and an agreement was made to secure spaces with cheap rents for artists (Rantisi and Leslie, "Le Mile End" 142). Although these decisions represented significant gains for Mile End's community, they remained limited to a very specific and small area of Montreal. This suggests that further work and mobilization will eventually be necessary, especially since the emphasis on creativity in the city's cultural policy continues to grow. In the end, this case exemplifies the negotiated process of defining what is included in the creative economy. The increasing local presence of transnational creative industries, like that of Ubisoft, means revising policy in light of the diverse, and sometimes contradictory, aims and needs of various actors inhabiting the district.

CREATIVE POLICY, STRATEGIES, AND DISTRICTS

Around the globe, districts and areas known for their intense artistic activities are being courted or appropriated by creative industries and, more broadly, by the creative economy. This process, paralleling gentrification, branding, symbolic capitalization, and commercial valorization, has been largely documented and critiqued in the social sciences and humanities (McRobbie; Rantisi and Leslie; Zukin; Vivant). This section further explores the role of policy and public action as facilitators of creative districts within this larger context.

Creativity as a cultural and economic industry term has been present in Montreal since the turn of the 21st century. As mentioned, specific projects were inspired by Richard Florida's influential thesis on the creative class. Florida was invited to produce an analysis of Montreal's creative index during the consultation process for the first cultural policy (Florida et al.). However, creativity—in the sense of "creative industries" and as a category for policy intervention—is a fairly recent phenomenon in the city. The necessity of drawing policy attention to "creative industries" was forwarded by the Board of Trade of Metropolitan Montreal (BTMM) incentive in 2013. Two strategic forums addressing art-business collaboration and the possibility for creative industries' growth organized by the BTMM first presented industries' role as the core of urban policy and economic development. The 2013 report *The Creative Industries: Catalysts of Wealth and Influence for Metropolitan Montréal*, produced by the BTMM, argued in definite terms for the creative industries as a legitimate economic sector, and it was the first city publication to quantify the value and economic weight of the creative industries in Montreal.[6] On top of giving the sector legitimacy solely through its economic importance, it provided guidelines for its constituents' activities and potential interventions for its growth.

While the notion of *creative class* refers to individual skills and the notion of *creative economy* refers to the broader economic or social contribution of creativity, *creative industries* are based on the production and marketing of creative products. The definition of creative industries used in the BTMM study is deliberately inspired by the one developed in 1998 by the United Kingdom, which has become somewhat of an international standard: "Industries that have their origin in the creativity, skills and talent of an individual and that have a high potential for growth and employment through the production and exploitation of intellectual property" (DCMS, cited in Bouquillon 8–9). The BTMM further states that "they are the result of a strong interaction between the arts and new technologies" (BTMM 1). The shaping of this new industrial category does not call for the development of a new sector as such. Rather, it is a matter of symbolically grouping under the same "new" name a set of pre-existing sectors whose respective modes of public support vary considerably—including, on one hand, the support focusing on cultural and artistic public institutions initiated in the 1950s and 1960s and, on the other hand, the industrial policies focusing on technological and multimedia businesses of the 1980s and 1990s.

These discourses have a clear impact on policy affecting the cultural sectors, and this was evident in the recent renewal of cultural policy at both the municipal (2017) and the provincial (2018) levels, which definitively integrated the notion of creative industries and made them a central axis of action. In the renewed policies, as in the BTMM publications, there is a certain contradiction between the role assigned to self-employed artists and cultural workers in the creative industries and the support measures that are to be put in place. Indeed, the artistic disciplines sector, supported by government programs for artists and non-profit cultural organizations, is presented as the city's "creative heart": "These are key sectors for artistic vitality, because they are sources of innovation, experimentation and influence. They account for a large share of 'underground' creativity, i.e., creativity developed outside formal organizations and institutions" (BTMM 16). Although they acknowledge a central position for artists in the creative industries, both policies fail to present specific measures to support or encourage their work and needs. Artists and art production are even completely absent from the digital creativity sector as portrayed and encouraged in strategic documents. Only commercial activities that can generate intellectual property are considered (Xn Québec).

The renewal of public cultural action based on creative industries instead takes the form of support for entrepreneurship. In both policies, the increased contribution of cultural activities to economic growth is envisaged at both levels of government through their role in "creating conditions conducive to [entrepreneurial] emergence and development" (Québec 44). Both the City of Montreal and the Quebec government want to focus on searching for new business models with stakeholders in the "ecosystem of artistic creation." If public support for the industrial side of culture is far from a new phenomenon, this way of making sense of and supporting cultural production nevertheless marked the starting point of business development (i.e., start-ups). The multiplication of video game studios, which rose in Quebec from 48 in 2009 to 198 in 2017, has been promoted as a model to follow (Xn Québec).

Through this lens, creativity becomes a commodity to be traded for business and economic development, and this new reality comes with a whole array of legitimation processes, such as producing economic portraits and statistics to convey its importance. The downside of this model of cultural development is that economic profits and start-up creation become the dominant dimensions through which we understand the value and function of arts and culture in neighbourhoods and cities. As Angela McRobbie has argued, educational programs, particularly post-secondary programs, also play an important role in the legitimation process, as they provide institutional recognition of the creative entrepreneur as a legitimate figure. In Montreal, much effort has been invested over the last five years in the creation of post-secondary and professional programs dedicated to creative entrepreneurship and creative industries management. Following the recent policy renewal, new college and university programs have been created in several public and private institutions in and around the city. One such example is a short program specifically dedicated to business creation in the creative and cultural industries sector.[7] The Ministère de l'Éducation et de l'Enseignement supérieur has also developed two educational hubs to promote programs related to digital creativity.[8] Finally, the Government of Quebec and the City of Montreal are helping to support a new school of "creative sciences," La Factry, which collaborates with design, advertising, and marketing agencies to offer training anchored in the job market.

These programs have a significant ideological impact as they support and socially value new jobs characterized by uncertainty while upholding an idea/ideal of independent creative production (McRobbie 34–5). They lend educational legitimacy to cultural work as the forerunner of flexibility in the workplace (Menger). In other words, the historical precariousness of artistic production, which has long been considered the opposite of work or even outside capitalism, has now become the dominant work model in the current context of urban creative industries and economy.

The figure of the creative entrepreneur plays a central and highly effective role in the paradigmatic shift toward creativity, and dedicated training courses correlate with this shift. In short, two phenomena are unfolding: first, the expansion of post-secondary and continuing education since the 1990s—particularly in the domains of the arts, communications, media, and the humanities—adjusting young artists and cultural workers to the idea of entrepreneurial culture; second, middle-classification processes that have come to be linked directly to entrepreneurship as an ideal. As McRobbie points out, this is not about social mobility but rather about an ideological effect where cultural workers and creative entrepreneurs feel they belong to the middle class. In this sense, neoliberalism succeeds in its mission to convince people of the rightful excitement and challenge of becoming a creative entrepreneur: "Concomitantly, when in a post-industrial society there are fewer jobs offering permanent and secure employment, such a risk-taking stance becomes a necessity rather than a choice. The two come together in a kind of magic formula" (McRobbie 11).

Another important objective of public policy in facilitating the creative industries and economy is creating spaces and places for the industries and entrepreneurs to bloom. Thus, in order to stimulate the development of the entrepreneurial "ecosystem," both provincial and municipal governments are involved in creating an organizational model based on incubating and accelerating cultural and creative businesses. To this end, governments offer funds, programs, and services to entrepreneurs and start-ups to encourage the transition from cultural production to entrepreneurship and international export. Montreal's cultural policy emphasizes the city's desire to stimulate the creation of these spaces for "entrepreneurial mutualization":

> Mutualization offers great potential for innovation in financing models and risk-sharing. The City will support the development of business models based on the collaborative economy. It will re-evaluate the eligibility criteria for its assistance programs in order to make the often atypical and innovative projects resulting from these new cultural management practices eligible (Ville de Montréal, *Politique de Développement Culturel 2017–2022* 42).

In this search for collaborative business models, the artist-run centre (administered by artist members), facilitating the sharing of workspace, appears as a typical case and serves as an inspiration. Thus, the incubators and accelerators set up to support creative entrepreneurship (La Piscine, Projet Zù, MTLab, etc.) to adopt both a physical presence, by setting up their offices in post-industrial buildings, as well as the legal status of non-profit organizations. This status is central to the city's programming structure, as it allows these organizations to legitimately obtain provincial and municipal public funding as well as private funding.

As Elsa Vivant explains in her work, the city becomes an ideal territory for creative industries—or, rather, the city is now "made" for them (Vivant, "Creatives in the City"). This process particularly affects artistic production districts that function as a resource and an organizational model for creative activities:

> the creative economy is indeed tending to become territorialized, to elect suitable spaces in metropolises where it will benefit from the logic of a network and face-to-face encounters between service providers. The resource district of artistic production functions as an archetype of the organizational modes of other creative activities, which find the resources for their development in the metropolis. (Vivant, *Qu'est-ce que la ville créative?* 50 [our translation])

If we map out the aforementioned components of the creative support system that is currently being established—new scholarly and professional programs for creative entrepreneurs and incubators to "catalyze" their potential for economic value, along with flagship companies that are being promoted as symbols of Montreal's creativity (such as Ubisoft, Sid Lee, and Moment Factory)—we can begin to understand how the system is being implemented in the material structure of the city and targeting specific districts. We highlight the integration and articulation of creative industries and entrepreneurialism in three particular areas: the Innovation District, the Quartier des Spectacles, and the Mile End/ Mile-Ex neighbourhood. The intentional ambiguity around the use and meaning of the term *creativity*, which otherwise justifies government support for creative entrepreneurship and creative industrial sectors, confusing it with support for the creative arts (Garnham), is taking shape in city space. The creative arts and creativity sectors are developing in parallel, through movements that are diverse and sometimes contradictory.

As Allen J. Scott writes: "the city is a powerful fountainhead of creativity," ("Cultural Economy and the Creative Field of the City" 115) and this can be understood in terms of a series of localized effects. Former industrial buildings became the leading sites for small-scale cultural production and artists' workshops; however, these same cultural producers are being pushed to the margins

Figure 1.1: Territorial Integration of the Creative Support System in Montreal[9]

Created by the authors.

Table 1.1: Icons for Types of Spaces in Territorial Integration of the Creative Support System in Montreal

Icon	Type of Space
	Scholarly creative industries programs
	Professional creative industries programs
	Incubators for creative start-ups
	Flagship creative companies
	Artists' workshops in former industrial buildings
·	Coffee shops
	Co-working spaces

Created by the authors.

of the districts as creative entrepreneurialism takes over their buildings. The same is occurring in the reshaping of third spaces such as coffee shops and co-working spaces as core domains of the creative economy and culture. What used to be marginal, or at least considered secondary, aspects of cultural and artistic scenes—the cafés, bars, and restaurants that sociologist Howard Becker called their "support system"—have become visible, and these spaces are now central actors in urban cultural development (Straw). As for co-working spaces, they were initiated by creative freelancers to cope with their flexible work reality and soon became a new type of business involving transnational franchises (de Peuter et al.).

As is generally the case in cities, the territorial integration of Montreal's creative industries follows the logic of the cultural regeneration of industrial spaces and places (Harvey, *The Condition of Postmodernity*). The space that creative industries occupy is mostly constituted by renovated industrial or heritage buildings. Logically, then, the process follows the territorial history of industrial Montreal, which is made up of three main axes (see the larger grey lines on the map in Figure 1.1). This territorial pattern also explains why studies so far have suggested that the main economic impact of creativity district policy is not related to creativity per se, nor its transmission or dissemination, and even less to cultural production, but rather linked to land value (Harvey, "The Art of Rent"). Even more so, it explains why the promise of a thriving and sustainable economy through the promotion of creative industries and districts has been repeatedly questioned and challenged. Detailed analyses of the economic portraits and statistics used to define creative industries and their case for the growth potential of creativity have shown methodological flaws as well as a preoccupation with the financial gains in specific sectors. Software and design make up a much larger proportion of the development effort than publishing, television, music, film, and the performing arts combined (Tremblay).

As mentioned, creative industries also establish mostly precarious working conditions with limited social support and increased responsibilities for workers. This is especially true for freelancers and the self-employed, who form a large part of these industries' workforces and face the burdens of continually updating their own training and finding workspaces (de Peuter; de Peuter et al.; McRobbie). Montreal is no exception: the portrait of the creative industries as presented by the BTMM is fragmented and characterized by a large proportion of self-employed workers and very small businesses that coexist with a few large multinationals, most of which are foreign owned. Andy Pratt also sheds light on the lack of inclusivity within these work environments. The proportion of female workers and racialized communities in these spaces is smaller than average in London, UK when compared to all industries. This led Pratt to conclude that "the new work that is being created so quickly, which is presented as the saviour and future of cities ... is some of the most unstable and precarious work, that reproduces the most regressive social and economic structure" (128). Issues of class, gender, and race in creative cities are not unique to London and have been highlighted and questioned across Europe, the United States, and Canada (Leslie and Catungal).

Furthermore, the discursive confusion around creativity seems to disfavour artistic practices and small-scale cultural production. Where government policy and strategies mention small-scale artistic producers, it is on the assumption that they will eventually work toward participating in Montreal's growing interurban competition that is happening on a global scale. As it was outlined in Britain's creativity policy:

> It is difficult to imagine where ... pathways in the creative industries that are intentionally small-scale and community-oriented would fit.... There are no provisions ... for grassroots cultural production that desires to remain at the grassroots level, and there is no vision of grassroots community development through small-scale creative industries. (Campbell, "Creative Britain and the Canadian Context" 125)

Such policy has encouraged the development of creative entrepreneurialism—in large part via the figure of the creative entrepreneur—which is now occupying the same or similar spaces as those used by artists, spaces with the same or similar artistic and post-industrial aesthetics. Yet, somewhat paradoxically, some artists have managed to benefit from these strategies and policies through making their demands heard by municipal authorities. As we will see in the following section, the revival of artists' mobilization for workplaces in the context of creative district policy creates new ways to assert their presence and find/hold on to a place in their transforming historical boroughs. This makes it so that the tensions between cultural production and creativity are experienced in large part through space and real estate.

REAL ESTATE AND CITIES' CULTURAL DEVELOPMENT: ARTISTS' WORKSHOPS AS FIELDS OF TENSIONS

Areas undergoing a process of transformation or branding as creative districts are divided in their responses. Along with local and international initiatives, various grassroots movements are still seeking to capture the various effects of the presence of creative industries, along with the spread of a creative culture. As we saw with the struggles in Mile End, this has the effect of making real estate developers important actors in cities' cultural development. In Montreal, the mobilization in Mile End was not an isolated case. The first large, organized mobilization of this kind took place in 2004. It involved forming a coalition, Sauvons l'usine Grover, to resist the eviction of three hundred cultural workers who had studios in an uninhabited industrial building that was being sold to build condos. Despite a two-year mobilization and solution seeking, the building still ended up being sold to a private developer. Nevertheless, it brought media and political attention to the vulnerability of independent artists' workplaces. The joint efforts of the cultural milieu and local development actors also led to the creation of Ateliers créatifs Montréal, a non-profit real estate developer. Their mandate is to protect but also develop affordable and sustainable spaces for professional visual artists, artisans, and cultural organizations. They do so by buying former industrial buildings or acting as an intermediate actor to provide very long–term leases. Although their aim has clearly been to take action beyond mobilizations on an ad hoc basis, it has been a challenge for them to do so due to a lack of funding and increased property taxes.

In 2018, as Quebec and Montreal were promoting their renewed cultural policy focusing on creative industries generally and digital creativity in particular, tenant artists were forced to come together once again. Two development projects near Mile End were beginning to threaten their expulsion: a new university campus and a centre of excellence for artificial intelligence, which attracted transnational companies like Microsoft. After the sale of three emblematic buildings and significant rent increases in others, another organization, Nos Ateliers, took shape. For one of the organization's founders, this meant being forced to move for the third time after having first been displaced from the Grover and then from Mile End. Nos Ateliers' focus was therefore not solely on the buildings that had been sold. It had a more general purpose: targeting political strategies that could be put in place to intervene proactively and avoid leaving artists fending for themselves in the process of mitigating the impacts of real estate speculation on their practices and on small-scale cultural production more broadly.

Thus, Nos Ateliers undertook an informal accounting of the general situation with artists' studios in Montreal. Apart from research produced in 2008 (Bellavance and Latouche), such a portrait was non-existent for the city. This approach thus aimed not only to increase their quantitative "weight" in potential negotiations but also to serve as a means to consolidate information on practices, various organizational models, problems encountered, and specific needs. The information could then serve as a basis for reflection on possible support models and potential measures that could be put in place. Simultaneously, the organization made a few appearances in local and national media to report on the critical situation. Joining forces with the borough's MP and Ateliers créatifs Montréal, they approached the city's administration, asking for action to be taken. Finally, as the situation got media and political attention, several conferences on the matter were organized in academic as well as artistic circles. In this work of consolidating artists' needs and promoting their place in creative districts, the language adopted was clearly tinged with that of creativity. The collection of data on the location of artist workshops is referred to as "creative hubs," and in order to respect the variety of actors implicated in the fight for affordable workspaces, the organization prefers to speak of "cultural innovation independents" rather than artists. While this designation is more inclusive in terms of practices, it is also very much in line with the definitions of the creative industries sector and the role assigned to artists within cultural policy.

As a result of this mobilization, the members of Nos Ateliers have been working since 2018 as the main contact on this issue (although they are not official representatives) with the City of Montreal and the Ministère de la Culture et des Communications. According to one of the city's representatives, the case was developed and prioritized as a cultural issue. Since then, the city has been working collaboratively with Nos Ateliers on a set of combined measures to create reserved and protected spaces that could guarantee their long-term presence: a comprehensive and exhaustive policy for the preservation, vitality, and viability of artists' studios. Several measures were studied, including regulatory tools pertaining to the transformation of industrial buildings, financial support in the form of grants, the implementation of a specific category of property tax for commercial properties dedicated mainly to artists' studios, as well as assistance to multiply the acquisition of buildings by cultural and artistic organizations. On its end, the Ministère de la Culture et des Communications announced a five-year, $25 million artist workshop upgrade program to complement and finance the city's own initiative, which will allow "the renovation and development of workspaces for artists and encourage collective ownership of workshops." The program took shape in 2021 and ended up focusing on grants to provide access to expert consulting and to help with renovations.

Despite the symbolic centrality of artists in political and marketing discourses on the creative industries, artists have struggled to be included in discussions about the city's creative future and its physical infrastructure. This work is completely voluntary. It requires a great deal of time and specific knowledge on topics such as zoning, building classification, property rights, and the property tax system, in addition to the efforts and expertise needed to manage their own organizations, which were set up exclusively for this work. One major concern is that social and political mobilization may take up all of the artists' creative time. In their negotiations with authorities, artists insist on the fact that they cannot all become non-profit organizations, long-term project managers, and owners. All these activities require knowledge and time, which diminishes the time they can allot to their artistic practices.

While some solutions are emerging that may support the sustainability of artists' presence in creative districts, it must be emphasized that the outcome of these struggles goes beyond the "win or lose" logic of the battle. The consequences do not only imply a forced displacement or, inversely, the ability to continue grounding artists' practices in the neighbourhoods in which they have invested through their organized and sustained resistance. These battles have also, in part, reorganized the relationships and tasks linked to artistic work, notably by placing the issue of real estate at the heart of small-scale artistic and cultural production. Although the new support program is welcome, several artists criticize the entrepreneurial and professionalizing tangent they must adopt to benefit from it. Not only do they have to be planning a major workshop project, but they also must take trainings and consult experts in finance and real estate. Some of them fear they are losing their capacity for self-organization in this process. What is at stake, in the end, is a place in creativity policy and grant programs for cultural and creative projects that neither are necessarily profit-oriented nor are intended to revitalize the district and land value.

CONCLUSION

Montreal's recent public policy encourages creative industries to bloom in central or post-industrial areas, and this context follows a larger wave of urban development in cities worldwide. However, a closer inspection of Montreal's singularity in terms of the development of creative industries and districts illuminates some key concepts to better understand the complex dynamics whereby artists' struggles, creative entrepreneurs' dreams, and real estate developers' ventures find themselves on shared ground.

Our analysis underlines a set of intertwined arguments. First, public policy ends up facilitating entrepreneurialism, which then mimics artistic networks and organizations and takes over artists' spaces rather than offering support for small-scale cultural production. Second, real estate developers have become key actors in the emergence of creative districts, just as they have during earlier waves of post-industrial development in cities (Jessop; Harvey; Scott). Their propensity l speculation and gentrification creates increasingly challenging working conditions for artists and small business owners who have largely contributed to the symbolic capital of these urban districts. However, at least in some cases (as discussed) in the context of Montreal, some artists have managed to secure public support to preserve their legitimate place along with their spaces in the material structure of the creative city. What remains murky, however, is the ways in which cultural production and creativity are entangled in higher education programs, in structural and cultural development initiatives and aesthetics, in the figure of the creative entrepreneur, and in the wider neoliberal ideology as it trickles down to local political economic and cultural transformations. In this chapter, we aimed to offer pathways to think about the increasing presence of the creative industries in Canadian cities in a multifaceted and critical manner. There are clearly unequal power relations at play in the shaping of creative districts, yet it would be too simple to frame the matter as the straightforward override of the interests of capital in urban settings. We think it is important to understand the ways in which artistic, cultural, entrepreneurial, and industrial incentives are articulated in ambiguous and sometimes contradictory ways, in weaving together creative enclaves and cultures in our cities.

CORE CONCEPTS

creative city: A city that aims to foster and promote a favourable environment for various forms of creativity. It is characterized by a concentration of cultural industries and related structures (economic, political, and built environment).

cultural and creative districts: Geographically defined areas in a city with a concentration of buildings and spaces dedicated to artistic, cultural, and/or creative activities.

cultural policy: Government measures to encourage or protect activities in various areas of culture. In Canada, it includes all artistic expressions along with communication sectors and mass culture (and creative) industries.

SUGGESTED ACTIVITIES

1. Find an independent artistic organization, an artistic company, or a citizen movement that has voiced its opinion or position regarding local creative development.

2. Identify a creative district in your city. Walk around the district and find its distinctive features.

3. Consult your municipal public policy and analyze the centrality of creativity. What are the given definitions or understandings of creative districts? What are the means of support offered for their development?

NOTES

1. This chapter is based on content analysis (media coverage, public reports, policies, strategic plans, etc.), a mapping of the structures supporting "creativity" in Montreal, and interviews with artists as well as with local authorities.

2. After having been active for several years, these two organizations no longer exist today.

3. The Mile End area has been the subject of mobilizations against possible zoning changes affecting its diversity and facilitating gentrification since the 1980s. In the mid-1980s, a local mobilization effort organized by residents and small business owners overturned a local government project to modify the existing mixed zoning of the Mile End. The historical existence of multipurpose zones, where, for example, apartments are authorized on top of retail trade shops, have slowed gentrification and the presence of big shopping centres (Rantisi and Leslie). The Mile End remained a mixed area where students, artists, small businesses, retail stores, and a vibrant social life and nightlife coexisted.

4. Ubisoft settled in Quebec because of the financial support offered (still to this day) to multimedia companies by the Quebec government, including tax breaks and wage subsidies.

5. He has since retracted these ideas. See his latest book, *The New Urban Crisis*, published in 2017.

6. For a more recent economic profile on creative industries, see https://www.ccmm.ca/fr/publications/etude/collaboration-art-affaires/industries-creatives-reussir-dans-un-environnement-en-mutation-rapide/.

7. For more information about Dawson College's programs, see https://www.dawsoncollege.qc.ca/news/dawson-community/dawson-college-and-ic-mtl-team-up-to-offer-new-instructional-program-to-budding-entrepreneurs/.

8. To learn more about these poles: https://polesynthese.com/en/study/ and https://polelavalartnumerique.com/.

9. This map was built using the open software *Umap*.

REFERENCES

Bachand, Raymond, et al. *Cadre, Principes Directeurs et Énoncé de La Politique Culturelle. Rapport Du Groupe-Conseil.* Ville de Montréal, 2003.

Bellavance, Guy, and Daniel Latouche. "Les Ateliers d'Artistes dans l'Écosystème Montréalais: Une Étude de Localisation." *Recherches Sociographiques*, vol. 49, no. 2, 2008, pp. 231–260.

Bouquillon, Philippe. "Les Industries et l'Economie Créatives, un Nouveau Grand Projet?" *Creative Economy, Creative Industries: des Notions à Traduire*, edited by Philippe Bouquillon, Presses Universitaires de Vincennes, 2012, pp. 5–46.

BTMM. *The Creative Industries: Catalysts of Wealth and Influence for Metropolitan Montréal*. Board of Trade of Metropolitan Montréal, 2013.

Campbell, Miranda. "Creative Britain and the Canadian Context: Youth, Education and Entrepreneurship." *Out of the Basement: Youth Cultural Production in Practice and in Policy*, McGill-Queen's University Press, 2013, pp. 121–147.

———. "Montreal, City of Strife? Agitation, Negotiation, and Visions of the Scene." *Out of the Basement: Youth Cultural Production in Practice and in Policy*, McGill-Queen's University Press, 2013, pp. 148–176.

Cochrane, Allan. *Understanding Urban Policy: A Critical Approach*. Blackwell, 2007.

Cohendet, Patrick, et al. "The Anatomy of the Creative City." *Industry and Innovation*, vol. 17, no. 1, 2010, pp. 91–111.

de Peuter, Greig. "Creative Economy and Labor Precarity: A Contested Convergence." *Journal of Communication Inquiry*, vol. 35, no. 4, 2011, pp. 417–425.

de Peuter, Greig, et al. "The Ambivalence of Coworking: On the Politics of an Emerging Work Practice." *European Journal of Cultural Studies*, vol. 20, no. 6, December 2017, pp. 687–706.

Florida, Richard. *The Rise of the Creative Class and How It's Transforming Work, Leisure, and Everyday Life*. Basic Books, 2002.

Florida, Richard, et al. *Montréal, Ville de Convergences Créatives: Perspectives et Possibilités*. Catalytix, 2005.

Garnham, Nicholas. "From Cultural to Creative Industries: An Analysis of the Implications of the 'Creative Industries' Approach to Arts and Media Policy Making in the United Kingdom." *International Journal of Cultural Policy*, vol. 11, no. 1, 2005, pp. 15–29.

Grenier, Line, and Martin Lussier. "Constructing Small Venus in Montréal: Theoretical Explorations on an Ongoing Project." *Musicultures*, vol. 38, 2011, pp. 173–190.

Harvey, David. "The Art of Rent: Globalisation, Monopoly and the Commodification of Culture." *Socialist Register*, vol. 38, 2002.

———. *The Condition of Postmodernity: An Enquiry into the Origins of Cultural Change*. Blackwell, 1989.

Jessop, Bob. "The Enterprise of Narrative and the Narrative of Enterprise: Place Marketing and the Entrepreneurial City." *The Entrepreneurial City: Geographies of Politics, Regime, and Representation*, edited by Tim Hall and Phil Hubbard, Wiley, 1998, pp. 1–99.

Le Bel, Pierre-Mathieu. "Choc des Mémoires Collectives et Espaces Thématiques dans ce Qui Reste du Red Light Montréalais." *Globe*, vol. 14, no. 1, 2011, pp. 197–213.

Leslie, Deborah, and John Paul Catungal. "Social Justice and the Creative City: Class, Gender and Racial Inequalities." *Geography Compass*, vol. 6, no. 3, 2012, pp. 111–122.

Lussier, Martin. "Le Quartier Comme Production Culturelle." *Canadian Journal of Communication*, vol. 40, 2015, pp. 315–332.

McRobbie, Angela. *Be Creative: Making a Living in the New Culture Industries*. Polity Press, 2016.

Menger, Pierre-Michel. *Portrait de l'artiste En Travailleur: Métamorphoses Du Capitalisme*. Seuil, 2002.

Peck, Jamie. "Struggling with the Creative Class." *International Journal of Urban and Regional Research*, vol. 29, no. 4, 2005, pp. 740–770.

Pratt, Andy. "The Cultural Contradictions of the Creative City." *City, Culture and Society*, vol. 2, no. 3, 2011, pp. 123–130.

Québec. *La Politique Culturelle Du Québec: Notre Culture, Notre Avenir*. Gouvernement du Québec, Ministère des affaires culturelles, 1992.

Québec, and Ministère de la culture et des communications. *Partout, la Culture: Politique Culturelle du Québec*. Open WorldCat, 2018, http://collections.banq.qc.ca/ark:/52327/3476686.

Rantisi, Norma M., and Deborah Leslie. "Materiality and Creative Production: The Case of the Mile End Neighborhood in Montréal." *Environment and Planning A: Economy and Space*, vol. 42, no. 12, 2010, pp. 2824–2841.

———. "Creativity by Design? The Role of Informal Spaces in Creative Production." *Spaces of Vernacular Creativity, Rethinking the Cultural Economy*, edited by Tim Edensor, Deborah Leslie, Steve Millington, and Norma M. Rantisi, Routledge, 2010, pp. 33–45.

———. "Le Mile End: Un Quartier Au Carrefour de La Vie Culturelle et Économique." *Montréal, La Cité Des Cités*, edited by Juan-Luis Klein and Richard Shearmur, Presses universitaire du Québec, 2017, pp. 126–145.

Roy-Valex, Myrtille. "Ville Attractive, Ville Créative : la Plus-Value de la Culture au Regard des 'Créatifs' du Jeu Vidéo à Montréal." PhD dissertation, Université du Québec, 2010.

Saint-Pierre, Diane. "Les Politiques Culturelles Du Québec." *L'État Québécois Au XXIe Siècle*, edited by Robert Bernier, PUQ, 2004, pp. 231–259.

Saint-Pierre, Diane, et al. "La Place de La Culture dans la 'Politique de Développement Intégré' de La Ville Québécoise." *Études Canadiennes*, no. 66, 2009, pp. 153–170.

Scott, Allen J. *The Cultural Economy of Cities: Essays on the Geography of Image-Producing Industries*. Sage, 2000.

————. "Cultural Economy and the Creative Field of the City." *Geograkisja Annaler Series B Geography*, vol. 92, no. 2, 2010, pp. 115–130.

Straw, Will. "Visibility and Conviviality in Music Scenes." *DIY Cultures and Underground Music Scenes*, edited by Andy Bennett and Paula Guerra, Routledge, 2018, pp. 21–30.

Tremblay, Gaëtan. "Industries Culturelles, Économie Créative et Société de l'Information." *Global Media Journal—Canadian Edition*, vol. 1, no. 1, 2008, pp. 65–88.

Ville de Montréal. *Conjuguer La Créativité et l'expérience Culturelle Citoyenne à l'ère Du Numérique et de La Diversité. Politique de Développement Culturel 2017–2022.* Montréal, 2017.

————. *Montréal Métropole Culturelle. Proposition de Politique de Développement Culturel Pour La Ville de Montréal.* Montréal, 2004.

Vivant, Elsa. "Creatives in the City: Urban Contradictions of the Creative City." *City, Culture and Society*, vol. 4, no. 2, June 2013, pp. 57–63.

————. *Qu'est-ce que la ville créative?* Presses universitaires de France, 2009.

Xn Québec. *Premier Profil de l'industrie de La Créativité Numérique Du Québec.* 2018, p. 57, https://www.xnquebec.co/portrait-industrie/.

Zukin, Sharon. *Loft Living: Culture and Capital in Urban Change.* Johns Hopkins University Press, 1982.

CHAPTER 2

Race and Representation in Canadian Public Podcasting: A CBC Study

Jeff Donison

INTRODUCTION

For people outside of mainstream media production, podcasting presents a potential space for voicing themselves. Podcasting requires only a basic understanding of digital applications and minimal economic investment. This alternative is notably liberating for racially and ethnically marginalized communities in Canada, who have often been silenced or spoken for by white, mainstream media (Henry and Tator 7). As Photini Vrikki and Sarita Malik argue, "In an international climate that bolsters populist rhetoric around minority cultural groups, podcasts occupy a rare marginal space for articulating the lived experiences of these groups, whilst challenging broader patterns of racialised disenfranchisement, including in the digital creative industries" (275). Racially and ethnically marginalized groups are using podcasting as a creative practice for producing social, political, and cultural discourse in meaningful ways for their communities (Florini 212). Podcasters and listeners can form intimate communities around podcasts as media texts (Llinares et al. 2).

The simultaneous process of self-representation and community interaction in podcasting is produced through "digital storytelling," which Nick Couldry defines as "personal stories now being told in potentially public form using digital media resources" (374). Podcasts as digital media resources are, in most cases, publicly available, self-representative stories that "promise to deliver authentic accounts of individual 'ordinary people'" (Thumim 4). Personal stories are commonplace in many podcast genres but are particularly prevalent in podcasts discussing race and ethnicity. In Canada, many racially and ethnically conscious podcasts explore attitudes, prejudices, and socialization toward racial and ethnic issues, and they revisit historical narratives and conceptualizations of Canadian identity and culture. In this way, podcasts can be defined as alternative media voicing "the social relations, issues, and experiences of groups that are often marginalized or excluded in corporate media" (Kozolanka et al. 3). Digital storytelling as a podcasting "technique for increasing understanding across generations, ethnicities and other divides" (Couldry 387) is important for voicing lived experiences that contest mainstream media representations of marginalized groups produced by settler Canadians.

But podcasting is not solely an alternative media practice anymore. Mainstream media are exercising podcasting's online affordances too, increasingly occupying the podcast industry by investing their time and money into production and online circulation to reach new audiences. Linda Kenix defines mainstream media as outlets that

> are situated completely within (and concomitantly co-creating) the ideological norms of society, enjoy a widespread scale of influence, rely on professionalized reporters and are heavily connected with other corporate and government entities.... Mainstream media have been traditionally viewed as ... relying on content that would appeal to the most ... readers and therefore ignoring the issues that are perhaps more important to smaller, minority groups. (3, 10)

The most popular podcasts in many Western countries are often produced by private, mainstream American media or public service media, including National Public Radio (NPR), the British Broadcasting Corporation (BBC), Australian Broadcasting Corporation (ABC), and the Canadian Broadcasting Corporation (CBC) (Berry 663; Simone Murray 201). Mainstream and public service media like the CBC are using their large infrastructures to collaborate with podcasters to produce programs that reflect their broadcasting mandates while reaching larger Canadian audiences.

Historically, many mainstream media outlets have disseminated information embedded in ideologies that "end up reflecting the 'preferred meanings' of a still dominant white society" (Jenkins 24). Whiteness has become naturalized and taken for granted while other races are represented in relation to whiteness as the status quo. When racialized groups are represented, they are predominantly portrayed negatively, in contrast to the discourse of whiteness as connotatively ideal within "the larger economy of representations prevailing within the mass media" (Jiwani 488). For example, Indigenous Peoples have been represented as savage, uncivil, lazy, and wild (Francis 482). Black people have been represented as criminal (Fleras 64; Henry and Tator 41). Immigrants have been represented as deviants, security risks, and fanatics based on non-Christian religious practices (Fleras 28). As Minelle Mahtani argues, "Negative depictions of minorities teach minorities in Canada that they are threatening, deviant, and irrelevant to nation-building" (100). Racialized groups are stereotyped and conflated in this discriminatory process of media representation, where European-settler culture has been positively portrayed and synonymous with Canadian identity (Smith 39).

In Canada, the CBC was developed as a remedy for privately produced, discriminatory media by developing content for all people based on public service media goals. Public service media (PSM) are defined as outlets that aim "to fulfill public interest obligations such as universal coverage, diversity and quality of programming, appeal to minority groups, emphasis on local and national content, and commitment to impartial standards of journalism" (Brevini 1). PSM exist on the media spectrum (Kenix 19) between mainstream and alternative media since PSM are funded, at least partially, by government agencies and have public influence and popularity, but they also reflect the voices and concerns of all regional groups. The CBC, as Canada's premier PSM, ideally provides opportunities for marginalized groups to produce representations within a media system that is publicly driven and nationally available.

The CBC is an important broadcaster to review because of its contradictory presence of popularity in the mainstream alongside its creation "to counteract the monopolization of the airwaves by the forces of wealth and power" (Basen 148). In a 2019 survey conducted by the Media Technology Monitor, Anglophone Canadians listed only two Canadian podcasts, *Ideas* and *Someone Knows* (both CBC produced), in their top 10 favourite podcasts. In Francophone communities, nine Canadian podcasts, seven of which are CBC produced, made the participants' top 10 list (CBC/Radio-Canada, "Enviroscan—2019" 19). Given the CBC's podcasting popularity in Canada, it is important to study if this PSM production through an initially alternative medium offers the same representative content produced by and for communities that are traditionally marginalized from mass media production. As Anamik Saha argues, people should consider to what degree "minorities are given the autonomy that would enable their creativity. The issue of diversity, representation, autonomy and creativity is at the core of discussions of public service media" (95).

By examining the CBC, this chapter offers an introductory exploration into PSM podcasting as a creative industry for racially and ethnically marginalized groups. Specific attention is paid to marginalized podcasters producing identities and representations within the CBC through critical podcasting narratives that address the cultural makeup of Canada in accordance with the CBC's broadcasting mandate. Media production can be an expensive and technologically complex artistic and commercial form requiring strategic access to financial, organizational, and marketing resources that are rarely available to marginalized storytellers. The CBC's podcasting is important to study to identify if the public model existing between mainstream and alternative media offers the same representative potential as independent podcasting for marginalized communities to contest oppressive mainstream media discourse using national broadcasting resources.

METHOD AND SAMPLE

This chapter begins with a brief overview of the CBC's mandate and entry into podcasting. The CBC is the object of inquiry because of its national broadcasting mandate to represent Canadian audiences, to exchange cultural expression, to contribute to national identity, to be widely accessible, and to "reflect the multicultural and multiracial nature of Canada" (CBC/Radio-Canada, "Mandate"). As Stacey Copeland and Lauren Knight argue, "Considering the continued use of 'multicultural' and 'diversity' language in CBC's governing documents, it is important to approach media produced by the government-funded public broadcaster with critical senses" (104). Following the overview of the CBC's mandate and podcasting is a textual analysis of two CBC podcasts, *The Secret Life of Canada* (*TSLOC*) and *New Fire*.

I chose *TSLOC* for analysis because it represents many non-white communities. *TSLOC* is a CBC original podcast that "highlights the people, places and stories that didn't make it into your high school textbook" (CBC/Radio-Canada, "About The Secret Life of Canada"). Produced in Toronto since 2018, *TSLOC* examines marginalized narratives as counter-discourses to dominant representations of Canadian history generally accepted as truth. Hosts Falen Johnson, who is Mohawk and Tuscarora Bear Clan from Six Nations, and Leah-Simone Bowen, a first-generation Barbadian Canadian, use this podcasting space to transmit alternative stories, or histories omitted altogether, about marginalized people across Canada. Johnson and Bowen conduct journalistic investigations, consult experts and historians, and invite people who have lived, or identify with, the stories being discussed to share their perspectives.

New Fire was also chosen for analysis because it represents the heterogenous and intersectional membership of various Indigenous nations across Canada. *New*

Fire is a CBC podcast that "brings you to the surprising heart of the conversations important to Aboriginal youth" (CBC/Radio-Canada, "New Fire"). As an "Urban Native Girl" and Tsilhqot'in writer from Tsi Deldel First Nation in British Columbia, host Lisa Charleyboy facilitates a podcasting space for Indigenous Peoples to discuss dating, home life, technology, sports, and other matters within various Indigenous communities across Canada. The podcast aired two seasons between 2015 and 2017, providing a space for Indigenous Peoples to share their experiences navigating their cultural identities within contemporary Canada.

Two episodes from each podcast were purposively selected based on their narratives addressing racially and ethnically marginalized identities and histories in Canada. The four-episode sample size is small in order to conduct a deeper listening of podcasters' and guests' perspectives within singular episodes. This deep listening offers an introductory understanding of how the CBC's small but increasing number of critical podcasts can support more representative discourse produced by, and for, marginalized communities about their intersectional identities in Canada. Episode narratives were assessed on their ability to represent marginalized legacies, experiences, and expressions nationally through the voices of those directly affected. These episode narratives are then compared with the CBC's mandate and podcast catalogue to identify how the CBC is becoming a production space for the racial representation of individual podcasters and their communities, who are un(der)represented in mainstream media. As Stuart Hall argues, the media "help to classify out the world in terms of the categories of race.… [But] they are also one place where these ideas are articulated, *worked on*, *transformed* and elaborated" ("The Whites of Their Eyes" 104; added emphasis). This chapter concludes with a short discussion of how the CBC, as an increasingly popular PSM podcast producer, can continue fostering meaningful inclusiveness moving forward through collaboration with independent podcasters and journalists.

THE CBC'S PODCASTING

The CBC has become a premier Canadian podcast producer after it began repurposing radio content as podcasts online in June 2005 (Cwynar 190; Simone Murray 201), releasing its first original podcast, *Campus*, in 2015, which chronicled the experiences and perspectives of students throughout the country (CBC/Radio-Canada, "Throughout the Years"). In 2020, the CBC had over 130 audio programs labelled as podcasts on their English website and had received over 200 million total podcast downloads (Canada, Canadian Heritage, *Creative Canada* 32). It is not surprising that the CBC increasingly invests resources into podcasting, since "25% of all podcast listeners in the country listen to at least one of its productions" (CBC/Radio-Canada, "CBC Podcasts"). The CBC's English-language podcasts are said to represent "a wide range of subjects, all explored with the finesse and uniquely *Canadian* viewpoint we've come to expect from this public broadcaster" (CBC/Radio-Canada, "CBC Podcasts"; added emphasis). But what is meant by a uniquely Canadian viewpoint?

National culture is partially constructed through a media system of representation via images, words, and symbols that produce meanings organizing our ideas and how we see ourselves (Hall, "The Question of Cultural Identity" 292). "Simply put, the media is responsible for the ways that Canadian society is interpreted, considered, and evaluated among its residents" (Mahtani 99). If media representations about Canadian identity are accepted nationally, they help shape public perceptions about what it means to be or act Canadian in tandem with other institutional representations. The media production of Canadian representations is therefore important to address when transmitted by the CBC, as the nationally representative broadcaster. According to Section 3(m)(viii) of Canada's *Broadcasting Act*, "the programming provided by the [Canadian Broadcasting] Corporation should reflect the multicultural and multiracial nature of Canada" (Canada, Canadian Heritage 5). Furthermore, Section 3(m)(vi) states that "the programming provided by the Corporation should contribute to shared national consciousness and identity" (Canada, Canadian Heritage 5). Although this 1991 legislation applies to broadcasting pre-Internet, its premised ideal presents the CBC as having a strong role in potentially producing podcasts voicing un(der)represented "ideas about racial and ethnic difference as embodied in these texts" (Saha 6). Furthermore, critical podcasts addressing racialized experiences in Canada help bridge knowledge and context gaps (Swiatek 173–74) between podcasters and different sociocultural communities across the country.

Since the CBC produced its first original podcast, its organizational strategy has emphasized reflecting contemporary Canada through staffing and content (CBC/Radio-Canada, "Your Stories, Taken to Heart"). Stories are the mainstay of podcasting, and based on national legislation and PSM frameworks, the CBC should create an inclusive space for marginalized groups to represent their experiences, histories, and identities through digital storytelling. Podcasting aligns with the CBC's overall organizational strategies. But is the CBC fulfilling the legislative aims and its organizational strategies through its podcasts? A small but increasing number of the CBC's podcasts are hosted by racially and ethnically marginalized groups who critically represent racial and ethnic issues, lived experiences, and histories. A few of these programs include *TSLOC*, *New Fire*, *Kiwew*,

Missing & Murdered, *Recovering Filipino*, *Telling Our Twisted Histories*, *Seat at the Table*, and *Sleepover*. These podcasts are emblematic of the CBC's products that "are expertly produced, [and] reflect the best documentary traditions of public broadcasting" (Taras and Waddell 137). What do these podcasts indicate about public podcasting's inclusivity for producing marginalized narratives? Here, the CBC's podcast narratives must be examined in detail.

THE SECRET LIFE OF CANADA

"The Indian Act"

Whether celebrating marginalized cultures or surveying harsh discrimination and histories of European colonialism in Canada, *TSLOC* presents a collaborative effort to reinterpret history by addressing systemic oppression and its lasting effects on communities today. In season two's tenth full episode, "The Indian Act," released on June 25, 2019, Johnson and Bowen evaluate the *Indian Act* (Canada, Department of Indian Affairs). The *Indian Act* is a federal law that has allowed the Canadian government to dictate how First Nations bands can operate and defines who qualifies as a status "Indian," among other forms of legal control. Criticizing this form of enfranchisement, Johnson notes that "non-Indigenous women who wanted to marry Indigenous men, they could get status. So, if you're a white woman, and you married an Indigenous man, you would become Indigenous, but it didn't work the other way around. So, an Indigenous woman who married a white man would lose her status" (CBC/Radio-Canada, "The Indian Act"). *TSLOC*'s episode reviews this policy, rooted in racist and sexist colonial ideology and renouncing Indigenous identity and sovereignty in exchange for assimilative Canadian citizenship and land control.

Johnson and Bowen invite Kaniehti:io Horn, Mohawk actress and host of podcasts *Coffee with My Ma* and the CBC-produced *Telling Our Twisted Histories*, to discuss how the *Indian Act*'s status rules perpetuate racism and sexism. "Our ways is like, you have a clan, you give it a name ... that's what makes you ... you identify ... through how you were raised and not by—because you're given a number" (CBC/Radio-Canada, "The Indian Act"). Horn voices her frustration about the Canadian government trying to define her identity for her and the possibility of being legally stripped of Indigenous status altogether. Johnson and Bowen's podcast provides perspectives like Horn's to illustrate the colonial struggle Indigenous Peoples face today stemming from the *Indian Act* (Canada, Department of Indian Affairs), which was created in 1876, and the government's attempted control and subjection of Indigenous identities.

However, Horn's perspective does not insist that Indigenous identities are successfully subjugated altogether. Rather, this episode celebrates Indigenous cultures and histories of resistance as much as it criticizes the *Indian Act*. Discussing former prime minister Pierre Trudeau's attempt to dissolve the Act in 1969, which was highly contested among First Nations, Bowen asks Johnson why the discriminatory legislation has not been dissolved completely. Johnson replies,

> It would terminate our identities and our rights as sovereign nations. Our reserve lands would be for sale, our treaties would be dissolved. To many Indigenous people, those treaties, those agreements, our ancestors made those, and they are sacred to us. It would also erase Canada's history and responsibilities. It means we would become assimilated. We would just become Canadians. (CBC/Radio-Canada, "The Indian Act")

Johnson is simultaneously acknowledging her ancestors' agreements to peacefully coexist with settler Canadians and the importance of maintaining the Act as proof of broken promises that Canada has continually dishonoured and uses to maintain power. Both her ancestral identity and the need for government accountability are solidified within the *Indian Act* and the peace proclamations before its construction in 1876. Johnson explains her rejection of identifying as Canadian since Canadian identity is synonymous with European settlement and is institutionally founded on the control of Indigenous Land and the erasure of Indigenous identities through legally enforced assimilation. As Métis writer Chelsea Vowel states, "Many Indigenous peoples do not identify as Canadian because at no point did they or their ancestors consent to becoming Canadian" (11). Overall, "The Indian Act" episode provides experiential Indigenous narratives to destabilize the very ontology of Canadian identity that dominant institutions, including mainstream media, have helped to construct discursively.

"Where Is Japantown?"

In "Where Is Japantown?," the second full episode of *TSLOC*'s third season released on May 12, 2020, Johnson and Bowen address Japanese internment camps in Canada during World War II. The hosts focus on the largest camp, Tashme, which held 2,600 Japanese Canadians after 1941. Johnson and Bowen explain the terrible conditions that the Canadian government forced people into based on their supposedly threatening ancestral identity. World War II rhetoric in Canada predominantly focused on Canada's support of the British Commonwealth overseas, yet rhetoric regarding internment camps on Canadian soil is often ignored or passively acknowledged within dominant media discourse (Oikawa 17). Johnson and Bowen's investigation reveals the displacement and dispossession these camps caused as well as the lack of critical accountability non–Japanese Canadians have taken for the treatment of Japanese Canadians historically.

Since many Japanese Canadian internment survivors have either passed away or do not publicly speak about their trauma, Johnson and Bowen invite two voice actors from *The Tashme Project*, Julie Tamiko Manning and Matt Miwa, to perform survivor testimonies they heard through their interviews with the Nisei. "'The Tashme Project' is a one-act verbatim theatre piece that traces the history and common experience of the Nisei … from Toronto, Hamilton, Kingston, Montreal and Vancouver" (*Tashme Project*). *TSLOC*'s podcast episode captures the "crucial communicative aspects of the voice such as … accent, dialect, and other elements of the emotional content of speech" (Bottomley 213) that Manning and Miwa produce on top of piano instrumentals to create an intimate environment between listeners and survivors. These individualized testimonies recall different stages of the internment camp process and the collective sense of foreign-ness the Nisei community felt within Canada. Together, the experiential stories create a poly-lithic narrative of living as a Japanese Canadian in the 1940s. *TSLOC* structures a participatory culture, where Manning and Miwa's testimonial performances of Nisei internment are centralized alongside Johnson's and Bowen's historical cri-tique of oppressive Canadian policy and ideology.

As an educational text about identity and displacement, *TSLOC*'s episode ad-dresses the larger struggle of Japanese Canadians being Othered, displaced, and excluded since internment. Paul Gilroy argues that major problems arise for "the half-different and the partially familiar" (*Against Race* 106) because this hybridity of sameness-difference is a threat to group pureness. In other words, Japanese Canadians during World War II were not seen as Canadians, which is a settler construction, but as homogenously Japanese and thus easier to manage and ex-clude. Although many of these prisoners identified as Canadian, the government did not view them as such based on physical traits and their symbolic meanings. *TSLOC*'s episode presents humanized testimonies that are often omitted from national narratives, and it confronts historical Canadian representations defining Japanese Canadian identity as foreign and threatening.

Mass media representations have helped shape the national imagination of supposedly peaceful settlement and egalitarianism between European settlers and racialized groups (Mackey 39). Mahtani argues that if these types of representa-tions remain owned, controlled, and produced by those in power, "the potential for greater diversity of stories that expose racial injustice, or tell other kinds of stories about minorities, for example, decreases" (112). *TSLOC* is one space with collaborative and representative value in "its ability to centre the role of the historian and invite the listener into this process" (Cuffe 555). As an e-diaspora, which is a dispersed community formed online with a common goal or movement (Hogarth and Fletcher 67), *TSLOC* is not restricted by singular ethnic, racial, or national identity. Instead, *TSLOC* is a collection of stories featuring marginalized histories and peoples in Canada, including Mohawk ironworkers, Black nurses, and the Nisei internment survivors. The podcast additionally produces "Shout Out" mini episodes that highlight individuals and their successes personally and professionally that are not regularly shown in mainstream media.

Identity markers and their meanings transform over time and across different cultural contexts. Therefore, identity allows podcasts like *TSLOC* to potentially contest naturalized representations of difference and enables marginalized podcasters and listeners to define themselves in a process of self-making. One of PSM's goals is to facilitate "a potentially enabling space for minority producers to intervene in the hegemonic construction of national identity" (Saha 159). The CBC's podcasting e-diaspora as a "multidimensional structure of similarities and differences" (Hall, "Nations and Diasporas" 172) supports marginalized peoples, like Japanese Canadians or the Mohawk in Canada, to negotiate self-representation and self-definition between multiple intersections. *TSLOC* is a production space for marginalized hosts, interviewees, and listeners to use PSM resources to represent themselves nationally and feel a sense of belonging in Canada while addressing discrimination.

NEW FIRE

"Young and Aboriginal in 2015"

New Fire is another critical CBC podcast that tells stories from Indigenous perspectives across Canada. In *New Fire*'s debut episode, "Young and Aboriginal in 2015," released on June 30, 2015, Charleyboy interviews Dustin Ross Fiddler, a Nêhiyaw actor and band councillor at Waterhen Lake First Nation. Fiddler shares his story about an acting audition where he was told that he did not look "Native" enough for the role because he did not wear a hair braid. Charleyboy also interviews Baillie Redfern, a Métis woman and Miss Indian World Pageant contestant, who similarly experienced discrimination based on Métis garments that she wore in her first competition. Both Fiddler and Redfern were individually expected to look and act a certain way based on a supposedly definable "Nativeness." These digital stories highlight the complexities of Indigenous identities (Lawrence 173) and assumptions about Indigeneity. Kathy Hogarth and Wendy Fletcher note that "to control people's culture and way of thinking is to control how they define themselves in relationships with others" (42). Fiddler and Redfern rejected external control and dominant ideologies within their respective creative industries and additionally define themselves through their podcasting representations.

Charleyboy also interviews Dr. Jules Arita Koostachin, a documentary director and Attawapiskat First Nation band member, who speaks on the oppressive force of Canadian colonization over the Cree. Echoing Fiddler's and Redfern's sentiments, she states:

> When you think of how we identify ourselves in terms of Néhiyawak, which is the Cree people, translates to the human beings, so essentially, when you are saying, "Oh, you're not Indian enough," or, "You're not Cree enough," you're basically saying, "Oh, you're not human enough." So I think there is something to be said around, you know, how we identify and how we relate to each other. (CBC/Radio-Canada, "Young and Aboriginal in 2015")

Koostachin argues that the us (white, human)/Other (non-white, inhuman) dichotomy perpetuated in dominant national discourse that idealizes whiteness as naturally Canadian and thus non-whiteness as Other is only one, and albeit detrimental, narrative working alongside colonial representations that help shape the settler imagination of who Indigenous Peoples are (Francis 474). More consideration should be placed on how people identify themselves and relate to each other, which podcasts help transmit, as comprising intersectional identities. Koostachin, Fiddler, and Redfern control their own identities and representations rather than have others dictate what it means to identify as Néhiyawak, Métis, or any other cultural affiliation. The guests resist external subjugation by using the CBC's openly dialogical podcasting space to represent themselves nationally.

New Fire is a form of oral storytelling that resembles Indigenous cultural practices of intimate oral performance as knowledge transmission over generations (Corntassel et al. 138). Participants like Koostachin, who is accompanied by her children in the episode, can speak across generations (time) and across Canada (space) to spread experiential stories about living in Canada as Indigenous Peoples. These lived experiences, articulated digitally, are emblematic of everyday stories that "have great social and political significance—and could potentially be indispensable for understanding the lives of those who lived the culture" (Bottomley 215).

"Where Are You From?"

In *New Fire*'s season two premiere, "Where Are You From?," released on June 29, 2017, Charleyboy interviews Rebecca Thomas, a Mi'kmaw writer and former Halifax poet laureate from Lennox Island First Nation. Thomas explains that as a multicultural person, "I've always existed as an 'other' person but haven't really recognized that 'til somebody decided to say some pretty terrible things to me" (CBC, "Where Are You From?"). Thomas explains that both settler and Indigenous communities often interpret an Indigenous person's "Nativeness" based on what cultural practices the person knows or how they look, which can cause internalization of Otherness. Thomas's internalization had forced her to feel belonging neither to the Mi'kmaq nor to her settler Canadian identity, to feel excluded from both identity groups and having to "walk that line" (CBC, "Where Are You From?"). Resembling Japanese Canadians in *TSLOC*'s "Where Is Japantown?" episode who viewed themselves as neither Canadian nor Japanese, Thomas highlights how her intersectional identity had caused her to feel excluded due to exterior essentialization dismissing half-difference as a form of control.

Charleyboy agrees with Thomas's feelings of displacement, narrating her own experience of learning more about her heritage while being a student in Toronto. Alluding to the episode title, Charleyboy and Thomas were both born in Canada, yet they explain that previously they did not have a definitive answer defining "where they are from." Even now, their intersectional identities can incite multiple answers since "identities deriving from the nation could be shown to be competing with subnational (local or regional) and supranational (diaspora) structures of belonging and kinship" (Gilroy, "British Cultural Studies" 394). For Thomas and Charleyboy, as much as for Koostachin, Redfern, and Fiddler, their intersectional identities are (re)defined and shared through podcast production that aims to represent various cultures in Canada, even if these specific podcasters and interviewees do not identify primarily as Canadians themselves, if at all, due to Canada's ideological association with whiteness.

THE CBC'S PRODUCTION PROCESS AND CATALOGUE

Both *TSLOC* and *New Fire* provide podcasting spaces for voicing perspectives that are not heard writ large in mainstream Canadian media. The CBC's mandate is to be a nationally representative broadcaster producing freely available content with, and about, the various cultures in Canada. *TSLOC* successfully fulfills the CBC's mandate by representing Canadian listenership through its interpretations of heterogenous cultures in Canada, by exchanging cultural expression through Johnson's and Bowen's journalistic commentary and by being widely, and freely, accessible to those with an Internet connection through major streaming apps and on the CBC's website. *TSLOC* additionally critiques Canadian identity by disseminating counter-discourses that more accurately reflect marginalized communities within Canada through representations of lived experiences. *New Fire* also successfully fulfills the CBC's mandate by representing Indigenous youth in Canada, exchanging cultural expression between various Indigenous Peoples and their lands, contributing to a reconstructed national identity grounded in Indigenous cultures and history, and being freely available on all CBC platforms and podcast aggregators.

The CBC's experiential podcasts surveyed here create a "process through which a person becomes a certain kind of subject owning certain identities in the social realm, identities constituted through material, cultural, economic, and psychic relations" (Smith and Watson 31). The hosts and guests use podcasting as a system of representation that articulates multiple potential identities (Hall, "The Question of Cultural Identity" 277). In other words, these podcasts implicitly critique monolithic representations of marginalized communities that influence public perceptions by alternatively transmitting a variety of perspectives within and across racial and cultural groups. By facilitating experientially diverse notions of individual and group identity for listeners, public podcasts can produce intimacies, "emotional experiences and personal connections in a comfortable space between interviewers and interview subjects, between the producers themselves, and between listeners, producers, and subjects" (Spinelli and Dann 77). Thus, PSM podcasters may use digital storytelling to transparently self-represent, just as Johnson, Bowen, and Charleyboy do, and the CBC then distributes these stories nationally to communities with Internet access who can identify with the content or learn from new perspectives.

TSLOC and *New Fire* together emphasize how freely accessible digital storytelling can help people address oppressive systems, define their own identities, and amend hegemonically constructed histories using PSM resources. Andrew Bottomley argues that "collective memory or collective consciousness of a society … can only be truly understood through the careful consideration of a plurality of subjective voices" (215). *TSLOC* and *New Fire* reassess national identity based on heterogeneity rather than ethnic, racial, or national homogenization. Both podcasts implicitly critique Section 3(m)(vi) of the national *Broadcasting Act* (Canada, Canadian Heritage) that instructs the CBC to produce content representing Canada. Shared consciousness and identity are currently produced generally through settler notions of diversity and what is deemed Canadian. Eva Mackey argues that "despite the proliferation of cultural difference, the power to define, limit and tolerate differences still lies in the hands of the dominant group" (83). However, *TSLOC* and *New Fire* critique the foundation of Canadian nationality itself from un(der)represented perspectives within a publicly driven, but still mainstream, media system. Collectively, the CBC's growing podcast catalogue includes an increasing number of critical podcasts produced by marginalized communities about the polylithic populations of Canada that are traditionally un(der)represented or misrepresented in mainstream media.

Seat at the Table is a CBC podcast launched in July 2017 and hosted by Martine St-Victor and Isabelle Racicot. In season two, St-Victor and Racicot "capture personal stories and perspectives on the Black Lives Matter movement, the urgency of this movement, and what it will take to move forward. Plus, they're ready to hold everyone (including themselves) accountable" (CBC, "Seat at the Table—About the Show"). St-Victor and Racicot interview Black academics, journalists, artists, and athletes about systemic racism within their respective fields while reflecting on their own experiences within Quebec as racialized people. One of the podcast's main objectives is to provide an opportunity (a seat) for marginalized peoples to talk about critical issues in privileged spaces (the table) like the media. *Seat at the Table* illustrates the range of perspectives within, and across, various racialized communities in Canada. A few episode guests include Robyn Maynard, Anthony Duclair, and Roxane Gay.

Missing & Murdered is a CBC podcast series hosted by Cree journalist Connie Walker. Each season centres on Walker's investigation into missing and murdered Indigenous women and girls (MMIWG) in Canada. The first season, in 2016, "unearths new information and potential suspects in the cold case of a young Indigenous woman [Alberta Williams] murdered in British Columbia in 1989." The second season, in 2018, follows the search for Cleo Semaganis Nicotine, a young Cree girl who was separated from her family in the 1970s "by child welfare authorities in Saskatchewan" (CBC, "Missing & Murdered"). Walker's journalistic podcast raises awareness about MMIWG in Canada that has, until recently, received minimal mainstream media attention. The podcast also addresses the history of colonization in Canada through systems like residential schooling and the Sixties Scoop, the effects of which are still present today. As Copeland and Knight argue in their study of Walker's *Missing & Murdered* season two, "it is mass media representation such as *Finding Cleo* by indigenous people about indigenous people that refuses to accept white civility but rather chooses to work within the structures given to break them down from the inside" (105).

Kiwew is another CBC podcast, hosted by award-winning Cree writer David A. Robertson. Spanning five episodes during 2020, Robertson "dives into his family's history and mysteries as he discovers and connects with his Cree identity" (CBC, "Kiwew"). *Kiwew,* which is Cree for "he goes home," refers to Robertson's return to his Cree identity accessed through the land and his family history. He uses audio recordings, interviews, and narration to sonically capture the process of learning about his father, including revisiting his father's trapline. The podcast underscores Robertson's effort as an Indigenous adult to connect with his Indigenous identity more closely than he did as a child. The podcast also highlights Robertson's hope for future Indigenous generations to be introduced to, and take pride in, cultural practices and ways of knowing at an early age. This is represented in the podcast when Robertson's daughter learns Cree from her grandfather, signifying the resurgence of Indigenous identity through language (Vowel 65).

Sleepover is a CBC podcast hosted by Sook-Yin Lee, a filmmaker, actor, artist, and broadcaster. The podcast brings together three strangers in a single place to have a conversation. "In each episode, with Sook-Yin's guidance, one stranger takes the spotlight and presents a problem from their life. The other two offer advice and bring up related experiences from their own unique perspectives" (CBC/Radio-Canada, "About Sleepover"). The guests articulate how they view themselves and their position in the world through these conversations. The setting of each sleepover is different, ranging from a cabin to a hotel room to Native Child and Family Services of Toronto. Lee's ability to incite and mediate conversations between podcast guests highlights the potential of podcasting for people to cross knowledge and context boundaries (Swiatek 173–74), where individuals can learn from one another across cultural divides between guests and among other listeners.

These CBC programs are only a few that illustrate how the CBC's PSM podcasting can support traditionally marginalized voices to critique dominant Canadian institutions and representations, produce individual and group identities through digital storytelling, and facilitate listening texts representing the collective makeup of Canada. Policies and practices producing representations of one nation too often create an idea of one people, yet each Western nation is a cultural hybrid that rarely facilitates equal expression. For many people living in Canada, to be Canadian is to identify with how mainstream media represent Canadianness, which homogenizes all races and ethnicities while Eurocentrically erasing their unique traces. Mahtani argues that "restricted frames of thinking and decisions about who is considered a 'real' Canadian determine which 'voices of the public' are collected and broadcast" (115). Mainstream media representations of Canadian culture have traditionally marginalized and homogenized diverse cultural practices in an attempted erasure of unique racial and ethnic histories and identities in striving for unitary nationhood through shared traditions. The CBC's podcasts, including *TSLOC* and *New Fire*, aim to reconstruct national identity by narrativizing marginalized identities and groups living within Canada, or they reject national identity altogether since dominant understandings of Canadian identity maintain settler narratives, and thus whiteness, as naturally Canadian. The CBC's podcasts are potential spaces to produce further dialogue and critical representations in long-form, non-commercial, and conversational structures created by marginalized communities through participatory PSM.

COLLABORATIVE EFFORTS

As mentioned in the introduction of this chapter, podcasting as a form of digital storytelling helps marginalized communities outside mainstream media production represent themselves independently. Freja Sørine Adler Berg argues, "The production of independent podcasts is different to institutional podcasts (e.g., produced by private or public media institutions) and branded podcasts as it is characterized by the highest degree of autonomy" (157). The independent model closely resembles alternative or community media (Brevini 3), advancing "compelling, real stories about people from all walks of life, unburdened by the necessity to cultivate large, mainstream audiences" (Sullivan 39). In her study on podcaster motivations, Kris Markman defines an independent podcaster "as someone who creates and distributes a regular podcast that does not have its origins in a pre-existing traditional media program or outlet" (552). Independent podcasting is effective in achieving diverse representation since podcasts capture "predominantly ordinary people ... [and] narratives and points of view that are rarely represented in other mass media, at least not with this level of attention and care" (Bottomley 214).

However, with podcasting becoming an increasingly popular creative industry, the dominance of privately and publicly produced podcasts in Canada has threatened independent podcasters from being widely heard. This is not to say that all independent podcasters cannot reach an audience without institutional affiliation (Swiatek 183) nor that all independent podcasters necessarily want to. It also does not mean that independent podcasters are silenced altogether. Yet the nature of podcasting's popularity, grounded in secretive algorithms and charting based on cyclical listenership (more listeners means more charting, which means more listeners, etc.), may create uncertainty for independents (Adler Berg 157) while sustaining dominance for established media organizations. Independent

podcasters have created collectives through shared resources, fanbases, and promotion of each other's podcasts (Sarah Murray 305) to thrive independently, but
there are multiple financial and production factors that can influence podcasters to
leave independent production. Independent podcasters or journalists may instead
choose to join established podcast networks like the CBC's if production goals
align and the opportunity for collaboration is available.

Volunteers and workers within independent podcasting may seek employment
with media companies while established networks may seek out independent
podcast(er)s reaching niche Canadian audiences who are underserved and underrepresented by mainstream media (Heeremans 71). Demonstrative of creative
industries, mainstream companies may use their recognized branding and for-
matting to promote a niche product with greater potential for success in a larger
market (Hesmondhalgh 556). Collaboration provides one opportunity for marginalized publics to reach larger audiences. Yet collaborative practice also raises
the issue of product ownership, since networks may request control in exchange
for their resources. A dilemma can result for podcasters who may have to navigate
their independence, creativity, and content production in exchange for potentially
wider listenership and increased access to resources.

Depending on program guidelines, independent podcasting may afford
relatively open and free communication since there are fewer restrictive policies
in place. However, the independent model is often not financially profitable.
Free-to-download podcast consumption "troubles simple notions of the podcast
as an agent of media democratisation" (Wilson 275) since everyone does not have
the means or privilege to produce podcasts for free. Although independent programs can receive subsidies and donations, there are limited national grants in
podcasting's large creative industry (Banks 133). This may force many independent
podcasters without access to mainstream production to wither away if profit is a
driving motivation, further marginalizing their voices.

PSM like the CBC have funding and resources for facilitating in-depth journalism and a larger audience reach compared to many independent programs who
share the same publicly representative goals. The CBC receives government funding that independent programs may not, though its financial support has been
threatened in the past (Taras and Waddell 177). However, if funding is sustained,
the CBC's community-driven podcasting can offer representative narrative production and freely accessible episodes for a national audience through its podcast website, the CBC Listen app, or other major aggregators. Saha argues that
a "PSM needs to fully commit to a remit that is focused on covering different
aspects of minority experience alongside a commitment to presenting them to

the mainstream" (175). The CBC's podcast catalogue is increasingly producing representations about marginalized experiences from within these communities through digital storytelling presented to the mainstream. Independent podcasters may thrive by collaborating with the CBC if given future opportunities.

The CBC should continue to grow their catalogue through racially and ethnically conscious podcasts that, while they may be niche, reflect a more representative (audio) picture of Canada compared to mass media productions, particularly in a Canadian industry dominated by American products. The national broadcaster can continue this task by using its resources to fulfill its community obligations, and it has begun this endeavour by openly inviting pitches for new, original podcast programs (CBC/Radio-Canada, "CBC Podcasts: Pitch Guide"), although this creative opportunity needs to be advertised more widely. Jeremy Wade Morris et al. argue that "podcasting offers both the potential to bring new voices into the mediascapes of everyday users and the possibility for sound workers to learn new skills and techniques for expressing and sharing ideas" (8). More financial and educational support should be provided to public initiatives to help people without financial or technical capital be introduced to podcast production and continually support independent podcasters.

CONCLUSION

Podcasts and podcasters in this chapter demonstrate that the CBC can be a space for enlightening public consciousness about omitted histories and experiences of racially and ethnically marginalized communities across Canada. The CBC's representative potential is grounded in its publicly driven and journalistically integral podcast production that addresses definitions of national history and culture constructed in an inclusive, niche industry. More importantly, racially and ethnically marginalized communities may use public podcasts to produce their own identities and derive their own meanings from within an established institution that has national reach. The CBC's podcasts, illustrated by *TSLOC* and *New Fire*, implicitly critique Canada's *Broadcasting Act*, requiring the CBC to produce content representing Canadian culture and identity. The programs do not represent a particular Canadian identity, but these digital stories—about the Nisei internment survivors, First Nations under the *Indian Act*, and Indigenous youth, for example—instead address the colonial construction of nationality, which is often absent from representations within mainstream media.

TSLOC's and *New Fire*'s e-diasporas are major alternatives for contesting institutionally constructed national identity, especially from within a national public broadcaster. E-diasporas reject national identity as natural and shared (Gilroy, *Against Race* 123). The CBC's growing podcast catalogue, including *Seat at the Table*, *Missing & Murdered*, *Kiwew*, and *Sleepover*, illustrates the possibility for a variety of podcasters to produce unique programs like Johnson, Bowen, and Charleyboy do to represent themselves and control their identities while critiquing generalized representations in Canada. In turn, listeners can identify with such perspectives or learn from them since these programs are available nationally to many sociocultural communities.

Overall, the CBC strives to be universally accessible in Canada by facilitating equal rights programming and circulation and producing quality content "to enhance public life, and enrich individual lives, rather than to serve advertisers. Its goals are cultural, rather than economic" (Rowland 8). Canadian government policy via the *Broadcasting Act* has attempted to intervene in media industries by promoting PSM produced and funded by the people, for the people. However, for a long time, "the people" in Canada has referred to dominant, white communities. The CBC aims to address this imbalance in racial representation through its critical podcast catalogue that includes programs produced by and for racially and ethnically marginalized communities. With podcasting becoming mainstream, it is evident that the CBC should facilitate more podcast productions about marginalized narratives, histories, and experiences moving forward. This representative effort can be fulfilled through collaboration with independent podcasters or journalists and through increased advertising of potential creative opportunities and education for people without access to podcast technology or training.

As Bottomley states: "That someone's life can become a *story*—a narrative that is heard by others and, in the process, recognized as having value—is one crucial way of showing that the person's experiences, and thereby the person's life, count" (221) (original emphasis). As a country considered post-racial and unitary but that maintains marginalization through mass media representations, Canada requires a representative and inclusive space for all people to be heard. The CBC's original podcasting, although in its infancy, may promise to be such an inclusive digital storytelling space if it continues to grow within this creative industry.

CORE CONCEPTS

digital storytelling: The practice of communicating lived experiences and histories through personal narration online using the technological affordances of available digital media like the computer, the Internet, the smartphone, and software programs.

e-diaspora: A collective that is not necessarily bound by identity but shares a common goal or movement as an imagined community. These goals or movements can change with the addition of new members and new interactions.

marginalized communities: Groups excluded from mainstream economic, political, social, and cultural participation because of identity markers like race, ethnicity, gender, sexuality, and class. Groups become marginalized based on their subordinate relationship to dominant groups who hold power in, and control over, society.

podcasting: The practice of audio recording speech for digital distribution that listeners can interact with on a webpage or through an application at any time. Its affordances include audience subscriptions, unrestricted episode lengths, low-cost production, and lack of fixed scheduling; it is also unregulated and targeted at niche audiences.

SUGGESTED ACTIVITIES

1. Locate a podcast episode and explain its use of digital storytelling.
2. Listen to an episode from *The Secret Life of Canada* (found on the CBC's podcast website https://www.cbc.ca/radio/podcasts) and describe how it supports marginalized communities to be heard. Consider the content's focus, the sources consulted, the people speaking, the racialized identities and/or ethnicities represented, and the episode's availability online.

REFERENCES

Adler Berg, Freja Sørine. "The Value of Authenticity and Intimacy: A Case Study of the Danish Independent Podcast *Fries Before Guys'* Utilization of Instagram." *Radio Journal: International Studies in Broadcast & Audio Media*, vol. 19, no. 1, pp. 155–173.

Banks, Mark. *Creative Justice: Cultural Industries, Work and Inequality*. Rowman and Littlefield International, 2017.

Basen, Ira. "The CBC and the Public Interest: Maintaining the Mission in an Era of Media Concentration." *Public Broadcasting and the Public Interest*, edited by Michael P. McCauley et al., Routledge, 2003, pp. 147–157.

Berry, Richard. "Part of the Establishment: Reflecting on 10 Years of Podcasting as an Audio Medium." *Convergence*, vol. 22, no. 6, 2016, pp. 661–671.

Bottomley, Andrew J. *Sound Streams: A Cultural History of Radio-Internet Convergence*. University of Michigan Press, 2020.

Brevini, Benedetta. "Public Service and Community Media." *The International Encyclopedia of Digital Communication and Society*, edited by Robin Mansell and Peng Hwa Ang, John Wiley & Sons, 2015, pp. 1–9.

Canada, Canadian Heritage. *Broadcasting Act*. Minister of Justice, 1991, https://laws-lois.justice.gc.ca/PDF/B-9.01.pdf. Accessed 3 August 2020.

———. *Creative Canada: Policy Framework*. Canadian Heritage, 2017, www.canada.ca/en/canadian-heritage/campaigns/creative-canada/framework.html#a1. Accessed 1 August 2020.

Canada, Department of Indian Affairs. *Indian Act*. Minister of Justice, 1985, https://laws-lois.justice.gc.ca/PDF/I-5.pdf. Accessed 3 August 2020.

CBC. "Kiwew." *CBC Listen*, www.cbc.ca/listen/cbc-podcasts/425-kiwew. Accessed 5 October 2021.

———. "Missing & Murdered—About the Show." *CBC Media Centre*, www.cbc.ca/mediacentre/program/missing-and-murdered. Accessed 3 October 2021.

———. "Seat at the Table—About the Show." *CBC Media Centre*, www.cbc.ca/mediacentre/program/seat-at-the-table. Accessed 17 March 2021.

———. "Where Are You From?" *New Fire*, 29 June 2017, www.cbc.ca/listen/cbc-podcasts/113-new-fire. Accessed 18 July 2020.

CBC Media Solutions. "CBC Podcasts." https://solutionsmedia.cbcrc.ca/en/platforms/cbc-podcasts/. Accessed 5 October 2021.

CBC/Radio-Canada. "About Sleepover." 16 October 2017, www.cbc.ca/radio/sleepover/about-sleepover-1.4348250. Accessed 5 October 2021.

———. "About The Secret Life of Canada." 18 September 2018, www.cbc.ca/radio/secretlifeofcanada/about-us-1.4828460. Accessed 28 July 2020.

———. "CBC Podcasts: Pitch Guide." 5 October 2018, www.cbc.ca/radio/podcastnews/pitch-us-1.4830131/. Accessed 1 September 2020.

———. "Enviroscan—2019." 1 November 2019, https://site-cbc.radio-canada.ca/documents/vision/strategy/latest-studies/enviroscan-public-en.pdf. Accessed 24 July 2020.

———. "Mandate." www.cbc.radio-canada.ca/en/vision/mandate. Accessed 10 July 2020.

———. "New Fire." www.cbc.ca/radio/podcasts/new-fire/. Accessed 29 July 2020.

———. "The Indian Act." *The Secret Life of Canada* from CBC, 25 June 2019, www.cbc.ca/radio/podcasts/documentaries/the-secret-life-of-canada/. Accessed 30 July 2020.

———. "Through the Years." www.cbc.radio-canada.ca/en/your-public-broadcaster/history. Accessed 2 August 2020.

————. "Where Is Japantown?" *The Secret Life of Canada* from CBC, 12 May 2020, www.cbc.ca/radio/podcasts/documentaries/the-secret-life-of-canada/. Accessed 19 July 2020.

————. "Young and Aboriginal in 2015." *New Fire* from CBC, 30 June 2015, www.cbc.ca/listen/cbc-podcasts/113-new-fire. Accessed 19 July 2020.

————. "Your Stories, Taken to Heart." *CBC/Radio-Canada*, May 2019, https://cbc.radio-canada.ca/en/vision/strategy/your-stories-taken-to-heart. Accessed 30 July 2020.

Copeland, Stacey, and Lauren Knight. "Indigenizing the National Broadcast Soundscape—CBC Podcast: *Missing and Murdered: Finding Cleo.*" *Radio Journal: International Studies in Broadcast & Audio Media*, vol. 19, no. 1, 2021, pp. 101–116.

Corntassel, Jeff, et al. "Indigenous Storytelling, Truth-Telling, and Community Approaches to Reconciliation." *English Studies in Canada*, vol. 35, no. 1, 2009, pp. 137–159.

Couldry, Nick. "Mediatization or Mediation? Alternative Understandings of the Emergent Space of Digital Storytelling." *New Media & Society*, vol. 10, no. 3, 2008, pp. 373–391.

Cuffe, Honae H. "Lend Me Your Ears: The Rise of the History Podcast in Australia." *History Australia*, vol. 16, no. 3, 2019, pp. 553–569.

Cwynar, Christopher. "More than a 'VCR for Radio': The CBC, the Radio 3 Podcast, and the Uses of an Emerging Medium." *Journal of Radio & Audio Media*, vol. 22, no. 2, 2015, pp. 190–199.

Fleras, Augie. *The Media Gaze: Representations of Diversities in Canada*. UBC Press, 2011.

Florini, Sarah. "The Podcast 'Chitlin' Circuit': Black Podcasters, Alternative Media, and Audio Enclaves." *Journal of Radio & Audio Media*, vol. 22, no. 2, 2015, pp. 209–219.

Francis, Daniel. "The Imaginary Indian: The Image of the Indian in Canadian Culture." *Race and Racialization: Essential Readings*. 2nd ed., edited by Tania Das Gupta et al., Canadian Scholars, 2018, pp. 473–484.

Gilroy, Paul. *Against Race: Imagining Political Culture Beyond the Color Line*. Belknap Press of Harvard University Press, 2000.

————. "British Cultural Studies and the Pitfalls of Identity." *Media and Cultural Studies: Keyworks*, edited by Meenakshi Gigi Durham and Douglas M. Kellner, Blackwell, 2006, pp. 381–395.

Hall, Stuart. "Nations and Diasporas." *The Fateful Triangle: Race, Ethnicity, Nation*, edited by Kobena Mercer, Harvard University Press, 2017, pp. 125–174.

————. "The Question of Cultural Identity." *Modernity and Its Futures*, edited by Tony McGrew et al., Polity Press, 1992, pp. 274–316.

————. "The Whites of Their Eyes: Racist Ideologies and the Media." *Selected Writings on Race and Difference*, edited by Paul Gilroy and Ruth Wilson Gilmore, Duke University Press, 2021, pp. 97–120.

Heeremans, Lieven. "Podcast Networks: Syndicating Production Culture." *Podcasting: New Aural Cultures and Digital Media*, edited by Dario Llinares et al., Palgrave Macmillan, 2018, pp. 57–80.

Henry, Frances, and Carol Tator. *Discourses of Domination: Racial Bias in the Canadian English-Language Press*. University of Toronto Press, 2002.

Hesmondhalgh, David. "Cultural and Creative Industries." *The SAGE Handbook of Cultural Analysis*, edited by Tony Bennett and John Frow, Sage, 2008, pp. 552–569.

Hogarth, Kathy, and Wendy L. Fletcher. *A Space for Race: Decoding Racism, Multiculturalism, and Post-Colonialism in the Quest for Belonging in Canada and Beyond*. Oxford University Press, 2018.

Jenkins, Cheryl D. "Newsroom Diversity and Representations of Race." *Race and News: Critical Perspectives*, edited by Christopher P. Campbell et al., Routledge, 2012, pp. 22–42.

Jiwani, Yasmin. "Doubling Discourses and the Veiled Other: Mediations of Race and Gender in Canadian Media." *Race and Racialization: Essential Readings*. 2nd ed., edited by Tania Das Gupta et al., Canadian Scholars, 2018, pp. 485–502.

Kenix, Linda J. *Alternative and Mainstream Media: The Converging Spectrum*. Bloomsbury Academic, 2011.

Kozolanka, Kirsten, et al. "Considering Alternative Media in Canada: Structure, Participation, Activism." *Alternative Media in Canada*, edited by Kirsten Kozolanka et al., UBC Press, 2012, pp. 1–22.

Lawrence, Bonita. *"Real" Indians and Others: Mixed-Blood Urban Native Peoples and Indigenous Nationhood*. University of Nebraska Press, 2004.

Llinares, Dario, et al. "Introduction: Podcasting and Podcasts—Parameters of a New Aural Culture." *Podcasting: New Aural Cultures and Digital Media*, edited by Dario Llinares et al., Palgrave Macmillan, 2018, pp. 1–13.

Mackey, Eva. *The House of Difference: Cultural Politics and National Identity in Canada*. Routledge, 1999.

Mahtani, Minelle. "Representing Minorities: Canadian Media and Minority Identities." *Canadian Ethnic Studies*, vol. 33, no. 3, 2001, pp. 99–133.

Markman, Kris M. "Doing Radio, Making Friends, and Having Fun: Exploring the Motivations of Independent Audio Podcasters." *New Media & Society*, vol. 14, no. 4, 2011, pp. 547–565.

Morris, Jeremy Wade, et al. "The PodcastRE Project: Curating and Preserving Podcasts (and Their Data)." *Journal of Radio & Audio Media*, vol. 26, no. 1, 2019, pp. 8–20.

Murray, Sarah. "Coming-of-Age in a Coming-of-Age: The Collective Individualism of Podcasting's Intimate Soundwork." *Popular Communication*, vol. 17, no. 4, 2019, pp. 301–316.

Murray, Simone. "Servicing 'Self-Scheduling Consumers': Public Broadcasters and Audio Podcasting." *Global Media and Communication*, vol. 5, no. 2, 2009, pp. 197–219.

Oikawa, Mona. *Cartographies of Violence: Japanese Canadian Women, Memory, and the Subjects of the Internment*. University of Toronto Press, 2012.

Rowland, Wade. *Saving the CBC: Balancing Profit and Public Service*. Linda Leith Publishing, 2013.

Saha, Anamik. *Race and the Cultural Industries*. Polity Press, 2018.

Smith, Antonia. "'Cement for the Canadian Mosaic': Performing Canadian Citizenship in the Work of John Murray Gibbon." *Race/Ethnicity: Multidisciplinary Global Contexts*, vol. 1, no. 1, 2007, pp. 37–60.

Smith, Sidonie, and Julia Watson. *Reading Autobiography: A Guide for Interpreting Life Narratives*. University of Minnesota Press, 2010.

Spinelli, Martin, and Lance Dann. *Podcasting: The Audio Media Revolution*. Bloomsbury Academic, 2019.

Sullivan, John L. "Podcast Movement: Aspirational Labour and the Formalisation of Podcasting as a Cultural Industry." *Podcasting: New Aural Cultures and Digital Media*, edited by Dario Llinares et al., Palgrave Macmillan, 2018, pp. 35–56.

Swiatek, Lukasz. "The Podcast as an Intimate Bridging Medium." *Podcasting: New Aural Cultures and Digital Media*, edited by Dario Llinares et al., Palgrave Macmillan, 2018, pp. 173–187.

Taras, David, and Christopher Waddell. *The End of the CBC?* University of Toronto Press, 2020.

Tashme Project. "About the Play and Company." www.thetashmeproject.com. Accessed 13 March 2021.

Thumim, Nancy. *Self-Representation and Digital Culture*. Palgrave Macmillan, 2012.

Vowel, Chelsea. *Indigenous Writes: A Guide to First Nations, Métis & Inuit Issues in Canada*. Highwater Press, 2016.

Vrikki, Photini, and Sarita Malik. "Voicing Lived-Experience and Anti-Racism: Podcasting as a Space at the Margins for Subaltern Counterpublics." *Popular Communication*, vol. 17, no. 4, 2019, pp. 273–287.

Wilson, Robbie Z. "Welcome to the World of Wandercast: Podcast as a Participatory Performance and Environmental Exploration." *Podcasting: New Aural Cultures and Digital Media*, edited by Dario Llinares et al., Palgrave Macmillan, 2018, pp. 273–298.

CHAPTER 3

Institutional Production of Heritage within the Culture Sector in Canada

Susan L. T. Ashley

INTRODUCTION

One definition of Canada's creative industries frames it as a set of commercial enterprises devoted to practices of symbolic creation, meaning making, and cultural production. Creative industries have become an important focus for governments' cultural policies, as Western societies after 1980 shifted from an industrial manufacturing system to a post-industrial economy based on services and information (O'Connor). Here, ideas of what culture is have moved away from elitist and paternalistic notions of "the arts" and toward associations with creativity and entrepreneurialism within economic development. Carried along with that shift were the many inequalities embedded in the production and consumption of arts and culture.

This chapter examines one sector of that cultural production within Canadian policy and institutions—the "heritage industry." The term was coined in the 1980s in response to the decline of the British industrial economy and the subsequent museumification of buildings and landscapes for tourism purposes (Hewison). The heritage industry preserves past forms of cultural economy and stores and presents those old ways of functioning while new cultural modes of cultural production evolve. This industry includes both public institutions and private enterprises—parks, galleries, and museums as well as living-history sites, zoos, and science centres—all key to tourism and entertainment economies worldwide. Not only locations for representations and products about nature, culture, and the past, these heritage institutions and businesses are sites for popular cultural expressions and for creative labour in today's post-industrial environments.

This network that makes up the heritage industry generates official or "authorized" discourses and representations on what is and was "valuable" about nature, culture, and the past (Smith). In Canada, for example, heritage narratives are celebratory accounts of wilderness settlers, heroic pasts, comfortable multicultural tolerance, and global citizenship. Such meanings, and their social and economic uses, are rife with intersectional inequalities. The heritage industry in Canada and internationally has perpetuated sector-wide erasures, misrecognition, lack of parity, and processes of power and precarity that limit access to decision making and employment.

This chapter poses the following questions: how, why, and to what effect do cultural policies, organizations, and practices assign value to aspects of the past as "our heritage"? How do political and economic decision making about heritage affect how we define Canadian identity and who belongs? Who makes these decisions about value, and who might be left out? The chapter outlines the ways that heritage has been used in Canada over the years to support the nation-state and economic development, including the relationship of heritage to multiculturalism policies. Two examples illustrate how cultural meanings are produced through heritage policies and institutions: the Royal Ontario Museum (ROM), Canada's largest institution devoted to heritage, and public community exhibitions and memorials developed within the federal Community Historical Recognition Program (CHRP). Both legitimize a celebratory official heritage through policies, systems, and practices. The chapter questions why institutions employ heritage-making strategies that appear to be participatory and democratizing but instead are underlain by hierarchies of unequal power driven by government policies and economic priorities.

HERITAGE AS A CULTURAL POLICY

Heritage is understood here as a cultural phenomenon, part of the symbolic, expressive, creative, or meaning making realm of society (Stanley). Holden has explored the interrelationship of culture and heritage as part of a regenerative cycle: "creativity becomes funded culture, which in turn becomes heritage, which then acts as a stimulus for further creativity" (27). At its heart, heritage is a process of deciding what is important about people's pasts—what has *value*, along with the performance of that valuation through action (Harrison). How value is ascribed, who is doing the valuation, for what reason, and who holds the power all decide the nature of this process. These nuances can be observed within the systems, discourses, and representations of heritage-making policies, institutions, and practices.

The influence of societal power dynamics on differing ideas about the value of the past has long been an issue in Canadian society. Cultural policy in Canada has historically been devised to build a national identity through the support of Canadian cultural production (Druick). One of the first instruments of cultural policymaking in Canada was the Royal Commission on National Development in the Arts, Letters and Sciences—the Massey-Lévesque Commission (1949–51). Aimed at examining high art and popular culture as well as scholarship and education in relation to Canadian identity, the report focused on protecting Canadian culture from the evils of mass American culture. The Massey commissioners valued high culture and the acquisition of elitist forms of knowledge and arts in Canada, while they saw popular culture as "the folklore, customs, and pastimes that traditionally existed in close relation to a people's social culture" (Litt 84–85). Both were perceived as threatened by American culture. While never using the word "heritage," the report expressed what Druick calls a postwar "melancholy" about "the loss of community, of pervasive amateur culture, of clear-cut values and traditions tied to European culture and religion" (170). Such ideas clearly privileged an idealized Anglo-European history and traditions, which they linked directly to a sense of Canadian nationalism:

> The work with which we have been entrusted is concerned with nothing less than the spiritual foundations of our national life. Canadian achievement in every field depends mainly on the quality of the Canadian mind and spirit.... These things, whether we call them arts and letters or use other words to describe them, we believe lie at the roots of our life as a nation. (Royal Commission 271)

The commission's recommendations guided the establishment of key cultural institutions in Canada meant to bolster Canadian identity and sense of heritage: the CBC; the National Film Board; the Canada Council; the National Gallery; the National Archives; the Social Sciences and Humanities Research Council, and the National Library. Concerning museums, the report recommended that they redefine their role from scholarly collecting and research to vehicles of adult education, although aimed at achieving nationalist goals. It recommended the creation of a Canadian History Museum, which was not followed through, but it was envisioned in line with the classical European and American museums at the time: important to the modern nation-state to the "civilizing" of its citizens (Bennett).

The report also encouraged changes to the National Historic Sites and Monuments Board to promote Canada's heritage buildings as well as significant investment in major restorations to historic sites such as the Halifax Citadel. These recommendations reflected a global trend in museums development and the preservation of historic "monuments and sites" (ICOMOS and the Venice Charter of 1964) but also, more relevantly, the world heritage movement (UNESCO and the World Heritage Convention 1972), all aiming to protect material aspects of culture and nature deemed significant for their (Western) scientific or artistic value (Harrison and Rose). The focus of this heritage-making was the listing of material things as "masterpieces," in line with ideals of heritage as an elite form of culture, as "the best that is thought and known" (Arnold) or "The Heritage"—the ascription of universality to white English heritage famously criticized by Stuart Hall (4).

While the Massey-Lévesque Commission report and the national institutions it generated reflected a "heritage-from-above" perspective, a shift to a more popular sense of culture and the valuing of "heritage-from-below" (Robertson) gained strength in postwar Canada and internationally. From the latter point of view, what was deemed heritage could be any aspect of anyone's past, not just nationalistic or privileged forms of culture and history. This broader views of heritage acknowledged its role in building identities and belonging on many scales—personal, local, national, or transnational. In Canada, popular rather than elitist ideas of culture became the basis of the heritage industry through the 1960s and 1970s, in a surge of Canadian nationalism that actively supported local histories. Canada's centennial year in 1967, marking one hundred years since Confederation, was a defining moment in this form of national heritage development. Led by the hugely successful World's Fair in Montreal, Expo 67, the year was celebrated through hundreds of arts, community, and heritage events across the country (Anderson and Gosselin). These activities foregrounded popular ideas of heritage, particularly pioneer history, within a federal government policy to bolster a shared Canadian identity (Mackey, *The House of Difference*). At the same time, the centennial events aimed to position the country on the world stage, in what might be seen today as a strategic "branding" effort. But Canada had difficulty in elucidating this unified brand because of the complexities of determining a single Canadian identity and heritage in a pluralist and multicultural nation (Aronczyk).

Leung writes that in the making of nations, there is an insistence on shared heritage: in Canada, this was "a fabled past from which something that can be deemed 'Canadian-ness' can emerge" (162). The many local and provincial museums and heritage centres created during the 1967 centennial year conveyed, for the most part, nationalistic imagining of Canada and its land that were dominated by Anglo and European settlement histories, with a similar mix of displays in national, provincial, and local institutions. Until the 1970s, recognition of Indigenous and non-Anglo cultures was either anthropological or non-existent. Indigenous narratives in Canada were often isolated either to detached spaces within natural history museums or to separate anthropological museums, effectively separating these collections and stories from mainstream representations of national heritage (Phillips). This reflected inequalities within heritage institutions globally, where, even in 2003, with the UNESCO Convention for the Safeguarding of the Intangible Cultural Heritage, protecting Indigenous or non-Western folklore from mass and globalizing culture was the paternalistic aim. This imposed fixed meanings and significance that did not acknowledge local views, contestation, or change (Kirshenblatt-Gimblett).

Canada positioned the word *heritage* as a central policy mechanism to achieve both internal unity and external branding when it established the Department of Canadian Heritage in 1993. It was to be the umbrella department for arts, culture, heritage, official languages, and all multicultural and citizenship programs. This move must be understood within the constitutional debates in Canada at the time, particularly the threat of Quebec's separation from the rest of Canada. The Heritage department would be a central cultural intervention to support a united nation and Canadian identity. As Prime Minister Jean Chrétien wrote in the Throne Speech of 1994, "Our cultural heritage and our official languages are at the very core of the Canadian identity and are sources of social and economic enrichment" (Hoag).

Canada's governmental emphasis on heritage through designating a specific department was unique within English-speaking countries (Sánchez-Carretero 388). The department oversaw matters "relating to Canadian identity and values, cultural development, heritage and areas of natural or historical significance to the nation" (Department of Canadian Heritage Act, S.C. 1995, c. 11). In 2001, the department's mission and objectives were reoriented toward "building citizenship" and "social cohesion," which de-emphasized heritage as a physical resource and stressed its intangible quality, specifically within the policy areas of stories and symbols, inclusion and participation, and values. Versions of the strategic objectives for the Heritage department from that period until 2013 deployed heritage as a national and civic resource for community building, arts and cultural activities, and tourism.

This strategy of heritage-making has been criticized as hegemonic, imposing dominant meanings on society. James argues that the nation-building and social cohesion qualities of heritage are a neoliberal process to contain and discipline citizens and their multiple cultures. Through departmental policy and institutional practices, inequalities of difference are then rendered into softer and powerless cultural expressions of "diversity"—a celebratory, feel-good construction.

Many critics point out how state-driven and passive framings of cohesion conveyed through Department of Heritage policies, with words like "shared values" and "tolerance," are paternalistic forms of culture. They bestow inclusion upon the minority cultures and mask social inequities (Bernard; Bannerji). Thus, governmental notions of heritage and national identity suffer from coercive effects of who gets to be included in that heritage and in which ways.

Issues with this framing of heritage link to the use of "multiculturalism" as a unifying concept. Multiculturalism has been interpreted politically through the Department of Heritage as a central component of the country's national identity and culture—its heritage—and how Canada defines itself both locally and to the world (Kymlicka). This interpretation attempts to reconcile the old version of white pioneer heritage with Indigenous and Black, Asian, and minority ethnic heritage, and it is often represented as being especially tolerant and inclusive. However, it ignores that social relations in Canada continue to have ongoing negative and often racist impacts on different people and groups. Multiculturalism was officially adopted as public policy with the *Canadian Multiculturalism Act* of 1985, which recognized the pluralist nature of its citizenry. The Act itself invoked heritage as an essential part of its policy:

> The Government of Canada recognizes the diversity of Canadians as regards race, national or ethnic origin, colour and religion as a fundamental characteristic of Canadian society and is committed to a policy of multiculturalism designed to preserve and enhance the multicultural heritage of Canadians.

In this way, multiculturalism in Canada is legislatively and intimately linked to the institutionalized promotion of heritage, administered through the Department of Canadian Heritage. Both rely on an ideal of "multicultural nationalism," which claims that both the identity of a national community and the identities of different communities within the nation can be simultaneously recognized and represented (Gordon-Walker). Many have criticized the policy, as white Anglo-dominance continues to prevail in most situations of power, including most mainstream institutions and media (e.g., Bannerji; Hogarth and Fletcher). They argue that there is an official portrait of Canadianness presented in public that purports a fully integrated multicultural social and cultural system in Canada, but in private spaces and the everyday world, non-whites are still excluded (Gomá). Multiculturalism policies have also been shown to "culturalize" racial difference by rendering deep structural and social inequalities as just cultural variations, often defined as heritage. In that process, ethnic difference is about "samosas, saris, steel bands," while society is held in place by the same whiteness beneath (Mackey, "Postmodernism" 408). This has also been interpreted as "civic" multiculturalism, which uses soft or symbolic approaches by the government aimed at nation building (Yan and Kim) and in which the heritage industry is fundamentally implicated.

National and provincial museums offer particular representations of multiculturalism in their exhibitions about Canadian heritage. Gordon-Walker examines the evolution of practices of the Museum of Alberta and the ways that "cultural communities" were curated separately from Western Canadian history in its exhibits or represented in temporary displays as discrete stories on the periphery—for example, lederhosen exhibited as representative of the experience of German immigrants in Alberta or a travelling exhibit exploring Chinese Canadian restaurants. The Canadian Museum of History in Ottawa, the primary national institution of Canadian heritage that portrays Canadianness for both citizens and foreign visitors, positions multicultural experiences at the end of the nation-story. Its Grand Hall depicts ancestral Indigenous history as the beginning of a national narrative, disappearing in the Canadian History Hall in a "progress across time." The History Hall then narrates the arrival of Europeans and "the diversity" of the Canadian experience. Canada's cultural histories of racialized minorities are placed at the end of a timeline, presented as evidence of its final national achievement of finding unity through diversity (Leung).

While heritage has clearly been used by the nation-state as a tool for particular identity and cultural representations both within its borders and globally, heritage has been heavily deployed in the economic sphere as well. Political uses of heritage are often combined with economic valuations and strategies. This reflects the global trend over the last 30 years where the primary policy justification for cultural sectors has become an economic one, with arts and culture positioned as central to economic development and innovation (Jameson). The creative economy discourse now drives most cultural policies, from UNESCO's to national governments' to urban municipalities'—and heritage institutions and built landscapes are often central to this.

On national, provincial, and local levels, notions of heritage drive a wide range of planning and development processes in Canada, functioning as political and socioeconomic resources. Creative cities initiatives often link heritage to these forms of development, among the "cultural resources" that contribute to urban development in a broader sense, clustered with the arts, festivals, community venues, and natural spaces (Baeker 40). Heritage is seen as intrinsic to place-based development, in its material form as historic districts or structures, or more intangibly as place-based crafts or traditional artistic forms. These historical cultural forms and expressions are tapped for entertainment and tourism but also as a source for creative content and intellectual property.

Cultural policies commonly signify heritage and a "sense of place" as part of branding and development schemes—for example, in the United Kingdom, conjuring up images of stately homes, royalty, and quaint rural villages as a resource for economic exploitation (Waterton and Watson), or, in Quebec, in the production of revised imaginings of rural land or terroir as *patrimoine* for new products and tourism strategies (Paquette et al.). In Ontario, a series of provincial government cultural planning forums in the mid-2000s resulted in several mid-size cities—such as Ajax, London, and Toronto (see culture plan in the next section)—developing culture/arts/heritage plans to guide their urban planning, recreation, and economic development (Kovacs).

Janes has written extensively on the ways that the language and organizational styles of economics and development have permeated museum management, as reflected in the following discussion on the Royal Ontario Museum. Economic pressures to survive have generated neoliberal responses in many museums: under a corporatized and commoditized museum model, the public is positioned as a consumer, public space becomes a marketplace, and the public good resides in exchange value through commercialized experiences like blockbuster displays. Janes insists that the real issues confronting mainstream museums must instead be addressing global environmental and societal change.

HERITAGE PRODUCTION IN CANADA: TWO EXAMPLES

Current policies and practices that drive heritage production in Canada, especially in relation to the place of multiculturalism, can be illustrated through two examples: the Royal Ontario Museum (ROM), Canada's largest institution of heritage, and the federal Community Historical Recognition Program (CHRP), specifically those community exhibitions and memorials developed by Italian Canadians. Both employ heritage as a resource for public policy and for economic generation. Each exemplifies different aspects of cultural production, representation, and participation in the heritage field in Canada, and both are public in the sense of being funded by governments to achieve policy aims, but they are also public in terms of serving "the public" as an audience and deploying strategies of publicness in their visibility, production, representation, and participation aims. Because of this public orientation, they can be used to question:

- What is represented as heritage and having heritage value in these examples?

- Who produces the meaning conveyed in their public presentations?
- How are diversity, equity, and inclusiveness enacted here—that is, in what way do publics who are racially or ethnically marginalized take part in these heritage-making processes?

Royal Ontario Museum

The Royal Ontario Museum (ROM) is an example of historical elitist ideals of what constituted heritage in Canada. It is the most well-known museum in Canada because of its long history, the breadth of its collections, numbers of visitors, and international reputation. Established in Toronto in 1912, like most "universal" museums in Western countries, its colonial lineage was clear: This was a time when huge numbers of objects were lifted from faraway places and deposited in museums without attracting moral and political uproar. The collections included global antiquities, Indigenous artifacts, and geological and natural history specimens, all initially attached to the University of Toronto for academic study. The museum was rooted in Victorian-age interest in progress, science, industry, and God, as well as the social value of knowledge and education, and the desire for civic respectability and status (Teather). These were unique things from around the globe that Canadians had never seen before, and by their positioning and exhibiting in a museum, their importance and significance were intended to enlighten and "civilize" the provincial population.

The museum functioned as a research and educational institution, initially affiliated with the university but then moved to the provincial education ministry, and it was an agency within variations of the Ministry of Culture from 1975 onward. For generations, the museum welcomed thousands of schoolchildren, and the populace of Toronto came to fondly regard this institution as the centre for knowledge about the past, material culture, and heritage. This was a site, Harold Innis would express, that was a "monopoly of knowledge," a centralized structure of power, situated in an imposing city building and controlling the preservation of historical knowledge and identity of the dominant culture, as well as world knowledge seen through the lens of the dominant culture. And this institution—then and now, a primary part of the cultural and heritage industries in the main city in Canada—continues to hold this power to define and signify what has value.

The most prominent example of this control over knowledge production and its dangerous impact was the ROM's exhibition *Into the Heart of Africa* in 1989–90, which became an internationally renowned exemplar of elite and colonial processes in heritage meaning making. Violent protests erupted over the exhibition on missionaries in Africa, denouncing its racism and white privilege (Tator et al.).

The museum administration and curators, generally supported by the press, employed the old argument of "academic freedom" rather than acknowledging the exhibit's visual and textual incompetence. The ROM has since been the subject of critical study on the *Into the Heart of Africa* exhibit, covered by several articles and a book on that subject (e.g., Butler; Mackey, "Postmodernism"; Reigel; Tator et al.).

The museum was forced to reorient its positioning after this controversy, although this was perhaps more in response to its aging exhibitions, declining relevance, and funding reductions. By 2000, the ROM had entered a new stage in its history, undertaking a redevelopment project worth more than $300 million, billed as a Renaissance (RenROM). As the lead project in a "cultural renaissance" in Toronto (Knelman) billed at positioning the city as an international cultural capital, it was one of a number of high-profile museum expansion projects across the globe in that decade (Message). Ashley studied cultural production and reception during this decade of development at the museum in her book *A Museum in Public: Revisioning Canada's Royal Ontario Museum*, interrogating the context, planning, staffing, decision making, and deployment of its public displays and activities. Under the guidance of star architect Daniel Libeskind and a dynamic new director, William Thorsell, RenROM restored the museum's heritage buildings and galleries, created a spectacular landmark—the Michael Lee-Chin Crystal—and launched a different museology: not only a new building and a new vision but a new way of doing heritage. Thorsell's new vision had two parts: to get as much of the collections as possible on display, to show off their richness and beauty in a striking piece of architecture that would achieve the status of world-class for the museum—what he called a "landscape of Desire"—and to reposition the institution as an "agora," a cultural common where assembly, debate, and discussion could take place (Ross; Thorsell). The twin locational goals of desire and agora meant attracting attention and status through visually striking objects and architecture, along with creating a common ground for provocative conversation.

The evolution of this institution, from its creation as colonial-minded educator intended to civilize the populace through to its current consumerist aim as a landscape of desire, demonstrates its key role in determining what aspects of Canadian heritage and culture have value and the changing ways that value has been determined over the years. In all instances, status enhancement continued as an important use for this institution, and thus its signification as "heritage" played a part in its reputational elevation. The establishment of a universal museum in the city in 1912 enhanced Toronto's and Canada's international profiles (Mak), and with the 2000 renovation, the museum was again promoted as a means for "greatness" and celebrity on the world stage (Ross). This example of old-style Massey-era heritage—the best—was combined with a modern version of the same thing—the greatest. As Thorsell wrote, "the Royal Ontario Museum offers a singular opportunity to create a new star in Toronto, Ontario and Canada … to retrieve the old and invent the new at the centre of Canada's leading metropolis."

RenROM fundamentally shifted the museum's cultural production to a capitalist orientation, where its new building and collections were displayed as gorgeous tools for global status, significance, and legitimation. This form of valuation was reflected in Toronto's 2003 *Culture Plan for the Creative City* and the concurrent construction or renovation of several large cultural institutions in the city, involving hundreds of millions of private and senior government dollars. The city's culture plan—which, according to their website, "aimed at positioning Toronto as an international cultural capital and placing culture at the heart of the city's economic and social agenda"—was textbook Richard Florida. This cemented the valuation of the ROM as a resource for economic utility, as a central part of creative cities planning and heritage industry development that generated financial benefit from "world-class" cultural status. The project consequently attracted many millions of dollars in support from elite stakeholders.

The ROM's history illustrates not only the ongoing use of heritage as an indicator of status but also the change in the valuation of culture and heritage from education/social improvement to commercial products for consumption. But the museum is also a good example of the lack of narratives and structures challenging notions of diversity, equity, and inclusion in cultural production, cultural participation, and representations within the heritage industry in Canada, as noted by this book. Late in 2008, the ROM changed its brand phrasing to "Engage the World" as the overarching philosophy of the new, revitalized ROM to reflect the importance of "communities," invoke the agora concept of the museum as a place for lively debate, and figuratively engage the museum with all the cultures of the world. Despite some good programming from dedicated cultural workers at the museum in education and audience engagement, the governance and representations within the museum are still dominated by elites and are even colonial in their offerings.

The permanent galleries about Canada and world cultures suffer from their essential nature as a place for collected "things." A heritage museum is a visual communicative medium, devoted to the social and cultural practices of showing, looking, and seeing. Viewing the ROM's Gallery of China or the unfortunately clustered Africa, the Americas and Asia-Pacific Gallery, or the art and culture features in the First Peoples Gallery—with rows upon rows of objects with brief context—gives a sense of a densely jammed retail shop. A once-only visitor would come away weary from too much "shopping" that has objectified these parts of the world in a very real way. These galleries also elicit a wonder at the sheer volume of materials taken from other peoples in the colonial era. Their display in separate Western-centric groupings and classifications reinforces their Otherness rather than encourages their sense of inclusive heritage.

Part of the problem during the RenROM development was not only the stated goal to focus on collections as jewels to be viewed but a perceived lack of time to undertake the kinds of consultation and collaboration required to produce community-centred exhibitions. As Thorsell indicated in an initiating memo to the exhibit Steering Committee, "everyone needs clear heads-up about the scope and pace of the project ... this will be a faster-paced project than most people have experienced, with more rigorous deadlines and targets." The challenge of the tight planning schedule might also be the reason that a stated "objects not narratives" design approach was adopted. The consequence was a form of gallery exhibition whose public function was simple and decorative more than complex and communicative. As well, expert advisors tended to be the focus of any curatorial-led consultations, to adhere to the rigorous deadlines. The African galleries, for example, were subject to extensive consultation according to one curator, but participants were experts and academics rather than people from African Canadian communities.

The ROM's temporary exhibitions and special programming have been more successful in tackling community and inclusion objectives. One example was *Stitching Community*, which aimed to give voice to community groups but also to "develop new audiences and support group sales" (ROM). The community consultation involved with this particular exhibit was aimed at social inclusion and cultural sensitivity—the desire to build bridges with Black community groups in reaction to the *Into the Heart of Africa* controversy. Shelley Ruth Butler, in a review of *Stitching Communities*, said that while the small exhibit filled a gap in that permanent Canadian gallery, it was "overwhelmingly silent on the social history of African Canadians" and it reinforced "a standard narrative that celebrates Canada as a land of freedom, without addressing in detail, the nuances and contradictions of this claim" (n.p.). Its curators had specifically designed the exhibit to insert new voices into this very colonial gallery, and they had spent a considerable amount of additional time and resources in selecting objects and oral histories to create the display.

The multicultural Friends of the Museum group, along with lectures, festivals, and special programs like the hugely popular Friday Night Live, attracts new audiences and offers new ways of looking at heritage in the museum. Admission to the First Peoples gallery is now free to the public and the museum has committed to ongoing anti-racist practice (ROM website). However, Ashley ("The Changing Face of Heritage") found that while some aspects of representation have improved, governance and operations personnel are still largely white and volunteers are mostly older and elite. Although the public-facing visitor services staff members are as multicultural as the city, the higher curatorial and management spheres responsible for cultural production at the institution are not yet as diverse, inclusive, or representative as they could be.

The heritage that was presented through the ROM's redevelopment exemplified celebrity publicness: what was heritagized and how, from the authority of the architecture to its prominence in public policy as an economic tool, to the public exhibitions and events in its externally facing spaces. The public face during RenROM was a rhetorical one that performed ideals of relevance and engagement but did not manifest these qualities behind the scenes. While its corporate positioning spoke of engagement and diversity, its actions in practice demonstrated historical preoccupations with ownership and governance bound to property and status. Boundaries persisted between institutional interests and practices and the lives and concerns of people for whom this institution of heritage existed.

The Community Historical Recognition Program

The Community Historical Recognition Program (CHRP) provides perhaps a more encouraging, grassroots, and inclusive example of heritage than at the ROM, aimed at communicating a national history shared by minoritized citizens. However, the workings of institutional cultural production, representation, and participation instead illustrate here how public policy controls bottom-up production and signification of heritage through its agenda-setting and funding strategies.

The CHRP was established in 2006 to support projects designed to recognize the "hardships placed on certain groups of people as a result of immigration restrictions and wartime measures previously imposed by the Government of Canada" (Citizenship and Immigration Canada vii). Its creation was spurred by demands for remembrance, reconciliation, and redress among several ethnocultural communities. The program funded books, theatre productions, exhibitions, online learning tools, and other heritage projects focused on historical hardships encountered by Ukrainian, Chinese, South Asian, Italian, Jewish, and other minoritized groups in Canada. Alongside the primary aim of recognizing past wrongs, the program nonetheless reinforced the longer tradition of multicultural policies that celebrated the contribution that these communities made to the nation.

The Canadian shift toward apology and restitution followed similar political moves worldwide in the 1990s, such as the Truth and Reconciliation Commission in South Africa and Sorry Day in Australia. Apologies and settlements referred to various historical events in Canada: the Chinese Head Tax, the internment of Japanese Canadians, the rejection of Sikh settlers on the ship *Komagata Maru*, the detainment of Italian and Ukrainian Canadians during World War II, and the settlement related to the spurning of Jewish refugees on the ship *St. Louis*. These many financial and symbolic resolutions were wrapped up in the CHRP. The promise was made to commemorate these processes and events and to "educate Canadians" about the experiences of ethnocultural communities with $34 million dedicated to heritage purposes, above and beyond other financial settlements (www.cic.gc.ca). Dozens of community museums, cultural centres, and websites received funding to generate public historical accounts of immigrant experiences in Canada.

The CHRP initiative, as a Conservative federal policy, clearly aimed to build a particular national narrative. But this form of heritage, like earlier multiculturalism policies, used a politics of recognition to legitimize the Canadian settler state. As James points out, "heritage redress builds directly on the turn from antiracism to sanitized discourses of heritage and cohesion that Abu-Laban and Gabriel link to the 1990s neoliberalization of multiculturalism under the Heritage ministry" (41). It reinforced Prime Minister Stephen Harper's use of a range of culture and heritage interventions to transform Canadian identity while he was in power between 2006 and 2015 (Wylie), including venerating Anglo-European history, the monarchy, and the military as crucial to the heritage narrative of Canada. This mindset was also endorsed in 2013 with the *Canadian Museum of History Act*, which reshaped and rebranded Canada's national museum in Ottawa, to the condemnation of historians, museum researchers, and the media (Leblanc).

CHRP funding entailed direct governmental influence on decisions about which heritage would be promoted. It targeted very specific historical incidents, depoliticized differences, and relegated to the past broader issues such as racism and inequalities. The new narratives distanced themselves from racism or prejudice and defused any idea that these might still be occurring, stating the program was "designed to address previous actions of the federal government, which are no longer consistent with Canadian values" (Citizenship and Immigration Canada 9). The emphasis on social cohesion was also clear: a stated desire to bring closure to affected communities and to focus on the need for integration. As Prime Minister Harper said in his address to Parliament about the apologies and the historical recognition process, "I rise today to formally turn the page on an unfortunate period in Canada's past"—in essence, saying *this is what happened then, this does not happen now, let's move on*. It allowed for the continued reconfiguration of what was regarded as the proper Canadian identity narrative.

The CHRP admitting historical wrongdoing affected how heritage is remembered in Canada generally and affected community heritage-making processes on the ground. The CHRP restitutions injected large amounts of money, suddenly, into a cluster of community organizations, which changed the way heritage was presented in these communities (Ashley, "A Museum of Our Own"). This form of heritagization inserted limitations into their spaces of heritage-making: James argues that groups were obliged to compete for finite resources and fit projects within policy objectives. The subject matter was focused on historicizing past racisms and on restitution as a solution, which suited CHRP objectives, thus limiting the tone, group subjectivities, and the agency expressed in their public histories, along with weakening any potential non-compliant narratives of anti-racism and equality.

The public culture produced by Italian Canadian communities across the country is an example of these effects, where a flurry of memorializing projects were funded as restitution for the World War II internment of Italian Canadians. Funds were allotted by project, specific to the restitution goals of the program. The exhibits, piazzas, statues, and murals selected to tell these stories had a celebratory rhetoric and future orientation. At the Piazza Dante wall memorial in Ottawa, CHRP funds enabled a bust of Dante Alighieri in the centre of a small, marble-tiled plaza and the naming of wartime dead and interned. The Columbus Centre in Toronto sponsored an exhibition on the internment, promoted activities and lectures, and published books. The Italian Cultural Centre in Vancouver sponsored live events and films, published a history book on Italians in Canada, and erected a temporary exhibit about family life of new immigrants and the effects of the internment. Several communities and groups in Ontario developed creative projects around the Italian internment, including travelling exhibits, documentary films, books, and magazine articles.

Gordon-Walker et al. explored the nature of the representations offered within these public heritage expressions. They noted that these commemorations, of those Italian Canadians who were harmed by their own government, offered therapy for the living by focusing on a sanitized celebration of the group's contribution to building a strong nation-state. Memorialization was seen by the communities as a tool to "officially rewrite Canadian history" (96). The impact of CHRP was to centralize stories of Italian victimization, the internment of Italian Canadians, as the most important aspects of their Canadian heritage. This was then resolved in the exhibits and media projects with celebratory stories of success, with immigrants becoming fine members of a strong multicultural Canada. In one case—the exhibition at the Columbus Centre—a more critical approach to its storyline, which was not resolved within multicultural nationalism, led to questioning issues of identity and ethnicity, the necessity of war, and the challenges of the rights of citizenship. Participants asked, "Can it happen again?" and asserted that "in trying to answer this question honestly, we begin the work of ensuring it does not."

The stories that emerged from the Italian community through their new public forms of history can be seen as liberating expressions of the complexities of Canadian heritage—or, instead, as mainstreaming sameness and assimilation. Likewise, this impact of policy intervention can be seen as a form of repentance and restitution for past wrongs that brings with it redistributive funding—or, more cynically, as invasive and manipulative. The CHRP exhibitions and other media were produced in a burst of funding in the period of 2006 to 2012, but the legacies of their productions have either disappeared or are fixed in place, growing old and dusty in small venues and community centres, with few follow-up programs. These narratives of groups marginalized by ethnicity have still not been significantly represented within mainstream heritage institutions at national and provincial levels. With the government singling out one act of restitution for public funding, and by placing the conversation outside of the mainstream, it did not get absorbed into Canada's popular historical consciousness. This is a classic issue within heritage production when used by dominant players to achieve a social end: The process acts to historicize, culturalize, marginalize, and send into the dim past any problem areas, thus sidestepping current-day, unresolved issues. Canada continues to be represented in its mainstream heritage spaces as a successful multicultural nation but with Anglo-Franco white histories as the norm. By isolating its Black or ethnic residents as immigrants or visible minorities, despite their long histories in Canada, this process thus perpetuates the lack of narratives and structures that challenge dominant forms of cultural and heritage production in Canada.

CONCLUSION

This chapter has demonstrated how heritage in Canada is a form of cultural production, a realm of public and private institutions that structure, represent, and signify particular ways of understanding the past. I have explored some of the policy and institutional processes by which heritage has been used by dominant agents to symbolize and perform Canadian identity over the years, including its elevation as the long-standing federal Department of Canadian Heritage.

Two examples were described to demonstrate the institutional signification of the past as a resource: the Royal Ontario Museum, Canada's largest institution devoted to heritage, and the federal Community Historical Recognition Program, one of the largest funding programs ever administered in the Canadian heritage field. Both examples were used to establish how embedded systems maintain historic inequalities in heritage production. Privileged and paternalistic notions of culture as "the arts" and "the best" are perpetuated in central institutions like the ROM, where art and culture are still employed for financial gain and status by dominant players. The same players are involved in shaping policies like CHRP, where minority ideas about heritage produced by community groups have been employed in public for political "apologies" but relegated to marginal locations outside of the civic gaze.

Both cases demonstrate that ingrained systems manipulate the celebratory aspects of culture and the past as spectacle for political, social, and economic gain, rather than as a source of democratic meaning making or even for social justice. Such systems still structure the agenda setting and resourcing of the heritage industry in Canada, continuing to entrench the many inequalities inherent in the nature of its production and consumption.

CORE CONCEPTS

heritage: Tangible and intangible aspects of the past that hold meaning for us and that we choose to pass on to future generations.

multiculturalism: The presence of, and support for the presence of, several distinct cultural or ethnic groups within a society.

value: The importance, worth, or usefulness of something. The capacity of art, culture, and aspects of the past to have effects or impacts on those who experience them, and the marking or raising of those activities or aspects as important to human lives.

SUGGESTED ACTIVITIES

1. What is Heritage? In pairs, how would you write a definition for the word "heritage"? Can you think of an example of Heritage defined as:
   A place
   An object
   An intangible process
   A practice

2. Visit the Royal Ontario Museum online, or a local heritage institution in your area, and find five objects, texts, videos, or other display items that engage with Black history. They cannot all come from the same display. Did any of these relate to Canadian Black history? What story did it tell?

3. Speak to a grandparent or an elder and ask them: if there was one thing they wanted to pass on about their "heritage" to you as part of the future generation, what would that be? Can they or you describe how this is "heritage"? Do you see this as part of Canada's mainstream narrative of Canadian identity?

REFERENCES

Abu-Laban, Yasmeen, and Christina Gabriel. *Selling Diversity: Immigration, Multiculturalism, Employment Equity, and Globalization*. Broadview Press, 2002.

Anderson, David, and Viviane Gosselin. "Private and Public Memories of Expo 67: A Case Study of Recollections of Montreal's World's Fair, 40 Years After the Event." *Museum and Society*, vol. 6, no. 1, 2008, pp. 1–21.

Arnold, Matthew. *Culture & Anarchy: An Essay in Political and Social Criticism*. Macmillan and Company, 1911.

Aronczyk, Melissa. *Branding the Nation: The Global Business of National Identity*. Oxford University Press, 2013.

Ashley, Susan. *A Museum in Public: Revisioning Canada's Royal Ontario Museum*. Routledge, 2019.

———. "A Museum of Our Own." *Museums and Migration: History, Memory and Politics*, edited by Laurence Gouriévidis, Routledge, 2014, pp. 153–163.

———. "The Changing Face of Heritage at Canada's National Historic Sites." *International Journal of Heritage Studies*, vol. 13, no. 6, 2007, pp. 478–488.

Baeker, Greg. "Cultural Economies." *Economic Development Journal*, vol. 16, no. 2, 2017, pp. 37–43.

Bannerji, Himani. *The Dark Side of the Nation: Essays on Multiculturalism, Nationalism and Gender*. Canadian Scholars, 2000.

Bennett, Tony. *The Birth of the Museum: History, Theory, Politics*. Routledge, 1995.

Bernard, Paul. "Social Cohesion: A Dialectical Critique of a Quasi-Concept." Strategic Research and Analysis, Department of Canadian Heritage, SRA-491e, 1999.

Butler, Shelley Ruth. *Contested Representations: Revisiting into the Heart of Africa*. University of Toronto Press, 2007.

Citizenship and Immigration Canada. "Evaluation of the Historical Recognition Programs." Evaluation Division Report, 2013.

Department of Canadian Heritage. "Canadian Multiculturalism Act R.S.C., 1985, c. 24 (4th Supp.)." Government of Canada, 2020. DOI laws-lois.justice.gc.ca/eng/acts/c-18.7/page-1.html. Accessed 8 January 2021.

————. "Department of Canadian Heritage Act, S.C. 1995, c. 11." Government of Canada, 2001. DOI laws.justice.gc.ca/eng/acts/C-17.3/section-4-20021231.html. Accessed 21 December 2020.

Druick, Zoë. "Remedy and Remediation: The Cultural Theory of the Massey Commission." *The Review of Education, Pedagogy, and Cultural Studies*, vol. 29, no. 2–3, 2007, pp. 159–174.

Florida, Richard. *The Rise of the Creative Class and How It's Transforming Work, Leisure, Community and Everyday Life*. Hazard Press, 2003.

Gomá, Marina. "Challenging the Narrative of Canadian Multicultural Benevolence: A Feminist Anti-Racist Critique." *OMNES: The Journal of Multicultural Society*, vol. 10, no. 1, 2020, pp. 81–113.

Gordon-Walker, Caitlin. *Exhibiting Nation: Multicultural Nationalism (and Its Limits) in Canada's Museums*. UBC Press, 2016.

Gordon-Walker, Caitlin, Analays Alvarez Hernandez, and Susan L. T. Ashley. "Recognition and Repentance in Canadian Multicultural Heritage: The Community Historical Recognition Program and Italian Canadian Memorializing." *Journal of Canadian Studies*, vol. 52, no. 1, 2018, pp. 82–107.

Hall, Stuart. "Whose Heritage? Un-Settling 'The Heritage,' Re-Imagining the Post-Nation." *Third Text*, vol. 13, no. 49, 1999, pp. 3–13.

Harper, Stephen. "Prime Minister Stephen Harper's Speech Thursday on the Chinese Head Tax." *Globe and Mail*, 22 June 2006, https://www.theglobeandmail.com/news/national/text-of-harpers-speech/article20414337/. Accessed 2 December 2020.

Harrison, Rodney. *Heritage: Critical Approaches*. Routledge, 2013.

Harrison, Rodney, and Deb Rose. "Intangible Heritage." *Understanding Heritage and Memory*, edited by Tim Benton, Manchester University Press, 2010, pp. 238–276.

Hewison, Robert. *The Heritage Industry: Britain in a Climate of Decline*. Methuen, 1987.

Hoag, Sarah. "Jean Chrétien: A Vision of Canada through an Analysis of His Throne Speeches." *Canada and Speeches from the Throne: Narrating a Nation 1935–2015*, edited by Alexander Washkowsky et al., University of Regina Press, 2020. Accessed 31 March 2021 at https://opentextbooks.uregina.ca/primeministers2020/chapter/jeanchretien/

Hogarth, Kathy, and Wendy Fletcher. *A Space for Race: Decoding Racism, Multiculturalism, and Post-Colonialism in the Quest for Belonging in Canada and Beyond*. Oxford University Press, 2018.

Holden, John. *The Ecology of Culture: A Report Commissioned by the Arts and Humanities Research Council's Cultural Value Project*. Arts & Humanities Research Council, 2015.

Innis, Harold. *The Bias of Communication*. University of Toronto Press, 1951.

James, Matt. "Neoliberal Heritage Redress." *Reconciling Canada: Critical Perspectives on the Culture of Redress*, edited by Jennifer Henderson and Pauline Wakeham, University of Toronto Press, 2013, pp. 31–46.

Jameson, Fredric. *Postmodernism, or, the Cultural Logic of Late Capitalism*. Duke University Press, 1991.

Janes, Robert R. *Museums without Borders: Selected Writings of Robert R. Janes*. Routledge, 2016.

Kirshenblatt-Gimblett, Barbara. "World Heritage and Cultural Economics." *Museum Frictions: Public Cultures/Global Transformations*, edited by Ivan Karp et al., Duke University Press, 2006, pp. 161–202.

Knelman, Martin. "It's a Bird! It's a Plane! No, It's SuperBuilder!" *Toronto Star*, 2 December 2001, p. D.02.

Kovacs, Jason F. "Cultural Planning in Ontario, Canada: Arts Policy or More?" *International Journal of Cultural Policy*, vol. 17, no. 3, 2011, pp. 321–340.

Kymlicka, William. "The Three Lives of Multiculturalism." *Revisiting Multiculturalism in Canada*, edited by Shibao Guo and Lloyd Wong, Brill Sense, 2015, pp. 15–35.

Leblanc, Daniel. "Ottawa's Plan for Museums Met with Skepticism, Outrage." *Globe and Mail*, 15 October 2012, https://www.theglobeandmail.com/news/politics/ottawas-plan-for-museums-met-with-skepticism-outrage/article4614604/. Accessed 21 March, 2021.

Leung, Carrianne K. Y. "Usable Pasts, Staging Belongings: Articulating a 'Heritage' of Multiculturalism in Canada." *Studies in Ethnicity and Nationalism*, vol. 6, no. 2, 2006, pp. 162–179.

Litt, Paul. *The Muses, the Masses, and the Massey Commission*. University of Toronto Press, 1992.

Mackey, Eva. *The House of Difference: Cultural Politics and National Identity in Canada*. University of Toronto Press, 2002.

———. "Postmodernism and Cultural Politics in a Multicultural Nation: Contests Over Truth in the Into the Heart of Africa Controversy." *Public Culture,* vol. 7, 1995, pp. 403–431.

Mak, Eileen Diana. "Patterns of Change, Sources of Influence: An Historical Study of the Canadian Museum and the Middle Class, 1850–1950." Unpublished PhD dissertation, University of British Columbia, 1996.

Message, Kylie. *New Museums and the Making of Culture*. Berg, 2006.

O'Connor, Justin. "Art and Culture after Covid-19." *Wake in Fright Blog*, 9 April 2020, wakeinalarm.blog/2020/04/09/art-and-culture-after-covid-19/. Accessed 20 April 2020.

Paquette, Jonathan, Aurélie Lacassagne, and Robin Nelson. "Patrimoine et territorialisations: les imaginaires culturels du terroir dans la région des Laurentides au Québec." *Journal of Canadian Studies/Revue d'etudes Canadiennes*, vol. 52, no. 1, 2018, pp. 193–216.

Phillips, Ruth B. "Show Times: De-celebrating the Canadian Nation, De-colonising the Canadian Museum, 1967–92." *Rethinking Settler Colonialism*, edited by Annie Coombes, Manchester University Press, 2006, pp. 121–139.

Reigel, Henrietta. "Into the Heart of Irony: Ethnographic Exhibitions and the Politics of Difference." *Theorizing Museums*, edited by Sharon Macdonald and Gordon Fyfe, Blackwell, 1996, pp. 83–104.

Robertson, Iain. *Heritage from Below*. Routledge, 2016.

Ross, Val. "Renaissance City: The Billion-Dollar Baby." *Globe and Mail*, 15 April 2006, https://www.theglobeandmail.com/arts/the-billion-dollar-baby/article1097767/. Accessed 8 January 2021.

ROM. Exhibition Selection [Powerpoint] n.d. c. 2010.

ROM. "Toward Greater Inclusion and Equity at the ROM." *Royal Ontario Museum*, https://www.rom.on.ca/en/about-us/toward-greater-inclusion-and-equity-at-the-rom. Accessed 26 May 2022.

Royal Commission on National Development in the Arts, Letters and Sciences. *Report*. King's Printer, 1951.

Sánchez-Carretero, Cristina. "Significance and Social Value of Cultural Heritage: Analyzing the Fractures of Heritage." *Science and Technology for the Conservation of Cultural Heritage*, edited by Miguel Angel Rogerio-Candelera et al., Taylor & Francis, 2013, pp. 387–392.

Smith, Laurajane. *Uses of Heritage*. Routledge, 2006.

Stanley, Dick. "The Three Faces of Culture: Why Culture Is a Strategic Good Requiring Government Policy Attention." *Accounting for Culture: Thinking through Cultural Citizenship*, edited by Caroline Andrew et al., University of Ottawa Press, 2005, pp. 21–31.

Tator, Carol, Frances Henry, and Winston Matthis. *Challenging Racism in the Arts in Canada: Six Case Studies of Controversy and Conflict*. University of Toronto Press, 1998.

Teather, J. Lynne. *The Royal Ontario Museum: A Prehistory, 1830–1914*. Canadian University Press, 2005.

Thorsell, William. "The Museum as the New Agora—Notes for an Address to the Empire Club." ROM news release, 3 May 2007, www.rom.on.ca/en/about-us/newsroom/press-releases/museum-new-agora-william-thorsell. Accessed 20 December 2020.

Waterton, Emma, and Steve Watson. *The Semiotics of Heritage Tourism*. Channel View Publications, 2014.

Wylie, Lana. "Revising Memories and Changing Identities: Canadian Foreign Policy under the Harper Government." *Mapping Nations, Locating Citizens: Interdisciplinary Discussions on Nationalism and Identity*, edited by Daniel. Hambly, 2017, pp. 108–120.

Yan, Miu Chung, and Andrew Eungi Kim. "Civic and Judicial Multiculturalism of Canada: A Critical Assessment of the Canadian Model of Diversity for South Korea." *Korea Observer*, vol. 44, no. 1, 2013, pp. 87–112.

PART II

PARTICIPATION: WORKING AND COMMUNITY BUILDING IN THE CREATIVE INDUSTRIES

CHAPTER 4

Laughter from the Sidelines: Precarious Work in the Canadian Comedy Industry

Madison Trusolino

INTRODUCTION

Canada is renowned as one of the great exporters of comedic talent. Not only has Canada produced countless internationally recognized comedians, but it also hosts the world's largest comedy festival, *Just for Laughs* (JFL). Despite the comedy industry's significant cultural and economic contributions, Canada does little to foster its own homegrown talent. For example, as per Canadian cultural policy, stand-up comedians are not considered artists, thus making them ineligible for Canada Council for the Arts funding. Similarly, Canadian comedians are also required to obtain costly visas in order to tour in the United States, while American comedians are not required to do so when they perform in Canada. In addition to being somewhat peripheral players in the Canadian cultural production scene, comedy workers operate in a grey area, like many freelance artists, and do not fit into a formal occupational category. Achieving artistic and financial success proves even more difficult for comedians with marginalized identities, who already face barriers to entry in an industry that is dominated by white, cisgender, straight men.

Most research on comedy focuses on its rhetorical attributes (Finley; Tomsett), emphasizing the importance of comedy as a tool of subversive education (Cooper; Davies and Ilott; Proulx). Cynthia Willet and Julia Willet argue that at its worst, comedy can act as a "tool of oppression"; while at its best, it can be a "source of empowerment, a strategy for outrage and truth telling, a counter to fear, a source of joy and friendship, a cathartic treatment against unmerited shame, and even a means of empathetic connection and alliance" (2). This literature provides important analyses of comedic content but does not include a fulsome account of *how* subversive comedy is produced and the political, economic, and cultural ecosystem in which it is created.

This chapter outlines the power relations embedded within the Canadian comedy industry, drawing on a political economic approach that attends to "labour-relations in cultural production" and conceives of "media and culture as sites of political and social struggle" (Cohen, *Writer's Rights* 23). Rooted in a historical analysis that considers not only the role of the state and capital but also the feminization and racialization of work, critical political economy of communication engages with the processes and relations of "social and cultural practices" (Mosco 72) and holds that "social change is ubiquitous" (38). I further consider the impact these relations have on marginalized comedians operating within an already precarious industry and how Canadian comedians have actively worked to address these concerns. Precarity is the "existential, financial, and social insecurity exacerbated by the flexibilization of labour associated with post-Fordism" (de Peuter 419). Comedians are emblematic of the new creative work environment, acting as eternal freelancers and gig workers with little formal support—thus falling squarely into the creative precarious workforce (Butler and Stoyanova Russell).

Due to a lack of research on the comedy industry and the difficulty of obtaining data in an industry largely populated by self-employed workers, demographic information comes primarily from journalistic and anecdotal evidence. What information can be gathered from the limited data points to the continued underrepresentation of women, BIPOC, and LGBTQ+ performers in comedy (Becker; Kachel and Sheaffer). Little research engages the complicated dynamics of race, gender, and sexuality within the creative industries (Conor et al. 1). Overlooking these workers' experiences helps sustain historical patriarchal structures as well as growing job insecurity, and it limits the inclusion of a diversity of voices in creative and artistic production. This chapter poses the question: how do women, BIPOC, and LGBTQ+ comedians experience and navigate the Canadian comedy industry? I engage with how marginalized comedians mitigate and resist sexist/racist booking practices; a lack of representation; financial instability; and increased risk of harassment through community building and interventions into teaching and production practices.

For this chapter, I define workers in the comedy industry as stand-up comedians, improvisers, sketch comics, and comedic storytellers. Although people employed in various roles in comedic films and television shows could also be part of the industry, the scope of this project is limited to those I have identified above. Aymar Jean Christian argues that creative industries research privileges "projects from corporate distributors" (7). With this in mind, this chapter is empirically and theoretically grounded in Toronto clubs and comedy nights as well as other community-driven spaces where artists from "intersecting communities" work collaboratively toward "professional advancement" (255) in order to tell their stories. This allows for a more thorough investigation of the obstacles and opportunities that shape women, BIPOC, and LGBTQ+ comedians' experiences of "coming up" in the comedy industry.

THE STUDY

The data in this chapter come from my larger study on women and LGBTQ+ comedians' experiences of work in the Canadian comedy industry. My fieldwork was conducted in Toronto, Ontario, which many consider the epicentre of the Canadian comedy industry; it is also home to a burgeoning women's and LGBTQ+ comedy scene. Participants were recruited through their publicly available email addresses and a shareable call for participants on social media. I interviewed 20 women and/or LGBTQ+ comedians in the spring/summer of 2020 over video-conferencing software. Because my research considers marginalization in the comedy industry, I sought to ensure a diverse pool of interviewees across gender (nine cisgender women, three transgender women, one gender-fluid person, two non-binary people, one agender person, and four cisgender men); race (nine white and eleven BIPOC people); and sexuality (twelve bisexual/pansexual people, two lesbians, one queer person, two gay people, one asexual person, and two straight people). This was made possible through the trust and relationships I had built by attending and volunteering at comedy shows primarily catering to women, BIPOC, and LGBTQ+ comedians over a period of three years. Because of the abundance of LGBTQ+ shows in Toronto, my data primarily centre the experiences of LGBTQ+ comedians. Although participants were provided with a list of population groups to choose from, they were also able to write in their own self-descriptions, which provided additional nuance to the study. Due to the reputation-based nature of the comedy industry, and the increased risk of harm that women, BIPOC, and LGBTQ+ comedians face, I have anonymized all participants' data and opted for the use of pseudonyms.

THE CANADIAN CEILING: CIRCULATION, MOVEMENT, AND DISTRIBUTION

Comedic careers in Canada are limiting. Nearly every participant said it was a struggle to make a livable wage and gain international, or even national, recognition in the Canadian comedy industry. When asked what needed to change to make the Canadian comedy industry more sustainable for performers, participants identified three areas: (1) recognition as artists by the Canadian government; (2) provision of more platforms for Canadian talent; and (3) expansion of cross-border North American mobility. Combined with the general precarity of working in the creative industries, comedians have a difficult time building successful careers. This section looks at how women, BIPOC, and LGBTQ+ comedians experience the structure of production in the industry and how it hinders the proliferation of Canadian comedy both nationally and internationally. By structure, I mean key institutions and gatekeepers, including corporate gatekeepers (Yuk Yuk's Comedy Club and JFL) and governmental institutions (granting bodies and the Canadian Broadcasting Corporation [CBC]). Although I foreground do-it-yourself comedy scenes in Toronto, it is important to first map out how these major players have shaped the culture and economics of the industry. This allows me to explore the political economy—including the "social relations, particularly the power relations, that mutually constitute the production, distribution, and consumption of resources" (Mosco 25)—of the Canadian comedy industry.

Canada is home to the world's largest comedy club chain: Yuk Yuk's has 12 clubs across Canada, and the agency Funny Business Inc. books comics for corporate events. Yuk Yuk's holds a monopoly on the industry. Originally marketed as a home for anti-establishment entertainment, Yuk Yuk's was founded in 1976 by Mark Breslin in the basement of what is now the 519 Community Centre—a Toronto hub for LGBTQ+ community services (Stebbins). Performing at Yuk Yuk's is seen as a major stepping stone to achieving success in the Canadian comedy industry—although its full-time comedians only make about $13,000 annually (Hannay) and are not allowed to perform at other clubs without explicit permission—which acts as an additional obstacle for women, as Yuk Yuk's has a reputation for not hiring women.

Grace, a stand-up comedian and actor, suggests that Yuk Yuk's is not a "thriving business" and most of Yuk Yuk's revenue comes from touring. The "road dog" (touring comedian) lifestyle, she argues, is not particularly appealing to most women in part because of their familial responsibilities. Although work-family conflicts are one of the many ways that cultural work is gendered, we should not merely credit their lack of representation or power in an industry to childcare responsibilities (Gill). Because Yuk Yuk's primarily tours smaller towns and cities, audience members, Grace thinks, are less likely to want to see BIPOC women like her. Other participants countered this, saying they have received positive feedback from smaller-town audiences. Women who do get hired are more likely to be dating rostered comedians who can share a hotel room and drive together, putting less of an economic strain on the venue. This business-centric approach erases the inequalities built into the model of the industry and, while acknowledging that women are underrepresented, eschews an analysis of how these inequities perpetuate exclusionary practices.

Yuk Yuk's has also been accused of supporting alleged abusers. For example, in 2019, Yuk Yuk's booked Louis C. K. for eight shows. In 2017, C. K. had been accused of alleged sexual misconduct by five women (Ryzik et al.). Breslin claimed that he was proud to book C. K. because, unlike with other accusations lodged against comedians and celebrities in the wake of the #MeToo movement, Breslin said there was "no assault" committed, just lack of "consent (followed by regret)" by C. K.'s accusers (Breslin). Breslin's comments were not only inaccurate but also followed a nefarious script used to delegitimize the experiences of survivors of abuse.

In addition to being home to the world's largest comedy chain, Canada is also home to the world's largest comedy festival, JFL, and other internationally renowned comedy festivals such as the Winnipeg Comedy Festival and the Halifax Comedy Festival. JFL's main festival takes place in Montreal, with two smaller festivals taking place in Toronto (JFL42) and Vancouver (JFL NorthWest). Although JFL is a Canadian festival, it provides notoriously little support for Canadian comedians, and it is, more or less, an American festival for American comics on Canadian soil. One participant who performed at JFL says that while she was grateful for the opportunity, she did not gain American representation or even get paid for her performance. Not paying comedians is a common practice among festivals and venues who argue that they pay comedians in exposure (Jeffries 8). Until 2019, JFL's famous "New Faces" shows, featuring up-and-coming comedians, did not feature Canadians. This speaks to the monopoly the United States has on the North American entertainment industry (Urquhart and Wagman), whereby American talent is valued and bolstered more than Canadian talent. This is surprising considering that, as Jack, a stand-up comic who works in the television industry, points out, American comedy is "structurally Canadian." Many internationally renowned comedians, like Catherine O'Hara, Andrea Martin, Eugene Levy, and John Candy, known for laying the foundation for modern comedy, got their start on the Canadian sketch comedy show *SCTV Comedy Network*, which ran from 1976 to 1984. Eeven the comedic staple *Saturday Night Live* was created by Canadian Lorne Michaels.

JFL also has a spotty history regarding gender-based violence. In 2018, Gilbert Rozon, the co-founder of JFL, was charged with rape—and although he was later acquitted, it caused him to step down (CBC News, "Just for Laughs"). This, however, was only the latest accusation against Rozon. In 1999, he was charged with forcible confinement of a 31-year-old woman and the sexual assault of a 19-year-old woman. The former charge was dropped due to a lack of evidence, but he pled guilty and was fined $1,000 and put on one year's probation for the latter (Sweet). He avoided a criminal record and jail time, which would have made him unable to travel for work, because the presiding judge believed that it would negatively impact JFL, which brings in tourists and provides hundreds of jobs. This means that the justice system prioritized JFL and its revenue over the safety of women.

Although this is disturbing, the prioritization of profit over people is perhaps unsurprising in dominant capitalist structures. Comedy festivals are important revenue streams for Canadian provinces, with JFL alone contributing $34 million to Quebec's GDP in 2016 (Everett-Green). Festivals also garner substantial sponsorships from corporations. Although comedians are generally undervalued and underpaid, festivals like JFL, the Winnipeg Comedy Festival, and the Halifax Comedy Festival have all received funding from granting bodies like the Department of Canadian Heritage. Stand-up comedians, on the other hand, are not considered artists by the Government of Canada, making access to arts funding difficult for these individuals. Improvisers and sketch comics have arguably more access because of their ability to apply as theatre companies. This is not unique to Canada, though. In the United Kingdom, comedy was only deemed an art form in 2020 when it became eligible for the Covid-19 Culture Recovery Fund as a form of theatre under Arts Council England. But the Department for Culture, Media and Sport stated that being included in this fund does not mean comedy clubs will be eligible for future funding (Richardson). In the United Kingdom, the main argument for comedy not being eligible for funding is that it is self-funded (Davis), but where comedy clubs run as a private business, this description does not apply to live comedic performers themselves. Despite this, there are more opportunities to perform in the United Kingdom than in Canada. With its smaller and more accessible geography and bigger population, the United Kingdom has a thriving comedy circuit, where comedians from other countries go to cut their teeth. Similarly, in the United States, comedy is not funded, but this is more in line with the country's private and market-based approach to funding. Nonetheless, the American monopoly on cultural production and access to Hollywood provides more upward mobility for comedic performers.

The Canada Council for the Arts (CCA), Canada's largest granting agency, has said that stand-up comedians are free to apply for grants if they can demonstrate their ability in other disciplines such as "circus performing, dance, or theatre" (Hannay). Comedians could, arguably, fit within the definition of professional artists set out by the CCA, defined as those who (1) have "specialized training in the artistic field (not necessarily in academic institutions)," (2) are "recognized as a professional by his or her peers (artists working in the same artistic tradition)," (3) are "committed to devoting more time to artistic activity, if possible financially," and (4) have a "history of public presentation or publication." Despite not being considered artists, comedians are counted as contributors to the arts and culture industry. Culture, according to Statistics Canada's "Canadian Framework for Culture Statistics," is defined as "creative artistic activity and the goods and services produced by it, and the preservation of heritage" (9). Expanding on this definition, the report outlines several domains used to group industries, products, and occupations. Comedy fits under domain B, "Live Performances" (50), contributing to the information and cultural industries' GDP, which saw a 6.9 percent rise between 2012 and 2018 (Statistics Canada, "Gross Domestic Product"). Comedy also contributes to the Arts, Entertainment, and Recreation sector GDP, which increased by 17.2 percent between 2012 and 2018.

Sophie, a comedian and theatre performer, does not consider this lack of recognition an obstacle and easily adapted her material, obtaining an Ontario Arts Council grant for her one-woman show. Nonetheless, these funding structures speak to a larger problem of the lack of legitimization and fostering of Canadian comedy and talent. This is especially egregious considering Canada prides itself on its investment in the arts and dedicated a substantial $1.9 billion to arts and culture over five years in the 2016 federal budget (Government of Canada). With few props, costumes, or sets needed, comedy is a relatively inexpensive and accessible art form, giving the impression of being low stakes. Lex, a stand-up comedian and drag performer, says they would like people to recognize that comedians are not merely "people who happen to be funny" but "hardworking performers," demonstrating that not only are comedians not taken seriously as artists, but they are also not considered workers.

This is a common problem within the creative industries, where, Kate Oakley says, creative workers are often disassociated from more "industrial" areas of work and are thus often seen as "artists" instead of workers. Oakley argues that the creative industries are populated by precariously employed workers and that "low pay and no-pay is rife." Because of creative work's special association with the arts, Oakley notes that workers in the creative industries tend to think that their work "should not be tainted by monetary consideration" and that "devoting oneself to it, even at the cost of one's health or relationships, is a noble pursuit." This narrative distances artistic labour from the "market economy, regulatory frameworks, state and employer policies" that shape their work and the ways that they work (Cohen,

"Cultural Work" 144). It also perpetuates the internal and external exploitation of creative workers, who generally discount their labour. For example, stand-up performer Max described comedy as an "obsession" or "a drug," feeding into the idea that precarity is the cost of "pursuing their passion" (Cohen, *Writer's Rights* 23).

Additionally, there are few major platforms in Canada that showcase Canadian talent. The CBC has produced and filmed live stand-up for CBC Gem, an online streaming platform inaccessible to audiences outside of Canada (Gem Support). These are almost exclusively filmed at one of the three major Canadian festivals, meaning comedians outside of the festival circuit are afforded few opportunities for publicity—an additional obstacle in gaining international name recognition. Canadian comedians struggle with finding mainstream success in Canada. Although Canada is a hub for film and television production, those productions are often not Canadian. Hollywood is incentivized to film in Canada because of the Film or Video Production Services Tax Credit, which, alongside provincial credits, significantly offsets the cost of filming (Epstein). Comedian and theatre performer Quinn says that the United States understands "that media is like information and media is starting to become the new cultural capital in the world."

Canada is thus at risk of a creative "brain drain" for the lucky few comedians who can obtain a visa to perform and work in the United States. Several participants mentioned potential moves to the United States or the United Kingdom, but the ability to perform in the United States is an arduous and expensive process. Comedians must qualify for an O-1 visa, also known as an "extraordinary person" visa. To obtain this non-immigrant visa, Canadians must demonstrate that they possess "extraordinary ability in the arts, sciences, education or athletics" or a "demonstrated record of extraordinary achievement in the motion picture or television industry" (US Citizenship and Immigration Services). The visa costs between $5,000 and $25,000, with a limit on the number of visas issued per year (Borys). To be considered, comedians must prove that they have "sustained national or international acclaim" and are "widely recognized as being one of the best" in their field (Maximilian Law Inc.). This adds an additional layer of difficulty considering the limited opportunities in Canada for comedians. If comedians perform in the United States without a visa, even at an unpaid gig, they could be banned from performing in the United States for five years. Unlike Canadians, Americans performing in Canada do not need to pay any fees and must simply provide proof that they have been booked at a festival, nightclub, or other venue. The risks, from this perspective, are minimal, perhaps non-existent.

Some comedians are unwilling/unable to take the risk to cross the border, including many transgender women, who fear how the legal system/border guards might treat them if they were caught performing. However, others have found ways around this. Comedians tell border agents they are on vacation, or they mitigate risk by concentrating all their comedic communications through one app, which they delete when they cross the border. Restricted access to the American comedy scene means most comedians exclusively tour in Canada. Touring clubs, or smaller venues, is a more consistent source of income, but it is also problematic because of Canada's vast geography, smaller population, and Yuk Yuk's and JFL's monopoly on the industry. Despite remaining powerful, though, these institutions do not present a fulsome picture of the performance spaces in which comedians, in particular marginalized comedians, have tirelessly worked to carve out their own unique scenes within the larger Canadian industry.

CASE STUDY: WORK IN TORONTO'S COMEDY SCENE

Toronto's comedy industry is home to a rapidly growing women's and LGBTQ+ comedy scene. Despite the major clubs in Toronto, my participants were more likely to perform at comedy nights taking place in bars, cafés, restaurants, and a handful of independent comedy venues. Finding the major chains unwelcoming at best and discriminatory at worst, my respondents actively worked to produce and create shows and spaces that provided alternative avenues for "coming up" in the industry.

Since new comedians have very little comedic experience, there are several ways they can "come up" in the Toronto comedy scene. Common among improvisers, and some stand-ups, is attending workshops at The Second City—a world-renowned comedy training centre and venue—or enrolling in the Humber College Program for Comedy Writing and Performance, where Breslin, co-founder of Yuk Yuk's, serves as producer-in-residence and artistic director. This overlap between Yuk Yuk's and the Humber College program reproduces already existing hierarchies in the comedy industry. For example, Ivy, a stand-up comedian and producer, says that when she attended, most of the instructors of the program were white, cisgender, straight men who are not in touch with the experiences of marginalized comedians. Despite this, the program allows emerging comedians to experiment with different comedic forms and build their networks. Another way comedians come up is through the open mic scene. Open mics provide free and, usually, unbooked stage time where comedians work on new material, scout out talent, and, importantly, network, since the audiences at open mics are usually composed of other comedians.

Participants stressed the importance of networking and relationship building in comedy, or what Rosalind Gill calls "compulsory sociality" (520). Compulsory sociality demands a level of time, energy, and resources to engage in networking activities that are not always available to comedians. Empirical work on the creative industries has shown that, due to a lack of formal hiring structures, reputation plays an important role in securing work and building careers. Bridget Conor et al. argue that "reputation is a key commodity" (10) blurring the boundaries of the workplace. Although being funny is important, Max says it is only about "30 percent of your job."

Social media platforms are one of the key ways that comedians network. In their study of comedians' use of social media, Rebecca Krefting and Rebecca Baruc found that it is an "industry imperative" (133), not only for networking but also for online promotion, content creation, and self-branding. Facebook was among the most popular tools for comedians, who used Messenger to connect with individual comedians and book gigs, and they posted and filled available spots through Facebook groups. For comedians who are less comfortable with networking in person, like Grace, social media can help create connection: "I've heard a lot of people say, 'I feel like we're just friends … because I see you on Instagram all the time.'" Networking online allows for Grace to remain on the radar of other comedians without having to put herself in situations that she finds uncomfortable or unappealing.

Comedians, particularly at the beginning of their career, rely almost entirely on other comedians for opportunities, are rarely paid, and often experience strenuous working environments. According to a report based on the 2016 long-form census, actors and comedians were found to make 57 percent lower (the median income for the group was $18,500) than the Canadian average income (Hill). To be counted in the category, individuals must list their primary occupation as actor or comedian, and only a small handful of the comedians I interviewed made the bulk of their income from comedy. Even those who considered themselves full-time comedians made most of their income writing, teaching comedy workshops, or working at theatres. Participants said that performing live contributed the least to their income among their various revenue sources and that they typically only made $0–$20 per set. On rare occasions, comedians may book corporate events, which can pay upwards of $1,000. The willingness to work for free, however, sets a dangerous precedent for others in the industry and drives everyone's prices down. This shows how, as Oakley writes, "there is no self-exploitation without exploitation of others." At the same time, working for free is often one of the only ways to get stage time when coming up. The normalization of working for free not only discounts individual comedians' labour but sets a precedent that is not sustainable for those who do not come from privileged backgrounds.

Many participants aspired to be full-time comedians, but they worked an array of other jobs, most commonly in the retail and restaurant industries, fitting into what Brooke Erin Duffy calls the "slash generation" composed of "individuals in their twenties and thirties whose worker identities span multiple professions" (xi). Duffy writes that creatives often try to "earn incomes from their so-called passion projects in the midst of a labor market that is rife with uncertainty" (xi). Not only do comedians work multiple non-comedy jobs, but they also occupy multiple roles within the industry, acting as their own agents and managers.

This hodgepodge of gigs and jobs, what Nicole Cohen calls the "hustle," is endemic to creative work. Cohen defines the hustle as the "mode of being for millions of precariously employed workers, who juggle multiple gigs, do what needs to be done to make money, and experience uncertain futures" ("Hustle"). In comedy, the "hustle" is better known as "the grind." The grind, according to Oliver, is the idea that "you have to do as many shows as possible every night." The grind is about actively pursuing and performing in all spaces, even those that are undesirable, but, as Elliot argues, "it shouldn't suck, comedy's fun … it shouldn't be this badge of honour that you lost a limb." Grind culture was referenced as exemplary of the ways in which comedy privileges straight, cisgender, and able-bodied men because it requires the ability to be flexible with one's time: doing multiple shows in one night most nights of the week and not turning down work in any particular venue. Those who are unable to participate in the grind are perceived as less committed to their craft. The privilege of success, then, often goes, as stand-up comedian Celine argues, to those who have "[t]he luxuries of a stable income and an identity that is not going to be met with hostility anywhere." The appreciation and privileging of grind culture may not explicitly come across as discriminatory, but my participants show how the mechanisms of comedy hold deeply rooted biases against marginalized comedians even when they appear to be "neutral" (Jeffries 139).

EMBEDDED INEQUALITIES: NAVIGATING THE INDUSTRY AS A MARGINALIZED PERFORMER

The lack of human resources (HR) in comedy was repeatedly referenced by my participants, who saw it as a huge barrier to their safety and security in the industry. Although some comedic institutions have HR departments, such as JFL and The Second City, most comedians I interviewed worked outside of, or across, institutions. Because of this, individual comedians confront varying degrees of risk, from having their reputation ruined and losing opportunities to facing legal charges for slander. Lex says that someone's power and status in the comedy community is constantly being put before the testimonies of the people they harmed. Thus, in addition to being their own manager and agent, stand-up and sketch comedian Avery says comedians are also their "own HR."

Several participants said they perform a kind of risk analysis, deciding whether an opportunity is worth the potential harm or distress it might cause. Grace says the problem is not that she gets harassed regularly; rather, it is on her to turn down opportunities where she does not feel safe. For example, she says she could be making more money if she was willing to do more out-of-town gigs, but she does not feel comfortable taking rides with groups of cisgender, straight men: "I refuse to be in cars with other male comedians where they'll be talking about how they hate their girlfriends and, you know, whatever super toxic things." Similarly, several comedians say they must closely navigate the open mic scene to avoid racist, homophobic, and transphobic content and treatment.

Participants also addressed the difficulty of working in comedy while maintaining their own reputation. The fragility of reputations can act as a silencing technique to quell dissent in the industry. Robin shared her experience of being harassed by a comedy club booker in his forties when she was eighteen, which ruined her relationship with the club. Although the booker was fired, she began to lose opportunities. After that, feeling she had little to lose, Robin began to address other experiences of violence and harassment in the industry, such as the booking of alleged sexual abusers at comedy clubs. This further isolated her in the industry, which is one of the reasons she began to produce her own shows. Annie had a bad experience confronting a comedian in a green room who was making jokes about rape: "He got very upset and was saying that I was calling him a rapist—which, to be fair, I did." After that, Annie never felt safe at shows where he was present. Because of how few women there are in the industry, green rooms are often spaces of unchecked toxic masculinity and many women find themselves in situations where, as the only woman on a lineup, they feel uncomfortable or at risk.

Marginalized comedians are often tasked with filling the diversity quota and/or being tokenized. Tokenizing in comedy occurs when members of marginalized groups are used in a "perfunctory way or as a symbolic gesture of inclusivity, lending a multicultural veneer" to a predominantly white show (Diffrient 43). Tokenization places comedians in a double bind in which they can get more stage time but they know they will be the only women/LGBTQ+/BIPOC comic on the bill. For some, this worked to their advantage, including Elliot, a stand-up comedian, who says that there were so few masculine-presenting queer comics of colour that they filled a diversity quota "vacuum." But Ada felt pressured to behave in the stereotypical way expected of them or else get sidelined: "So if you're not gay enough, if you're not Black enough, if you're not willing to be 'hon,' 'babe,' whatever, then you get benched because you're deemed difficult."

During Black History Month or Pride, comedians often felt used on shows produced by straight, cisgender, white men. For example, one such producer suggested a Pride show where half the comedians booked were LGBTQ+ and the other half were homophobic. This was not only an attempt to profit from the work of LGBTQ+ comedians but also a situation where they would be put in danger. During the height of the global Justice for George Floyd/Black Lives Matter protests in the summer of 2020, Lex, who is Black, was asked by a white producer to do an online show for free. They agreed because the donations made by the audience were going to go toward Black-led organizations, but upon reflection they realized how inappropriate it was for a white producer to book Black comedians and not pay them.

Sara Ahmed, in her work on diversity initiatives in the university, argues that diversity often acts as a "technique of arranging things" so that institutions can appear "better" or "happier" (98) without doing the work that disrupts the status quo. This is likewise present at comedy festivals and shows that tend to use marginalized comedians to commodify difference rather than work to address deeper institutional problems. Ivy says these producers "don't actually want to represent these people" and just want to open the demographics of their audience. Festivals and shows then use marginalized comedians to appeal to niche audiences. Niche marketing segments social groups through "identifying characteristics" (Christian 114) and considers representation a commercial imperative rather than an ethical or moral one (Saha).

My participants had an ambivalent relationship with the idea of representation. Although tokenization adds undue pressure for marginalized comedians, my findings echoed Jeffries' in that they felt they were "breaking through glass ceilings and being an example or role model for other group members to emulate" (172). Many interviewees experienced moments with audience members that affirmed the importance of their work. Mary, a transgender woman, recounted the excitement of a transgender audience member after seeing her perform. Gwen, a Black queer improvisor, spoke of seeing a Black queer audience member with tears in her eyes because she saw herself represented on stage by Gwen. This demonstrates the importance of seeing oneself reflected in the media. Several participants said that they did not pursue comedy until they saw other women, BIPOC, and LGBTQ+ comedians perform. In Christian's study of web television shows, he found that because producers were able to bypass traditional network television gatekeepers, they could provide representations that "connect sincerely with their communities" (155). Similarly, marginalized comedians can provide intimate portrayals of their lives that might not be considered marketable to mainstream club audiences. Unfortunately, this means that they also take on the added risks of intervening in the production process in an already precarious industry.

COMMUNITY BUILDING: FORMAL AND INFORMAL ORGANIZING IN THE COMEDY INDUSTRY

Despite the low (or no) pay and precarious and uncertain career trajectories, there have been few attempts at formal labour organizing in the comedy industry. This reflects a larger trend within the creative industries, where "individual coping strategies" (Cultural Workers Organize)—ranging from working multiple jobs to mitigate financial strain to self-care—are celebrated over collective responses to precarity. Two notable exceptions exist: One being the attempted cross-Canada strike in the 1980s by comedians against Yuk Yuk's (Deveau 132); the other was the successful 1979 Los Angeles Comedy Store strike, where comedians managed to negotiate a US$25 per-set payout from the Comedy Store after discovering a pay gap between the main room (where comedians were paid) and the other rooms (where they were not) (Zoglin). The strike was deemed a seminal moment in the history of comedy, turning stand-up from a hobby into a profession (Stebbins). Among my study participants, several were members of either acting or writing unions, but they remained outside of formally organized comedy.

In 2017, motivated by the lack of recognition for Canadian comedy and comedians, comedian Sandra Battaglini, along with a small group of fellow comedians, formed the Canadian Association of Stand-Up Comedians (CASC). CASC began after Battaglini sent a letter to the prime minister calling on the government to provide funding for comedy projects. This led to a meeting with her local member of Parliament to discuss how to get stand-up comedy recognized as an art form (Hannay). CASC has over six hundred members and has hired lobbyists to advocate for them on Parliament Hill. The purpose of the group is to "advocate on behalf of professional Canadian comedy writers and performers and collaborate with private and public sector stakeholders in the comedy industry" and to "promote and insist on a harassment-free environment for comedy professionals that fosters racial, social, economic, physical, mental, and gender justice and equality" (CASC, "About").

Many of my study participants respect CASC's mission but are still hesitant to become due-paying members. Even among its own founders, there has been some confusion about CASC's purpose. Battaglini has maintained they are a lobby group, stating that while she believes in workers' right to unionize, "creating a union for comics is difficult because the work is so precarious" (*Interrobang* staff). On the other hand, another founding member, Jay Freeborn, said CASC is "somewhere between a union and a representation group" (Smith). CASC is still working to solidify its role in the industry and build trust with comedians.

The publicity surrounding CASC inspired discussions around recognizing the cultural and economic importance of the Canadian comedy industry. Toronto-based venue The Theatre Centre held a week-long festival entitled "Comedy Is Art," comprising a diverse lineup of Canadian-produced shows, and created a residency spot for artists working in comedy. CASC was also part of the fight against JFL's attempt to limit an important financial resource for Canadian comics after, in 2019, the festival took over Canada Laughs, a Sirius XM radio channel broadcasting exclusively Canadian comedy. Before the takeover, many Canadian comedians relied on the royalties garnered from the channel. Instead of amplifying Canadian content, JFL intended to platform "international comics, decades-old routines, and recordings that Just for Laughs owns" (Van Evra). Not only was Canada Laughs an important revenue stream, but it also assisted in helping Canadians gain the exposure necessary to help with international mobility (Bond). Taking to social and news media, comedians applied public pressure, leading JFL to commit to maintaining Canada Laughs' previous commitment to 100 percent Canadian content.

While formal organizing is still rare in the comedy industry, informal organizing happens regularly. Facebook groups are an important organizational tool for comedians, especially for women and LGBTQ+ comedians. These groups function not only as spaces for networking and sharing opportunities but also as whisper networks to warn one another of, for example, bad producers or predatory comedians, away from the view of cisgender, straight men. Quinn, a group moderator, admits that these groups are far from perfect spaces and, like the entertainment industry, are largely populated by white artists, meaning that the onus is often on BIPOC members to step up and educate the group. This speaks to the added labour that marginalized, and specifically BIPOC, comedians take on in the industry. Lisa Nakamura argues that the labour of educating "white men and women about racism and sexism is difficult, valuable, and unappreciated." Furthermore, it puts BIPOC comedians at greater risk of being "harassed, trolled, and threatened" (108). For example, Ada says that as a Black woman she was nervous about the repercussions for posting in support of Black Lives Matter in 2014 because it was still perceived as a "terrorist group."

Comedians also use their routines as a form of subversion within the industry. Zoe, a writer and stand-up, is often the first transgender person her audience members encounter. Knowing this, she writes her set as a "trans 101" and views it as an opportunity to educate her audiences: "There's something about getting people to laugh along with you that you can kind of sneak in information without them noticing." Elliot, a person of colour on the asexuality spectrum, enjoys going into spaces where "someone has never seen someone that looks like me, introducing them to the concept that I exist, and then getting them to laugh along with me." This aligns with previous research showing that comedy acts as an accessible educational tool (Cooper 2019), covertly teaching audiences about people, topics, and communities they might not have otherwise engaged with.

Other comedians try to transform the ways comedians navigate the industry, whether it be through workshops or producing inclusive shows that not only elevate marginalized performers but facilitate inclusive audiences. Improvisers Ada and Gwen both integrate anti-oppression training into their comedy workshops through discussions of unconscious bias in comedy. Another group of comedians, recognizing the difficulties (and sometimes dangers) of the open mic scene, started an open mic exclusively for women and non-binary comedians. These mics provide an opportunity to make entry into comedy less turbulent while still allowing comedians room to fail and grow. Several comedians also saw the gap in BIPOC, women's, and queer-centred shows and, as Ivy says, rather than "wait(ing) for anyone to give us that space," actively carved out a niche for themselves. Not only does this provide a platform for marginalized voices, but, as Grace notes, it is a smart marketing decision that helps comedians "cultivate their own audience."

Importantly, abuses of power are not only relegated to the world of comedy primarily occupied by cisgender, straight men. Several comedians brought up an instance of alleged abuse within the Toronto queer comedy scene where an up-and-coming queer comedian used their power to silence dissent. This demonstrates the weakness of what Dave O'Brien et al. call the "demography and representation approach" (274) that underpins many strategies to address inequality, where the assumption is that if a workforce mirrors a nation's demographics, it will have a positive impact on cultural representation. This approach does not consider how precarity and entrepreneurialism perpetuate exclusionary and unsafe practices lacking a fulsome understanding of "inequalities and power imbalances" (275) that shape the industry. Nonetheless, the opening of LGBTQ+, feminist, and BIPOC comedy spaces has had a remarkable impact on the comedy scene in Toronto.

Toronto has long been home to pockets of women-, BIPOC-, or LGBTQ+ centric shows—note, for example, the festival We're Funny That Way, a queer comedy festival launched in 1996 that supports LGBTQ+ charities. In the past five years, there has been a surge of shows that centre women, BIPOC, and LGBTQ+ comedians and audiences. Because of the relatively small number of comedians in Toronto—in comparison to other North American urban centres—LGBTQ+ comedians have an easier time getting to know and providing opportunities for one another, thus offering a unique opportunity for up-and-coming comedians in Canada. For example, Celine was, in part, prompted to move from Edmonton, Alberta, to Toronto after she came out as a transgender woman. After her transition, she began to feel alienated and noticed diminishing opportunities: "I stopped being able to do the road, I stopped getting booked on certain shows, I stopped being able to work with certain people." Celine's experience reminds us of the limited opportunities for marginalized comedians outside of Canada's largest city.

These interventions by marginalized comedians into the Canadian comedy industry demonstrate the tensions between the mainstream comedy scene and the growing women's and LGBTQ+ comedy scene(s). As this chapter has demonstrated, comedy is still overwhelmingly dominated by white, cisgender, straight men, who are considered the standard and form the lens through which comedians and comedy are seen. Because of this, diversity in the industry is presented as a binary between white, cisgender, straight men and, as Ivy says, "the rest of us" (Saha 92). By opening these spaces of resistance, marginalized comedians are platforming their own voices rather than waiting for opportunities and showing that, as Elliot says, "we can be successful outside of those spaces and we can be visible and talented and funny and successful."

CONCLUSION

This chapter has outlined the precarious and shifting terrain of the Canadian comedy industry and emphasized how race, gender, and sexuality impact comedians at various stages of their artistic production. I have outlined the microstructures of comedic work and the "broader economic, political and cultural context" to gain a better understanding of how women and LGBTQ+ comedians "exercise agency" (Saha 48) in the production of comedy. Researching how marginalized comedians navigate the industry allows for a deeper understanding of how "social patterning and social inequality in production" impact the "representation and consumption of culture" (O'Brien et al. 272). While not denying the importance of textual analysis, a focus on production demonstrates the tensions around the concept of representation.

Most participants felt as though they had limited access to either mainstream comedy clubs, festivals, or international audiences. As I have demonstrated, there is a significant contingent of artists who are not seen or supported as artists in Canada. This has a chilling effect on the production of Canadian culture and the flourishing of Canadian talent. With little support from the Canadian government, major media, and comedy institutions, comedians, and more explicitly marginalized comedians, are working to create meaningful alternatives to the mainstream route to success. At the same time, without support for Canadian talent, the Canadian comedy industry is likely to remain on the periphery of global entertainment industries.

CORE CONCEPTS

freelance artists: Artists who work contract to contract or gig to gig rather than have stable and long-term employment.

the grind: The taking on of as many jobs and opportunities as possible, no matter how bad, with the belief that this will eventually lead to financial and artistic success.

political economy: The study of the social relations that determine the allocation of resources from production to distribution.

precarity: The increasing social and financial insecurity and flexibilization of work and labour.

tokenism: The expectation of an individual to represent a whole identity category, such as race, gender, or sexuality.

SUGGESTED ACTIVITIES

1. Comedy is not considered an art form in Canada. Develop a policy proposal advocating for, or against, its recognition by the Canada Council for the Arts. Consider comedy's economic and cultural contributions and definitions of the performing arts.
2. Choose a local comedy venue and compile its roster of comedians for a recent week. Who is represented on the bill? Who is not? What does this say about the potential social and political dynamics of the industry?

REFERENCES

Ada. Personal interview. 20 July 2020.

Ahmed, Sara. *Living a Feminist Life*. Duke University Press, 2017.

Annie. Personal interview. 18 July 2020.

Avery. Personal interview. 6 May 2020.

Becker, Kristen. "Is the Comedy Club Business Model Outdated? Part 1: Diversity." *The Interrobang*, 29 March 2016, https://theinterrobang.com/comedy-club-business-model-outdated-part-1-diversity/. Accessed 3 April 2021.

Bond, John-Michael. "Canadian Comedians Almost Lost One of Their Biggest Revenue Streams to the Just for Laughs Festival." *Paste Magazine*, 28 February 2019, https://www.pastemagazine.com/comedy/just-for-laughs/canadian-comedians-almost-lost-one-of-their-bigges/. Accessed 3 April 2021.

Borys, Christian. "'Extraordinary Person' Visas and the Plight of Canadian Comedians." *Vulture*, 1 December 2014, https://www.vulture.com/2014/12/extraordinary-person-visas-and-the-plight-of-canadian-comedians.html. Accessed 3 April 2021.

Breslin, Mark. "Breslin: Why I Brought Louis C.K. Back from the Dead." *The Canadian Jewish News*, 8 November 2019, https://thecjn.ca/arts/breslin-why-i-brought-louis-c-k-back-from-the-dead/. Accessed 3 April 2021.

Butler, Nick, and Dimitrinka Stoyanova Russell. "No Funny Business: Precarious Work and Emotional Labour in Stand-Up Comedy." *Human Relations*, vol. 71, no. 2, 2018, pp. 1–21.

Canada Council for the Arts. "Professional Artist" (Glossary page), https://canadacouncil.ca/glossary/professional-artist. Accessed 5 November 2020.

Canadian Association of Stand-Up Comedians. "About," https://www.canadianstandup.ca/about/. Accessed 4 November 2020.

CBC News. "Just for Laughs Founder Gilbert Rozon Acquitted in Rape, Indecent Assault Trial." *CBC News*, 15 December 2020, https://www.cbc.ca/news/canada/montreal/gilbert-rozon-rape-trial-1.5842309. Accessed 3 April 2021.

Christian, Aymar Jean. *Open TV: Innovation Beyond Hollywood and the Rise of Web Television*. NYU Press, 2018.

Celine. Personal interview. 25 July 2020.

Cohen, Nicole. "Cultural Work as a Site of Struggle: Freelancers and Exploitation." *TripleC*, vol. 10, no. 2, 2012, pp. 141–155.

———. "Hustle." *Nicole S. Cohen*, 3 February 2017, https://nicolescohen.com/2017/02/03/hustle/. Accessed 3 April 2021.

———. *Writer's Rights: Freelance Journalism in a Digital Age*. McGill-Queen's University Press, 2016.

Conor, Bridget, Rosalind Gill, and Stephanie Taylor. "Part 1: Introduction, Gender and Creative Labour." In *Gender and Creative Labour,* edited by Bridget Conor et al., Wiley Blackwell/Sociological Review, 2015, pp. 1–22.

Cooper, S. Katherine. "What's So Funny? Audiences of Women's Stand-Up Comedy and Layered Referential Viewing: Exploring Identity and Power." *The Communication Review*, vol. 22, no. 2, pp. 91–116.

Cultural Workers Organize: Researching Collective Responses to Precarity. "About," https://culturalworkersorganize.org/about/. Accessed 4 November 2020.

Davies, Helen, and Sarah Ilott. "Gender, Sexuality and the Body in Comedy: Performance, Reiteration, Resistance." *Comedy Studies*, vol. 9, no. 1, 2018, pp. 2–5.

Davis, Hazel. "Why Isn't Comedy Funded by the Arts Council?" *Guardian*, 3 November 2009, https://www.theguardian.com/stage/2009/nov/03/comedy-funded-arts-council. Accessed 3 April 2021.

de Peuter, Greig. "Creative Economy and Labor Precarity: A Contested Convergence." *Journal of Communication Inquiry*, vol. 35, no. 4, 2011, pp. 417–425.

Deveau, Danielle J. "English Canadian Stand-Up Comedy as a Field of Cultural Production." PhD dissertation, Simon Fraser University, 2010, https://summit.sfu.ca/item/12496.

Diffrient, David Scott. "Beyond Tokenism and Tricksterism: Bobby Lee, MADtv, and the De(con)structive Impulse of Korean American Comedy." *Velvet Light Trap*, no. 67, 2011, pp. 41–56.

Duffy, Brooke Erin. *(Not) Getting Paid to Do What You Love: Gender, Social Media, and Aspirational Work*. Yale University Press, 2017.

Elliot. Personal Interview. 7 May 2020.

Epstein, Edward Jay. "Northern Expenditure: Why Are So Many Movies Still Being Shot in Canada?" *Slate Magazine*, 13 February 2006, https://slate.com/culture/2006/02/why-are-so-many-movies-shot-in-canada.html. Accessed 3 April 2021.

Everett-Green, Robert. "Will Gilbert Rozon's Fall Kill the Just for Laughs Festival He Founded?" *Globe and Mail*, 17 November 2017, https://www.theglobeandmail.com/arts/theatre-and-performance/will-gilbert-rozons-fall-kill-the-just-for-laughs-festival-hefounded/article37017844/. Accessed 3 April 2021.

Finley, Jessyka. "Raunch and Redress: Interrogating Pleasure in Black Women's Stand-Up Comedy." *Journal of Popular Culture*, vol. 49, no. 4, 2016, pp. 780–798.

Gem Support. "Can I Watch CBC Content on Gem if I'm Outside Canada?" *CBC Help Centre*, https://cbchelp.cbc.ca/hc/en-ca/articles/115003517273-Can-I-watch-CBC-content-onGem-if-I-m-outside-Canada-. Accessed 4 November 2020.

Gill, Rosalind. "Unspeakable Inequalities: Post Feminism, Entrepreneurial Subjectivity, and the Repudiation of Sexism among Cultural Workers." *Social Politics: International Studies in Gender, State and Society*, vol. 21, no. 4, 2014, pp. 509–528.

Government of Canada. "Chapter 5—An Inclusive and Fair Canada," *Budget 2016*, 22 March 2016, https://www.budget.gc.ca/2016/docs/plan/ch5-en.html#_ Toc446106809. Accessed 18 October 2021.

Grace. Personal interview. 11 May 2020.

Gwen. Personal interview. 24 July 2020.

Hannay, Chris. "Beating Them to the Punchline: How Canadian Stand-Ups Are Trying to Change the Funny Business." *Globe and Mail*, 23 November 2018, https://www. theglobeandmail.com/arts/theatre-and-performance/article-canadian-stand-up-comedians-lobby-for-artist-status-in-bid-for-better/. Accessed 3 April 2021.

Hill, Kelly. "A Statistical Profile of Artists in Canada in 2016." *Hill Strategies Research Inc.*, November 2019, https://hillstrategies.com/wp-content/uploads/2019/11/sia49_ artists_canada2016_revised.pdf. Accessed 3 April 2021.

Interrobang staff. "Behind Canada's New Artists Collective: Canadian Association of Stand Up Comedians." *The Interrobang*, 30 March 2018, https://theinterrobang. com/behind-canadas-new-artists-union-canadian-association-of-stand-up-comedians/. Accessed 3 April 2021.

Ivy. Personal interview. 21 May 2020.

Jack. Personal interview. 30 May 2020.

Jeffries, Michael P. *Behind the Laughs: Community and Inequality in Comedy*. Stanford University Press, 2017.

Kachel, Meredith, and Austin Sheaffer. "What's the Deal with Stand-Up Comedy Bookings?: Using Data to Show Discrepancies in Gender in Chicago's Stand-Up Comedy Scene." *Meredith Kachel*, https://www.meredithkachel.com/gender-and-comedy. Accessed 3 November 2020.

Krefting, Rebecca, and Rebecca Baruc. "A New Economy of Jokes?: #Socialmedia #Comedy." *Comedy Studies*, vol. 2, no. 6, pp. 129–140.

Lex. Personal interview. 27 July 2020.

Mary. Personal interview. 11 May 2020.

Max. Personal interview. 14 May 2020.

Maximilian Law Inc. "O-1 Visa for Canadian Citizens of Extraordinary Ability." *Canadians in the USA*, https://canadiansinusa.com/work-visas/o1/#:~:text=The%20 O%2D1%20visa%20is,industry%20(O%2D1B). Accessed 4 November 2020.

Mosco, Vincent. *Political Economy of Communication*. 2nd ed., SAGE, 2009.

Nakamura, Lisa. "The Unwanted Labour of Social Media: Women of Colour Call Out Culture as Venture Community Management." *New Formations*, vol. 86, no. 86, 2015.

Oakley, Kate. "Artists as Workers. A Response to John Bellamy Foster." *Centre for the Understanding of Sustainable Prosperity*, 29 March 2017, http://www.cusp.ac.uk/ themes/m/koakley_m1-3/. Accessed 3 April 2021.

O'Brien, Dave, Kim Allen, Sam Friedman, and Anamik Saha. "Producing and Consuming Inequality: A Cultural Sociology of the Cultural Industries." *Cultural Sociology*, vol. 11, no. 3, 2017, pp. 271–282.

Oliver. Personal interview. 20 August 2020.

Proulx, Melanie. "Shameless Comedy: Investigating Shame as an Exposure Effect of Contemporary Sexist and Feminist Rape Jokes." *Comedy Studies*, vol. 9, no. 2, 2018, pp. 183–199.

Quinn. Personal interview. 13 July 2020.

Richardson, Jay. "Live Comedy Will Receive Government Funding." *British Comedy Guide*, 20 July 2021, https://www.comedy.co.uk/live/news/5852/live-comedy-government-support/. Accessed 18 October 2021.

Robin. Personal interview. 8 May 2020.

Ryzik, Melena, et al. "Louis C. K. Is Accused by 5 Women of Sexual Misconduct." *New York Times*, 9 November 2017, https://www.nytimes.com/2017/11/09/arts/television/louis-ck-sexual-misconduct.html. Accessed 18 October 2021.

Saha, Anamik. *Race and the Cultural Industries*. John Wiley & Sons, 2018.

Smith, Peter. "Canadian Stand-Up Comedians Form Union to Demand Government Recognition." *The Daily Hive*, 16 August 2020, https://dailyhive.com/vancouver/casc-comedians-stand-up-2018. Accessed 2 April 2021.

Sophie. Personal interview. 7 May 2020.

Statistics Canada. "Canadian Framework for Culture Statistics." 2011, https://www150.statcan.gc.ca/n1/pub/13-607-x/2016001/1247-eng.htm. Accessed 3 April 2021.

———. "Gross Domestic Product (GDP) at Basic Prices by Industry, Annual A=Average (x 1,000,000)." 9 April 2018, https://www150.statcan.gc.ca/t1/tbl1/en/tv.action?pid=3610043403. Accessed 3 April 2021.

Stebbins, Robert A. *The Laugh-Makers*. McGill-Queen's University Press, 1990.

Sweet, Doug. "Discharge for Laugh-Fest Boss Rozon Draws Fire." *Montreal Gazette*, 3 March 1999, https://montrealgazette.com/news/local-news/from-the-archives-discharge-for-laugh-fest-boss-rozon-draws-fire. Accessed 3 April 2021.

The Theatre Centre. "Comedy Is Art," http://theatrecentre.org/?p=13660. Accessed 4 November 2020.

Tomsett, Ellie. "Positives and Negatives: Reclaiming the Female Body and Self-Deprecation in Stand-Up Comedy." *Comedy Studies*, vol. 9, no. 1, 2018, pp. 6–18.

Urquhart, Peter, and Ira Wagman. "Considering Canadian Television: Intersections, Missed Directions, Prospects for Textual Expansion." *Canadian Journal of Film Studies*, vol. 15, no. 1, 2006, pp. 2–7.

US Citizenship and Immigration Services. "O-1 Visa: Individuals with Extraordinary Ability or Achievement." *Working in the United States*, https://www.uscis.gov/

working-in-the-united-states/temporary-workers/o-1-visa-individuals-with-extraordinary-ability-or-achievement. Accessed 4 November 2020.

Van Evra, Jennifer. "'A Huge Blow': Canadian Comedians Say Changes to Comedy Station Could Be Devastating." *CBC Radio*, 28 February 2019, https://www.cbc.ca/radio/q/blog/a-huge-blow-canadian-comedians-say-changes-to-comedy-station-could-be-devastating-1.5033101. Accessed 3 April 2021.

Willet, Cynthia, and Julia Willett. *Uproarious: How Feminists and Other Subversive Comics Speak Truth*. University of Minnesota Press, 2019.

Zoe. Personal interview. 11 May 2020.

Zoglin, Richard. *Comedy at the Edge: How Stand-Up in the 1970s Changed America*. Bloomsbury, 2008.

CHAPTER 5

Film in Canada's Creative Industries: Old Barriers and New Opportunities

George Turnbull

INTRODUCTION

Since the beginning of the 20th century, films—which involve the transformation of stories into moving images—have offered a distinctive mechanism to create meaning and to shine a light on the human condition and, more specifically, on the Canadian experience. In this country, however, where the economics of commercial filmmaking are unfriendly and the industry operates in the shadow of global competition, both the participation in the making of films and the creation of audiences have been challenging. How have we managed to create meaning through film in Canada? How have we built audiences for this kind of storytelling? What supportive network exists made up of government bodies, producers, artists, and disseminators for Canadian filmmaking—and where does the future lie? Those are the central questions examined here.

Filmmaking has had a troubled history in Canada, with a small domestic market divided into two separate communities. For well over a century, those involved in Canada's industry have tried to work out a distinctively Canadian solution. The Lumière brothers and Edison Studios created the first films shot on location in Niagara Falls, with the first public screening in Montreal on June 28, 1896 (Lacasse 6–7). Since then, the industry has largely flourished in the province of Quebec, but English Canadian filmmakers have depended on government funding and Canadian audiences have mostly looked to Hollywood. There has never been any shortage of creative genius in Canada, though. Now, with new technological opportunities in the 21st century, new sources of funding, support from film production associations, and a growing range of distribution channels, it is possible that Canadian filmmakers are about to discover that elusive "Canadian" solution.

Film is one of the world's most dynamic and lucrative creative industries. In Canada, however—especially English Canada—filmmaking has floundered in the shadow of Hollywood. With cinema networks largely controlled by foreign interests, filmmakers in English Canada have struggled to build audiences. Furthermore, an adverse regulatory environment has meant that feature films lack the Canadian content protection long enjoyed by television and radio. While many talented artists have emerged, there has been a persistent tension between "art versus entertainment, culture versus commercial, and realism versus spectacle" (Preston 353).

Culture matters, not only in enhancing people's quality of life but also in inspiring a nation with common values and ideas. Film, as one of the most accessible and broadly referenced cultural forms today, is thus central to nation building. Yet, because of fierce and well-funded competition in the English-speaking world, English-speaking Canada has struggled to create its own film industry. However, in Quebec—with fewer international competitors; vibrant local support by local directors, actors, technical experts, and audiences; and available sources of funding—the domestic film industry has thrived.

This chapter outlines the history of the feature film industry in Canada, with particular reference to barriers that have prevented the sector from flourishing. The chapter identifies current challenges and opportunities, especially new digital media and platforms that could liberate Canadian filmmaking from the past. I examine screendance as an example of how filmmaking has thrived despite the difficulties and consider what the future might hold.

HISTORY OF FILM IN CANADA

Historical and geographical conditions in Canada have hindered the development of a national film industry. In countries that developed early, successful industries all began with "well established vaudeville, music hall, and theatrical traditions" (Morris 28). Canada, with its huge size and small population, had no such foundation. Theatre was mostly limited to touring productions from abroad, and Canada had no convenient theatrical communities eager to make the leap to screen (28). In the early 20th century, most films shown in Canada were either imported or made in Canada by foreign practitioners: the Canadian Bioscope Company, for example, was staffed entirely by British filmmakers (33).

As for the kind of films produced, there were only a few early attempts at fictional storytelling. Most Canadians producing films in the early 20th century—Léo-Ernest Quimet (Montreal), Henry Winter (Newfoundland), and James Scott (Toronto)—limited themselves to newsreels or travelogues. In English Canada, the Canadian Pacific Railway (CPR) was the first filmmaker, and it produced a number of short films for a purely practical purpose—to attract immigrants to the Canadian West.[1] Those promotional films dominated Canadian filmmaking into the 1930s. There were, however, exceptions to the rule, and, in 1903, the CPR made Canada's first fictional drama: *Hiawatha, The Messiah of the Ojibway* (1903), a 15-minute film based on the work of American poet Henry Wadsworth Longfellow (Melynk 21) and shot on location with Indigenous actors (Morris 36). A few years later, *Evangeline* (1913) was arguably the first feature-length film in English ever produced in Canada (49). Made by the Canadian Bioscope Company, it dealt with the Acadian Expulsion of 1755. The film was a financial and critical success in Canada and the United States (Zoe 50). After making a few more films—none as successful as *Evangeline*—the company folded in 1915.

Over the next few years, several new film companies emerged: the British American Film Company of Montreal produced only one well-known film, *The Battle of the Long Sault* (1913); the Conness Till Film Company of Toronto made comedy and adventure films in 1914–15; and the All Red Feature Company of Windsor produced a drama about the War of 1812, *The War Pigeon* (1914) (Morris 51–52). The most successful Canadian film producer, however, was Ernest Shipman. Married to American author, actress, and film producer Nell Shipman, Shipman produced *Back to God's Country* (1919), partly filmed on location in Alberta—a revolutionary approach in its day (106). Nell Shipman's groundbreaking nude appearance in the film may have helped make it a financial success, as it earned a 300 percent profit (107). Although technically a US-Canada co-production, many regard this film as the first Canadian blockbuster. As another first, Shipman made several films based on Canadian novels: *God's Crucible* (1920); *Cameron of the Royal Mounted* (1921); *The Man from Glengarry* (1922); and *The Rapids* (1922). Shipman's innovative work created a minor boom in Canadian silent filmmaking.

This promising beginning led nowhere, as the rise of Hollywood, after the First World War, stifled further growth in English-language filmmaking in Canada. And there was another growth-limiting factor—biculturalism. With audiences carved in two, with two distinct cultures and languages, English Canada lacked the market to support a national feature film industry. This limited domestic market combined with strong foreign competition to make Canada into an importer of feature films and an exporter of talent, with actresses such as Mary Pickford[2] and

Marie Dressler[3] heading south to Hollywood. Canadian filmmakers responded by taking the industry in a positive new direction: they began to specialize in documentaries. The National Film Board (NFB) was established under the 1939 *National Film Act* with part of its original mandate to develop propaganda to promote support for the Second World War. By 1950, its mandate was to "create, produce, and distribute distinctive and original audiovisual works that reflect the diverse realities and perspectives of Canadians, and to share these works with the people of Canada and the rest of the world" (*National Film Act* 1950). The NFB's John Grierson, Canada's first film commissioner, encouraged NFB filmmakers to work on developing documentary and animation expertise, a focus that "has never completely left Canadian cinema" (Cavell 21). The NFB also expanded into the North, where it made over "two hundred films documenting life in the Arctic" (MacKenzie and Stenport 127).

Even as English Canada became famous for its documentaries, feature filmmaking was recognized in official circles as a lost economic opportunity. After the war, Canada negotiated with the United States to redress balance-of-payment inequities, with filmmaking included as one of the affected industries (Melynk 85), and the Canadian Cooperation Project (CCP) was established to encourage Hollywood to make films in Canada. As Pendakur writes, the government's support of CCP was merely "a way of covering up their lack of policy initiatives to encourage the production of indigenous film" (141). The development of a feature film industry in English Canada was simply not seen as a priority (Melnyk 86).

Meanwhile, Quebec had a very different experience. It had not encountered the same level of foreign competition, and what competition did exist from French filmmaking dwindled almost to nothing during the Second World War. Growing demand in the 1930s for Quebec-centred narratives had created a pool of writers and actors serving Radio-Canada's popular radio dramas, and they were ready to exploit the dearth of foreign material that prevailed from 1939 onward. From 1944 to 1953, in the so-called Golden Era of French-language feature films in Quebec, films such as *Le Père Chopin* (1945) and *Tit-Coq* (1953) were produced. The good times appeared to end in 1952, with the advent of French-language television and Radio-Canada's revival of radio drama. Writers, actors, and audiences migrated toward those media, new and old, while Quebec's fledgling film industry was gradually replaced with blockbuster films made outside Canada. Interest in domestic filmmaking was reinvigorated, however, in the 1960s—a period of new nationalism, with renewed interest in Quebec culture. Not only were Quebec producers once again motivated to tell their own distinctive stories; they were newly inspired by French productions in *cinéma vérité, cinéma d'auteur, cahiers du cinéma,* and the *nouvelle vague* to tell those stories in new ways. These novel forms tended to use amateur actors—often paid less than professionals—and the creative focus shifted from actor to director.

GOVERNMENT AND THE CANADIAN FILM INDUSTRY

The film industry would not exist in Canada without government support at both national and provincial levels. Indeed, government involvement is "among the most significant defining characteristics of film in Canada" (Morris 127). The rationale for that support has changed over time and included "encouraging immigration, supporting the war effort, inculcating ideas of national identity, communicating social policies, attracting tourism, and developing a feature film industry in the shadows of Hollywood's extensive global reach" (Wagman 3). In this process, the provinces have shouldered much of the responsibility. For example, the regulation of Canadian film content, distribution, and exhibition has fallen under provincial jurisdiction, and the provinces have established some landmark institutions. In 1911, Ontario notably established the first censorship board in North America, and the other provinces followed suit. As for production, in 1917, the Ontario Motion Picture Bureau (OMPB) became the world's first state-sponsored film organization, with a mandate to promote the province. Private companies in Toronto produced the earliest OMPB films (Morris 70). The bureau then purchased Trenton Studies and began making its own films. With production and distribution systems becoming gradually outdated, the OMPB closed in 1934.

As for the federal government, it broke new ground in establishing the Canadian Government Motion Picture Bureau in 1918, the world's first national film production organization (Melnyk 41). The consciousness of Hollywood looming to the south, however, meant that feature films were seen as a dead end, and the government limited its own early filmmaking to the promotion of Canadian trade and industry. As a wartime creation in 1939, the NFB had completely replaced the bureau by 1941, with an original mandate to develop war-oriented propaganda. In the postwar period, "propaganda" gradually shifted to "education," and a new mandate encouraged the NFB "to interpret Canada to Canadians and to other nations" (*National Film Act* 1950). The films that followed became gradually "more delicate, personalized and experimental" (Handling, "The National Film Board" 47). The NFB also developed as a vehicle to promote education across Canada through a "system of travelling theatres, moving … from … village to village, playing the schools and village halls and the factories, bring[ing] Canada's expanding affairs alive to a million people a month" (Grierson 66). After that, it was a short step from education to cultural expression. In 1967—Canada's Centennial—the question of Canadian identity was paramount, and there was new awareness of the power of film to promote Canadian culture. That year, the government recognized feature films as a means to convey a domestic narrative when it established the Canadian Film Development Corporation (CFDC) "to foster and promote the development of a feature film industry in Canada" (Handling, "Telefilm Canada" 1).

Even with a healthy budget of $10 million, the effectiveness of the CFDC was hindered by lack of a clear mission and competing priorities. In making loans to the industry, should CFDC focus on "(1) overall industry growth, (2) production of popular films, or (3) production of culturally-significant films" (Tepperman 2)? Two different factions emerged, which Peter Harcourt defined as the "Nationalists" (wanting to create distinctively Canadian films) and the "Continentalists" (wanting to compete with Hollywood to produce films for international audiences) (156– 59). Without protectionist measures—for example, a quota system for film exhibition or a tax on box-office receipts—the goals of the Nationalists could never be realized (Preston 355), although policies were devised to help develop films with international appeal. In particular, the Capital Cost Allowance (CCA) was expanded "to allow 100 percent income write-off for anyone who invested in a Canadian film production" (Acheson and Maul 263– 64, quoted by Preston 355). This encouraged private financing to complement the CFDC's investments (355) and resulted in an increase from 18 feature films made in 1975 to 76 in 1979 (Melnyk 113–14). Co-production treaties with other nations "created yet another way for Canadian producers to finance projects" (Dorland 1983, quoted by Preston 355). The Nationalist dream withered, however, as these new films ignored genuinely Canadian stories in favour of stories with international interest. Furthermore, though more Canadian films were being produced, a lack of distribution channels remained a fundamental barrier, and efforts to introduce quotas for Canadian films in the 1970s faltered in the face of lobbying by the powerful Motion Picture Association of America (MPAA). In 1984, the CFDC was renamed Telefilm Canada, and its mandate expanded to include domestic television shows.

In a new century, it was time for a new approach with the production of more "audience-friendly" films. In 2000, the Department of Canadian Heritage adopted a policy called "From Script to Screen" to boost Canadian audiences with a goal to increase domestic box-office viewership of Canadian films to 5 percent of the total market (Tepperman 2). The government committed substantial funding to its new policy, providing $15 million in 2000–01, with subsequent payments amounting to $50 million beginning in April 2001 (Minister of Public Works and Government Services Canada 2). The production of "audience-friendly" films did increase, but auteur filmmaking by previously successful directors decreased (Tepperman 2). Films began to be gauged in financial rather than creative terms, with box-office success overshadowing artistic accomplishment. The metric shifted from director to producer, and the careers of many rising Canadian directors were damaged. After 10 years, the policy was acknowledged as a failure. Since then, Telefilm Canada—which operates as a financing partner for filmmakers—has adjusted its focus from encouraging box-office success to helping the industry improve the distribution of films (including indie films)—for example, at film festivals, through streaming, and on home screens and personal devices. Telefilm Canada continues working to this day to stimulate domestic demand, especially for English-language films. It remains a major source of investment, it supports the development of new media and music, and it gives grants to Canadian film festivals. As well, it administers co-production agreements with over 60 countries (Telefilm Canada 2020). As examples of its work, *Room* (2015) and *Brooklyn* (2015) in 2016 were both nominated in the Best Picture category at the 88th Academy Awards, and *Room* won the coveted prize. Funding for individual filmmakers is more problematic, but some financial support is available.[4]

How to support diversity has always been a major challenge for the Canadian government. Although officially a multicultural country, biculturalism has been the rule, with Canada's English and French communities dominating the industry (Gittings 231). New policies and filmmaking competitions have been put in place, notably the "NFB's Ontario-based Reel Diversity Competition 2001 and Its Documentary West Unit's Diversity in Action Programme 2001–2002" (232). Telefilm and a number of other funders, including initiatives like the Bawaadan Collective,[5] have programs that support Indigenous filmmakers and filmmakers of colour. Marchessault and Straw point to issues raised by the recent Truth and Reconciliation Commission and insist it is time "to decolonize all aspects of Canadian life, [and] then those who make films—like those who study them—must be part of this process" (xxii).

The role of the government in Canadian filmmaking has proven to be both life support and a major headache. Wagman concludes that Canadian government support of the film industry is "bureaucratic in nature" (16). To make a movie in Canada, he writes, "is to be in constant dialogue with government agencies and to develop the practical know-how to make use of the various techniques—subsidies, quotas, tax credits, and controls on ownership—to help bring a project to fruition" (16). Critics argue that government policies have actually hindered the development of Canadian cinema. It may be time, they say, to loosen the bonds and allow creativity and diversity to shine.

FILM PRODUCTION, DISTRIBUTION, AND EXHIBITION IN THE CANADIAN ECONOMY

In the early days of film, countries in Europe faced many of the same issues as Canada, but—unlike Canada—they took steps to protect their young film industries. By the 1920s, European governments had already moved to protect against American domination, mainly by setting quotas for domestic production, distribution, and exhibition. Canada did not follow suit, and, as a result, film production, distribution, and exhibition in Canada have always been dominated by vertically integrated American studios such as Paramount, RKO, 20th Century Fox, MGM, and Warner Brothers, which—tellingly—include Canadian revenues in US domestic statistics. Since 1922, Canada has operated as a subsidiary of the Motion Picture Producers and Distributors Association of America and as a branch plant of the American studios. There are various associations in Canada that coordinate the exhibition of films—for example, Motion Picture Exhibitors and Distributors of Canada (formed in 1924, renamed in 1940 to the Canadian Motion Picture Distributors Association and in 2011 to the Motion Picture Association—Canada). Nevertheless, American companies dominate exhibition everywhere in Canada except Quebec. In 1923, Famous Players (owned by Paramount Pictures) bought out the Canadian-owned Allen Theatres, and, to this day, the distribution network is controlled by the American studio system. Most Canadian films are handled by American distributors or shown in smaller or repertory theatres, and, currently, there are no Canadian content regulations applying to Canadian movie theatres. Though festivals do provide some audience exposure for Canadian films, Canadian films today rely mostly on the negotiation of television carriage and streaming rights with such broadcasters as the Canadian Broadcasting Corporation (CBC), Crave, HBO, Hulu, and Netflix.

Against this backdrop, it is not surprising that the contribution of filmmaking by Canadians to the Canadian economy has been disappointing. In terms of direct revenues, Canadian Media Producers Association (CMPA) data from 2017 show that Canada's English-language films account for only about 1 percent ($8.6 million) of the domestic market (Pinto 2), although the figure is 20 percent in Quebec (Tepperman 2). The highest grossing Canadian film in 2019 brought in less than $6.5 million in revenues.[6] The industry has survived, however, and there are pockets of relatively higher performance in Toronto and Vancouver, Canada's "Hollywood of the North," which have attracted American companies to invest in filmmaking in Canada. The result has been to turn filmmaking in this country into a multibillion-dollar industry (Magder et al., "1974 to Present" 13), creating some 190,000 jobs and generating some $9.3 billion for the economy in 2018–19. The secret of success has been government support, tax incentives, and financing by film collectives and arts council grants. American productions, attracted to Canada by tax breaks and by periodically favourable exchange rates, have brought more than money into the economy; they have also bolstered professional development by hiring professional Canadian crews and building a state-of-the-art studio infrastructure.

CANADIAN DIRECTORS

The NFB, as well as producing many of Canada's earliest film products, also nurtured talent. Many early directors began at the NFB—Norman McLaren, for instance, who was originally a NFB animator. His film *Neighbours* (1952) won Canada's first Academy Award for a short film (Melnyk 72). In the 1960s, Don Owen made a film, initially a NFB-financed short, and it was later expanded into *Nobody Waved Good-Bye* (1964). One of English Canada's first and most admired narrative feature films, it tells the story of teenage rebellion. Canadian experimental filmmaker Michael Snow also emerged from the NFB to make the internationally acclaimed avant-garde film *Wavelength* (1967). Technically brilliant and utterly original, this film still tops critics' lists of the best one hundred films of the 20th century. In 1970, Don Shebib's *Goin' Down the Road* told the story of two young men setting off from the Maritimes in search of fame and fortune. The film was a commercial success at home and abroad (Melnyk 110) and is still recognized as one the top 10 Canadian films ever made. The same sort of trajectory occurred with French-language films. The NFB established a French production unit in the 1950s, and a number of French Canadian filmmakers—Pierre Perrault, Gilles Carle, Claude Jutra, Michel Brault, Gilles Groulx, and Denys Arcand (Melnyk 125–45)—emerged from there to develop "direct cinema" or "*cinema verité*," with a focus on the Québécois experience. Claude Jutra's *Mon oncle Antoine* (1971), a tale of the great Asbestos Strike of 1949 told through the eyes of a 15-year-old boy, made money and won international recognition and a place near the top of any list of great Canadian films. It remains a monument to the cultural creativity of Quebec's Quiet Revolution (Melnyk 139).

Until recently, however, the experience of Canadian directors has generally been a discouraging one overall. The public, especially in English Canada, has typically undervalued Canadian films, and many directors—artists such Norman Jewison, Arthur Hiller, Ted Kotcheff, Jason Reitman, Paul Haggis, and James Cameron[7]— left Canada to pursue their art elsewhere. Canadian actors also have fled the country to seek success in Hollywood, including Norma Shearer, Christopher Plummer, Donald Sutherland, Michael J. Fox, Keanu Reeves, Jim Carrey, and many others. This may be changing, though. David Cronenberg and Atom Egoyan are arguably the most important English Canadian filmmakers working from the 1960s to today (Melnyk 146–66), and they did not follow the bright and shiny road to Hollywood. Cronenberg, beginning as an experimental filmmaker, succeeded in finding commercial success in the science-fiction and horror genres—e.g., *Shivers* (1975) and *Videodrome* (1981)—without leaving home. Later, he adapted the work of other artists and novelists to film—e.g., *The Dead Zone* (1983), *Spider* (2003), *A History of Violence* (2005), and *Cosmopolis* (2012). Atom Egoyan, born in Egypt and raised in British Columbia, followed Cronenberg's example in a number of ways, not least by continuing to work in Canada. Cronenberg's influence also expressed itself in Egoyan's work through its concern with the "transformation power of technology, perhaps a uniquely Canadian obsession largely influenced by Marshall McLuhan" (Magder et al., "Notable Films" 17–18). Egoyan made his first feature film, *Next of Kin,* in 1984, moving later in his career to small-scale character dramas such as *The Captive* (2016).

Since the mid-1980s, the world has become much more aware of Canadian directors and their work, with international recognition (Melynk 11) increasing steadily over time. Anne Wheeler was the first Canadian woman to achieve prominence with *A War Story* (1981) and *Loyalties* (1986) (Melnyk 169). In the 1980s and 1990s, the Ontario Film Development Corporation supported many emerging indie directors, including Atom Egoyan, Bruce McDonald, Peter Mettler, Ron Mann, Patricia Rozema,[8] John Greyson, Jeremy Podewsa, and Don McKellar. These directors belonged to the Toronto New Wave film movement, which, according to Longfellow (167–200), flourished with support from a combination of local film collectives, arts councils, and regional and national film agencies at a time when those bodies were open to low-budget, art-house fare. At the same time in Quebec, the film industry was being revitalized by such directors as Denys Arcand—*Le déclin de l'empire américain* (1986) and *Jésus de Montréal* (1989)—and Jean-Claude Lauzon—*Un zoo la nuit* (1987) and *Léolo* (1992) (Melynk 201).

A success story of a different kind unfolded in 2001, when Zacharias Kunuk directed *Atanarjuat (The Fast Runner)* (2001), the first feature film ever made in Inuktitut; it won best feature at the Cannes Film Festival and many Genie Awards.[9] It was a great start to a decade in which Deepa Mehta's *Water* (2005) was nominated for an Academy Award and distributed in the United States to critical acclaim (Tepperman 9). In 2006, Sarah Polley's *Away with Her,*[10] the bilingual *Bon Cop, Bad Cop,*[11] and the English-language *Trailer Park Boys: The Movie* all won acclaim.

At the same time, Canada's French-language directors were being feted for such notable films as Jean-Marc Vallée's *C.R.A.Z.Y.* (2005), which was a box-office hit in both Canada and France. The list of winners continued into the next decade, with feature films by Quebec directors achieving critical and commercial success as well as being nominated for best foreign language film at the Oscars or featured at Cannes. The most notable of these were *J'ai tué ma mère* (Xavier Dolan, 2009); *Incendies* (Denis Villeneuve, 2010); *Monsieur Lazhar* (Phillipe Falardeau, 2011); *Rebelle (War Witch)* (Kim Nguyen, 2012); *Dallas Buyers Club* (Jean-Marc Vallée, 2013); *Mommy* (Xavier Dolan, 2014); *Sicario* (Denis Villeneuve, 2015); and *The Bleeder* (Phillipe Falardeau, 2016). As Loiselle writes, "quality art films, with their edgy antiheroes, and complex narratives that can move, educate, and delight the cultural elites, are the works that generally represent Québec on the international stage" (367).

Given the success of many Canadian directors, national and local film production associations have emerged that support both amateur and professional productions. These include such associations as the CMPA; the Calgary Society of Independent Filmmakers (CSIF); the Documentary Organization of Canada; the Film and Video Arts Society of Alberta (FAVA); the Peace Region Independent Media Arts Association (PRIMAA); and Women in Film and Television Alberta (WIFTA). These associations may encourage the evolution of new Canadian filmmakers in the future.

FILM FESTIVALS AND THE BUILDING OF AUDIENCES

Without film festivals—which, for over 70 years, have been attracting new audiences, investment, and media attention for Canadian films—the market would be even smaller than it is. Many festivals, however, have come and gone. The first commercial film festival in Canada was organized in Saskatchewan in 1950 by the NFB's James Lysyshyn: the Yorkton International Documentary Film Festival (Pâquet and Wise 1). Since 1977, this festival has screened Canadian films only, and winning films tour the province. Various other festivals were held between the 1950s and 1970s, but most have now folded. A few, such as the Ottawa International Animation Festival, founded by the Canadian Film Institute in 1975, continue to be held biannually. Some annual festivals from the 1980s have survived, including the Atlantic Film Festival (held in Halifax since 1981) and the Vancouver International Film Festival (since 1982). There are also a few enduring regional festivals sponsored by various cities or groups.[12] The Hot Docs Canadian International Documentary Festival, established in 1994, has grown into the premiere documentary film festival in North America. The brainchild of Wyndham Wise, then executive director of the Canadian Independent Film Caucus (now the Documentary Organization of Canada), the festival originally showcased only Canadian films, but the mandate was broadened in 1978 to include international documentaries. In Quebec, the Festival International du Film de Montréal (now the Montréal World Film Festival) was established in 1960, and, throughout its existence, it has attracted leading industry protagonists from Quebec and the world. A second festival, the Festival international du film en 16 mm (later renamed the Festival du nouveau cinema), was founded in Montreal in 1971. As the second longest running film festival in Canada, its focus is on avant-garde, experimental, and underground films.

Canada's longest running festival—and the largest film festival in North America—is the Toronto International Film Festival (TIFF) (formerly the Toronto Festival of Festivals). Film producers Bill Marshall and Henk van der Kolk, in association with lawyer Dusty Cohl, founded TIFF in 1976. Two years later, Wayne Clarkson of the Canadian Film Institute took over running the event, followed, in the 1980s, by Helga Stephenson and Piers Handling. The story of TIFF is one of continual development. In 1984, the festival introduced "Perspective Canada"[13] as part of its program to focus on Canadian filmmakers. It also launched an annual publication, *Film Companion*, edited by notable Canadian film historian Peter Morris.[14] That same year, the festival inaugurated a poll of critics to identify the top 10 Canadian films of all time; that poll is updated every 10 years or so.[15] The Toronto festival was renamed in 1994 and began offering year-round, national programs, including the TIFF Kids International Film Festival, and various projects to support Canadian filmmakers and actors. The program today showcases feature films, documentaries, and experimental films and gives awards in such categories as "Best Short Film" and "Best Canadian First Feature." Fully open to the public, TIFF operates as a testing ground for audience appeal and as a gauge for potential financial success. The festival is something of a financial success in its own right, every year generating more than $200 million of economic activity in Toronto and Ontario. Determined to ensure that Canada's industry stays open to a diversity of filmmakers in the future, TIFF also prioritizes "normalizing gender parity and equality" (TIFF 2020). The pandemic year of 2020 was challenging for TIFF. The number of films featured shrank from hundreds down to 50, with the usual 300,000 viewings declining to a mere 50,000. Live screenings were held at only a few theatres, and audience size was limited to ensure physical distancing. To compensate, however, films also were shown at drive-in venues and online. Red-carpet events, press conferences, and industry talks also went virtual. Only time will tell whether this is the new reality for film festivals in Canada. If so, then TIFF 2020 offered a model on which to build.

International festivals continue to promote some of the best work produced by the Canadian film industry. As Chahine writes, international film festivals such as Cannes continue "to be vital to the visibility of a Canadian cinema still largely shunned by its national audience" (47). Hopefully, these international film festivals will continue to be held in the future (even virtually) as a venue from which to launch Canadian feature films to the world. It should also be firmly stated, however, that smaller, regional film festivals are equally important to the building of national audiences for Canadian film.

SCREENDANCE: A CASE STUDY FOR THE CANADIAN FILM INDUSTRY

Screendance, as an art form, illustrates many features of the Canadian film industry—the dependence on government funding, the seminal role of NFB practitioners, the brilliance of Canadian creators, the challenge of building domestic audiences, the importance of festivals in creating interest, and the opportunities offered by new technologies both in terms of production and distribution. What is most significant, however, is that technically and artistically screendance may well be showing the way into a new future for Canadian filmmaking.

Screendance—also called "choreocinema," "cine-dance," "motion-picture dance," "video dance," "dance for camera," "dance on screen," "dance film," and "choreography for the camera"—has been delighting Canadian audiences since the days of Busby Berkeley and Stanley Donen in the 1920s and 1940s. It also has roots in the "early surrealist dance films by Ukrainian-born artist Maya Deren in the 1940s" (De Rosa and Burgess 61). As a hybrid discipline that operates at the intersection of film (image in motion) and dance (body in motion), screendance is variously defined. According to Pottratz, it "is a moving image work, the content of which has choreographic compositional intention, combined with the technical and creative language of cinema" (182). Heighway's broader interpretation insists that "dance in screendance need not be 'dance' movement, nor human motion, but anything kinetically driven, full stop" (45). In fact, research suggests that "the broadness of screendance includes anything from Hollywood and Bollywood musicals to experimental or avant-garde films—any intersection of dance and movement made with the frame of the screen in mind" (Turnbull 32).

Canadian screendance developed first in Quebec, and practitioners in that province continue to dominate the form. In the rest of Canada, even a limited amount of government support (notably from the NFB, which controlled the genre in its early stages) has turned screendance into a vehicle for some breathtaking artistic experimentation. Norman McLaren, whom John Grierson recruited to the NFB in 1941, began to integrate dance into his films in the 1960s. In *Pas de deux* (1968), the movement of two dancers is "staggered and overlaid by the optical printer to produce a stroboscopic effect" (Szporer 170). In *Ballet Adagio* (1971), McLaren developed a technique called "chronophotography" (170), using time lapses to create what is described as "a work of exquisite beauty, a hymn of flesh, muscle and grace, which is both deeply erotic and sublimely moving" (Elley 101). Another NFB-supported director, Philippe Baylaucq, adapted McLaren's techniques in *Lodela* (1996) to create moving "canvases" (Szporer 171). He created an illusion of bodies moving "in space on horizontal, vertical and diagonal planes ... [to depict] the transmigration of the soul from death to new life" (171).

As discussed, funding and festivals are the dual pillars supporting the ongoing success of filmmaking, including screendance, in Canada. In the 1990s, with support from the Bravo!FACT Foundation, the NFB, federal and provincial arts councils, and the CBC, the number of screendance practitioners grew and production increased. Nevertheless, funding is an area of real vulnerability. Screendance suffered from the recent cancellation of the Canada Council's Dance on Screen Production Fund, and practitioners were left scrambling to find alternative sources of support. Clearly, activists need to work harder to persuade federal and provincial arts councils to recognize screendance as a discipline of artistic importance. Screendance equally depends for its success on the continuing efforts of a number of screendance festivals—the most important being the Moving Pictures Festival of Dance on Film and Video (MoPix)—which are vital to the building of audiences. Founded by Kathleen Smith and Marc Glassman in 1992 and benefiting from extensive public funding, MoPix was held annually in Toronto until 2006 in a period that Smith dubbed the "mini-Golden Era" of screendance in Canada (1). The festival featured works by Canadian and international screendance artists in "all kinds of formats, from video and 16mm film to installation and multimedia. ... Almost without competitors in its early years, MoPix throughout its fifteen-year life fed the artform and challenged the film and arts community in Canada to embrace the multi-faceted work of screendance" (Turnbull 34). Canadian works shown at this festival included *Roxana* (Moze Mossanen, 2006), *Revolver Tango* (Pascale Marcotte, 2004), and *a pairing of SwanS* (Veronica Tennant, 2004). Unfortunately, the availability of funding and the viability of festivals is linked. In 2006, when funding and broadcast opportunities for screendance collapsed, MoPix folded, and its archive of films was lodged at Dance Collection Danse in Toronto. Since then, screendance film festivals have made something of a comeback as a means to create interest, develop audiences, and encourage practitioners. In 2013, screendance artist and teacher Kathleen Rea founded the Contact Dance International Film Festival in Toronto, focusing on "momentum-based dance" (Turnbull 35) built around the themes of accessibility and diversity. Many leading Canadian practitioners have shown work at this festival, where dancers with disabilities or those representing cultural, ethnic, or demographic minorities are encouraged to submit work. In Montreal, Priscilla Guy, a Montreal-based dance artist and consultant, launched the Regards Hybrides International Festival, which combines a theme-based program with presentations, screenings, live performances, panel discussions, workshops, and networking opportunities. In Vancouver, Sophia Wolfe and Kristina Lemieux established the F-O-R-M festival in 2015 with a focus on youth, "featuring artists of all body types and abilities and encouraging submissions from Indigenous and LGBTQ2+ artists" (36). Also, in Vancouver in 2014, Jen Ray founded the CASCADIA Dance and Cinema Festival to bring together screendance artists from Canada and the world.

Funding issues and the need for festival support are old topics. The key to the future may lie just as much in the seizing of new technological opportunities. Certainly, the recent resurgence of screendance is the result of using novel cinematic techniques and mediated software products (e.g., 3D, computer choreographic software, video projections, motion capture technologies, augmented reality, and virtual reality [VR]), devices (e.g., Oculus Rift, Samsung Gear VR, and Google Cardboard), and platforms (e.g., YouTube, Facebook, Instagram, and other social media, web channels, company websites, and interactive museum and gallery installations). Interactive sites are being developed where viewers can even become the creators of their own screendance works. Philip Szporer is a professor at Concordia University whose company—Mouvement Perpétuel—is helping to reshape screendance through the use of 3D technologies (38), for example. Freya Björg Olafson, a multimedia artist and professor of screendance at York University, creates films at the intersection of video projection, 3D, VR, and interactive technologies (38). Elias Djemil-Matassov incorporates abstract movement into storytelling. Izabella Pruska-Oldenhof, a professor at Toronto Metropolitan University, draws inspiration from the work of Maya Deren and Amy Greenfield as she explores connections between bodies and technology. Allen and Karen Kaeja have directed and choreographed a body of internationally acclaimed work focusing on the Holocaust. Thecla Schiphorst, a professor at Simon Fraser University working with Tom Calvert, founded Life Forms (now DanceForms), which is an interactive animation software to create "DIY" screendance films.

Despite funding issues, screendance in Canada is clearly entering a new phase of creativity, innovation, and technological advancement. As Kathleen Smith writes, "Even with the changing technological, funding, and political environment for dance on camera, the relationship between the moving body and the camera remains as vital as ever ... luring more artists, not just dance artists, into deep explorations of what it means to move and have a body, in more and different ways than would have seemed possible back in 1992" (10). The barriers are real, but the power of screendance as an artistic form is such that they are likely to be overcome. With its technological innovations, it is an example of an art form that could be adapted by the broader Canadian film and creative industries community in the future.

THE FUTURE OF FILM IN CANADA

Even as new sources of funding become available, Canada's English-language film industry will continue for the foreseeable future to remain largely dependent on the government for financing. That means that public priorities will continue driving production in Canada, including the funding of Indigenous and racially diverse filmmaking as well as niche filmmaking genres like screendance. Quebec filmmakers, on the other hand, will continue to produce films as part of a distinctive cinema supported by a large Quebec audience. As Loiselle writes, "none of the top-grossing films produced in Quebec over the past seventy years focus on the diverse experiences of Indigenous people or emigrants" (368).

The disruptions caused by Covid-19 in 2020 and 2021 will likely recede into the past, but some of the changes may remain—for example, the trend toward on-demand streaming on such platforms as Gem (CBC), Netflix, Crave (Bell Media), Hulu, Disney Plus, and Prime Video. That trend existed before the pandemic; it was bolstered by the pandemic; and, after the pandemic, it will likely continue to affect the way that films are produced, distributed, and exhibited. As for Canadian content, Gem has been working with Telefilm to bring more Canadian films to its digital platform (Pinto 1), and by 2021 Netflix was already encouraging Canadian production companies and directors to submit proposals for future films and television series. In addition, as of 2021, an exhibition quota for Canadian films on international streaming services is under discussion, along with a requirement for global streaming services to air Canadian films, all of which would tend to increase audiences for Canadian work. If Canadians are to benefit fully from these new opportunities, however, new support for the development of and streaming and self-distribution of Canadian content is needed, and Canadian filmmakers need to "embrace multiple methods of marketing" (Bracey 2).

As for production, the shift from 4K to 8K cameras, the evolution of specialized editing software, and changes in special effects and animation capacities have led to the use of more computer-generated imagery (CGI), motion capture, and VR in filmmaking. With an array of new technical and artistic possibilities, the government is likely to support the use of new digital technologies in filmmaking, making the Canadian industry more creatively competitive as a result. As for that oldest of Canadian genres, the documentary, it has been reborn in the 21st century, notably in the form of interactive works produced by independent filmmakers and the NFB. As Mulvogue explains, these films are "branching out to virtual reality (VR) and other immersive storytelling practices such as 360-degree screens" (420). These interactive films may be the way of the future, providing new and exciting immersive experiences in which Canadian practitioners can excel.

Funding remains a barrier, but the 21st century offers new hope. As well as traditional sources of support, filmmakers in Canada have begun to explore novel sources of financing such as "crowdfunding," which involves the use of the Internet to attract a multitude of small-scale investors. *Code 8* (2019), for example, directed by Jeff Chan, was largely crowdfunded, with some support from Telefilm, and with Elevation Pictures handling Canadian distribution and XYZ Films handling foreign sales (Pinto 3). Private equity investment from Canada and the United States is also expected to continue growing in importance. In addition, the broader definition of funding criteria that not only assesses past financial success but also considers inclusion, diversity, and equity will result in new stories being told in new ways.

CONCLUSION

A person without a voice lacks power; a country without a voice will be overwhelmed by the voices of others. Films, as perhaps the single most accessible and popular art form in the world, can and should play a significant role in helping Canadians to understand and to appreciate what makes their culture unique and valuable. Filmmaking in English and French Canada—with multiculturalism on one hand and a unified cultural identity on the other—has never coalesced into a single national industry, and English-language filmmakers have never rivalled the success of their colleagues in Quebec, much less in the United States. Yet, despite many persisting barriers, Canadian directors have produced a considerable body of internationally recognized work over time, and, as partners in American filmmaking, they have developed considerable technical and creative strength in support of the industry. Screendance is just one example of this flourishing. Even so, Canadian audiences have not supported their own cinema, choosing instead to watch big-budget films imported from the United States and other countries. Many promising Canadian filmmakers have left the country as a result or have reluctantly abandoned filmmaking altogether. We are in danger, as a country, of falling silent.

In the 21st century, technology is flattening the competitive field, and talented Canadian filmmakers have new opportunities to succeed. Today, Canadian filmmakers can deploy new technologies not only to produce dynamic films but also to deliver them in new ways to new audiences. In terms of content, however, the industry needs to play to its strengths. It needs to make a virtue of the diversity in English Canada and to speak more engagingly to its various audiences, using—for example—such richly hybrid vehicles as screendance. This is a new world in so many ways. Who knows? When it comes to filmmaking, the 21st century may well belong to Canada. The world is listening, so what have we got to say?

CORE CONCEPTS

digital film technology: The process of recording moving images using digital image sensors instead of film.

documentary film: A non-fictional film intended to present reality for the purposes of instruction or to create an historical record.

experimental film: A mode of filmmaking that re-evaluates cinematic conventions and explores non-narrative forms or alternatives to traditional forms.

feature film: A fictional narrative film with a running time long enough to allow it to stand alone in a program.

screendance: A hybrid, movement-based art form, defined not by the moving subject alone but also by the movement of the camera, frames, and editing process, which exists only as it is rendered in film, video, or digital technologies.

SUGGESTED ACTIVITIES

1. Documentaries: Brainstorm a number of documentary subjects from a Canadian perspective, break into teams to develop compelling storylines for the various topics, and then present these in class.
2. Film festivals: Review existing festivals and brainstorm gaps and opportunities for a new festival (genre[s], location, audience appeal, funding, in-person versus online, etc.).

3. Screendance: Watch a short feature film, then break into groups to discuss how to reconfigure it as a screendance production, outlining an artistic concept in terms of overall approach, setting, music, choreography, etc.

NOTES

1. A Manitoba farmer, James Freer, in 1897 became the first person to make a Canadian film (Morris 30). His films depicting life on the Canadian Prairies were *Arrival of CPR Express at Winnipeg, Pacific and Atlantic Mail Trains*, and *Six Binders at Work in a Hundred Acre Wheatfield*. CPR sent Freer to tour England in 1898 with movies collectively entitled *Ten Years in Manitoba*. The successful tour was repeated in 1902 with funding from the Government of Canada (Melnyk 16).

2. Mary Pickford (1893–1979), born in Toronto, was known as "America's Sweetheart" after moving to Hollywood and becoming the most popular actress of the silent film era (Melnyk 27).

3. Canada "lost many of those who might have helped establish and sustain a film industry" (Morris 28), including actors like Marie Dressler, who left Ontario for Broadway and later launched a film career spanning the 1920s and 1930s.

4. For information on funding sources for individual Canadian filmmakers, visit www.reelshorts. ca/filmmaking/resources/fundinding-sources/, which features links to the following organizations: Alberta Foundation for the Arts; Alberta Media Fund; Canada Council for the Arts; Canada Media Fund; Harold Greenberg Fund; Independent Production Fund; NFB Filmmaker Assistance Program; and Telefilm Canada.

5. Bawaadan Collective represents Indigenous artists who create content and support each other in the collective creation of films. See www.bawaadancollective.com/.

6. The top grossing Canadian films of 2019 were (1) *Menteur*, $6.3 million; (2) *La course des tuques*, $2.6 million; (3) *Il pleuvant des oiseaux*, $1.8 million; (4) *Merci pour tout*, $1.1 million; and (5) *La Femme de mon frère*, $750,000 (Playback Staff 2).

7. James Cameron directed two of the highest-grossing films of all time, *Avatar* (2009) and *Titanic* (1997), which together grossed an estimated $6 billion worldwide.

8. Patricia Rozema is one of Canada's earliest female directors. Her film *I've Heard the Mermaids Singing* (1987) won an award at Cannes (Melnyk 174) and became one of the most profitable films ever made in Canada, grossing more than $6 million worldwide.

9. In 2015, *Atanarjuat (The Fast Runner)* (2001) was named the best Canadian film of all time. The film combines self-representational Indigenous storytelling with non-Indigenous filmmaking techniques and practices (Raheja 1165).

10. In 2008, Sarah Polley won a Genie Award and an Oscar nomination for *Away with Her* (2006), based on her screenplay adaptation of Alice Munro's short story "The Bear Came Over the Mountain."

11. In 2007, *Bon Cop, Bad Cop* (2006) became the highest-grossing Canadian film of all time, earning more than $13 million domestically (Magder et al., "1974 to Present" 14).

12. Some of the many regional film festivals held regularly in Canada include Montréal World Film Festival; St. John's International Women's Film Festival; Cinéfest Sudbury International Film Festival; Inside Out Toronto LGBT Film and Video Festival; Toronto's Images Festival of Independent Film and Video; Calgary International Film Festival; Edmonton International Film Festival; and the Victoria Film Festival.

13. "Perspective Canada" helped a number of Canadian filmmakers win recognition in Canada and internationally, including Atom Egoyan; Bruce McDonald; Denys Arcand; Jean-Claude Lauzon; Leá Pool; Don McKellar; Peter Mettler; Patricia Rozema; John Greyson; Clement Virgo; Deepa Mehta; and Jeremy Podeswa.

14. Peter Morris wrote *Embattled Shadows: A History of Canadian Cinema, 1895–1939*, detailing the early history of Canadian film. He curated the Canadian Film Archives, 1963–75, and was founding president of the Film Studies Association of Canada.

15. The top 10 Canadian films of all time (updated in 2015 by TIFF) are (1) *Atanarjuat (The Fast Runner)* (Zacharias Kunuk, 2002); (2) *Mon oncle Antoine* (Claude Jutra, 1971); (3) *The Sweet Hereafter* (Atom Egoyan, 1997); (4) *Jésus de Montréal* (Denys Arcand, 1989); (5) *Léolo* (Jean-Claude Lauzon, 1992); (6) *Goin' Down the Road* (Don Shebib, 1970); (7) *Dead Ringers* (David Cronenberg, 1998); (8) *C.R.A.Z.Y.* (Jean-Marc Vallée, 2005); (9) *My Winnipeg* (Guy Maddin, 2007); and (10) *Stories We Tell* (Sarah Polley, 2012) / *Les Ordres* (Michel Brault, 1974).

REFERENCES

Acheson, Keith, and Christopher Maul. "It Seemed Like a Good Idea at the Time (Financing of Canadian Films)." *Canadian Journal of Communication*, vol. 16, no. 2, 1991, pp. 263–276.

Bracey, Leon. "Rich Past, Bright Future." *Business in Focus Magazine*, www.businessinfocusmagazine.com/2013/03/canadian-film-production/. Accessed 15 August 2020.

Cavell, Richard. "Canadian Cinema and the Intellectual Milieu." *Canadian Cinema*, edited by Janine Marchessault and Will Straw, Oxford University Press, 2019, pp. 21–33.

Chahine, Joumane. "On the Road—Canadian Cinema and the World." *Canadian Cinema*, edited by Janine Marchessault and Will Straw, Oxford University Press, 2019, pp. 35–51.

De Rosa, Maria, and Marilyn Burgess. *Canadian Dance Mapping Study: Literature Review*. Canada Council for the Arts, 2012.

Dorland, Michael. "Quest for Equality: Canada and Co-Productions: A Retrospective (1963–1983)." *Cinema Canada*, vol. 100, 1983, pp. 13–19.

Elley, Derek. "Rhythm 'n' Truths: Norman McLaren." *Canadian Film Reader*, edited by Seth Feldman and Joyce Nelson, Peter Martin Associates, 1977, pp. 94–102.

Gittings, Christopher. "Multicultural Fields of Vision." *Canadian National Cinema: Ideology, Difference and Representation*, Routledge, 2002, pp. 231–262.

Grierson, John. "A Film Policy for Canada." *Documents in Canadian Film*, edited by Doug Fetherling, Broadview Press, 1988, pp. 51–67.

Handling, Piers. "The National Film Board of Canada: 1939–1959." *Self Portraits: Essays on the Canadian and Québec Cinemas*, edited by Pierre Véronneau and Piers Handling, Canadian Film Institute, 1980, pp. 42–53.

———. "Telefilm Canada." Online. *The Canadian Encyclopedia*, 2006. Updated 28 May 2014. Accessed 15 August 2020.

Harcourt, Peter. *Movies and Mythologies: Toward a National Cinema*. CBC, 1977.

Heighway, Anna. "Understanding the 'Dance' in Radical Screendance." *International Journal of Screendance*, vol. 4, 2014, pp. 44–62.

Lacasse, Germain. "Cultural Amnesia and the Birth of Film in Canada." *Cinema Canada*, vol. 108, June 1984, pp. 6–7.

Loiselle, André. "Popular Québec Cinema and the Appeal of Folk Homogeneity." *Canadian Cinema*, edited by Janine Marchessault and Will Straw, Oxford University Press, 2019, pp. 367–389.

Longfellow, Brenda. "Surfing the Toronto New Wave: Policy, Paradigm Shifts and Post-Nationalism." *Self Portraits,* edited by André Loiselle and Tom McSorley, Canadian Film Institute, 2006, pp. 167–200.

MacKenzie, Scott, and Anna Westerståhl Stenport. "The Polarities and Hybridities of Arctic Cinemas." *Canadian Cinema*, edited by Janine Marchessault and Will Straw, Oxford University Press, 2019, pp. 125–146.

Magder, Ted, et al. "Canadian Film History: 1974 to Present." Online. *The Canadian Encyclopedia*. Updated 29 November 2019. Accessed 15 August 2020.

Magder, Ted, et al. "Canadian Film History: Notable Films and Filmmakers 1980 to Present." Online. *The Canadian Encyclopedia*, 2019. Updated 21 November 2019. Accessed 15 August 2020.

Marchessault, Janine, and Will Straw. "Introduction." *Canadian Cinema*, edited by Janine Marchessault and Will Straw, Oxford University Press, 2019, pp. xii–xxii.

Melnyk, George. *One Hundred Years of Canadian Cinema*. University of Toronto Press, 2002.

Minister of Public Works and Government Services Canada. *From Script to Screen: New Policy Directions for Canadian Feature Film*. Canadian Heritage, Government of Canada, 2000.

Morris, Peter. *Embattled Shadows: A History of Canadian Cinema, 1895–1939.* McGill-Queen's University Press, 1978.

Mulvogue, Jessica. "The World Navigated—Interactive Documentary in Canada." *Canadian Cinema*, edited by Janine Marchessault and Will Straw, Oxford University Press, 2019, pp. 409–422.

National Film Act 1950. Government of Canada, www.onf-nfb.gc.ca/en/about-the-nfb/organization/mandate/. Accessed 8 September 2020.

Pâquet, André, and Wyndham Wise. "Film Festivals." Online. *The Canadian Encyclopedia*, 2010. Updated 17 October, 2014. Accessed 15 August 2020.

Pendakur, Manjunath. *Canadian Dreams and American Control: The Political Economy of the Canadian Film Industry.* Wayne State University Press, 1990.

Pinto, Jordan. "The Future of Canadian Cinema in an OTT World." *Playbackonline.ca* 18 September, 2019. Accessed 15 August 2020.

Playback Staff. "2019's Top-Grossing Films at the Canadian Box Office." www.playbackonline.ca/2020/01/2019s-top-grossing-films-at-the-canadian-box-office/. Accessed 8 September 2020.

Pottratz, Wyn. "Screendance Cannot Be Everything: Defining the Form Ten Years after the *(Hu)Manifesto*." *International Journal of Screendance*, vol. 6, 2016, pp. 182–185.

Preston, Scott. "The Blood Brood—Canadian Horror Cinema—Past and Present." *Canadian Cinema*, edited by Janine Marchessault and Will Straw, Oxford University Press, 2019, pp. 351–366.

Raheja, Michelle. "Reading Nanook's Smile: Visual Sovereignty, Indigenous Revisions of Ethnography in *Atanarjuat (The Fast Runner)*." *American Quarterly*, vol. 59, no. 4, 2007, pp. 1159–1185.

Smith, Kathleen. "The Evolving Story of Dance on Film: An Overview of New Forms Then and Now." *Dance International*, Summer 2018.

Szporer, Philip. "Northern Exposures: Canadian Dance Film and Video." *Envisioning Dance on Film and Video*, edited by Judy Mitoma, Routledge, 2002, pp. 168–175.

Telefilm Canada 2020. www.telefilm.ca/en. Accessed 8 September 2020.

Tepperman, Charles. "Bureaucrats and Movie Czars: Canada's Feature Film Policy since 2000." *Media Industries*, vol. 4, no. 2, 2017, pp. 1–17.

TIFF 2020. www.tiff.net/about-tiff-20. Accessed 8 September 2020.

Turnbull, George. "The Shoestring Renaissance." *The Dance Current*, May/June 2019, pp. 32–39.

Wagman, Ira. "Three Canadian Film Policy Frameworks." *Canadian Cinema*, edited by Janine Marchessault and Will Straw, Oxford University Press, 2019, pp. 3–20.

Zoe, Constantinides. "The Myth of *Evangeline* and the Origin of Canadian National Cinema." *Film History: An International Journal*, vol. 26, no. 1, 2014, pp. 50–79.

CHAPTER 6

Inclusion, Access, and Equity: Diversity Initiatives in Canada's Game Industry

Matthew E. Perks and Jennifer R. Whitson

INTRODUCTION

To many, a career in Canada's game industries sounds like a dream job that bridges arts, culture, and tech worlds. Digital distribution and self-publishing on platforms such as Steam, Apple, and Google Play have fostered the growth of hundreds of small independent studios. The industry is expanding—employing 27,000 Canadians in just under seven hundred studios. This expansion is accompanied by economic growth, contributing $4.5 billion to Canada's GDP in 2019 (Nordicity). To meet this perceived demand, education and training programs increased five-fold from 2010 to 2017, with over three hundred post-secondary institutes offering games-focused courses, certificates, and degrees as of 2017 (Liu et al.).

Despite this rosy outlook, a career in Canada's game industries also sounds like a nightmare. Industry expansion is coupled with increasingly intense competition. Hundreds of games are released daily, leading to what some refer to as the "Indiepocalypse," and the concentration of profits are in the hands of a relatively few large multinationals, such as Nintendo, Ubisoft, and Electronic Arts (Kerr). For decades, game industries have faced critique for exploitative working conditions, long hours, and unpaid overtime (Dyer-Witheford and de Peuter). More recently, they face additional criticism due to toxic workplace cultures and misogynistic and racist player communities (Gray). Ultimately, one's gender has a clear impact how one participates in paid gameswork.

This chapter takes a critical approach to analyzing just who can participate in Canadian game development, focusing on how policy frameworks act to promote more diverse participation in gameswork by acting as influential symbols for local gamesmaking communities. In section 1, we examine why the game industries seem to be perpetually young and perpetually male. In section 2, we outline common approaches to diversify Canada's game industries. And in section 3, we apply a case study approach, using interview data from small and mid-size game studios in Montreal to examine how external pressures such as funding policies work at a local level to influence who is hired and promoted and who participates in video game development.

WHAT DO GAME INDUSTRIES LOOK LIKE AND WHO WORKS IN THEM?

From *Candy Crush* to *Fortnite*, edu-games to e-sports, contemporary games and game industries are heterogeneous, varying in terms of business model, production team scale and process, budget, and infrastructure. Rapid changes in technology, audience demographics, business models, and other factors have created an unstable ecosystem that makes it difficult to generalize about the organization of game development work. Game production processes are currently undergoing a shift, moving from releasing games as a final "boxed" product largely played on consoles and PCs to instead developing games as a "live" service with continual content releases and incremental updates, played on a broad array of platforms (Dubois and Weststar). Regardless of production model, some players—and power imbalances—remain the same: (1) development studios create games; (2) publishers finance and/or promote games, often exerting creative oversight; and (3) platforms (e.g., consoles and online services) ensure select games reach player audiences. While game studios arguably shoulder the most work and risk, publishers and platforms act as essential market gatekeepers, negotiate significant profit shares and intellectual property ownership, and commonly leave studios with a fraction of overall sales revenues. Aphra Kerr demonstrates how a small number of hardware and digital platform providers (e.g., Sony, Microsoft, Nintendo, Apple, and Valve) now generate significant revenues from controlling access to both physical distribution (e.g., game consoles) and digital distribution (e.g., app platforms), while "a huge number of independent game developers, wholly owned subsidiaries, in-house development team and amateurs provide the content to fill the voracious appetite of the online networks, consoles and mobile devices" (3).

Canada's own game industries are composed of a very small number of very large multinational studios, such as Electronic Arts, Ubisoft, and Square Enix, and hundreds of small "indie" studios. While more than half of Canada's game studios employ fewer than five people, the vast majority (79 percent) of those employed in games work for large companies of over one hundred people (Nordicity). Game studios are located across Canada (Parker and Jenson); however, 82 percent are found in British Columbia, Ontario, and Quebec, particularly in larger "hub" cities like Vancouver, Toronto, and Montreal. British Columbia's history of film and media tax incentives, Quebec's strong financial support for arts and culture, and Ontario's media development funds have each encouraged this growth.

Hub cities often are centred around one or several larger studios that act as "trees." These large "tree" studios employ and train gamesworkers, who may later leave to seed their own smaller independent "acorn" studios. For example, the introduction of a large Ubisoft studio in Montreal encouraged both the growth of pre-existing independent game studios and seeded new ones. It also heralded the introduction of multimedia labour tax credits that encouraged additional multinational studios to create satellite locations in Montreal to take advantage of both the talent and the financial incentives (Della Rocca). Similar seeding has occurred in other large cities in Canada, clustered around studios such as Electronic Arts in Vancouver and BioWare in Edmonton. Members of these hubs commonly socialize, network, and share advice at local meetups.

The surging growth of independent development in Canada is a direct result of low-cost and accessible development tools and reduced gatekeeping in distribution channels. While smaller studios struggle with long-term economic sustainability, they are seen as sites of creativity, risk-taking, and innovation that feed forward into a risk-averse mainstream industry via the transfer of skilled personnel, technologies, processes, and ideas. There is a multi-directional flow of gamesworkers as they move back and forth between large multinationals, scrappy independent studios, and everything in between. More research is needed to ascertain whether independent studios are a viable model for diverse participation and labour equity in gameswork. Indie games commonly cater to "niche" markets and express more diverse viewpoints, but this might have more to do with mainstream studios' focus on mass markets and not the actual demographics of independent gamesworkers. Moreover, the economic precarity of independent studios reinforces destructive labour practices, such as only hiring those who are able to work long hours at low (or no) pay—commonly young, mobile, childless men (Whitson et al.).

The average developer in Canada is 31, white, male, and has no dependents. Women comprise only 19 percent of the workforce (Nordicity). This differs from the overall Canadian labour force, where the average worker is 45 years old and nearly as likely to be female (47.4 percent) as male (Statistics Canada). This parallels global industry trends. A large survey conducted by the International Game Developers Association in 2019 reports that most (81 percent of) gamesworkers are white, and Black and Hispanic/Latinx populations are underrepresented.[1] In the next few paragraphs, we outline four intersecting pressures that help explain the over-representation of white heterosexual males in game industries and in technology sectors more generally.

Games (and Computer Science) Are for Boys?

While video game development requires a range of skill sets, including project management, 3D modelling, animation, and art, as well as sound, narrative, and level design, many other positions require backgrounds in computer science and engineering. However, at the post-secondary level, these fields also demonstrate a gender divide, with women's enrolment hovering at around 20 percent. This has not always been the case. Computer science as a field was traditionally dominated by women (Hicks), a history recently popularized via films such as *Hidden Figures*. The association between computers and "women's work" only started to decline in the decades after Second World War as the status of the work increased and women were pushed out of this workforce. Up until the 1980s, women's enrolment in post-secondary computer science programs was still increasing, reaching highs of 37 percent before precipitously declining (Hayes). This decline has been attributed to the rise of personal computers and video game consoles (Margolis and Fisher).

In the absence of a ready-made market, these products and the associated gaming and programming magazines were explicitly marketed to boys (Kline et al.), who then grew up immersed in computer culture. As a result, entry-level programming curriculum changed, assuming students were already familiar with coding. This inadvertently excluded girls and all others who did not grow up immersed in games, reinforcing wider cultural associations between "rational" computer technologies and masculinity (Fisher and Jenson). This fuels (mis)perceptions that "computers are for boys" and that girls are uninterested or unskilled in computer-related fields, despite evidence that there are no actual gender differences found in quantitative measures of students' abilities and performances (Singh et al.).

Gender Segregation and the Pay Gap

Cultural assumptions linking capabilities and skills to one's gender feed into demographic patterns in the workplace. Roles in games and other creative industries are segregated by gender, with men dominating both more prestigious creative roles and technical work while there are high concentrations of women in production and "service" roles associated with human resources (HR), community management, and coordination (Hesmondhalgh and Baker). This holds true in Canadian game industries—only half (52 percent) of women work directly on games (Nordicity). Instead, they are clustered in lower-status, lower-paid positions, such as HR. Globally, there is a gender wage gap in games, with women being paid 15 percent less than men for the same work (Graft). This echoes trends in Canada's technology sector more generally: women with a bachelor's degree or higher earn nearly $20,000 a year less than their male counterparts in the same job. This gap widens if they are Indigenous or part of a visible minority (Deschamps).

Passion, Labour, and Working Conditions

The 2020 *State of the Game Industry* report found that the industry was "driven by young workers who tend to depart within a decade." Commissioned and conducted by the Game Developers Conference (the industry's "premiere professional event"), the report surveyed more than four thousand international gamesworkers. Game development is a career path that "frequently demands and normalizes extended working hours, lacks job stability, and is often unpredictable and without clear trajectories for growth or advancement" (Liu et al. 20). Hiring is predicated upon demonstrating one's passion for games (Consalvo). This necessarily narrows hiring to those—mostly men—who grew up gaming. Additionally, "passion" is linked to a general willingness on the part of young, highly skilled workers to accept otherwise exploitative work practices. This commonly takes the form of "crunch," sustained periods of overtime to meet milestones. In 2019, 41 percent of gamesworkers reported crunch, with a further 35 percent reporting long or extended hours—for example, exceeding 50 hours per week (38 percent) or 60 hours per week (32 percent). Only 8 percent received paid overtime (Weststar et al., "Developer Satisfaction"). Employees feared losing their jobs and so complied with overtime requests.

Workplace instability is increased by larger workplace precarity and studio closures. There are few, if any, "forever" careers, and gamemakers frequently shift jobs (Weststar et al., "Developer Satisfaction"). Employment instability and the associated need to move one's family for work is related to increased stress, work anxiety, and depression (Crevoshay et al.). These workplace conditions place pressures on those with families, particularly women, who work "double shifts" by taking on most domestic and caregiving work at home. Simply put, gamesworkers are forced to choose between families and careers, leading to a continual "churn" and loss of senior expertise. Those wanting to start families, searching for more stability, feeling burnt out, or simply desiring work-life balance leave the industry and are quickly replaced by the next cohort of eager graduates. Ultimately, only a third of gamesworkers remain in the industry for 10 years or more (Game Developers Conference).

Toxic Cultures

The well-documented toxicity in tech and game industries is an additional factor explaining why women and members from LGTBQ+ and racialized communities fail to pursue game development as a career, and when they do, they leave prematurely (Weststar et al., *Diversity Among Videogame Developers*). Women who make games, or even just play games, are routinely harassed and threatened both online and off. Most notably, this has taken the form of #GamerGate, an online harassment campaign targeting women gamesworkers, players, journalists, and academics (Mortensen) that ultimately resulted in many leaving the industry. Toxic gamer culture is broader in scope than #GamerGate, targeting any players who do not align with white male heterosexual identities, particularly communities of colour (Gray).

Patterns of toxicity are replicated within the workplace. This can take the form of employers insufficiently protecting marginalized employees from online harassment from player communities. However, much of this toxicity is internal and directly related to workplace sexual harassment, as evidenced most recently by gamesworkers and streamers outing abusers online in a similar fashion to Hollywood's #MeToo movement. For example, two popular American development studios, Activision Blizzard and Riot Games, face multiple lawsuits filed by both the State of California and female employees, who accused their employers of endemic gender-based discrimination and sexual harassment. In 2020, sexual misconduct allegations were levelled against high-level executives at Ubisoft, leading to many resignations, including Yannis Mallat, president of Ubisoft Canada, and Cecile Cornet, Ubisoft's global head of human resources. Notably, it seemed HR staff were aware of numerous incidents and failed to respond. Toxic attitudes and cultures fostered within game studios, and condoned by upper management, directly impact who feels safe participating in game industries.

There is some indication that these patterns are changing. The 2019 International Game Developers Satisfaction Survey reported a 10 percent increase in the representation of female gamesworkers—up to 24 percent from 14 percent in 2017—and this is attributed directly to diversity efforts. These increases were also coupled with growing numbers of gamesworkers who have dependents (35 percent compared to 29 percent in 2017) and an increasing average age, which the authors attribute to gamesworkers feeling supported enough to stay in the industry longer term (Weststar et al., "Developer Satisfaction"). These changes may also be linked to structural changes and growing support for workplace structures that reduce precarity and inequity. Notably, over 75 percent responding gamesworkers support unionization efforts (Game Developers Conference).

In the following section, we talk about "meritocracy" and whether it explains who can have a career in game development, explore "pipeline" models for conceptualizing women's lack of participation in game industries, and finally, discuss two strategies for intervention: gender mainstreaming and diversity management.

PROBLEMATIZING MERITOCRACY

In 2012, science-fiction author John Scalzi wrote a blog post arguing that in "the role playing game known as The Real World, 'Straight White Male' is the lowest difficulty setting there is." Extending this metaphor of life as a game, he argued that gaining points and "levelling up" are by default easier for males due to historical structural inequalities. In contrast, a "Gay Minority Female," through no choice of their own, plays through life on what amounts to a "hardcore" setting. Due to structural inequalities related to one's gender, race or cultural group, economic standing, and various other factors, players never start from the same place, and there are simply fewer barriers to getting into university, getting a job, or receiving a raise if you are straight, white, and male. The post went viral, largely due to how it challenges the notion of meritocracy and the belief that everyone who works hard will be equitably rewarded.

The notion of a meritocracy pervades both game industries and game cultures. Because games themselves are built on systems of hierarchies—rewarding effort and skill at "levelling up"—there is a misconception that everyone starts on an equal setting and hard work is fairly rewarded. But this ignores history, differential access to resources, and all the intersectional head starts that allow some individuals to succeed where others fail. These same ideals also impact what games are made, the mechanics they feature, and the stories they tell (Paul).

Ideals of meritocracy, that the most qualified candidate is the most talented and best suited for the role, direct attention away from structural issues that "stack the odds" in favour of specific individuals. Gender inequality results in profound differences in working experiences and conditions. While creative industries argue they are "open, tolerant, and based upon democratic and meritocratic principles"

(Gill 510), the reality is that they mirror tech industries—unevenly distributed along lines of gender and race, resulting in an inequitable distribution of rewards, power, and autonomy (Banks). Women and racialized people are less likely to grow up with games, they are less likely to enter and graduate from computer science programs, and they are less likely to be recruited and hired by game companies. Once they gain a foothold within the industry, they are more likely to work in lower status, lower paid, and part-time positions, and they are paid less than white male counterparts for the same work. They commonly face harassment both from player communities and their own colleagues. Many simply leave game industries within a few years of entering (Weststar and Legault). While data on class, sexuality, and ability are limited and much more research is needed (Weststar et al., *Diversity Among Videogame Developers*), similar patterns likely shape the career trajectories of other marginalized developers. So, what is being done to improve these structural conditions that limit who can meaningfully participate in Canada's game industries?

Pipelines

Efforts to increase the number of women in game industries have been conceptualized in terms of a "pipeline," where simply getting more women and girls to enter STEM (science, technology, engineering, and mathematics) education (especially computer science) results in a more diverse, creative industry down the pipeline. The pipeline model frames four different stages where interventions may be made: (1) increasing girls' and women's exposure and access to games; (2) increasing women's participation in education and training; (3) providing access to early job experiences and mentorship; and (4) sustaining longer-term careers in the field. As argued by Harvey, this "evokes a vision whereby if enough force is imposed at one end of the pipeline—be it pumping entrants in or 'priming' students for employability—students will inevitably be propelled toward success" (Harvey 758). Despite the proliferation of STEM pipeline initiatives in past decades, women's enrolment in STEM programs such as computer science has *declined* since the early 1980s, as has the percentage of jobs held by women in computer science (Singh et al.).

In short, pipeline models assume that initial exposure to games leads to further reinforcement through formal schooling, which leads to successful early job experiences and long-term careers in the field. There is a large body of research on early gameplay experiences and gender, emphasizing that it is not a dislike or disaffinity for games that keeps girls and women from playing. Rather, it is the association between boys and games that effectively reduces girls' access to games

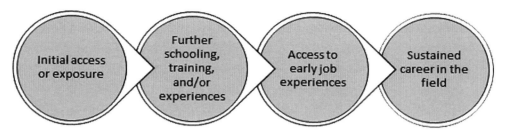

Figure 6.1: General Model of a Traditional Career Pipeline

Adapted with permission from RightsLink: Springer Nature: Women's Experiences on the Path to a Career in Game Development by Weststar and Legault (2018).

and devalues feminized forms of play. This "limits and delegitimizes their experience and expertise in the face of dominant, masculine interpretations of technical competence and the industry-maintained hegemony of 'real' games" (Weststar and Legault 110; see also Fron et al.). While 50 percent of Canadian players are female, women are commonly associated with mobile puzzle and "casual" games (NPD Group). These gendered patterns in play fuel gatekeeping of who is deemed a "real gamer" and the harassment of those deemed to not belong.

Initially, it was thought that offering formal games programs at the post-secondary level (e.g., colleges and universities) would increase diversity by replacing informal routes into games that were premised on masculinized player cultures and exclusionary "insider" social networks (Deuze et al.). However, this assumes all students enter game industries through post-secondary programs in game development and computer science. There are three reasons why this assumption is an issue. First, "only a minority of women follow the assumed pathway, enroll in good proportions in appropriate training programs, obtain and remain with jobs in the industry" (Weststar and Legault 106). Most women in game industries did *not* enter through this pipeline, so a focus on improving women's participation in post-secondary STEM programs via male-dominated pipelines misses alternative pathways that may be more effective.

Second, this pipeline creates a hierarchy of job skills that places computer science at the top of this creative industry and devalues all other essential work. While most gamesworkers have post-secondary degrees, there are gendered differences in the type of education obtained. Men outnumber women in computer science and software engineering degrees by more than four to one (Cimpian et al.), while women outnumber men two to one in animation, art and design, and graphic design. A focus on STEM pipelines allows industry leaders to explain away gender pay gaps and the industry-wide underrepresentation of women and other minorities as *solely* due to the lack of diverse enrolment in computer science and programming courses, while programming is only one of *many* skills needed for game development.

Third, post-secondary institutions struggle to address the institutional and structural forces that disproportionately impact underrepresented and marginalized people in STEM-related fields. For example, in games-related programs, students are still largely young, white, and male. Despite the widening of games audiences, as well as the propagation of STEM diversity initiatives, women in games education remain underrepresented and must deal with a range of implicit and explicit forms of policing to succeed. Women and gender minority students are defined by their status of "not male" and found lacking when their skill sets, game preferences, or social habits deviate from "default" male norms (Harvey).

Finally, a focus on getting women into a specific pipeline and making sure they do not leave misses the fact that careers at the end of the pipeline are often inhospitable to women and others who do not fit the norms or expectations of that pipe (Weststar and Legault). Simply put, women who enjoy both games and programming may not pursue education and careers in these fields because gaming cultures and workplaces are well known to be toxic. A focus on STEM pipelines and education also ignores the reasons why women and minorities leave the industry mid-career (Harvey). This draws attention away from addressing the social and cultural factors outlined in section 1 that lead women to avoid or leave the male-dominated industry. For example, nearly half of 2015 International Game Developers Association's Developer Satisfaction Survey respondents felt there was not equal treatment and opportunity in game industries. And when compared to males, "twice as many females reported experiencing inequity in recruitment and hiring processes, four times as many females reported experiencing inequity in the promotion process, five times as many females reported inequity on monetary grounds, six times as many females reported microaggressions in the workplace (verbal, behavioral, and environmental indignities), and seven times as many females reported experiencing inequity in both discipline and social/interpersonal interactions" (Weststar and Legault 114). Accordingly, there is increasing pressure to intervene in industry practices themselves. We address two methods of workplace interventions in the next section.

Strategies to Increase Representation

Gender mainstreaming and diversity management represent two strategies to shift organizational practices in both government and industry toward more feminist goals. As outlined by Elisabeth Prügl, these strategies are comparable and frequently intersect, but they illustrate different underlying rationales, logics, and measures of success. While gender mainstreaming follows a bureaucratic logic of addressing structural inequities via more formalized policies and procedures, diversity management leverages individual entrepreneurial logics to frame difference as creatively and economically productive—and thus something that industries should proactively seek out and encourage.

Gender mainstreaming emerged from international development agencies and public administration in the 1990s, acknowledging that policies and practices that seem to be gender-neutral affect women and men differently. They often privilege men's experiences over women's and result in pervasive (if unintended) discrimination on a structural level. The solution, for gender mainstreaming practitioners, is to make such failings conscious, recognize difference, utilize bureaucratic measures to "level the playing field" between men and women, and thus correct structural inequalities. While we can identify initiatives for racialized, Indigenous, and other marginalized communities that align with mainstreaming, they are far less developed, perhaps pointing to the difficulty in categorizing, measuring, and accounting for more complex, intersectional identities and oppressions on a bureaucratic level. In game industries, gender mainstreaming takes the form of anti-bias training, gender equity knowledge campaigns, pay scale reviews, and formal equity policies related to recruitment, hiring, and promotions, as well as initiatives aimed at improving working conditions and health benefits. These can be seen in nearly all large studios' recruitment websites, which emphasize diversity and inclusion, empowerment for all, and positive descriptions of studio culture.

In contrast, diversity management emerged from the private sector. Rather than concentrate only on gender differences, diversity management "starts from the assumption that a diverse workforce—including not only women but also people with all kinds of differences—adds to creativity and the bottom line" (Prügl 73). Companies adopted diversity management initially because they feared lawsuits under new equal opportunity requirements and gender equality laws. Diversity management assumes that a more broadly diverse workforce—along vectors that include race, gender expression, ability, and citizenship status—increases profit. Different viewpoints improve communication and information flow, foster creativity, and allow companies to represent and meet the needs of an increasingly diverse customer base. Using diversity management rationales, hiring women makes economic sense: Their creative influence may result in games that appeal to wider, non-male audiences.

Diversity management contrasts gender mainstreaming by viewing difference as productive and largely disregards the systemic inequalities that gender mainstreaming seeks to address. Diversity management takes a neoliberal approach, moving away from gender mainstreaming's bureaucratic-level, top-down policy solutions, and instead encourages individuals to become "entrepreneurs of the self" who capitalize on their unique perspectives and diversity (Prügl 83). Examples of diversity management in game industries include training to help recognize and appreciate diversity, guidelines for hosting inclusive workspaces and events, and developing communication and collaboration skills that emphasize how to work effectively within diverse teams. For example, in Montreal, the non-profit organization Pixelles runs workshops on how to write job postings that attract a wider range of applicants and avoid masculinized language.

Gender mainstreaming works at the institutional level, while diversity management shifts responsibility to individuals themselves. The end goals of gender mainstreaming and diversity management differ substantially. Diversity management locates success in market results and increased profit. This is straightforward to measure. Gender mainstreaming, in contrast, has a more difficult task in measuring, assessing, and evaluating whether the negative structural impacts of gender have been effectively addressed. As Prügl notes, evidence of whether diversity leads to market results is inconclusive and contradictory, but "a proliferating discourse about the superior performance of companies with a substantial representation of women in management supports the claim" (83). Whether diversity management increases profitability or not, there is a marked benefit for governments to back diversity management initiatives, as this encourages corporations to self-govern and address discriminatory practices without government intervention or resources.

Overall, the tension between gender mainstreaming and diversity management is characterized by competing views about diversity. Gender mainstreaming initiatives are expensive to implement and focus primarily on binary gender, but there is little evidence that diversity management initiatives actually create better workplaces for marginalized individuals (Proctor-Thomson). While a diverse workforce may increase the profits of creative firms, the reality is that women and other marginalized groups are still not well represented in these workplaces. Because they are not in positions of power, they do not share in the profit (Hesmondhalgh and Baker; Proctor-Thomson). Without the structural shifts supported by gender mainstreaming interventions, stereotypes of women are reinforced in these workplaces. Instead of being seen as bringing creativity and profit to a firm, women are relegated to "supportive" roles. In lead positions they are viewed as controlling and manipulating. This results in a revolving door of "diversity hires," as women are hired, lack internal support, burn out, and subsequently leave.

It is one thing to talk about abstract pipelines and initiatives to increase women's participation in Canada's creative industries, but what does this look like on the ground? What types of interventions do policies make? And how do they impact those already in the industry? To explore these questions, we outline a short case study detailing one small policy change made by the Canada Media Fund (CMF) in 2017, focusing on how it was received by a local community of gamesworkers in Montreal, how it impacted participation in the local industry, and what the inherent tensions between gender mainstreaming and diversity management are.[2]

CASE STUDY: GENDER EQUITY INITIATIVES

The CMF is a not-for-profit corporation that allocates over $350 million in funding annually to support the production of Canadian television and digital media content. In 2017–2018, the CMF introduced gender initiatives expressly aimed at increasing the representation of women in CMF-funded projects, including their Experimental Stream, which provides funding for game studios. This echoes initiatives from other media firms, such as the CBC, the NFB, and Telefilm. The CMF's initiatives included ensuring that juries evaluating proposed projects have gender parity, participation in third-party gender balance initiatives, and changing internal policies. The latter included how funding applications are scored and evaluated, awarding three percentage points to applications where the leadership team was composed of at least 40 percent women. This was referred to as reaching "gender parity." The "gender parity" initiative became the focus of our case study.

The gender parity policy takes a gender mainstreaming approach by introducing a gender quota. It focuses only on women, not broader representations of diversity (although the CMF has other programs for Indigenous content creators). The announcement of the policy acknowledged that talented women are already employed but lack opportunities. The 3 percent advantage was intended to "trigger" opportunities and help "level the playing field" by incentivizing the promotion of more women into leadership roles. However, the initiative was promoted in strongly diversity management tones by the president and CEO of CMF, Valerie Creighton, who noted that "[s]ocieties that maximize diverse views offer a competitive advantage." She then went on to cite that the American FX channel increased the diversity of their directors from 12 percent in 2014 to 51 percent in 2016 and received a record number of Emmy nominations as a result (Canada Media Fund, *CMF Announces Initiatives*). So, while specific gender quotas and policies are gender mainstreaming tactics, ultimately the CMF's diversity initiative was advertised in diversity management terms and justified to creative industry studio heads as driving creativity and profit.

In a sense, the initiative attempts to increase the "flow" of women through game industries pipelines, providing studios financial incentive to promote women and thus fix "blocked" and "leaky" pipelines that lead to the lack of women in leadership positions. Initial results reported by the CMF after the first year were small but positive. Of the 329 applications in the Experimental Stream—which included games, software, web series, and interactive content—96 teams had at least 40 percent female leadership. In terms of determining who received funding versus who did not, 19 projects were successful due to the additional gender points, while a further 31 projects near the funding cutoff point were refused because they did not meet gender parity (Canada Media Fund, *Gender Parity*). In games specifically, 29.5 percent of "key personnel" for funded game projects were women, a figure higher than the industry average. However, more detailed data on games-specific projects were not available publicly, leading to speculation from gamesmaking communities about whether these policies made a difference, whether they were fair, and whether their impact was positive. To answer these questions, we interviewed game studio leaders.

In fall of 2018—a year after the CMF policy was implemented—we conducted interviews with 20 participants in Montreal, Quebec. These participants were recruited through purposive sampling from previous projects and networks and continued with snowball sampling following participant recommendations. All interview participants were given pseudonyms to protect their anonymity. Our interviews focused on perceptions of diversity in game industries, reactions to and experiences with the CMF policy, and individual experiences with diversity and gender diversity policies. Our participants were mainly studio founders, co-founders, and industry intermediaries; eight were women and twelve were men. Of the twenty, eleven had applied to recent CMF funding rounds: six received funding, five did not. We organized our findings into three intersecting areas, each described below.

The Fairness of Diversity Initiatives

While the first two sections of this chapter outlined the ways in which the game industry can be inequitable and unfair to women and other marginalized individuals, most of the interviews focused on an entirely different perception of inequality—whether policies to address gender inequalities are fair to studios or not. Given that we interviewed gamesworkers, perhaps it is not surprising that many framed the new CMF policy in terms of a game with rules one must strat-egize around in order to "win." Interviewees more often framed this funding "game" in terms of competing with other studios for scarce resources—namely a limited number of women in the industry—and argued that this new emphasis created an uneven playing field between studios of different size. Ultimately, these narratives tokenized women and framed them as undeserving of promotion, reify-ing sexist bias rather than addressing it.

Multiple interviewees framed multinational studios as competitors for limited human resources and commonly mentioned Ubisoft Montreal, which employed approximately 3,500 gamesworkers at the time. Even if multinationals were not applying for the same funds, they had larger budgets to recruit and hire women. As one interviewee notes:

> A female programmer is like a shiny Pokemon. It's extremely rare, and when you see one, you'd like to have it. So Ubisoft says: "well, I'll pay you $10,000 a year more, because then I get to have you, and I show that I have a diverse work group, basically." The issue with us is that we don't have that power. (Erik, M)

This statement aligns with the pipeline issues discussed above, attributing fail-ures to hire diverse employees with the broader scarcity of women with computer science degrees who want to work in the industry. Importantly, this focus on pro-grammers overlooks all other leadership roles and skill sets.

The thematic emphasis on rules and resources also included multiple refer-ences to how the system could be "gamed." For example, some felt larger studios could find loopholes and subvert the intent of the policy, as studios with more staff and multiple ongoing projects could reassign senior women to projects that were applying for funding:

> So, if you have a four-hundred-person company ... even if you have 5 percent of women leaders, you can probably do all your CMF projects with women as leaders and the rest of the projects will be led by men. (Santiago, M)

Larger studios were seen as able to create a false impression of gender parity by reallocating existing women strategically to CMF projects without necessarily changing their practices or broader leadership structure. Because smaller studios only work on one or two games at a time, reaching gender parity at the project level necessarily equated to much larger changes in studio leadership.

Meritocracy

The most referred to method of gaming the system was by "falsely" promoting women. As put by one interviewee, the quota could be manipulated via temporary female contract employees, who could appear on multiple applications from multiple studios:

> Freelancers probably with a good resume can be used on one more than the project. Or probably if they're women inside the company, they're in the application, they take a leadership position even though it's not really a leadership position. (Nikolay, M)

Here, women could be double-counted and used as placeholders for the de facto leaders—promoted in name only, without changing their roles and responsibilities.

Many of these discussions centred on meritocracy and whether those promoted were deserving of their position, particularly in comparison to male employees. As put by one interviewee:

> Those people aren't there, and when they are, we're all competing to get them, to get that diverse point of view. So it makes it very, very difficult to hire these people, or we have to hire people that aren't as good at the job as others but that we're gonna train into a role that we think that they can have.... I don't feel that way now, but at the time I felt like I was being forced to hire people that might not be the best people for the job just because the government had decided that parity was the thing. (Jin, M)

Another interviewee echoed this sentiment, noting that while they supported the policy, their own studio lacked the budget to hire more experienced women, and moving less-experienced women through the pipeline without first developing leadership skills would risk jeopardizing the studio:

> We can't take a junior and hire them in and then be like, "Great, you're in charge now." That's gonna just destroy the organization.... Well, the policy makes sense so I'm not up in arms over it but I'm also ... it's kind of difficult for us to do anything about it. Or, at least, it's gonna take many many years for those changes to happen. (Santiago, M)

The interviewee expressed frustration at losing points for something they felt they could not control. Hiring, training, and mentoring more junior women into leadership roles would take years, and it came with the continual risk these women would be "poached" by larger studios offering higher salaries and more developed diversity initiatives. Thus, policy emphases on gender quotas in leadership were seen as a form of "positive discrimination" that set social characteristics in opposition to actual skill or merit.

Many in the game industries argue that initiatives expressing "the need for greater diversity was acceding to political correctness and therefore to less deserving, less talented, less meritorious pretenders" (Harvey 763). This sentiment and pressure to promote women may unintentionally harm the very people the policy was intended to support. As one female interviewee reflected:

> I think it's hard to deal with imposter syndrome even when you have tons of experience, and having some guys that you know [give] you this title just so that they could have money. That could be destructive to your identity and your own self-confidence. (Briar, F)

Even when qualified for the role, women's accomplishments would be diminished and doubted—including by the women themselves. The studios that promoted women simply to "get the points" were seen as effectively using women without changing their own perceptions. Another female interviewee echoed this sentiment, noting:

> I think there's also imposter syndrome for women that were promoted for this sole purpose. I've spoken with some. And some of them were like, "I'm not sure if I deserve this, but I'm not sure if I'm being used." And that was the terminology used. (Shanna, F)

While interventions may force firms to hire more women, they do not account for how this frames women's work as founded only in their "difference" rather than "merit" (Proctor-Thomson).

Impacts

The impact of policies like these on local industries is still unclear, including how many studios in Montreal received or lost funding due to the 3 percent. But it is very clear that the CMF policy forced studios to reflect upon and change their internal studio practices. The policy signalled new values, generating conversations and friction within local game development communities.

Many of the interviewees were part of what is colloquially referred to as the Cabal, a network for small and mid-size studio leaders in Quebec that collectively shares knowledge and advice about day-to-day operations, such as recommending tax experts, networking, and navigating bureaucracies. Similar networks exist in the other Canadian hub cities, including Full Indie in Vancouver, Toronto's Gamma Space, and local International Game Developers Association (IGDA) chapters in cities like Edmonton. According to interviewees, the CMF policy change initiated a flurry of posts to the Cabal email listserv, which until that point had not featured diversity-related topics. Nearly a year afterward, all interviewees referenced these discussions, emphasizing their role in shaping individual viewpoints on diversity.

In the days following the initial announcement, some studio heads on the Cabal mailing list responded in frustration about how they might "game" the system and made crude jokes about applying for a change of gender on their provincial identification so they could meet the quota. The response to this was quite polarizing, but it also led to a number of studio heads taking on educational roles, pointing out the transphobic nature of the jokes, explaining why structural inequality and the lack of diversity in game industries is a problem for the local community, and recommending further resources on gender parity. This led to an apology from the initiating parties. While this tension may have been seen as a watershed moment in the local community, it also ended the discussion on the listserv.

While we are unable to verify the exact details of their applications, at least one interviewee expressly noted that without the additional gender parity points, their application would have been denied. A year after the initiatives were introduced, our interviewees felt that the initial discussions they had within their local networks, particularly the Cabal conversations, had a large impact on how they felt about gender equity. A few of the interviewees noted that at the time, they disagreed with the policy, but after the tense exchange, they read into the issues more and subsequently worked to hire more women. In this sense, social pressure at both the CMF and local levels changed how studios hired, or at least talked about hiring, something that studios would not have done on their own.

All interviewees broadly supported increased diversity in game industries, most framing their responses in diversity management terms, linking gender parity with concrete benefits such as increased audience share, funding, profits, or recognition. However, one interviewee pointed to a tension between gender mainstreaming and diversity management approaches, arguing that increased diversity was inherently important.

It's unfortunate that our culture often tries to pose diversity as a business advantage, because I think, that's a red herring. I don't think that that is what we should be focusing on or what we should be valuing over human lives and experiences, but also I'm not actually sure it's true. I think it might in fact be a disadvantage in some ways and that's fine. I think it's worth it. I think it has other advantages, but it's not necessary. You don't have to have diverse creators to make diverse content. (Briar, F)

The above quote problematizes the assumed links between representation, content creation, and profit, noting that diverse content *can* be created by non-diverse individuals and that—while desirable—fostering more representative workforces may be economically *disadvantageous* and thus undermine diversity management rationales for increasing diversity.

There were also mixed feelings as to whether it was the place of the CMF to address gender inequalities and tie funding directly to whether studios hired or promoted women. Interviewees were uncomfortable with funding agencies "forcing" studios to have more diverse representation:

I'm always very iffy when there's requirements that come with money, because yeah, that's definitely controlling, but I do also … the CMF as a public entity I think has a role to play.… If as a society we have decided that this is a thing that we want, then I think it is a good thing to have an incentive. (Selena, F)

Here, the fact that the CMF was seen not as a corporate agency but as a public entity linked with state funding, the larger social good, and democratic values justified their actions. Beyond the CMF, many gamesworkers did not feel it was their own individual responsibility to address structural equality:

I think at the time, I felt like it was kind of.… It sucked that they were putting the onus on business owners instead of putting it on the education or in the environment or on bringing these people to have the opportunity to go to school, to get good at these jobs and then they could get hired. (Jin, M)

For this interviewee, the lack of women in the game industry was not located at the studio or even industry level but at education. They evoked the pipeline metaphor, arguing that efforts should be concentrated at the start of the pipeline, including increasing the number of girls and women in educational programs.

Most of the interviewees felt that the policy was ineffective in the short term but would lead to longer-term structural change if connected with other, wider industry-level initiatives. One interviewee notes CMF funding policies that simply count the number of women on a project are a poor measure of actual diversity and inclusivity:

> It was trying to enforce [equity] in a weird way, but they are trying, and I think that's pretty important … it's going to force many of those studios to rethink. I don't think it will come with good intentions from the studios itself or themselves.… I don't think [policies like the CMF's] are tackling the important issues like the bias, like toxic environments for work. (Shanna, F)

So, while the external pressures might change studio practices, the interviewee doubted whether studios themselves would recognize structural inequality without more training and support. In this sense, the top-down 3 percent on its own was seen as superficial, at least in the short term.

However, there was evidence that this rather minor initiative had more immediate positive impacts. One interviewee reflected upon how the policy changed their own role at the studio, hiring practices, and larger studio culture:

> It impacts me.… We actively made more efforts to make my role as a producer more defined and give me more responsibility production-wise, because we wanted to kind of put that in the forefront, because that's one of the key roles that they recognize. (Selena, F)

They also noted a shift in who and how they recruited:

> We more actively sought women and tried to think about how do we make positions attractive to women?… Thinking about your biases and your hiring process and things like that. (Selena, F)

Here, the interviewee reflects on the larger impact of gender quotas, what changes they enable, but also what they *did not* change:

> It has also kind of brought out more discussions of gender equity in the studio in general, which also brought me to be a little bit more forward with the fact that we might have some sort of parity when it comes to roles, because we've had the three points from the CMF for our last project, but the lowest paid employees remain the women in our studio, so there is still some gender

inequity. It has brought us to kind of think about "how do we put our money where our mouth is?" (Selena, F)

While emphasizing positive impacts, the quote above emphasized the amount of work still to be done in terms of addressing more deeply rooted inequities. It is worth pointing out that many of these inequities surfaced in our interviews, with repeated assumptions that women were less skilled than men and very little recognition of the structural barriers that women face.

CONCLUSION

As we have demonstrated in this chapter, there are clearly acknowledged issues that limit just who can meaningfully participate in game industries, metaphors that help us understand some of the difficulties women and other marginalized populations face, and models that shape where and how interventions are made. In short, there is an uneven playing field that determines who can play and is welcomed into game spaces, who enters and succeeds in educational programs, and who is recruited, hired, and promoted. Most of those in the industry are young, white, male, and without children, and they simply may not recognize the additional hurdles that others face, or if they do, they do not believe it is their responsibility to remove these hurdles. Framing the problem of who participates in game industries as a pipeline shapes proposed solutions and ignores other critical issues. These solutions prioritize jamming more women and girls into the access end of STEM-oriented pipelines and addressing "leaks" and "blockages" in the hopes that a wider, more diverse talent pool will result.

The way diversity initiatives are introduced and talked about, in terms of diversity management or gender mainstreaming, shapes how individuals respond. The framing presented by the CMF presents a problem by utilizing both logics. It takes a gender mainstreaming approach by introducing gender quotas to reduce women's barriers to promotion but markets itself in diversity management terms of profit. While diversity management effectively markets diversity as "good for business," by linking women to money, it may conversely undermine more long-term efforts for change. For example, in the case of the CMF, focusing efforts primarily on counting women risks turning women into game pieces to win funding and tokenizing their contributions. This aligns with larger critiques of pipeline models: increasing numbers of women and other marginalized groups will not have the desired participatory effects unless the underlying structural and cultural factors that devalue their contributions are addressed first.

CORE CONCEPTS

diversity management: Emerging from the private sector, diversity management sees all forms of diversity—not just gender—as something individuals can leverage to their benefit. Diversity management argues that a diverse workforce is more creative and thus more profitable than a non-diverse workforce.

gender mainstreaming: Emerging from international development agencies and public administration in the 1990s, gender mainstreaming recognizes that policies and interventions are not neutral and may impact women and men differently. To address this inequality, gender mainstreaming takes the form of policy interventions and bureaucratic measures to reduce the workforce inequality of women in various industries.

meritocracy: A system of norms that argues that innate skill, talent, or achievement are the defining standards to evaluate the worth of individuals. Meritocracy does not account for structural differences and inequalities that may impact ability or access for all individuals.

pipeline: A metaphor largely used in science, technology, engineering, and math (STEM) for conceptualizing the pathway individuals pass through, from early childhood interest in a certain field, through education, to a sustained career in these fields. The pipeline metaphor argues that increasing the number of individuals (gender and sexual minorities, BIPOC, etc.) at the start of the pipeline, and addressing leaks and blockages along the way, increases participation and presence in the downstream workforce.

SUGGESTED ACTIVITIES

1. Search online for images or videos of game advertisements from various decades (1970s, 1980s, 1990s, 2000s, 2010s) and collect five for each decade. For each, identify who is represented by age, gender, racialization, and role (e.g., player, spectator, game character, parent). Organize your counts into a table. Reflect on what significant shifts, if any, occurred over time.

2. The Game Developers Conference (GDC) is the largest international professional conference for gamesworkers. Visit its website and explore past talks in its advocacy stream (https://gdconf.com/). What are some commonly identified areas for advocacy? What range of interventions are suggested? What part(s) of the pipeline does it focus on?

3. Gender parity programs can be found in many different institutions. Check your university's or college's website to see if there are any programs targeting gender or racialized minorities to increase enrolment in certain programs. Thinking about the key concepts of diversity management and gender mainstreaming, can you identify these concepts in the strategies and methods employed?

NOTES

1. While most game industries data treat gender as a binary and only collect basic demographic information, the 2019 IGDA study includes data on a wider range of gender and sexual expressions, including non-binary identification, as well as data on disability and neurodivergence.

2. This study was funded by the Social Sciences and Humanities Research Council of Canada as part of the ReFiguring Innovation in Games grant.

REFERENCES

Banks, Mark. *Creative Justice: Cultural Industries, Work and Inequality.* Rowman & Littlefield International, 2017.

Canada Media Fund. *CMF Announces Initiatives to Increase the Contribution of Women.* https;//www.cmf-fmc.ca/news/cmf-announces-initiatives-to-increase-the-contribution-of-women/.

————. *Gender Parity 2017–2018 Annual Report.* https://ar-ra17-18.cmf-fmc.ca/funding/gender_parity/. Accessed 5 September 2018.

Cimpian, Joseph R., et al. "Understanding Persistent Gender Gaps in STEM." *Science,* vol. 368, no. 6497, 2020, pp. 1317–19, https://doi.org/10.1126/science.aba7377.

Consalvo, Mia. "Crunched by Passion: Women Game Developers and Workplace Challenges." *Beyond Barbie and Mortal Kombat: New Perspectives on Gender and Gaming,* edited by Yasmin B. Kafai et al., MIT Press, 2008.

Crevoshay, Eve, et al. *State of the Industry 2019: Mental Health in the Game Industry.* White Paper, Take This, 2019, p. 64, https://www.takethis.org/wp-content/uploads/2019/07/TakeThis_StateOfTheIndustry_2019.pdf. Accessed 8 October 2021.

Della Rocca, Jason. "The Montreal Indie Game Development Scene … Before Ubisoft." *Loading…,* vol. 7, no. 11, 2013.

Deschamps, Tara. "Pay Gap between Women, Men in Canadian Tech Jobs Is Nearly $20K per Year: Study." *Financial Post*, 23 January 2019, https://business.financialpost.com/pmn/business-pmn/pay-gap-between-women-men-in-canadian-tech-jobs-is-nearly-20k-per-year-study. Accessed 8 October 2021.

Deuze, Mark, et al. "The Professional Identity of Gameworkers." *Convergence*, vol. 13, no. 4, 2007, pp. 335–353.

Dubois, Louis-Etienne, and Johanna Weststar. "Games-as-a-Service: Conflicted Identities on the New Front-Line of Video Game Development." *New Media & Society*, March 2021, pp. 1–22.

Dyer-Witheford, Nick, and Greig de Peuter. "'EA Spouse' and the Crisis of Video Game Labour: Enjoyment, Exclusion, Exploitation, Exodus." *Canadian Journal of Communication*, vol. 31, no. 3, 2006, pp. 599–617.

Fisher, Stephanie, and Jennifer Jenson. "Producing Alternative Gender Orders: A Critical Look at Girls and Gaming." *Learning, Media and Technology*, vol. 42, no. 1, 2017, pp. 87–99.

Fron, Janine, et al. "The Hegemony of Play." *Proceedings of the 2007 DiGRA International Conference: Situated Play*, vol. 4, Digital Games Research Association, 2007, pp. 309–318.

Game Developers Conference. *GDC State of the Game Industry: Game Devs Shifting Focus to Next-Gen Consoles*. https://gdconf.com/news/gdc-state-industry-devs-shifting-focus-next-gen-consoles. Accessed 8 October 2021.

Gill, Rosalind. "Unspeakable Inequalities: Post Feminism, Entrepreneurial Subjectivity, and the Repudiation of Sexism among Cultural Workers." *Social Politics: International Studies in Gender, State & Society*, vol. 21, no. 4, 2014, pp. 509–528.

Graft, Kris. "Game Developer Salary Survey 2014." *Gamasutra*, 2014, https://www.gamedeveloper.com/audio/game-developer-salary-survey-2014-the-results-are-in-. Accessed 8 October 2021.

Gray, Kishonna L. *Intersectional Tech: The Transmediated Praxis of Black Users in Digital Gaming*. Louisiana State University Press, 2020.

Harvey, Alison. "Becoming Gamesworkers: Diversity, Higher Education, and the Future of the Game Industry." *Television & New Media*, vol. 20, no. 8, 2019, pp. 756–766.

Hayes, Caroline Clarke. "Computer Science." *Gender Codes*, edited by Thomas J. Misa, John Wiley & Sons Ltd., 2010, pp. 25–49.

Hesmondhalgh, David, and Sarah Baker. "Sex, Gender and Work Segregation in the Cultural Industries." *The Sociological Review*, vol. 63, 2015, pp. 23–36.

Hicks, Marie. *Programmed Inequality: How Britain Discarded Women Technologists and Lost Its Edge in Computing*. MIT Press, 2018.

Kerr, Aphra. *Global Games: Production, Circulation and Policy in the Networked Era.* Routledge, 2017.

Kline, Stephen, et al. *Digital Play: The Interaction of Technology, Culture, and Marketing.* McGill-Queen's University Press, 2003.

Liu, Zhenyan, et al. "The State of Video Game Education: Canadian, American, and Californian Post-Secondary Programs." *ReFiguring Innovation in Games Conference,* 2019.

Margolis, Jane, and Allan Fisher. *Unlocking the Clubhouse: Women in Computing.* Revised ed., MIT Press, 2003.

Mortensen, Torill Elvira. "Anger, Fear, and Games: The Long Event of #GamerGate." *Games and Culture,* vol. 13, no. 8, 2018, pp. 787–806.

Nordicity. *The Canadian Video Game Industry 2019.* Entertainment Software Association of Canada, 2019, p. 43, https://theesa.ca/wp-content/uploads/2019/11/ CanadianVideoGameSector2019_EN.pdf. Accessed 8 October 2021.

NPD Group. *Real Canadian Gamer: Essential Facts 2020.* Entertainment Software Association of Canada, 2020, p. 32, https://theesa.ca/wp-content/uploads/2020/11/ RCGEF_en.pdf. Accessed 8 October 2021.

Parker, Felan, and Jennifer Jenson. "Canadian Indie Games between the Global and the Local." *Canadian Journal of Communication,* vol. 42, no. 5, 2017.

Paul, Christopher A. *The Toxic Meritocracy of Video Games: Why Gaming Culture Is the Worst.* University of Minnesota Press, 2018.

Proctor-Thomson, Sarah B. "Feminist Futures of Cultural Work? Creativity, Gender and Difference in the Digital Media Sector." *Theorizing Cultural Work: Labour, Continuity and Change in the Cultural and Creative Industries,* edited by Mark Banks et al., Routledge, 2013.

Prügl, Elisabeth. "Diversity Management and Gender Mainstreaming as Technologies of Government." *Politics & Gender,* vol. 7, no. 1, 2011, pp. 71–89.

Scalzi, John. "Straight White Male: The Lowest Difficulty Setting There Is." *Whatever,* 15 May 2012, https://whatever.scalzi.com/2012/05/15/straight-white-male-the-lowest-difficulty-setting-there-is/. Accessed 8 October 2021.

Singh, Kusum, et al. "Women in Computer-Related Majors: A Critical Synthesis of Research and Theory from 1994 to 2005." *Review of Educational Research,* vol. 77, no. 4, *American Educational Research Association,* 2007, pp. 500–533.

Statistics Canada. *Labour Force Characteristics by Sex and Detailed Age Group, Annual.* 5 April 2019, https://www150.statcan.gc.ca/t1/tbl1/en/tv.action?pid=1410032701. Accessed 8 October 2021.

Weststar, Johanna, and Marie-Josée Legault. "Women's Experiences on the Path to a Career in Game Development." *Feminism in Play,* edited by Kishonna L. Gray et al., Palgrave Macmillan, 2018, pp. 105–123.

Weststar, Johanna, et al. *Developer Satisfaction Survey 2019*. International Game
    Developers Association, 2019, p. 38.

———. *Diversity Among Videogame Developers*. International Game Developers
    Association, 2017, p. 39.

Whitson, Jennifer R., et al. "The Missing Producer: Rethinking Indie Cultural
    Production in Terms of Entrepreneurship, Relational Labour, and Sustainability."
    European Journal of Cultural Studies, vol. 24, no. 2, 2021, pp. 606–627.

CHAPTER 7

Creative Hubs: Sites of Community and Creative Work

Mary Elizabeth (M. E.) Luka

INTRODUCTION

In this chapter, I examine ways that we can understand the purposes of and assess Canada's creative hubs focused on arts, culture, and media. Creative hubs are useful in a number of ways: to develop a cultural district; to offer co-working or presentation spaces for professional creative workers to share skills, networks, or their current work; to spark innovation; or to involve citizens, clients, and users in the creative sector in more collaborative ways. Such spaces are important because the culture sector (including artists, arts organizations, and cultural industries) is a crucial element of our social fabric and the economy. In my own research, I have examined arts, culture, and media-based creative hubs such as cSPACE (a co-working building) and National accessArts (a multidisciplinary disability arts organization) in Calgary, Alberta (discussed below); BC Artscape (a social service and arts co-working building) in Vancouver, British Columbia; Yukonstruct (a social enterprise and business incubation centre) in Whitehorse, Yukon; the New Dawn Centre for Social Innovation in rural Nova Scotia; and the European Network of Living Labs. A recent study by Crossick and Kaszynska examined cultural districts and creative hubs around the world. They found that the social contributions of creative hubs such as those above include the availability of deeply varied cultural offerings and creative practices situated within or nearby vital public spaces; supporting education in strategic creative practices; building local and community identity and cohesion; advancing the livability of a city or region; and captivating the attention of creative and knowledge workers, investors, and tourists alike. Creative hubs and networks also enable communities—including marginalized, dissenting, or underrepresented voices—to come together in more inclusive and sustainable ways (Hassan; Luka, *Creative Hubs in Canada*; Yung, "Impact Evaluation," *Generator*). All these outcomes act to evaluate impact. The term *impact evaluation* refers to what is assessed and counted as "success" for an organization or sector. While culture sector activities are often evaluated using economic measures of success—such as ticket sales, merchandise sales, or more broadly diversified revenue streams (e.g., Dempwolf et al.; Essig), this chapter uses the overarching concept of creative citizenship (Luka, "Towards Creative Citizenship," *Scratching the Surface, A(rtSpots) to ZeD*) to consider broader ways of assessing the impact of the culture sector and creative economy. A broader, more inclusive approach to impact measurement for creative hubs in our communities also leads to findings that the many different types of creative hubs that now exist ought to be supported through funding and policy. The idea of creative citizenship helps frame these more inclusive definitions of creative hubs. To help understand creative citizenship from a practical point of view, I examine the role of creative labour in the hubs, including the ways in which creative workers and communities operate in interlocked ways with the systems in which they find themselves. This leads me to examine and update the relevance of triple-bottom-line (i.e., socio-cultural, environmental, and economic) measures (Elkington) by combining these with a more complex understanding of the importance of cultural and social vitality (Hawkes) in the creative industries as complements to economic models and implications.

To illustrate these ideas, I turn to some of the hubs and networks I have investigated over a five-year period, as well as funders and policymakers I have spoken with about these sites. I explore how creative citizenship and a wholistic approach to impact assessment for creative hubs and networks generates a broader definition of creative hubs than currently exists in government funding programs. Using this approach, I offer a sustained critique of core funding models and the exclusionary nature of the definitions used to decide which creative hubs are eligible for funding. I also use exemplars in this chapter to suggest how varied creative networks and hubs can pragmatically reshape policy and practice as well as production and distribution environments. Finally, the chapter concludes with three activities that will help you undertake your own research on creative hubs.

CANADA'S CREATIVE HUBS AND NETWORKS

In their 2016 evaluation of creative hubs and networks across the United Kingdom, Dovey et al. found that a creative hub often functions as a flexible, aggregative mode of organizing innovation, business, and talent development by bringing emergent creative economy organizations together. This is particularly true of creative hubs focused on arts, culture, and media. As spaces, Dovey et al. claim, creative hubs operate in neighbourhoods, sometimes acting as an anchor for the area, including Watershed in Bristol, United Kingdom (described below). Physical buildings that host creative hubs can include a wide range of creative activity by artists, social entrepreneurs, and service organizations that address social, cultural, and economic needs and practices, such as Culture Link CIC in Halifax, Nova Scotia. On Flin Flon's main street in Manitoba, several creative businesses and studios are located side by side rather than in one building. But creative hubs are not limited to physical spaces; indeed, they are increasingly virtual or distributed operations that share values and sometimes missions and mandates to provide collective cultural supports, production, and distribution channels (Dovey et al.). Examples include the Centre for Social Innovation (CSI) in Toronto, which operates in physical spaces but also as a virtual network; Canadian Public Arts Funders—a network of arts councils that informally support creative hub activities; and Etsy and Copass—the latter being two internationally distributed networks that bring creative workers together to share a selling platform or access to co-working spaces worldwide, respectively. Other examples of physical creative hubs include the Banff Centre for Arts and Creativity in Alberta; the non-profit organization Qaggiavuut and its proposal for Qaggiq as a central hub for arts and culture activities across northern Canada; and Lunenburg, Nova Scotia's regional creative economy, which is a loosely affiliated group of creative businesses and individuals (Luka et al.; Luka, *Creative Hubs in Canada*; Wallace and Luka; Nordicity; Déziel and Duchesneau).

However, rather than incorporate a definition of creative hubs that includes the above range, the Department of Canadian Heritage narrows eligibility to access the Canada Cultural Spaces Fund. The focus is on physical buildings incorporating tenant or co-working spaces ("a multi-tenant facility that brings together professionals from a range of arts or heritage sectors and creative disciplines … with shared space, equipment and amenities") and a range of business models, including non-profit, social enterprise, for-profit, and individual creative workers. Functionally, the creative hub must provide "opportunities for idea exchange, collaboration and/or professional development [as well as] space and programming that is accessible to the public" (Department of Canadian Heritage). Virtual and distributed operations are not supported.

This rather narrow eligibility criteria in the Canadian context influences comparable funding programs in provincial/territorial and municipal jurisdictions.

While it is helpful to have leverage once you are on the list of eligible organizations, the narrowness of the definition acts to gatekeep against particular forms of creative hubs. This is especially true for organizations that are systemically disadvantaged because of distance, social inequities, or size, such as those found in dispersed rural environments or run by women or marginalized groups. I saw this in my research, for example, at cSPACE in Calgary and Culture Link CIC in Halifax, both of which embody a classic creative hubs structure. They include buildings that rent facilities and offer services to cultural clients and creative workers and are able to leverage multiple levels of government funding based on the traditional federal definition. Interestingly, cSPACE is a registered non-profit, while Culture Link CIC uses a form of incorporation known as a community interest company (i.e., a for-profit organization with a mission that benefits the community; see, e.g., Smith). In contrast, Flin Flon's main street and the Winnipeg Cultural District (WCD) are co-located sets of buildings—often in declining neighbourhoods—that are tenanted or owned by creative businesses, or, in other words, distributed creative hubs. The WCD has not been able to secure Cultural Spaces funding, although it aspires to serve many arts, culture, and creative enterprises. Flin Flon has not even applied. National accessArts Centre (NaAC; formerly the Indefinite Arts Centre) was only recently able to secure funding for its building in Calgary but not for the networking and collaboration it does outside the building context, which I discuss in more detail below (Luka, *Creative Hubs in Canada*; Luka et al.; personal communications). I argue that the Canadian government's definition could be fruitfully expanded to become consistent with more expansive international approaches, thereby reflecting today's realities for many other kinds of creative hubs: distributed, international, virtual, local, and those responsive to marginalized communities and to realizing equity in the field.

While the rapid shift to virtual operations in the culture and business sectors during the Covid-19 global pandemic made even more visible the limits of the Canadian federal definition, extensive current research in Canada and the United Kingdom (e.g., AHRC; Déziel and Duchesneau; Dovey et al.; Luka et al.) highlights a way forward. Flexible knowledge-sharing and collaborative approaches developed in locally specific creative hubs and networks are better positioned to mitigate—and benefit from—rapid changes in the field, whether sudden or expected. To this end, knowledge sharing and collaboration are also crucial opportunities for the creative ecosystem to leverage the strengths of the almost two hundred creative hubs and networks focused on arts, culture, and media in Canada. To help with knowledge sharing, over the last five years I facilitated the creation of the Creative Hubs and Networks Mapping Initiative (CHNMI), a research database that collected and now shares information about these two hundred hubs and networks (https://criticaldigitalmethods.ca/creative-hubs-and-networks-database/). The database reports on organizational mission and vision; location(s); users; programs and services; business models; funders; and marketing and outreach. While each hub or network is quite unique, many also have much in common with other hubs. Researchers, creative workers, funders, and others can use this database to examine the many kinds of creative hubs and networks in Canada, including incubators, creative service providers, experimental arts laboratories, community hubs, and co-working spaces. These sites can include bricks-and-mortar buildings or organizations distributed over wide geographic spaces, or membership-based and virtual operations, each featuring a multitude of forms of arts, media, and digital innovation, as I explore below.

To better understand how today's creative hubs developed, it is useful to look at two classic creative hubs that brought professional artists together in a building and subsequently into a network of other creative workers, alongside customers, viewers, or users. Almost 40 years after Bristol's Watershed convened key stakeholders to raise money to renovate a series of unused harbourfront spaces (a process known as making a building refit for purpose), the notion of co-location and co-working creative hubs has powerfully taken hold globally. This includes refit-for-purpose urban development commitments to revitalize moribund heritage or industrial sites and attract people to a part of a city that has fallen into disuse. Founded in 1982, Watershed is one of the key international models for creative hubs and related partners and activities, not just in Bristol but worldwide. It currently encompasses the Pervasive Media Studio—where experimental and interactive media are developed and produced—a cinema, shops, a café, and social enterprise start-up supports inside a non-profit structure. In its wake, as an anchor organization along the revitalized waterfront, multiple businesses, restaurants, and cultural tourism sites have come to exist. The comparable groundbreaker in Canada is Toronto's Artscape, founded in 1986 (https://www.artscape.ca/). Artscape is a non-profit umbrella organization with a number of social enterprises contained within it. Artscape's creative hubs house arts and culture organizations, artists, and artist-led families in a variety of neighbourhoods, with different facilities designed to address the needs of the local communities. Some buildings highlight creative placemaking with designed spaces. Others feature a curated group of tenants, providing affordable workspaces to arts organizations and artists as well as live-work spaces to individual creatives. The most recently launched Artscape creative hub, Daniels Launchpad, is its only member-operated business incubation site, with a variety of professionalizing programs, spaces, and services for its members. Together, Artscape's system of creative hubs is well positioned to be a leader in knowledge sharing for creative hubs in Canada. They do this through their DIY website (https://www.artscapediy.org/) and a collaborative initiative for creative workers, Artsunite.ca. The Artscape model has proliferated across the country, including at BC Artscape, with its focus on affordable housing for artists and financially accessible programs for the local community. Although many of the individual Artscape operations can be described as *classic* or *traditional* creative hubs in their own right (some of which were groundbreaking when founded), it is also a network of creative hub *buildings* as well as a network of *creative workers*. Additionally, Artscape's alumni are a network of *leaders* for the creative hubs system across Canada because Artscape was the first to achieve the scale and variety it now helps nurture in the ecosystem. Similarly, the Centre for Social Innovation is now a classic co-working space and was one of the first in North America. Co-working spaces rent offices and studios out to creative workers on sliding scales of size, cost, and time commitments (e.g., one desk for three months; a studio shared with other artists). Both Artscape and CSI act as models for newer but still traditional co-working and arts presentations spaces such as cSPACE in Calgary and the emergent Culture Link CIC in Halifax.

CREATIVE CITIZENSHIP AS A FOUNDATION FOR INCLUSION IN CREATIVE HUBS

While the early creative hubs for arts, culture, and media focused on reclaiming historical spaces and on the gentrification of derelict or underutilized neighbourhoods, more recent types of creative hubs have moved toward a broader mandate of social inclusion and community dynamism. To examine whether and how inclusion is defined by various hubs, I use the key concept of *creative citizenship*. There are four intersecting elements woven together in creative citizenship as I have previously developed it (Luka, "Towards Creative Citizenship," *A(rtSpots) to ZeD*). Conceptually, the idea draws on cultural citizenship, convergence culture, and nation-state policy directives, which I discuss below. Practically speaking, the four core factors for creative citizenship are (1) stakeholders and participants who embody a set of narrowcast audiences develop shared objectives together, (2) to cultivate a series of networked and sometimes innovative creative production practices (*creation*), and (3) to find new, often collaborative, ways to share content and knowledge (*distribution*) that (4) are inclusive and thereby reflect embedded and explicit policy commitments to equity and diversity. By narrowcast audiences, I am referring to groups of people who share values, interests, and/or types of jobs, and they also often share demographic characteristics (Bazalgette). Narrowcast audience examples include Canadian curators, Black creative workers, or regional public media producers.

Creative citizenship also updates the notion of cultural citizenship (originally explored in Andrew et al.), which emphasizes the production of nation-state identity through cultural practices and outcomes. Reconceptualizing cultural citizenship is important, because over the last decade, the notion has become a normative, somewhat blurred expression in Canada and elsewhere to describe often passive nation-state cultural heritage and production protections. (See Ryan Phillips' chapter in this collection for a complementary critique of cultural citizenship in the context of hockey.) Catherine Murray's essay in the 2005 anthology *Accounting for Culture* mobilized the concept of cultural citizenship to analyze the evolution of cultural diversity and inclusion in media in Canada, the United States, and Australia (among other countries). Murray pointed to important ways in which ideas about pluralism and cultural diversity (or the lack thereof) are promoted in government policy statements, often in relation to economic goals, but are not necessarily realized in everyday actions and practices. In contrast, creative citizenship operates more locally and precisely. It is active rather than passive. Creative citizenship asks individuals and groups or communities with complex identity affiliations to create and network together original works of their own cultural expression, including circulating them in inventive ways, rather than using them as ways to protect nation-state, genre-specific, or traditional understandings of historical or pre-existing cultural artifacts and ephemera. Creative citizenship also connects analyses of precarious labour within the culture sector and media industries to the examination of innovation and social inequities, including as both relate to cultural policy. Creative citizenship thereby provides an approach to examine today's creative economy beyond its economic drivers. Creative citizenship shares the idea of building audiences or community collaboratively with aspects of commercially driven convergence culture (where viewers and users are also producers and creators; see Jenkins) and of the creative economy. But the concept of creative citizenship is also intended to find practical ways to understand specific efforts toward inclusion as a lever for social change in the creative sector, in more activated ways than cultural citizenship did.

A pertinent example of how creative citizenship aims to find practical, everyday ways, grounded in local communities and groups, to support equitable and quite divergent practices of production and distribution in creative hubs is NaAC. This is an organization with a 45-year history of serving artists with developmental disabilities in Calgary, Alberta. NaAC has proposed to bring together a networked group of sister organizations to be amalgamated under its banner for the purposes of developing a national creative hub for *social change* (personal communication). Currently, NaAC offers its artists a wheelchair accessible lounge, a kiln room, a fibre studio, 2D and 3D capabilities, as well as digital photography suites. Their programming is flexible except for some thematic workshops, and their operating model is on a fee-for-service basis. NaAC envisions a fully accessible building that will serve at least three hundred artists a week (and the potential to double that number), as well as 150 support workers, 50 volunteers, and 20 staff members, along with a virtual and distributed system of programs and services. Design plans for the building include a digital and visual media centre, a fully accessible black box theatre, and rehearsal spaces, as well as a social enterprise space that will include a craft shop, a gallery, and a community-based café that would employ disabled people. The NaAC will also provide an artist residency suite that will host disabled artists from across the country for approximately three weeks at a time. In addition, NaAC plans to coordinate and support similar activities at sites across the country. The idea for this type of creative hub (a building in Calgary plus distributed, offsite services) emerged out of accessArts' conversations with sister organizations looking to form a partnership that embodies accessibility, especially from a disability perspective. Through this cross-country programming, the organizations involved will realize their dual mandates as social service *and* arts organizations, including providing artists with the tools for self-advocacy.

Similarly, at the international level, much larger networks committed to social change are operated through Ideo.org (globally) and URBACT (in Europe). These social change creative hubs emerged from efforts by organizations, policymakers, and creative workers to activate shared values through policy and practices, including international agreements such as the UNESCO Convention on the Protection and Promotion of the Diversity of Cultural Expressions (De Beukelaer et al., Luka, "Towards Creative Citizenship"). *Social changers* are committed to the triple bottom line (TBL), including the realization of social vision, mission, and values, not just to providing co-working spaces or services to a single local creative worker community, as at Artscape or CSI. The basic idea behind the TBL is to incorporate sociocultural, economic, and environmental measures to assess success (Elkington; Hawkes). Social change–oriented creative hubs and networks concentrate proactively on the production of meaning and social cohesion on the ground, including the tensions embedded in these relationships. URBACT is a socially aware, cultural, and sustainable urban development initiative supported by the European Union and other countries, while Ideo.org is the non-profit arm of the global design company Ideo, which builds public-private-third sector partnerships to design solutions to global problems.

THE WORK THAT HAPPENS AT CANADA'S CREATIVE HUBS

To more critically examine creative hubs, especially in terms of their everyday practices, it is important to consider the much-documented *precarious nature of creative work*, including evaluating how this is ameliorated at specific creative hubs. The promise of arts and media creative hubs is that they are physical, virtual, and distributed sites where professional practice in the creative fields can come together, providing a sense of community and stability. Creative hubs enable creative workers to share skills and networks, develop and discuss innovative approaches, and invite users, clients, and citizens to pursue their own creative goals. In the "gig economy," creative workers and artists assemble short-term contracts, volunteer promotional "opportunities," micro-enterprises (e.g., Etsy), and commissions that often result in low or no-pay career trajectories incorporating both material and emotional labour (Wallace). Conversely, creative hubs hold the promise of ameliorating the isolation of gig-based "freedom" through sharing collective resources, space, and, in some cases, group health benefits, which precarious workers may not otherwise access.

Unpacking a nuanced understanding of the precarious structuring of creative work complicates matters in an important way. Scholarly and industry research provides extensive evidence of the precarity of creative work in the arts and media sectors, including its lack of inclusivity or fair pay. For example, Hill Strategies Research has been analyzing Statistics Canada data for several years on behalf of various cultural agencies, including the Canada Council for the Arts and provincial/territorial arts councils (see "A Statistical Profile," "Mapping Artists," "Arts and Culture"). Their findings confirm the precarity of the Canadian artist and creative worker's existence. In the early 2000s, the centrality of the urban creative worker as an economic engine for the Western world was just beginning to show its new shape in analyses of the loose collection of cultural industries that would purportedly employ individuals in a rewarding and fulsome future of creativity (see Florida). While creative economy analyses are, by definition, primarily driven by the economics of culture (Throsby) rather than a triple bottom line (Elkington; Hawkes) or the actions of individual artists, studies consistently showed that the value realized in the sector is at the cost of the creative labourers who drive it (e.g., Hermus et al.; Burgess and De Rosa; ARCA and IMAA; Jeannotte and Pineau; Wallace).

This is important because creative economy analyses often subsume non-economic considerations relevant to artistic/creative, social/physical, and knowledge-sharing, or sense-making analyses of equivalent value, even while dismissing or ignoring the precarity of creative workers. For example, valuing the aesthetics of creative work might include assessing the ability of a creative worker or company to design compelling logos or an original way to use 3D imagery. A social/physical analysis might assess the accessibility of a space by asking the following questions: Is it quiet? Are there ramps as well as stairs? A sense-making analysis might involve understanding that a creative hub provides social services such as free meals as well as co-working spaces for inexpensive rent for traditionally underpaid artists. This combination of considerations will complicate an economic analysis, which then might consider how well creative workers are being paid as well as how many tickets are sold for a performance. In Canada, understanding that economic measures are not the only measure of success has led to recognizing the systemic inequalities of the job market for specific demographic groups (e.g., when women make 75 percent of what men do for the same job) or in terms of role models or access to opportunities. Scholars such as Mirjam Gollmitzer and Catherine Murray have analyzed artist income against gender and the need to have many part-time jobs to make a living. Bateman and Karim have analyzed ongoing rates and forms of racial inequality. *Women in View* reports from 2012 through 2019 enumerate ongoing gender inequities in the Canadian broadcast system, including for racialized groups. Although some economic information is generated by Statistics Canada's Cultural Satellite Account, that information does not include detailed data breakdowns such as gender, ethnicity, or part-time, piecework, or full-time data. In fact, the lack of detailed current information is so dire that the annual analysis provided by Hill Strategies Research and a sponsoring consortium that includes the Canada Council for the Arts, among others, was suspended due to lack of available data (Hill Strategies Research, "Lack of Data"). There has been even less information sharing in the last decade about how to best generate relationships between artists and creative workers involved in creative hubs with their specific communities, cultures, and subcultures, which is one of the reasons the CHNMI database and others like it are so useful to these groups. (See also https://aso-map.massculture.ca/, a mapping of the self-defined arts service organizations in Canada.)

To help find strategies to address precarious forms of creative labour and programming (Alacovska and Gill), it is useful to consider how funders and creative hubs know when they have been successful. For this, I turn to the idea of using *sustainable*, *relevant*, and *responsive impact measures*, including self-generated and external measures of success. Both pragmatic and analytical, this "logic-model" approach (Herranz) brings together triple bottom line analysis with individual creative (artist or creative worker) and structural impact measures (e.g., business models, mission/visions) to focus on a broad collection of flexible goals and objectives. It also activates the concept of creative citizenship by assuming that self-assessment and wholistic evaluation processes are crucial to understanding success on its own terms at specific creative hubs. Assessments of activities, programs, services, and structures include looking at relationship and community building (whether with professionals or with broader publics) as well as how to achieve more equitable working and living conditions for artists and creative workers. In a recently completed research with Jacqueline Wallace, Helen Yung, Katy Ilona Harris, Claudia Sicondolfo, and Hillary Walker for the Department of Canadian Heritage, we took a wholistic approach to researching 195 studies on impact assessment literature and frameworks. Wallace, Yung, and I identified a wide spectrum of potential measures, some of which are reproduced in this chapter's Appendix. We developed a streamlined logic model (see Figure 7.1, below) to incorporate four key types of measures: artistic and creative; business and economic; social and physical (access, inclusion); and knowledge sharing and sense-making. During the same period, I worked with digital librarians Kirsta Stapelfeld, David Kwasny, and Paulina Rousseau and with graduate students Samarth Singhania and Rachel Barber-Pin to organize the CHNMI, the database of creative hubs that Jacqueline Wallace

Figure 7.1: Schematic of Key Impact Measures for Creative Hubs

Luka et al.: Luka, *Creative Hubs in Canada.*

and I first developed in 2018 and that has since been augmented and validated with other research by Nordicity and Déziel and Duchesneau.

For creative hubs, impact measures that can show how to build and maintain a physical environment that encourages cross-pollination, comfortable working conditions, and a compatible surrounding area are important. For example, are supportive services, potential audiences, or collaborators nearby (Daldanese and Cerreta; Esmaeilpoorarabi et al., "Urban Quality Framework," "Enhanced Community Engagement," and "Innovation Districts")? To actively design an organizational culture in creative hubs that is collaborative (Whitham et al.), it is important to look for impact measures that show how, when, and why people assemble to work, talk, and create together (online or otherwise). So, for example, while some creative hubs (such as NaAC, Artscape, or URBACT, described above) feature networks under one roof (whether physical, virtual, or distributed) and some feature multiple international partnerships or collaborations, others (such as Art Hives in Montreal) connect multi-sited, community-run arts studios for people to visit, make art, share skills, and talk in hands-on ways.

Many other exemplars of *knowledge-sharing and sense-making* creative hubs exist, including the Tett Centre in Kingston, Ontario; maker spaces in libraries, community centres, and universities; and community-specific operations such as Wonder'neath in Halifax, Nova Scotia. Knowledge-sharing and sense-making social changers exist in an open system that can respond to highly localized conditions. The community-centred approach and commitment to art-making as a vehicle for civic engagement often means that these sites operate as safe spaces for inclusive community dialogue. For example, the Tett Centre is a multidisciplinary arts hub owned by the City of Kingston that first opened its doors in January of 2015 (personal communication), while Wonder'neath opened in 2010 (see below). Like classic creative hubs such as Artscape or CSI, revenue is generated from renting studio space to artist tenants, but the Tett Centre and Wonder'neath also rent or lend out equipment and event spaces for community groups, along with offering summer camps and open houses and other one-off events throughout the year. Additional programming is offered by artist tenants at the Tett, some commissioned by and some simply supported by the Tett website and promotional strategies. The Tett creates partnerships with other organizations—such as offering their gallery space to marginalized groups—and employs a small organizing staff with a tenant committee and a community engagement committee under the direction of a volunteer board of directors. The building itself is fully accessible, while free programming is available in addition to paid programming, ensuring that there is a spectrum of offerings in a safe, welcoming community space.

Similarly, Wonder'neath Studio in Halifax, founded in 2010 as an ad hoc shared studio space, developed into a non-profit organization in 2014 and a charitable organization in 2018.[1] Wonder'neath introduced an open studio initiative in 2014, which provided artist expertise, art supplies, and a community drop-in space to create work, including a rapid conversion to curbside pickup kits to comply with Covid-19 regulations in March 2020 (personal communications). As of March 6, 2020, Wonder'neath workshops, guest artists, and all-ages creative work sessions had seen 16,770 people come through the doors, and they had offered more than three thousand home art kits between mid-March and July 2020 (the first few months of the Covid-19 global pandemic). Wonder'neath is led collaboratively by Melissa Marr and Heather Wilkinson with the assistance of 10 artist facilitators. The studio's thoughtful approach to cultural and community inclusion includes Art Bikers—comprised of a diverse artist team founded on principles of deep caring—as well as an artist commission to advance and share knowledge about formal practice and several partnerships. For example, the open studio has partnered with the Mi'kmaw Native Friendship Centre, Mount Allison University, the Nova Scotia College of Art and Design, the Halifax Animation Festival, and the Charlottetown-based artist-run centre called this town is small. Wonder'neath has presented programming and educational workshops, including with Visual Arts Nova Scotia, the Heart of the City national conference, and the international Art Hives gathering. One such partnership was a project called Field Trip in 2020, which explored the following question: "Who has access to the arts and how can arts organizations create welcoming spaces?" The project involved 15 sessions with six community organizations and 155 participants across multiple generations and segments of the various communities with which Wonder'neath regularly becomes involved. Using creative methodologies, the experiential and inclusive research conducted by Wonder'neath feeds an ongoing relationship with the Veith Street Gallery Association, Mulgrave Park, and the North End Community Care Circle, organizations that serve marginalized groups and communities. For example, Wonder'neath and its partners created an Art Hive experience with the Halifax Down Syndrome Society, building relationships among artists who have Down syndrome and the broader creative community.

CREATIVE CITIZENSHIP AND THE CORE BUSINESS OF CREATIVE HUBS

The logic model presented in Figure 7.1 for measuring success—or impact—is clearly not intended to be linear. Instead, all four sets of measures are meant to be used simultaneously. However, by starting with the cultural, artistic, and creative assessment measures, creative hubs are thereby always evaluated through the lens of their core creative work and the challenges of aiming to describe, use, and analyze intrinsic and extrinsic creative measures (Dovey et al.; UNESCO). In no particular order, an evaluation process might consider business models and economic factors in service to core creative functions and goals. Similarly, knowledge sharing and sense-making measures could be used to illustrate how important and revealing self-assessment is in evaluation in combination with artistic and creative outputs. Completing the analysis by using equity-driven social and physical design measures ensures that broad social, civically engaged, and cross-sectoral considerations are being used to assess success, not just how much money came in the door or how much artwork went out.

The logic model also works as an expression of creative citizenship. The four groups of flexible and responsive assessment measures enable the identification of creative stakeholders and participants who hold shared objectives, often articulated as creative and artistic outcomes. These participants cultivate a series of viable and sometimes innovative creative production practices (blending business/economic measures with creative/artistic impact measures). Participants also find new, often collaborative, ways to share content and knowledge (knowledge sharing and sense-making combined with business/economic and creative/artistic measures). In the full expression of creative citizenship, the aforementioned activities reflect embedded and explicit policy commitments to equity and diversity (which can also be assessed using social/physical measures, often in combination with but not in service to business/economic measures). This approach de-emphasizes the priority traditionally given to economic and business considerations, in contrast to the definition of creative hubs at the Department of Canadian Heritage. Using the concept of creative citizenship to build the more encompassing logic model presented in this chapter also enables acknowledgement of marginalized or traditionally excluded organizations that rely on prioritizing equity, access, artistic/creative considerations, or sense-making endeavours rather than on turning a profit or being cost effective, to the detriment of other measures. Examples of equity-seeking or traditionally excluded groups served by creative hubs include NaAC or remote or distributed operations such as in Flin Flon, Lunenburg, or Qaggiavuut, or two newer outlier organizations, examined below: UKAI and Skwachàys.

UKAI Projects and its Ferment incubator aim to explore what artists need to sustain themselves in the contemporary, more distributed arts ecology.

By distributed I mean organizations that are not physically located in the same buildings but prefer a looser affiliation or process for bringing their collective work together. Additionally, some forms of equity-focused distributed organizations, such as UKAI, strongly deprioritize economic measures of success. UKAI subverts the typical transactional arts model with one that is centred on generosity and reciprocity; these are values that can be made legible in the more comprehensive logic model in Figure 7.1. This distributed and primarily virtual organization was developed and founded by Gerrold McGrath to address gaps in the ecosystem based on experience working as a program director for the Banff Centre in Alberta as well as Artscape Launchpad in Toronto. The UKAI creative hub is also a producing partner with organizations that lack the infrastructure to confidently solicit funds or deliver on the strategic priorities of government and private funders. Examples of projects include video storytelling for clients, helping for-profit firms develop core business models and investments that benefit communities, and digital prototyping for non-Western culturally specific music practices. A major difference between UKAI/Ferment and a traditional creative hub model as defined by the Department of Canadian Heritage is the prioritization of the human values of compassion and love in their processes. There is a strong focus on enriching connections among all actors rather than producing specific outcomes.

Similarly, Skwachàys is an Indigenous-run boutique art hotel and artist residency for Indigenous artists. Skwachàys was designed to incorporate the principles of the healing lodge model, which supports members of Indigenous communities who come to larger urban centres for medical purposes. Affordable housing and community care for Indigenous people, whether for health, social, or cultural reasons, are core to the operation. The hotel comprises three floors of boutique hotel rooms, three floors that follow the healing lodge model, and three floors of residential suites for Indigenous artists that connect to a ground floor art gallery showcasing their work. There is an artist workshop in the basement. Artists-in-residence tend to stay between six months and three years. The artist residency program has included people who became mainstream television and Hollywood film actors as well as lesser-known creative luminaries. First opened in June of 2012, the current iteration has been in operation since August 2014. The first of its kind in Canada, the operation has received international recognition, including coverage by Condé Nast in New York, the Canadian Broadcasting Corporation, and CTV/Bell Media in Canada, a Korean broadcasting company, and was named one of the one hundred greatest hotels in the world by *Time* magazine in 2018.

CONCLUSION: HOW WE DEFINE OURSELVES IS HOW WE SUSTAIN OURSELVES

Two critical conclusions about creative industries have emerged from my investigation of creative hubs. One is an overdependence on using business models and economic factors as primary indicators of the viability or success of a creative hub. This holds as true for a linked creative network distributed across a broad geographical area as for a traditional creative hub found in one building. The second is the connected and leveraged way in which government departments or agencies use definitions that—inadvertently or otherwise—exclude hubs of activity that may not be located in a specific building. As I have shown in this chapter, such definitions reject more equity-focused or distributed operations, less populated regions or marginalized groups, and virtual creative hubs. The Department of Canadian Heritage definition examined in this chapter determines funding for national, substantial, or emergent creative hubs by requiring "bricks and mortar" to be in the mix. The definition ignores or downplays other important core commitments to creative work, social and physical factors, or knowledge sharing, demonstrated by different kinds of creative hubs in the arts and culture sector. In particular, creative/artistic and social/physical accessibility goals are downplayed. This is made more complicated by the challenges of measuring ambiguous, individualized, or community-focused intrinsic impacts. Similarly, impacts that require generations to realize or are highly interlocked with other variables and factors tend to be ignored, including ways to measure the social or long-term impacts that are a common function of cultural and artistic endeavours.

At the individual level, the emphasis on having to pay for physical studio, office, or live-work spaces (whether as co-tenants or co-owners), combined with the precarious gig economy, ensures that artists (hard-pressed to generate cash for space rental or ownership) cannot fully participate in creative hubs or the creative economy. In the creative hub environment, and even in hubs that claim to look at a broad spectrum of considerations, my research shows that success tends to be narrowed down to financial, physical, or output-oriented measures, such as the commercializability of programs and services rather than on social, cultural, or knowledge-sharing considerations. Commercial practices include not sharing market-based or other knowledge, emphasizing competition rather than collaboration, and discounting self-generated forms of impact assessment such as sense-making. This emphasis reinforces elements of the for-profit system as the dominant model even in arts and culture, with its much longer history of community-centred, social, and aesthetic outcomes. Understanding and encouraging complex measures of "success" in the policy framework that structures this rapidly evolving ecosystem is therefore of deep importance, not just because the growing creative economy already represents 2.7 percent of Canada's GDP and 3.5 percent of jobs (Statistics Canada) but also to become more inclusive and rounded. We also know that the sector—and community-building activities such as those that take place at creative hubs—generates positive sociocultural impacts such as better health and social cohesion while simultaneously developing production and distribution systems for the creative economy, remaking profoundly varied communities, identities, and culture (Ashley; Cunningham; Luka, *Scratching the Surface*). Consequently, by using evaluation measures and funding protocols that prioritize a balanced mix of artistic/creative, social/physical, knowledge sharing and sense-making as well as business/economic measures, the creative industries and culture sector can become more inclusive in pragmatic ways for populations that have previously been marginalized or systemically discriminated against, including, for example, racialized groups, working class artists, or rural or isolated communities.

CORE CONCEPTS

creative citizenship: Creative citizenship (Luka, *A(rtSpots) to ZeD*; "Towards Creative Citizenship") involves (1) stakeholders and participants who embody a set of narrowcast audiences to develop shared objectives together, (2) to cultivate a series of networked and sometimes innovative creative production practices (creation), and (3) to find new, often collaborative, ways to share content and knowledge (distribution) that (4) are inclusive and thereby reflect embedded and explicit policy commitments to equity and diversity.

impact measures: Flexible impact measures for organizational activities in the creative industries (the work undertaken by creative hubs, for example) incorporate four broad categories of assessment: aesthetic/artistic and cultural; business and economic; social and physical; and knowledge sharing and sense-making elements.

triple bottom line: A term coined by John Elkington to draw attention to the social, environmental, and economic costs of capitalism. Rather than simply focusing on profit models, the TBL asks us to consider a more wholistic approach to the impact of business activity. This is made more complex by Hawkes and others' assertion that the idea of *social* includes the cultural and civic impacts of the culture sector and creative industries.

SUGGESTED ACTIVITIES

1. Find a creative hub in your area and identify the core values and principles of how they operate. For example, collect information on organizational mission and vision; primary users and audiences or communities engaged; location(s) and programming or membership scope; and knowledge-sharing initiatives. Do they have virtual operations? What is the geographic scope of their activity? What is the governance or management model used by the organization? Do they have partners or community collaborators?

2. Document the kinds of professional work that take place in two different creative hubs (compare and contrast). Find one that uses a primarily for-profit model and another that uses a social equity model. Which one employs or houses more artists and creative workers? Which kinds of creative roles are directly or indirectly supported? In what ways? What are the professionalization activities that take place in these creative hubs? How often? In what ways does their marketing and social media activity support these programs, services, and spaces?

3. Using the four categories of impact indicators enumerated in the appendix (artistic/cultural; business/economic; knowledge sharing/sense-making; social/physical), examine the business, creative, and operational models used to support community activity and creative workers at one or more creative hubs in your community or field.

NOTE

1. Wonder'neath has periodically partnered with Narratives in Space + Time Society, the collaborative artistic organization that I co-founded.

APPENDIX: EXAMPLES OF IMPACT MEASURES FOR CREATIVE HUBS

The examples of impact measures presented in the table below are based on a synthesis of 195 studies on impact measurement related to the creative industries and culture sector (Luka et al.). There are many more specific examples that could be developed under each type of overarching impact measure.

Type	Examples of potential measures of assessment
Cultural, artistic, and creative measures	• Dedicate resources to the development of entrepreneurship and professionalizing networks and practices in the cultural sector. • Practice leadership, facilitation, and inclusive skills development. • Construct or make available conditions for new opportunities to a broader spectrum of artists, creative workers, and community members. • Develop a rich cultural life for/with the local community. • Build community through appealing and/or inclusive programming. • Actively pursue cross-industry awareness, support, and, ultimately, collaboration to build community over the long term. • Participate in and produce public debates, discussions, and civic engagement opportunities. • Encourage a collaborative and accommodating organizational culture (communities of practice). • Operate collectively: work on joint projects; share information; share skills; participate in dynamic genre and operational discussions. • Understand that urbanity or proximity is not the only (or even the most crucial, though clearly helpful in some cases) component of building communities of practice (see also physical indicators).
Economic and business measures	• Basic start-up / entrepreneurship financial management metrics. • Classic and wholistic non-profit management, accountability, and leadership measures. • Economically viable live-work spaces for creative workers. • Collaborative, networked multi-tenant hubs that also address social issues. • Robust digital community, including open-source elements. • Sustainable arts-based accelerators and incubators.
Knowledge sharing and sense-making measures	• Knowledge sharing: information gathering; peer-exchanges; ecology growing. • Sense-making: narratives of start-up or experimental ingenuity or creative entrepreneurship combined with arts, culture, and creative practices. • Sense-making: understanding audiences or personas, users and non-users for marketing and identity purposes.

Type	Examples of potential measures of assessment
Social and physical measures	• Accessibility (physical, material, sensory, linguistic).
	• Basic proportional inclusion (representation) of societal groups.
	• Third spaces as co-work and creative hubs and the impact of collaborative labour.
	• Community and cross-sector measures.
	• Geographic-economic impact of maker, hacker, Fablabs, accelerators as co-creation spaces.
	• Urban renewal, revitalization, and vibrancy.
	• Innovation of urban governance and collaborative planning.

REFERENCES

AHRC. *Creative Exchanges: The AHRC Knowledge Exchange Hubs for the Creative Economy Report*, 2017, https://ahrc.ukri.org/documents/project-reports-and-reviews/creative-exchanges-ke-hubs. Accessed 1 March 2017.

Alacovska, Ana, and Rosalind Gill. "De-Westernizing Creative Labour Studies: The Informality of Creative Work from an Ex-Centric Perspective." *International Journal of Cultural Studies*, vol. 22, no. 2, 2019, pp. 195–212.

Andrew, Caroline, Monica Gattinger, M. Sharon Jeannotte, and Will Straw, eds. *Accounting for Culture: Thinking Through Cultural Citizenship*. University of Ottawa Press, 2005.

Artist-Run Centres and Collectives Conference [ARCA] and Independent Media Arts Alliance [IMAA]. *Employment Standards in Artist-Run Centres and Independent Media Arts Centres*, 2010.

Ashley, Susan, ed. *Diverse Spaces: Examining Identity, Heritage and Community within Canadian Public Culture*. Cambridge Scholars Publishing, 2013.

Bateman, Katherine, and Karim Karim. "Canadian Legislation, Regulations, and Guidelines on the Representation of Diversity." *Canadian Journal of Communication*, vol. 34, no. 4, 2009, pp. 741–748.

Bazalgette, Peter. "Public Service Narrowcasting." *Prospect Magazine*, 28 February 2009.

Burgess, Marilyn, and Maria De Rosa. *Recommended Employment Standards and Human Resource Management Tools in Canadian Artist-Run Media Arts Organizations*, 15 November 2009, IMAA.

Crossick, Geoffrey, and Patrycja Kaszynska. "The Social Impact of Cultural Districts." *Global Cultural Districts Network* (GCDN), 2019, https://gcdn.net/product/the-social-impact-of-cultural-districts/. Accessed 17 September 2019.

Cunningham, Stuart. *Hidden Innovation: Policy, Industry and the Creative Sector*. Queensland University Press, 2013.

Daldanese, Gaia, and Maria Cerreta. "PLUS Hub: A Cultural Process for Pisticci Regeneration." *BDC: Universita degli Studi di Napoli Federico II*, vol. 18, no. 1, 2018, pp. 127–145.

De Beukelaer, Christiaan, Miikka Pyykkönen, and J. P. Singh. *Globalization, Culture, and Development: The UNESCO Convention on Cultural Diversity*. Palgrave Macmillan, 2015.

Dempwolf, C. Scott, Jennifer Auer, Michelle D'Ippolito, and College Park. *Innovation Accelerators: Defining Characteristics Among Startup Assistance Organizations*, November 2014. DOI: 10.13140/RG.2.2.36244.09602.

Department of Canadian Heritage. Canada Cultural Spaces Fund Application Guidelines, "Glossary." Government of Canada, https://www.canada.ca/en/canadian-heritage/services/funding/cultural-spaces-fund/application-guidelines.html. Updated 4 October 2018. Accessed 20 January 2020.

Déziel, Marie-Odile, and Guillaume Duchesneau. *Exploring the Phenomenon of Creative Hubs*. Telefilm Canada, 2019.

Dovey, Jon, Andy C. Pratt, S. Moreton, Tarek E. Virani, J. Merkel, and J. Lansdowne. *The Creative Hubs Report*. British Council, 2016.

Elkington, John. "25 Years Ago I Coined the Phrase 'Triple Bottom Line.' Here's Why It's Time to Rethink It." *Harvard Business Review*, 25 June 2018.

Esmaeilpoorarabi, N., T. Yigitcanlar, and M. Guaralda. "Towards an Urban Quality Framework: Determining Critical Measures for Different Geographical Scales to Attract and Retain Talent in Cities." *International Journal of Knowledge-Based Development*, vol. 7, no. 3, 2016, pp. 290–312.

Esmaeilpoorarabi, N., T. Yigitcanlar, M. Kamruzzaman, and M. Guaralda. "How Can an Enhanced Community Engagement with Innovation Districts Be Established? Evidence from Sydney, Melbourne and Brisbane." *Cities*, vol. 96, 2020.

———. "How Does the Public Engage with Innovation Districts? Societal Impact Assessment of Australian Innovation Districts." *Sustainable Cities and Society*, vol. 52, 2020.

Essig, Linda. "Value Creation by and Evaluation in Arts Incubators." *International Journal of Arts Management*, vol. 20, no. 1, 2018, pp. 32–45.

Florida, Richard. *The Rise of the Creative Class and How It's Transforming Work, Leisure, Community and Everyday Life*. Basic Books, 2002.

Gollmitzer, Mirjam, and Catherine Murray. *From Economy to Ecology: A Policy Framework for Creative Labour*. Canadian Conference of the Arts and Simon Fraser University—Centre for Policy Studies in Culture and Communities, 2008, http://ccarts.ca/wp-content/uploads/2009/01/CREATIVEECONOMYentiredocument.pdf. Accessed 31 January 2020.

Hassan, Zahib. *The Social Labs Revolution: A New Approach to Solving Our Most Complex Challenges*. Berrett-Koehler Publishers, Inc, 2014.

Hawkes, Jon. *The Fourth Pillar of Sustainability: Culture's Essential Role in Public Planning*. Common Ground Publishing Pty, 2001.

Hermus, Greg, Joseph Haimowitz, David Redekop, and Tony Fisher, with assistance from Alison Howard (Campbell), P. Derek Hughes, and Douglas Watt, for the Cultural Human Resources Council. *Cultural HR Study 2010: Labour Market Information Report for Canada's Cultural Sector*. Conference Board of Canada, 2010.

Herranz, Joaquín. "The Logic Model as a Tool for Developing a Network Performance Measurement System." *Public Performance & Management Review*, vol. 34, no. 1, 2010, pp. 56–80.

Hill Strategies Research Inc. "Arts and Culture in Nova Scotia: Stats and Gaps for Arts Nova Scotia, Creative Nova Scotia Leadership Council and NS Department of Communities, Culture & Heritage" [PowerPoint presentation], 26 October 2012.

———. "A Statistical Profile of Artists in Canada." *Statistical Insights on the Arts*, vol. 3, no. 1, 2004, www.hillstrategies.com. Accessed 10 February 2020.

———. "Lack of Data Leads to Suspension of Statistical Insights into the Arts Series. 11 May 2016, http://www.hillstrategies.com/content/lack-data-leads-suspension-statistical-insights-arts-series. Accessed 10 February 2020.

———. "Mapping Artists and Cultural Workers in Canada's Largest Cities." 9 February 2010, www.hillstrategies.com.

Jeannotte, Sharon, and Alain Pineau, eds. *Flat-Lined but Still Alive: Analyses of the Provincial and Territorial Budgets from the Perspective of Arts, Culture and Heritage*. Canadian Conference of the Arts and Centre on Governance, University of Ottawa, February 2013.

Jenkins, Henry. *Convergence Culture: Where Old and New Media Collide*. New York University Press, 2006.

Luka, Mary Elizabeth. *A(rtSpots) to ZeD: 21st Century Arts Documentary Production*. Forthcoming.

———. *Creative Hubs in Canada: Knowledge Networks and Opportunities*. Department of Canadian Heritage, 2018.

———. *Scratching the Surface: Rethinking the Roots of Canadian Communication Policy*. CRTC, 2016.

———. "Towards Creative Citizenship: Collaborative Cultural Production at CBC ArtSpots (1997–2008)." Doctoral dissertation, Concordia University, 2014, https://spectrum.library.concordia.ca/979003/.

Luka, Mary Elizabeth, and Jacqueline Wallace, with Helen Yung, Katy Ilona Harris, Claudia Sicondolfo, and Hillary Walker. *Towards a Measurement Framework for Creative Hubs.* Department of Canadian Heritage, 2020.

Murray, Catherine. Cultural Participation: A Fuzzy Cultural Policy Paradigm. In *Accounting for Culture: Thinking Through Cultural Citizenship*, edited by Caroline Andrew, Monica Gattinger, M. Sharon Jeannotte, and Will Straw, University of Ottawa Press, 2005, pp. 32–54.

Nordicity. *Hubs and Business Skills Training for the Culture and Creative Sector—What's Working?* WorkInCulture, 2017.

Smith, Natasha. "An In-Depth Look at Nova Scotia's New Community Interest Companies. Miller-Thomson." *Social Impact Newsletter,* 6 July 2016.

Statistics Canada. "Cultural Satellite Account." *Provincial and Territorial Culture Indicators 2018*, https://www150.statcan.gc.ca/n1/daily-quotidien/201022/ dq201022a-eng.htm. Accessed 15 March 2020.

Throsby, David. *The Economics of Cultural Policy.* Cambridge University Press, 2010.

UNESCO. *Convention on the Protection and Promotion of the Diversity of Cultural Expressions.* United Nations, 2005, https://en.unesco.org/creativity/sites/creativity/ files/passeport-convention2005-web2.pdf. Accessed 28 August 2020.

Wallace, Jacqueline. "Handmade 2.0: Women, DIY Networks and the Cultural Economy of Craft." PhD dissertation, Concordia University, 2014, https:// spectrum.library.concordia.ca/978912/.

Wallace, Jacqueline, and Mary Elizabeth Luka. *Creative Hubs Inventory Report to the Department of Canadian Heritage.* Government of Canada, 2018.

Whitham, Roger, Simon Moreton, Simon Bowen, Chris Speed, and Abigail Durrant. "Understanding, Capturing and Assessing Value in Collaborative Design Research." *International Journal of CoCreation in Design and the Arts*, vol. 15, no. 1, 2019, pp. 1–7.

Women in View. *Women in View on TV*, 2012, http://womeninview.ca/reports/. Accessed 1 August 2020.

————. *Women in View on Screen*, 2015, http://womeninview.ca/reports/. Accessed 1 August 2020.

————. *Women in View on Screen*, 2017, http://womeninview.ca/reports/. Accessed 1 August 2020.

————. *Women in View on Screen*, 2019, http://womeninview.ca/reports/. Accessed 1 August 2020.

Yung, Helen. "Impact Evaluation for the Arts for the Kingston Arts Council." Laboratory of Artistic Intelligence, 2020.

————. *Generator and the RISER Project: Sector Developers for Independent Theatre in Toronto.* Toronto Arts Foundation with the support of the Metcalf Foundation and Toronto Arts Council, 2017.

PART III

PEDAGOGIES: TEACHING AND LEARNING
THROUGH THE CREATIVE INDUSTRIES

CHAPTER 8

Don Cherry's "You People" Rant: A Critical Race Approach to Understanding Corporate Nationalism, Audience Commodification, and Cultural Citizenship

Ryan J. Phillips

INTRODUCTION

In November 2019, *Hockey Night in Canada* (*HNIC*) commentator Don Cherry created a national controversy following remarks made in a Remembrance Day rant. The now infamous rant involved Cherry berating immigrants ("you people who come here … you love our way of life") for not wearing poppies—a popular symbol of Remembrance Day observance in Canada (Cherry). The racist and xenophobic implications of Cherry's comments—especially given the historical context of Remembrance Day—were widely criticized across Canada. While Cherry was no stranger to controversy (he has ranted about women, Europeans, and "commies" over the course of almost 40 years), his "You People" rant sparked a national backlash and popular calls to remove him from the program. Ultimately, Sportsnet (the private broadcast company owned by Rogers, which now also owns *HNIC*) fired Cherry several days after the incident—citing Cherry's unwillingness to apologize for his comments.

Cherry's rant was interpreted by many as being contrary to Canada's purported values of multiculturalism, diversity, and inclusion. His subsequent firing was then widely recognized as the appropriate response to intolerance and ignorance in a liberal democratic society. However, this popular narrative ignores the fact that Cherry had already been espousing intolerant views and using exclusionary rhetoric for decades on the Canadian Broadcasting Corporation (CBC) and Sportsnet. It is also important to note that Cherry was not fired for his "You People" rant—he was fired for not apologizing afterwards. In this chapter, I argue that the persistent normalization of Cherry's racist and xenophobic rhetoric on *HNIC* reveals a disconnect between Canada's purported values of diversity and inclusion and the actually existing public pedagogies of national identity. Ultimately, I argue that Cherry's tenure and the circumstances surrounding his eventual firing are more reflective of Canada's ongoing acceptance of corporate nationalism.

Cherry's career, his "You People" rant, and his eventual firing provide entry points to interrogate the ways in which things like national identity, race, market forces, and conceptions of citizenship become interconnected through Canada's creative industries. In this chapter, I use this interrogation to better understand how and why Don Cherry—and *HNIC* more generally—works to both (re)produce national symbols, values, and histories for audiences and (re)produce audiences as commodities for corporate advertisers. I apply a critical race lens to Cherry and hockey broadcasting in Canada as a way of exploring the concepts of audience commodities, corporate nationalism, and cultural citizenship. Finally, I also consider alternatives to the existing structures of hockey broadcasting in Canada by addressing the concept of civic audiences.

BACKGROUND ON DON CHERRY AND "COACH'S CORNER"

Cherry was born in Kingston, Ontario, in 1934. He played in various North American hockey leagues throughout the 1950s and 1960s and coached the Boston Bruins for several seasons in the 1970s. After coaching the Colorado Rockies for one season in 1979, Cherry moved into his broadcasting role as a commentator for *HNIC*. Though an unremarkable hockey player, Cherry embedded himself into the collective cultural consciousness of Canadian hockey throughout his decades of sports broadcasting. In 2004, Cherry was voted the 7th "Greatest Canadian" in the CBC's *Greatest Canadian* series—Tommy Douglas placed first (CBC, "And the Greatest Canadian").[1] Cherry was also the subject of the two-part, made-for-TV biopic *The Don Cherry Story* (2010; 2012), which starred *Letterkenny*'s Jared Keeso and *Less Than Kind*'s Tyler Johnston (as adult and teen Cherry, respectively). The biopic itself is cheesy, self-aggrandizing, and not particularly memorable as a media product—yet its existence is testament to Cherry's status as a Canadian state celebrity (Cormack and Cosgrave, "Theorising the State Celebrity").

"Coach's Corner" was added as a segment to the popular CBC show *HNIC* during the early 1980s.[2] During each segment, Cherry and his co-commentator (originally Dave Hodge, who was later replaced by Ron MacLean) would discuss the first period of the game, as well as other recent hockey news and highlights. "Coach's Corner" recreated the sort of dialectics that arise naturally in bars and living rooms (i.e., the spaces in which hockey games are typically watched) in order to explain the game to non-hockey players and fans, thereby attracting a larger audience. Since the beginnings of "Coach's Corner," Cherry served as the program's most popular commentator, effectively becoming synonymous with Canadian hockey broadcasting within only a few years. The "Coach's Corner" segment proved incredibly popular among traditional hockey fans and non-fans alike, and it lasted until Cherry's firing in 2019.

Cherry's tenure on "Coach's Corner" was marked by his inflammatory and exclusionary rhetoric, which often manifested as asides aimed at immigrants and racialized peoples. For example, Cherry has dismissed the seriousness of the genocidal war in the Balkans as "Lower Slobovia attacking Slimea" and criticized Canada's official multiculturalism on the grounds that it allowed Europeans to play in the NHL ("you love them here, with your multiculturalism") (as cited in Brean, para. 2–3). Cherry has also been openly hostile toward legitimate concerns of systemic racism in hockey and Canadian society. Regarding the harsh treatment of Ojibwa players Chris Simons and Ted Nolan in 2007, Cherry ranted that Indigenous players should "go out and get [their] own fair shake in life and work for it!" (as cited in Ho, para. 3). The flip side of Cherry's berating of immigrants and racialized peoples has been his persistent self-victimization of white English-speaking Canadians. In the late 1990s, for example, Cherry criticized government spending on the Alberta Francophone Games on the grounds that they excluded English players, complaining that "if you don't speak French, you're out!" (as cited in Denis and Dallaire 415). Denis and Dallaire argue that Cherry's vocal animosity toward non-white and non-English demographics is thus in line with other nativist sentiments in Canadian history, such as the anti-immigration platform of the Reform Party, Canadian Alliance, and (more recently) the People's Party.[3] Indeed, Allain argues that Cherry's racism and xenophobia are often implicitly presented through his valorization of white, working-class, English-speaking hockey players—particularly those from rural Ontario and the Prairies.

Despite these behaviours, Cherry served as the public face and voice of "Coach's Corner" since the segment's inception. His boisterous personality, folksy vernacular, and controversial statements quickly registered as synonymous with hockey broadcasting in the popular Canadian imaginary, and Cherry soon became a cultural icon. Many viewers tuned in to *HNIC* every week just to see Cherry's outlandish suits and listen to his colloquial rants about hockey, politics, or whatever other topic happened to fly into his mind (Young; Phillips). Indeed, Cherry became a Canadian cultural icon specifically because he was useful in (re)producing audiences as commodities for the CBC to sell to advertisers.

Despite his often controversial positions and talking points, Cherry was incredibly profitable for the CBC (and, later, Rogers Communications). But Cherry did more than just reproduce audiences—he also taught national cultural values and consumption habits to Canadians. In this sense, Cherry's role on "Coach's Corner" (especially in the wake of his "You People" rant) can be understood as a sort of racialization or perversion of what is sometimes called "cultural citizenship"—the idea that citizenship and community belonging are (at least in part) culturally dependent. In particular, Cherry's perversion of cultural citizenship regularly involved an equivocation of culture and racial identity that was allowed to persist in the interests of capital accumulation through audience commodification.

HOCKEY BROADCASTING THROUGH A CRITICAL RACE LENS

Critical race theory (CRT) offers an appropriate critical lens through which to interrogate and make sense of the implications of Cherry and his "You People" rant. CRT questions and critiques the historical, social, cultural, and economic relationships between race, racial identity, and power. Unlike traditional liberal approaches to race, however, which have historically emphasized rationality, individualism, and other Enlightenment values as means by which to address racism, CRT questions the fundamental bases upon which our existing institutions and social orders are premised (Delgado et al.). In other words, CRT examines the structures and institutions that (re)produce racism, rather than individual instances of explicit racism. In the Canadian context, for example, a critical race approach to the over-policing of Black and Indigenous people might emphasize the historical developments of policing as an institutional mechanism for oppressing and marginalizing groups or individuals (Chan and Chunn). Furthermore, CRT attunes to the ways in which racism has increasingly come to manifest in expressions of cultural differences rather than physical or biological differences (Cordeiro-Rodrigues). When asking questions about the relationships between citizenship and culture, then, we can likewise sensitize ourselves to the potential ways in which implicit (or even explicit) racial biases perpetuate themselves through creative industries and promotional intermediaries like Cherry.

An important dimension of CRT is that implicit or institutionalized forms of racism and bias are often perceived as normal. Because of this perceived normalcy, many regular manifestations of racism are made invisible in everyday life and therefore become difficult to address or cure (Tenenbaum and Ruck; Delgado et al.). As such, only blatant cases of racism tend to receive widespread attention or calls to action. For example, Cherry's rants about a foreign hockey coach whose name "sounds like dog food" or his criticism of foreign aid to Haiti following deadly hurricanes sparked controversy throughout Canada for their racist and xenophobic implications (as cited in Brean, para. 3). However, we also see invisibly normal racism at work on the part of CBC and Sportsnet—while Cherry has made explicitly racist and xenophobic remarks at various points throughout his career, broadcasters consistently refused to remove him from *HNIC*. Allowing Cherry to remain on the popular program despite a pattern of problematic behaviours presented his commentary to audiences as legitimate points of controversy rather than inherently problematic. The enabling of Cherry's racism and xenophobia on the part of broadcasters thus represents how even explicit instances of racism can be systemically normalized or made invisible to audiences.

In a pedagogical sense, the allowance of Cherry's exclusionary rhetoric serves (in effect) to teach a normalized racism to Canadian audiences in three ways. First, Cherry's comments were regularly broadcast to millions of *HNIC* viewers every Saturday night for 39 years, thus disseminating racism and xenophobia to a large national audience. Second, Cherry's cultural connection to hockey in the popular imaginary of Canadians served to metonymically convey a connection between hockey and racism. Cherry's connections to both hockey and racism thus implied a connection between hockey itself and racism. Finally, the perpetual reluctance of CBC and Sportsnet to reprimand Cherry for his racist behaviours conveyed to audiences that Cherry's rhetoric was normal (albeit controversial) rather than inherently problematic. Thus, Cherry acted as a state celebrity who taught audiences that Canadian identity, ice hockey, and casual racism were all culturally intertwined.

Cherry's perpetual normalization of racism also served a material purpose for broadcasters—at least until 2019. The idea that racism is useful for already dominant socioeconomic groups (and corporate interests in particular) is another core dimension of CRT. In Cherry's case, his normalized racism was part of an outlandish persona that proved useful for broadcasters in attracting and commodifying the attention of audiences. Advertisers also typically prioritize the attention and buying power of white audiences over racialized audiences (particularly during prime time programming hours), given that white audiences are perceived as being more wealthy and thus more likely to purchase advertised products and services (Gandy Jr.). This discrimination of audiences affects the programming decisions of broadcasters, whose goal is to maximize advertising revenue by attracting the most profitable audiences. Cherry's racism was therefore excused by broadcasters on the grounds that it served the material interests of corporate creative industries in Canada (Denis and Dallaire). Indeed, the insidiousness of Cherry's specific instances of racism can only be understood through a comprehensive understanding of the corporate media structures in place, which both perpetuate and benefit from the reproduction of normalized racism.

CORPORATE NATIONALISM

The ideal of public broadcasting is meant to embody a sense of cultural citizenship and belonging, yet the realities of Cherry's career (and the CBC more generally) have often drifted more into the realm of corporate nationalism. This is largely due to the CBC's status as a mixed-model public broadcaster, which requires a close (and often uncomfortable) relationship between the public institution and corporate interests. While Cherry's role on *HNIC* should have reflected and encouraged a sense of cultural citizenship among Canadian audiences, it ultimately represented a boisterous example of Canadian corporate nationalism that was characterized by consistent bouts of racist and xenophobic rhetoric.

Corporate nationalism is an insidious form of nationalism that exists at the nexus of consumer capitalism and national identity. It involves the appropriation of nationalism (including symbols, identities, and popular myths) in order to sell products and services, as well as the use of promotional or commercial strategies to sell (or teach) national identity to audiences (Weedon; Koch). Corporate nationalism is insidious because it involves exploiting peoples' deeply held senses of community and belonging in order to increase profits for companies that are largely disinterested in the well-being of a nation or its citizenry. Hudson's Bay Company, Tim Hortons, and Canadian Tire have all built their respective brands around the affective value of corporate nationalism—if a consumer is thinking about purchasing a new BBQ, blender, or basketball, then an ingrained sense of nationalism might prompt them to make the purchase at Canadian Tire (even if the price might be lower at Wal-Mart). Even large international companies like Coca-Cola and Apple will routinely imbue their Canadian ads with (sometimes stereotypical) nationalistic sentiments—which are almost always related to hockey in some way or other.

Corporate nationalism is meant to elicit emotional responses in audiences through appeals to patriotism, nostalgia, stereotypes, and/or popular myths in order to increase consumption and, therefore, profit for private companies. In many ways, corporate nationalism warps the concept of cultural citizenship by equating culture with national identity and equating citizens with consumers. But how have Don Cherry, "Coach's Corner," and *HNIC* contributed to the reproduction of corporate nationalism in Canada? Furthermore, how can we reimagine (and potentially restructure) these cultural institutions to better contribute to a common sense of cultural citizenship? To answer these questions, it is important to look closer at the historical development and contemporary state of hockey broadcasting in Canada.

Canadian philosopher John Ralston Saul differentiated between positive and negative iterations of nationalism in an increasingly globalized world. According to Saul's conceptualization, positive nationalism is similar to cultural citizenship—both recognize the existence and cultural significance of communities and strive to make those communities as inclusive, just, and democratic as possible. Because of nationalism's typical relationship to geopolitical space, positive nationalism can best be understood as a spatial dimension of cultural citizenship. On the other hand, negative nationalism is exclusionary, jingoistic, and xenophobic (Saul). Negative nationalism is the ideological force that allows for individuals to perceive their own nation as fundamentally superior to others. Importantly, negative nationalism is also uncritical and unreflective—it does not allow for critical self-reflection or the possibility that one's nation might have problems or ever be in the wrong. While positive nationalism is aspirational and democratic, negative nationalism is blindly authoritarian. Cherry thus represents a sort of negative nationalism that is closely tethered to corporate interests, capital accumulation, and racial traits.

Advertising and the Corporate History of Hockey Broadcasting in Canada

The history of hockey broadcasting in Canada has always been tethered to corporate nationalism. This phenomenon began with popular radio programs during the 1920s, wherein announcers (such as Foster Hewitt) would offer audiences a play-by-play of live games. In 1929, MacLaren Advertising purchased exclusive broadcasting rights for all Toronto Maple Leafs games—meaning that any corporate sponsors had to pay MacLaren Advertising in order to have ads appear during games. The history of hockey broadcasting in Canada is also closely tied to the history of the nation's public broadcasting institution—the CBC. The CBC was created in the 1930s, with *HNIC* quickly becoming its most popular radio program (Phillips). Unlike other public broadcasters (such as the BBC in the United Kingdom), the CBC is a mixed-model public broadcaster, meaning that it is partially funded (though not directly overseen or influenced) by the federal government and partially reliant on advertising revenue. In 1936, Imperial Oil became the primary advertising sponsor of *HNIC*, and by the end of the 1930s, the program's weekly audience had increased from one million to two million viewers—resulting in increased advertising revenue both for the CBC and MacLaren Advertising.

The widespread adoption of television during the postwar period continued to increase the *HNIC* audience and advertising revenue, with an audience of over 5.5 million viewers by the end of the 1960s. Cherry was added to *HNIC* in the early 1980s in order to attract greater audiences, which in turn meant greater advertising revenue for the CBC. In 1988, Molson replaced MacLaren Advertising as the rights holder for NHL hockey broadcasts in Canada, and the program was subsequently renamed *Molson's Hockey Night in Canada*. Molson forced the CBC to drastically change the format and aesthetic of the program in an attempt to increase audiences and, therefore, advertising revenue. However, audiences were not receptive to these changes and the corporate rebranding of *HNIC*, with viewership declining during the Molson years. In 2001, Molson ended its partnership with the CBC, leaving the public broadcaster in a state of relatively decentralized advertising partnerships with various smaller companies and organizations. Post-Molson, *HNIC* audiences and ratings began to grow once again.

By the mid-2000s, private media companies such as CTV-TSN began competing with the CBC for broadcast licensing rights to NHL games. This resulted in the CBC paying an astounding $600 million for a six-year contract in 2008—significantly more than had ever previously been spent on a bid for hockey broadcasting rights. In 2014, however, Rogers Communications outbid the CBC for NHL hockey broadcasting rights with a contract reportedly worth $5.2 billion—a bid against which the CBC could not possibly hope to compete. Since the Rogers takeover in 2014, viewership and ratings for *HNIC* have been declining, the CBC has had to fill hundreds of hours of Canadian content requirements with other programming, and access to NHL hockey broadcasts has become more limited and expensive for audiences—the subscription model now costs approximately $200 per year for access to regular season games. The point, however, is that while hockey broadcasting in Canada has always been tied to corporate interests to some degree, the Rogers takeover in 2014 represents the full privatization of a public and cultural institution.

The Rogers takeover of *HNIC* included the acquisition of "Coach's Corner," Cherry, and his audience. Given Cherry's effectiveness at producing audiences for advertisers, it is no surprise that Rogers opted to retain the commentator. Assuming ownership of "Coach's Corner" also meant that a private, for-profit company now owned a Canadian cultural institution and symbol of Canadian national identity. Indeed, the Rogers takeover of *HNIC* and "Coach's Corner" represents the most significant instance of media privatization in recent Canadian history. Cherry's firing by Sportsnet also demonstrates that private profit is always the ultimate driving force behind corporate nationalism. In the following section, I look at the political, economic, and cultural implications of Rogers amplifying the commodification of *HNIC* audiences.

THE (RE)PRODUCTION OF AUDIENCE COMMODITIES

The privatization of *HNIC* highlights the significant role of audiences in advertising-dependent media systems. Until the 1970s, communication scholars had been preoccupied with studying the ideological dimensions of advertising. As such, there existed a lot of scholarly work on the messages of advertising but almost no work on the economics of how ads work. In 1977, however, influential Canadian economist Dallas W. Smythe published an important paper in which he theorized how the economics of advertising work. Smythe's ("Blindspot") paper led to a long scholarly debate among economists, communication scholars, and industry professionals about the nature of advertising.[4]

The lay conception of advertising, as well as the language people tend to use in reference to advertising, is such that content creators sell ad space or time to advertisers. For example, a half-hour time slot of television programming might contain 22 minutes of content and 8 minutes of commercial time that companies can purchase in order to advertise their products or services. However, the actual economics of advertising are dependent on audiences. According to Smythe's ("Blindspot") *audience commodity theory*, audiences *are* (literally) the product being produced and sold in advertising-dependent media markets—not advertising space or time. Smythe ("Blindspot") argued that content creators produce materials (sitcoms, podcasts, magazines, sporting events, etc.) that serve as a sort of free lunch to attract viewers. In the case of television, for example, after purchasing the initial media infrastructure (i.e., the television set), viewers are able to watch content without having to purchase individual episodes or segments other than any basic subscription packages. The attention of viewers (i.e., their potential buying power) is then commodified and sold to advertisers with valuation based on factors such as audience size and demographics.

Rather than purchasing ad space or time, then, advertisers purchase audiences from content creators, based on the fact that advertisements without audiences are worthless (Smythe, "Blindspot"). The viewing (or listening, reading, etc.) time of audiences thus represents a sort of exploited labour, given that simply being exposed to advertisements produces significant value for advertisers and content creators without fairly reimbursing audiences (Smythe, "Rejoinder"; Jhally; Phillips). Jhally thus argues that the leisure time of audiences is increasingly being turned into a new form of working time, wherein audiences work to learn which products and services to purchase—thus creating greater overall value for advertisers. According to audience commodity theory, then, consumers purchase media infrastructure not in order to gain access to content but rather in order for content creators to transform viewers into audiences that can then be commodified and sold to advertisers.

Audience commodities have also always existed according to racially based consumer segmentations. While the attention and buying power of audiences are commodified in capitalist and advertising-dependent media systems, not all audiences are valued equally by creative industries. Historically, broadcasters and advertisers in North America have prioritized the attention and buying power of white English-speaking viewers above that of racialized (especially Black and Indigenous) viewers (Gandy Jr.). The logic behind this systemic discrimination is that, due to other ongoing elements of systemic racism, Black and Indigenous consumers are often perceived as less wealthy and thus less likely to purchase the products and services being advertised. Creative industries professionals have therefore opted to prioritize programming that will appeal to the greatest number of white English-speaking viewers in order to (re)produce the most profitable audience commodity for advertisers (Gandy Jr.). According to this discriminatory logic, Cherry's perpetual valorization of whiteness and his berating of immigrants and racialized peoples were tolerated by CBC and Sportsnet for decades, given that these behaviours did not threaten corporate profits. Only after advertisers began threatening to rescind sponsorships (following the 2019 "You People" rant) did Sportsnet finally relent and remove Cherry from the program. For corporate creative industries, then, racism and exclusionary rhetoric only become problematic when they threaten the profitability of audience commodities.

While Smythe's ("Blindspot"; "Rejoinder") audience commodity theory initially sparked a heated debate within communication studies, professional advertisers and media content creators noted that this was the commonsensical assumption according to which their industry had operated for decades. Smythe's audience commodity theory is now generally accepted, though with some refinements and additions from other scholars (e.g., Jhally; Gandy Jr.). It is also important to note that, while Smythe was primarily concerned with the economics of advertising, he agreed that the ideological dimensions of ads were also significant

("Rejoinder"). In the case of Don Cherry, the commentator was important in both propagating cultural messages as well as generating advertising revenue—though Cherry's ability to produce audiences ultimately proved to be his most significant role for broadcasters.

Because the CBC has always been a mixed-model public broadcaster (i.e., it has always relied at least partially on advertising revenue), it has continuously needed to consider how best to commodify audiences while still providing culturally relevant content. Cherry's role on "Coach's Corner" thus presented a perfect opportunity for the CBC to attract greater audience attention (especially white English-speaking attention, which could then be commodified and sold to advertisers) during its already incredibly popular *HNIC* program. Communication scholars and CBC executives have noted that Cherry was valued by the public broadcaster specifically because his charismatic personality, folksy vernacular, flashy suits, and non-technical commentary succeeded in attracting new audiences for hockey broadcasting, including more female viewers and non-hockey fans (Young; Phillips). The CBC, therefore, tolerated Cherry's controversial rants and public statements for decades because the commentator was so productive in the commodification of audiences. Cherry also quickly gained celebrity status within the culturally significant realm of Canadian hockey broadcasting. Ultimately, however, Cherry was fired by Rogers following his "You People" rant because the commentator had finally become unprofitable for the private company—in addition to not reflecting Canadian cultural values.

Cherry is problematic in that he has long been a (profitable) Canadian cultural icon, yet he has always stood in opposition to Canadian cultural values. The cultural and economic dimensions of Cherry's firing are thus noteworthy for two reasons. First, according to the logic of cultural citizenship, Cherry could reasonably have been fired by the CBC decades ago for any one of his xenophobic, racist, or sexist rants. Yet the CBC retained Cherry as a commentator precisely because his controversial nature helped (re)produce profitable audience commodities. Given the mixed-model funding of the CBC, then, we can deduce that the public broadcaster's reliance on advertising revenue was such that the CBC felt the need to prioritize profitability over cultural citizenship.

Second, Cherry was fired by Rogers because he became unprofitable for the private company (i.e., for economic rather than cultural or moral reasons). The privatization of *HNIC* represents an intensification of corporate nationalism in Canada. However, Cherry's firing demonstrates the fact that advertising-dependent entities (such as Rogers and, to a lesser extent, the CBC) will always tend to prioritize profitability over cultural citizenship. Indeed, this has been a key historical reason why nationalists distrust capitalism—for-profit entities are self-interested rather than community focused (Edwardson). Advertising and cultural citizenship are thus often (if not always) in tension with one another. In the final section of this chapter, I look at one way in which this conflict can be addressed—how corporate nationalism and audience commodities can be replaced with genuine cultural citizenship through public broadcasting reform in Canada.

CULTURAL CITIZENSHIP

Most modern discussions about citizenship revolve around the legal or institutional definitions of the term. According to this view, "citizenship" is a formal, legal status that is granted to individuals by the state in order to bound those individuals to a geopolitical entity (Donaldson and Kymlicka). In other instances, citizenship is sometimes explicitly understood to be based on racial, religious, genealogical, or ancestral factors that allow for (supposedly) unambiguous identification of geopolitical group members—a conception usually referred to as ethnic citizenship (Troyan; Kriszta et al.; Kende et al.). Arguably, Cherry's pattern of racist rhetoric heavily implies that he qualifies Canadian citizenship according to racial or ethnic traits. Yet both citizenship and race remain contentious forms of social identity, and the negotiated intersections of these identities further complicate each in their own right (Delgado et al.).

Cultural citizenship exists as an alternative conceptualization to institutional and legal citizenship on the one hand and racial or ethnic citizenship on the other. It conceptualizes membership within a civic community as being culturally relevant, and it includes the right to "know and speak" in culturally relevant ways (Miller 34). Cultural citizenship means that individuals belonging to a particular civic community or geopolitical region should have equal rights and abilities to participate in cultural practices, including access to culturally relevant historical knowledge (e.g., libraries, archives, museums, and heritage sites), arts, entertainment, and other forms of cultural production. In Canada, for example, ice hockey has been legislated as the nation's official winter sport—with lacrosse being the official summer sport (*National Sports of Canada Act* 1994). Indeed, hockey has been identified in scholarly works and perpetuated through popular culture as a significant cultural symbol in Canada (see Young; Gruneau and Whitson; Elcombe; Bociurkiw; Phillips and Martin). A cultural conception of citizenship would thus suggest that to be Canadian should mean having access to playing hockey, discussing hockey, and knowing hockey (i.e., consuming hockey-related media). It is also important to note that the right and ability to engage in culturally relevant practices does not mean that participation in these practices should be compulsory for citizens. In the Canadian example of hockey, cultural citizenship means that everyone should be able to engage with the sport in some way if they so choose but that engagement with hockey is not a requirement for belonging in the civic community (Phillips and Martin).

In Cherry's "You People" rant, however, we see an individual in a position of cultural power and influence in the creative industries using one cultural symbol (i.e., hockey-related media) as an avenue for berating racialized people perceived as not engaging with another national cultural symbol (i.e., poppy wearing). As many commentators have noted, Cherry would have had no way of knowing who is (or is not) an immigrant based on anecdotal accounts of passing people on the street—particularly in racially and ethnically diverse metropolitan regions like Cherry's city of residence, Mississauga. His problem with immigrants (i.e., "you people who come here") not wearing poppies thus reflects a more specific (and, arguably, more problematic) concern for non-white people not wearing poppies.

Racism and racial biases are not always explicit or immediately apparent (Delgado et al.). Rather, racism often manifests itself in subtle, implicit, or institutionalized ways. When Cherry ranted on a national hockey program about certain people not wearing poppies, he effectively did two things. First, Cherry's rant implied that cultural and civic belonging are necessarily tethered to racial and ethnic traits. Cherry received warranted criticism for these implications and was fired soon thereafter as a direct result of the racist message—or, rather, for failing to apologize for the message. The second, more problematic effect of Cherry's rant, however, was that it reflected the sort foundational racism that persists in Canada, despite the national mythos of Canadian diversity and inclusion. In other words, Cherry's "You People" rant said the quiet part loud—it made visible the invisible ways in which hockey is too often associated with Canadian culture, citizenship, and whiteness. Cherry's firing thus served as a useful scapegoat for liberal hegemonic order—by identifying Cherry's behaviour as racist and removing him from the program, Sportsnet created the impression of having addressed racism writ large. By doing so, however, Sportsnet avoided having to grapple with the widespread and deeply rooted institutional racisms that allowed for Cherry's popularity in the first place. Clearly, Cherry's removal from the program was a justified action (on both moral and economic grounds). But failing to then also critically interrogate why and how Cherry's persistent exclusionary rhetoric remained so popular for so long indicates a failure of creative industries in addressing more systemic bases of racism.

National symbols (such as hockey and poppies) are only one dimension of cultural citizenship. Cultural citizenship also includes the recognition and appreciation of cultural values. In Canada, our purported cultural values have traditionally revolved around things like civility and public etiquette (Kingwell; Reid). The continued existence of official multiculturalism also suggests that respect for diversity is itself an aspirational Canadian cultural value (Parekh). As an important caveat, the purported values of inclusion, diversity, and multiculturalism are real in the sense that they continue to exist in the popular imaginary or mythology of Canada. Whether or not these ideals ever materialize in the everyday lived experiences of individuals or groups is another question altogether, particularly in regard to racialized citizens. As noted above, cultural citizenship also means access to learning about and contributing to Canada's ongoing history, which has always depended on immigration. When considering these other dimensions of cultural citizenship, then, it becomes clear that Cherry's "You People" rant—and indeed, many of his exclusionary rants throughout his broadcasting career—ignored the mythologized Canadian cultural values of civility and respect for diversity, in addition to ignoring the important historical role that immigration has played (and continues to play) in the country.

As Scherer and Rowe argue, cultural citizenship is now largely negotiated through media. This is so in the sense that media (particularly public media) is incredibly effective in (re)producing national symbols, teaching and entrenching cultural values (both implicitly and explicitly), and explaining shared histories to audiences. In the Canadian context, the CBC's role in cultural production and nation building is enshrined in its mandate to tell distinctly Canadian stories to Canadians—a mandate that involves both *reflecting* existing Canadian culture as well as *generating* new dimensions of Canadian culture over time. Cormack and Cosgrave thus suggest that "the CBC is a place where Canada gets made and remade" (*Desiring Canada* 18). In this sense, Cherry's attempt to co-opt the cultural symbolism of hockey and poppies in order to generate an exclusionary understanding of what it means to be Canadian—particularly based on racial or ethnic traits—represents a perversion of the ideals of cultural citizenship. More concerning still is the fact that Cherry's perversion of cultural citizenship was itself reflective of the ongoing failures of Canadian creative industries to adequately encourage a more meaningful sense of inclusive civic culture.

Pedagogy and the Racialized Perversion of Cultural Citizenship

Cultural citizenship ought to serve as a means through which people are made able to participate in—and contribute to—their cultural, communal, or national affinities. Cherry's history of exclusionary rhetoric thus seems contrary to the idealized conception of public broadcasting as a negotiator of cultural citizenship.

To understand how, I now turn to breaking down and unpacking the historical and cultural contexts of Cherry's "You People" rant.

Cherry's habitual racism and xenophobia on "Coach's Corner" were always at odds with Canada's official multiculturalism and aspirational commitments to diversity. Cherry was vocally opposed to the inclusion of European players in the NHL and regularly belittled the accomplishments of French Canadian players (Brean). The regular incivility and breaches in discursive etiquette for which Cherry became known led to CBC producers placing a several second delay between filming and airing "Coach's Corner" segments, just in case anything Cherry said needed to be haphazardly edited out of the program. Despite these precautions, however, Cherry still managed to stir controversy for decades by deriding the purported cultural values of civility and respect for diversity in Canada.

Cherry's "You People" rant represents a nexus of racism and xenophobia, which manifest themselves in the commentator's preoccupation with wearing poppies in November. This is evident in the fact that Cherry's rant was directed at racialized immigrants specifically rather than citizens in general.[5] While cultural citizenship seeks to allow for people to engage with national cultural practices (again, if they so choose), Cherry's rhetoric instead attempted to establish racialized boundaries between who does and does not count as a Canadian citizen. Cherry thus represents a racialized perversion of cultural citizenship—seeking to exclude non-white people and groups from the national cultural community rather than trying to make cultural participation more open, inclusive, and democratic. Yet Cherry maintained his role as a controversial commentator for decades despite his antipathy toward inclusive cultural citizenship—specifically because of his usefulness in accumulating profits for private corporations via audience commodification.

CIVIC AUDIENCES: AN ALTERNATIVE TO CORPORATE NATIONALISM

In order to address the demands of cultural citizenship and overcome corporate nationalism's complacency in systemic racism, it is important to reconceptualize audiences as democratic participants rather than racialized commodities. Such a reconceptualization would have as its starting point the fundamental belief that all members of a given community deserve free and equal access to culturally relevant news, education, and entertainment. This notion of *civic audiences* thus serves as a potential remedy to the ongoing segmentation and commodification of audiences in capitalist-based media (Phillips and Martin). Indeed, an emphasis on civic audiences would help to fulfill the mandate of the CBC by producing and distributing content that is in the best interest of the citizenry, rather than content that is most efficient at commodifying audiences.

Given its cultural and symbolic significance in Canada, I use hockey broadcasting as an example of culturally relevant entertainment that could benefit from reform—especially in the wake of the Rogers takeover and Cherry firing. For example, the CBC could begin producing content featuring women's leagues' and local hockey leagues' games—both of which have been largely overlooked by the CBC in the past (see Phillips). Hockey is a cultural institution in Canada, and its diverse manifestations remain popular throughout the country across demographics—despite hockey's perpetual underfunding by successive governments (Phillips). Yet broadcasters have been fixated on the NHL for almost a century, to the extent that "watching hockey" has largely become shorthand for watching an NHL game. This equivocation between hockey and the NHL does not necessarily need to be the case, though in order to democratize hockey broadcasting, Canada will need to address three issues: funding for the CBC, protecting the CBC's broadcasting rights, and what Elcombe has called the "moral equivalent of Don Cherry" (194).

First, the CBC needs much more funding. As noted earlier in the chapter, Canada's public broadcaster has had its annual budget cut consistently since the 1980s by Liberal and Conservative governments. While the Trudeau Liberal government increased the CBC's funding by $675 million in 2016, this was barely a drop in the bucket considering the decades of funding cuts and effects of inflation (Bradshaw). In order to reconceptualize audiences as democratic cultural citizens (i.e., civic audiences), the CBC needs to become fully publicly funded. Increasing funding for the CBC and moving the public broadcaster away from its current mixed-model (i.e., advertising-dependent) structure would allow for hockey programming to become more diverse, inclusive, and reflective of its national audience—including broadcast time for women's leagues and local leagues.

It is also important to note that fully funding the CBC does not necessarily mean removing all advertising and promotions—only those from for-profit companies that consume segmented audiences as commodities. Advertising could still exist in a fully funded CBC wherein the information being presented is in the interest of the audience. Brief news updates, information about upcoming elections, and promotions for other CBC programs could all still fill the time gaps between hockey periods. Especially during hockey broadcasts, civic-oriented hockey organizations such as Hockey 4 Youth and Hockey Diversity Alliance could promote their activities and campaigns.[6] Rather than constantly being subjected to the same corporate messages telling us to buy a new iPhone or Honda, audiences could be learning about the state of their national and local communities during promotional breaks.

Second, Canada needs to develop and implement listed broadcasting events (LBE) policies to protect the free-to-air broadcasting rights of the CBC. Several states (including the United Kingdom, Belgium, and Argentina) have already created LBE policies, which legally protect the free-to-air broadcasting rights of a public broadcaster for listed events that are deemed to be of national or cultural significance (Scherer and Rowe; Phillips and Martin). Typically, these LBE policies have focused on culturally significant sporting events, such as cricket in the United Kingdom and football in Argentina. The idea behind LBE policies is that some cultural events ought to be freely accessible by cultural citizens, rather than requiring citizens (or at least, those who can afford to do so) to purchase private broadcasting access. Adopting LBE policies in Canada would thus legally protect the ability and cultural right of citizens to engage with their national winter sport.

Finally, we need to seriously reconsider the democratic role of Cherry and "Coach's Corner" in the context of civic audiences and cultural citizenship. Elcombe has argued that one way of doing so would be for us to think about what the "moral equivalent" of Don Cherry might look like (194). While Cherry has always been a polarizing and largely problematic figure in Canadian popular culture, Elcombe argues that Cherry's role in national public discourse is an important one—or at least, it could be important if someone with a greater sense of future-oriented moral reasoning could serve that role. In other words, the idea of Don Cherry is perhaps more important than the man himself or his brand.

Cherry's platform granted him a large and regular audience, among whom Cherry was able to elicit significant normative discourses about hockey and, by symbolic extension, about Canadian culture and society. While Cherry did this in a shallow way that perpetuated and normalized racism, there is the possibility for someone intelligible to use this platform in a more constructive manner (Elcombe 201). Other Canadian public intellectuals like Naomi Klein, John Ralston Saul, and David Suzuki influence the democratic discourses of citizens in a much less direct and much less frequent way. What is needed in hockey broadcasting, then, is someone as captivating as Cherry but with the moral rectitude that is becoming of a public intellectual. As Elcombe further suggests:

> In a strange, simplistic way, Don Cherry *functionally* serves as Canada's "accidental" Socrates. He addresses issues through highly visible media sources that initiate debates about morally relevant topics in the most "airy public spaces" of Canada—in homes, office water coolers, sport bars, and the popular media to name a few. (202)

The problem, however, is that while Cherry espoused a boisterous sense of national pride in his rants, he lacked any sense of *national hope*. Drawing from philosopher Richard Rorty, Elcombe argues that some form of national pride is a necessary requirement for functional democratic societies, in the same way that self-respect is a necessary requirement for the individual to flourish (205). However, pride in one's national community is a necessary but not a sufficient condition for democracy— democracy also requires a sense of national hope, or some future-oriented sense of how best to achieve social justice in our national community (Elcombe 209). While national pride allows someone to feel a deep-seated connection to their civic community, national hope enables someone to envision how their civic community might overcome historic or existing shortcomings in the pursuit of social justice. In other words, national hope allows people to care enough about their civic community to want to try and make that community better.

Cherry's role as a prominent public figure thus limited peoples' abilities to think about and discuss how they might best rectify the existing moral shortcomings of the nation. Worse still, Cherry's persistent exclusionary rhetoric further fanned the flames of racism and xenophobia being taught through Canada's creative industries. Now that Cherry has been removed from "Coach's Corner," however, he could be replaced with a better representation of Canadian culture— someone charismatic and entertaining, able to ignite a more inclusive moral discourse among audiences, and who espouses both a sense of national pride and national hope.

CONCLUSION

In this chapter, I explored the concepts of cultural corporate nationalism, audience commodities, cultural citizenship, and civic audiences through a critical race lens. In doing so, I critically identified the ways in which Cherry's "You People" rant encapsulated the normalization of racism and xenophobia throughout his career. In this sense, Cherry's final rant (and indeed, much of Cherry's career) can be understood as a sort of perversion of the democratic ideals of cultural citizenship. Rather than attempting to make the cultural symbol and practice of hockey more inclusive, Cherry served as a barrier to realizing a greater cultural citizenship in Canada. For almost 40 years, Cherry retained his platform on "Coach's Corner" because of his national fame and profitability for advertisers—and despite his perpetual racism and xenophobia. With the public backlash to his "You People" rant, however, it became apparent that Cherry's polarizing persona was no longer efficient at producing audience commodities. Ultimately, if we hope to address systemic racism and strengthen any genuine sense of cultural citizenship in Canada,

l to reconceptualize audiences as democratic citizens rather than com-
ιis will require, among other things, grappling with what the "moral
f Don Cherry" might entail and promoting a sense of national hope
through creative industries.

CORE CONCEPTS

audience commodity theory: The understanding that, in consumer capitalist-based media systems, the attention and buying power of audiences are the primary market commodities being produced and consumed. According to this theory, media content is provided to audiences as a "free lunch" in order to attract their attention, commodify their buying power, and teach audiences what to buy.

civic audiences: An alternative to both corporate nationalism and audience commodities that conceptualizes audiences as democratic citizens of a given geopolitical place.

corporate nationalism: The phenomena in which either (1) private corporations appropriate and commodify national symbols for profit or (2) governments partner with private corporations in a symbiotic relationship. In either case, the drive for increased corporate profits is prioritized over any appeals to national pride, unity, or hope.

critical race theory (CRT): A critical way of interrogating the systemic manifestations, effects, and legacies of racism in society. Rather than focusing on individual instances of racism or racist behaviours, CRT addresses structural and institutionalized racism—particularly in colonial and imperialist societies.

cultural citizenship: The notion that citizenship ought to be, at least in part, culturally based and also that citizens have a right to access cultural forms of production relevant to their geopolitical and national affiliations.

public broadcasting: The provision of news, education, and entertainment to (and supported by) the public; a democratic alternative to both private/corporate broadcasting and state broadcasting. While public broadcasting is publicly funded, it remains operationally independent from government influence.

SUGGESTED ACTIVITIES

1. Have a conversation with a friend or family member about Don Cherry. How much of the conversation centres around hockey? How much of it centres around Cherry's personality, politics, or suits? What does this tell you about

Cherry's role in Canadian consciousness and his influence as a state celebrity? Do they agree or disagree with Cherry's firing? Why or why not?

2. Watch a *Hockey Night in Canada* game (they are still freely available through the CBC on Saturday nights) with a friend, family member, or roommate. What Canadian cultural symbols, values, and histories are being (or not being) represented? Who is being (or not being) represented on screen? Which corporations are being promoted, and do any of them use Canadian cultural symbols, values, or histories in their ads? What versions of Canada are being communicated, and how?

3. This chapter suggests several possible alternatives to Don Cherry as public intellectuals: Naomi Klein, John Ralston Saul, and David Suzuki. What other individuals might help communicate positive nationalism through hockey broadcasting? How can we best incorporate considerations of socioeconomic class into decisions regarding our public intellectuals? How might we reform the CBC (and public broadcasting more generally) in order to better promote social justice?

NOTES

1. A subsequent poll by the predominantly conservative *National Post* newspaper ranked Cherry as the #1 greatest Canadian of all time. The contest was by no means scientific, and Don Cherry (#7) and Wayne Gretzky (#10) encouraged their own fans to vote for Sir John A. MacDonald and Terry Fox, respectively. A subsequent (and equally unscientific) poll by the predominantly conservative National Post newspaper ranked Cherry as the #1 greatest Canadian of all time.

2. Although the segment was added in 1980, the title "Coach's Corner" was not officially used until 1982.

3. I might also include staunch militarism and its implied Islamophobia post-9/11 or support for Donald Trump's US presidency and its racial undertones to Cherry's list of racially charged rhetoric in the 21st century.

4. While the theory of audience commodities caused some initial controversy in academic circles, many advertising professionals noted that they had been operating according to this economic logic for decades.

5. After the fact, Cherry noted that he should have said "everybody" rather than "you people," though he still refused to apologize for the xenophobic undertones of his rant (CBC, "I Should Have Said Everybody").

6. Hockey 4 Youth is a charitable organization that works to remove social and economic barriers to hockey for new Canadians and at-risk youth in addition to providing educational and life skills training. Hockey Diversity Alliance is a non-profit working to "eradicate systemic racism and intolerance in hockey."

REFERENCES

Allain, Kristi A. "'A Good Canadian Boy': Crisis Masculinity, Canadian National Identity, and Nostalgic Longings in Don Cherry's *Coach's Corner*." *International Journal of Canadian Studies*, vol. 52, no. 1, 2015, pp. 107–132.

Bociurkiw, Marusya. *Feeling Canadian: Television, Nationalism, and Affect*. Wilfrid Laurier University Press, 2011.

Bradshaw, James. "Federal Budget Pledges $675-million in CBC Funding." *Globe and Mail*, 22 March 2016, https://www.theglobeandmail.com/report-on-business/liberals-pledge-675-million-in-cbc-funding/article29354285/. Accessed 23 October 2020.

Brean, Joseph. "'Europeans and French Guys': A Selection of Don Cherry's Hits Over the Years" *National Post*, 11 November 2019, https://nationalpost.com/news/lower-slobovia-attacking-slimea-a-selection-of-don-cherrys-hits. Accessed 15 March 2021.

CBC. "And the Greatest Canadian of All Time Is . . . " *Canadian Broadcasting Corporation*, 29 November 2004, https://www.cbc.ca/archives/entry/and-the-greatest-canadian-of-all-time-is. Accessed 27 October 2020.

———. "I Should Have Said Everybody: Don Cherry Tells CBC He Regrets His Choice of Words." *Canadian Broadcasting Corporation*, 12 November 2019, https://www.cbc.ca/player/play/1640859715856. Accessed 7 October 2020.

Chan, Wendy, and Dorothy Chunn. *Racialization, Crime, and Criminal Justice in Canada*. University of Toronto Press, 2014.

Cherry, Don. *Hockey Night in Canada*. Sportsnet, 9 November 2019.

Cordeiro-Rodrigues, Luis. "Animal Abolitionism and 'Racism without Racists.'" *Journal of Agricultural and Environmental Ethics*, vol. 30, no. 6, 2017, pp. 745–764.

Cormack, Patricia, and James F. Cosgrave. *Desiring Canada: CBC Contests, Hockey Violence, and Other Stately Pleasures*. University of Toronto Press, 2013.

———. "Theorising the State Celebrity: A Case Study of the Canadian Broadcasting Corporation." *Celebrity Studies*, vol. 5, no. 3, 2014, pp. 321–339.

Delgado, Richard, Jean Stefancic, and Angela P. Harris. *Critical Race Theory: An Introduction*. 3rd ed., New York University Press, 2017.

Denis, Claude, and Christine Dallaire. "'If You Don't Speak French, You're Out': Don Cherry, the Alberta Francophone Games and the Discursive Construction of Canada's Francophones." *Canadian Journal of Sociology*, vol. 25, no. 4, 2000, pp. 415 (1–20).

Donaldson, Sue, and Will Kymlicka. *Zoopolis: A Political Theory of Animal Rights*. Oxford University Press, 2011.

Edwardson, Ryan. *Canadian Content: Culture and the Quest for Nationhood*. University of Toronto Press, 2008.

Elcombe, Tim. "The Moral Equivalent of 'Don Cherry.'" *Journal of Canadian Studies,* vol. 44, no. 2, 2010, pp. 194–218.

Gandy Jr., Oscar H. "Audiences on Demand." *Toward a Political Economy of Culture: Capitalism and Communication in the Twenty-First Century,* edited by A. Calabrese and C. Sparks, Rowman & Littlefield Publishers, 2004, pp. 327–341.

Gruneau, Richard, and David Whitson. *Hockey Night in Canada: Sports, Identities, and Cultural Politics.* University of Toronto Press, 1993.

Ho, Solarina. "Don Cherry's History of Controversial Comments." CTV News, 11 November 2019, https://www.ctvnews.ca/sports/don-cherry-s-history-of-controversial-comments-1.4680505. Accessed 22 March 2022.

Hockey Diversity Alliance. "Our Purpose." https://hockeydiversityalliance.org/#our-purpose. Accessed 26 October 2020.

Jhally, Sut. *The Codes of Advertising: Fetishism and the Political Economy of Meaning in the Consumer Society.* Routledge, 1990.

Kende, Anna, Nora A. Lantos, and Peter Kreko. "Endorsing a Civic (vs. an Ethnic) Definition of Citizenship Predicts Higher Pro-Minority and Lower Pro-Majority Collective Action Intentions." *Frontiers in Psychology,* vol. 9, no. 1, 2019, pp. 1–17.

Kingwell, Mark. *A Civil Tongue: Justice, Dialogue, and the Politics of Pluralism.* Penn State University Press, 1994.

Koch, Natalie. "The Corporate Production of Nationalism." *Antipode: A Radical Journal of Geography,* vol. 52, no. 1, 2020, pp. 185–205.

Kriszta, Kovacs, Kortvelyesi Zsolt, and Nagy Aliz. "Margins of Nationality: External Ethnic Citizenship and Non-Discrimination." *Perspectives on Federalism,* vol. 7, no. 1, 2015, pp. 85–116.

Miller, Toby. "Before, During, and After the Neoliberal Moment: Media, Sports, Policy, and Citizenship." *Sport, Public Broadcasting, and Cultural Citizenship: Signal Lost?,* edited by Jay Scherer and David Rowe, Routledge, 2014, pp. 30–47.

National Sports of Canada Act. Statutes of Canada, c. 16, Department of Justice, 1994. Accessed 15 September 2020.

Parekh, Bhikhu. *Rethinking Multiculturalism: Cultural Diversity and Political Theory.* Palgrave-Macmillan, 2006.

Phillips, Ryan. J. "An Inquiry into the Political Economy of *Hockey Night in Canada:* Critically Assessing Issues of Ownership, Advertising, and Gendered Audiences." *Canadian Journal of Communication,* vol. 43, no. 2, 2018, pp. 203–220.

Phillips, Ryan J., and George Martin. "Listing and Protecting Culturally Significant Events: Intangible Cultural Heritage and Policy Considerations for Hockey Broadcasting in Canada." *International Journal of Cultural Policy,* vol. 26, no. 5, 2020, pp. 584–596.

Reid, Dylan. *Toronto Public Etiquette Guide.* Spacing Media, 2017.

Saul, John Ralston. *The Collapse of Globalism and the Reinvention of the World.* Overlook Press, 2005.

Scherer, Jay, and David Rowe. "Sport, Public Service Media, and Cultural Citizenship." *Sport, Public Broadcasting, and Cultural Citizenship: Signal Lost?*, edited by Jay Scherer and David Rowe, Routledge, 2014, pp. 1–29.

Smythe, Dallas W. "Communications: Blindspot of Western Marxism." *Canadian Journal of Political and Society Theory,* vol. 1, no. 3, 1977, pp. 1–28.

————. "Rejoinder to Graham Murdock." *Canadian Journal of Political and Social Theory,* vol. 2, no. 2, 1978, pp. 120–127.

Tenenbaum, Harriet R., and Martin D. Ruck. "Are Teachers' Expectations Different for Racial Minority than European American Students? A Meta-Analysis." *Journal of Educational Psychology,* vol. 99, no. 2, 2007, pp. 253–273.

Troyan, Brett. "Ethnic Citizenship in Colombia: The Experience of the Regional Indigenous Council of the Cauca in Southwestern Colombia from 1970 to 1990." *Latin American Research Review,* vol. 43, no. 3, 2008, pp. 166–191.

Weedon, Gavin. "'I Will Protect This House': Under Armour, Corporate Nationalism and Post-9/11 Cultural Politics." *Sociology of Sport Journal,* vol. 29, no. 3, 2012, pp. 265–282.

Young, Scott. *The Boys of Saturday Night: Inside Hockey Night in Canada.* Macmillan, 1990.

CHAPTER 9

When Black History Month Media Posts Double as Pedagogical Tools: Appraising Existing Black History Month Coverage and Proposing Future Directions

Selina Linda Mudavanhu

INTRODUCTION

Every February, Canada marks Black History Month. The formal recognition of Black History Month first started at the beginning of the 1950s when the Canadian Negro Women's Association organized several events (Manitoba Education). The successful petition to the City of Toronto in 1978 by the Ontario Black History Society resulted in February being recognized as Black History Month (Thompson). After a motion in 1995 by the Honourable Jean Augustine, the first Black Canadian woman to be elected to Parliament, the House of Commons formally established February as Black History Month in Canada (Government of Canada, "About Black History Month").

Black History Month is intended as a time to "honour the legacy of Black Canadians, past and present" (Government of Canada, "Black History Month"). Ojo observes that, among other things, the annual month-long celebrations are about recognizing and celebrating the diverse nature of Black people in the country.

While there have been instances when some institutions have been accused of neglecting Black History Month (Peng), in general many commemorate it. Across the country, February is replete with different events to mark the month. Given their role of informing, educating, and entertaining (Lule), media sources often carry stories on Black History Month. The case study in this chapter examines the coverage of Black History Month in content posted between 2018 and 2020 on websites of the Canadian Broadcasting Corporation (CBC), the CTV Television Network, the *Globe and Mail*, and the *Toronto Star*. These media organizations were selected because of their size, reach, and significant positions in the Canadian media landscape.

Founded in 1936, the CBC is Canada's national public broadcaster. It provides Canadians with radio and television services as well as content on the Internet and other emerging platforms (Government of Canada, "Canadian Broadcasting Corporation"). The CBC's mandate includes contributing to a collective national consciousness and reflecting the cultural and racial diversity in Canada. CBC News, a division of the CBC, was founded in 1941. CBC News gathers and reports on local, national, and international news as well as produces current affairs programs. CTV is the largest privately owned Canadian terrestrial television network, founded in 1961. CTV is part of Bell Media and broadcasts in English. The *Globe and Mail* was established in 1844. It is one of the leading newspapers in Canada that is circulated nationally and reaches more than six million audience members weekly through digital and print formats. The *Toronto Star* was founded in 1892, and it is the country's largest daily newspaper, publishing in the Greater Toronto Area. By 2015, both the *Globe and Mail* and the *Toronto Star* were among the country's top five newspapers (News Media Canada).

The aim of this chapter's case study is to understand the ideas that the aforementioned media prioritized during Black History Month. It is important to focus on media coverage and representations because the media generally plays an important pedagogical role in society. Gidengil et al. argue that outside of family and acquaintances, the media are major information sources for many. In addition, Hackett (199) observes that "the media influence public perceptions of what exists, what is important, what is good and valuable, what is bad and threatening, and what is related to what." Hackett (199) elaborates that the media does this "through their ability to focus public attention on some events and issues, and away from others."

In justifying the focus on Black History Month, it is important to state that February is one of the only times in the year when there is a deliberate, specialized, and concentrated focus on Black Canadians and their histories. Manitoba Education (9) explains that Black History Month "provides a focal point for the celebration of Black experiences, perspectives, and history." Further, Ishimwe argues that Black History Month "helps those who lack knowledge to learn more on culture and Black history." Manitoba Education (9) adds that Black History Month has become a key component of "multicultural and anti-racism programming and approaches." Henry characterizes Black History Month as facilitating a "learning space" for "[celebrating] Black joy, and [envisioning] transformative Black futures," among other things. Henry further argues that "acknowledging

Black History Month in the way it was intended is antiracist pedagogy." If Black History Month is the rare opportunity for the rest of Canada to hear and learn about their fellow Black compatriots' experiences and histories, it is imperative to pay attention to what the media communicate to their audiences. Similar to classroom spaces, the media have the potential to "positively affirm the identities of Black [people]" if they are intentional about their "use of stories and images of Black life to challenge dominant Euro-Canadian historical national narratives, normalized white identities, white supremacist power structures, and anti-Black sentiments" (Henry).

REPRESENTATIONS

When examining how various media sources cover Black History Month, it is important to state that these organizations are not neutral purveyors of information. Tolley contends that the media "play an active role in determining which stories are covered, how subjects are portrayed, and the standards by which events, issues, and personalities are understood and evaluated" (15). Buckingham (57) concurs: "the media do not offer us a transparent window on the world but a mediated version of the world. They don't just present reality, they represent it." Fürsich (115) adds that the media "create reality and normalize specific world-views or ideologies." In representing or constructing reality, the media are involved in selection processes to determine what is included (foregrounded) and excluded (backgrounded) in publications and broadcasts (British Broadcasting Corporation). The media engage in what Entman refers to as framing: "To frame is to select some aspects of a perceived reality and make them more salient in a communicating text, in such a way as to promote a particular problem definition, causal interpretation, moral evaluation, and/or treatment recommendation" (52). The implication of framing is that not everything about a topic is covered. Neary and Ringrow (297) explain that the media cannot offer an impartial and comprehensive picture because of "spatial and time constraints, perceived newsworthiness, dominant societal norms, audience considerations, [and] political views of media outlets."

Scholars are concerned about media representations because they provide audiences with ways of understanding and engaging with topics they cover (British Broadcasting Corporation). Commenting on the centrality of representations, Tawil asserts that positive depictions have the potential to fight typecast or stereotypical portrayals, as the latter often have deleterious repercussions for individuals and groups of people. In addition, positive representations favourably impact the ways in which society views different people. On the other side, negative representations have the opposite effect (Tawil).

In Canada, the media have been taken to task over the unsatisfactory manner in which they have represented racialized Canadians (Cukier et al.; Tolley; Fleras). In the context of politics in Canada, for example, Tolley argues that the representations of racialized candidates leave a lot to be desired, elaborating that "visible minority candidates' coverage is more negative, less prominent, more filtered, and more likely to include a photograph (a subtle way of cuing candidate race) than is the case for white candidates" (47). Another study by Cukier et al. on representations of women and racialized minorities in Canadian television concludes that these groups are underrepresented as expert sources in selected public affairs programs. Cukier et al. further argue that racialized women in particular get the short end of the representational stick.

Problematic portrayals of racialized groups cannot be separated from questions of newsroom demographics. Malik and Fatah contend that although Canada's population has become more diverse in the last 20 years, this has not been reflected in the staffing and content of many news organizations. In a statement issued in January 2020, the Canadian Association of Black Journalists (CABJ) and Canadian Journalists of Colour (CJOC) asserted that "Canadian newsrooms and media coverage are not truly representative of our country's racial diversity." In the same statement, the two journalism groups called for—among several other things—the employment of more racialized reporters and editors. CABJ and CJOC argued that "a more diverse news team translates into more diverse coverage."

While the media provides audiences with ways of looking at the people and events they cover, it is important to note that audiences are not dupes that passively imbibe dominant meanings. Hermes argues that audiences actively produce meanings from media texts—and their experiences and identities impact the ways they construct meanings from messages presented to them. In that regard, while it is critical to examine content by the media, audience studies are necessary to provide an understanding of how real people interact with ideas that are prioritized in these venues.

CRITICAL RACE THEORY: COUNTER-STORYTELLING

When examining the ways the media covers a topic like Black History Month, it is crucial to understand critical race theory, particularly the idea of counter-storytelling. Conceptually, critical race theory emerged from the critical legal studies movement in the United States. Ansell (345) argues that critical race theory is regarded as "a new generation of US civil rights scholars and activists dissatisfied with traditional civil rights discourse, the slow pace of racial reform, and the seeming inability of mainstream liberal thinking on race to effectively counter the erosion of civil rights accomplishments." Prominent thinkers who developed and advocated for critical race theory include Derrick Bell, Kimberlé Crenshaw, Richard Delgado, Alan Freeman, Cheryl Harris, Charles Lawrence, Mari Matsuda, and Patricia Williams (Ansell). Critical race theory has since been used as a scaffold for research in disciplines such as communication studies, education, political science, and sociology, and, as Delgado and Stefancic observe, the community of critical race theory scholars has expanded beyond the United States. There are now a number of critical race scholars located in countries like Canada, Australia, India, and Spain.

There are several ideas that critical race theory scholars propose. They argue that racism is endemic and embedded in the fabric of society (Delgado and Stefancic). These scholars argue that liberal notions such as colour-blindness and meritocracy mask the invisible manifestations and workings of white power (Bodenheimer). Additionally, critical race theory scholars insist on analyses that are both contextual and historical (Muñoz), contending that the experiential knowledge of Black people has to be taken seriously (Hiraldo). Critical race theorists also insist that oppression is intersectional (Columbia Law School).

In addition to these ideas, critical race scholars have used counter-storytelling as a tool to refute, challenge, and resist racist representations of social life (Yosso). Alemán (75–76) argues that "majoritarian stories function as master narratives and reinscribe the myths of meritocracy and colour-blindness, purport neutrality and common sense, and invoke stereotypes that vitiate people of colour as dim, criminal, and depraved and exalt whites as intelligent, lawful, and moral." Counter-storytelling centralizes the experiential knowledge of people whose narratives have been relegated to the discursive margins. Martinez (37) elaborates that counter-storytelling "recognizes that the experiential and embodied knowledge of people of colour is legitimate and critical to understanding racism that is often well disguised in the rhetoric of normalized structural values and practices." Yosso contends that, in addition to deconstructing hegemonic narratives, counter-stories work to build solidarity and community in marginalized groups as well as bridge dominant and subordinate groups by "adjusting perceptions about the supposed shortcomings about people of colour and revealing the inner workings of white entitlement" (Alemán 76).

In view of these arguments, the concept of counter-storytelling provides an important framework for understanding the coverage of Black History Month and the stories that are prioritized during this time.

THE CASE STUDY

The case study that follows takes a qualitative approach to understand how Black History Month was represented in posts on websites of the CBC, CTV, the *Globe and Mail,* and the *Toronto Star.* The case study focuses on the online spaces of the aforementioned media because research shows that Canadians increasingly access news from websites and social media platforms like Facebook and Twitter (Canadian Internet Registration Authority; Canadian Journalism Foundation). Precisely because the media play a pedagogical role in society, as stated earlier in the chapter, this case study is interested in responding to the following questions:

1.   What ideas did the selected media prioritize during Black History Month?
2.   What were the implications of these choices?

The search term "Black History Month Canada" was used to find posts to examine. The search yielded mixed and "messy" results. There were posts from 2015, 2016, and 2017 that came up that could not be included because the study focused specifically on 2018, 2019, and 2020. Some material that came up had been posted outside of February. A few of the posts had nothing to do with Black Canadians, their histories, or their experiences. Purposive sampling, a non-probability sampling technique, was used to select posts included in the case study. Only information-rich posts with content on Black people in Canada posted in February 2018, 2019, and 2020 were picked. The sampling process continued until a saturation point was reached (Fusch and Ness).

Thematic analysis was used to examine the posts. Though the actual process of conducting the thematic analysis was iterative, the steps suggested by Nowell et al. for this type of analysis were useful in examining the identified posts. The initial step entailed documenting all posts that came up from the search. URLs, headlines, introductory paragraphs (where applicable) of all posts were copied and pasted into a spreadsheet. A summary of each post was made. In the second step, preliminary codes were produced. This was followed by steps 3 (finding themes) and 4 (reviewing themes in the data). Below are some preliminary themes that were identified: "History of Black History Month," "Revisiting the history of Black people in Canada," "Naming and honouring archivers in the Black community," "Celebrating Blackness," "Personal experiences of being Black and handling racism," "Naming racism," "Events commemorating Black History Month," "Pleasure: food, music, dance," and "Beyond Black History Month/activism." Some of these themes were combined while other themes with little evidence were left out of the write-up. The last two steps (naming themes and writing the chapter) occurred concurrently while revisiting previous steps.

FINDINGS

It is important to reiterate the central role that media plays in communications during Black History Month. In the context of formal education, "there are no mandated learning expectations on the 400-year Black presence in Canada" (Henry), which has resulted in Black History Month serving as a "curriculum intervention" (Henry). In broader Canadian society, Black History Month content published and posted by the media industries plays a similar stopgap pedagogical role to get Canadians au fait with Black Canadian histories and experiences. Given the significant role the media play in teaching and learning about Black History Month, it is important to pay attention to the kinds of content that they prioritize. In addition to critical appraisals of the status quo, it is imperative to provide recommendations on future directions that the media could explore when covering Black History Month and beyond.

Coming back to the case study, four themes were dominant in content on Black History Month posted on websites of the selected media. There was a focus on certain histories of Black Canadians as well as posts in which Black people who contributed to the country were named and honoured. Also covered in the posts were Black people's experiences of prejudice in Canada. In addition, the media featured the country-wide events that happened to commemorate Black History Month.

Black Histories in Canada

In Canadian mainstream historical narratives, the histories of Black people have not always been prioritized. As Black studies professor Rinaldo Walcott avers, "Canadians have been able to write a history of Canada that has rendered Black people very absent" (Miller). Walcott further argues that mediators of history and media in the country have toned down Black experiences (Miller). Speaking about the paucity of Black Canadian histories in the context of educational materials, the Honourable Jean Augustine contends:

> I was an educator.… I recognized that the classroom curriculum was saying very little about African Canadians. The same thing was done to Indigenous peoples—if there was any reference, it was either in the footnote or as a sideline. Black Canadians were not part of the script and were not shown contributing to Canadian society. (McLeod)

Partly in response to such neglect, several posts during Black History Month featured histories of Black Canadians. In a post on the CBC News website, historian Adrienne Shadd nuanced the narrative of the arrival of Hamilton's Black community, arguing that not all Black people came to the city as liberated slaves. Shadd argued that some Black families came as free people (Carter). The post "Demeaned, Overworked and All Called George: How Black Train Porters Transformed Canada" (Yang) detailed the history of Black train porters in Canada and the ways in which they revolutionized the country. Also, among the posts on histories of Black Canadians was the under-the-radar trade of rum and fish between Newfoundland and Jamaica (CBC News, "Artistic Director Andrew Craig").

Some histories featured during the month were personal experiences of individuals' and families' early settlement in Canada. Moser contends that such narratives are "right there in front of us ... seemingly silent below the noise of the national narratives we have been told." Moser explains these histories require "a deep form of listening to be heard." In the CTV post "Sask. Family Has Deep Roots in Province's Black History," Carol Lafayette-Boyd discussed the history of her family settling in Saskatchewan in the 1900s. Another post, "'We Are the Roots': New Documentary Chronicles Triumphs of Alberta's Black Pioneering Families" (CBC News) focused on a documentary in which Black families' histories of settlement in the Canadian Prairies are foregrounded.

Other posts featuring personal histories included "One of Nova Scotia's First Black Nurses Recalls Struggles and Triumphs" (Colley). In this post, retired nurse Clotilda Yakimchuk narrated her journey of becoming the first Black graduate at the Nova Scotia Hospital School of Nursing. She discussed how her journey was marked by racism and how she overcame it. In a different article on the CBC News website, "'Honey with the Medicine': Singer-Songwriter Khari McClelland on How Music Can Help Tell Difficult Truths" (Nair), McClelland narrated the history of how Kizzy, his great-great-great-grandmother, came to Canada fleeing slavery in the United States. In the account, Kizzy struggled to secure accommodation—among other challenges—in Ontario, which eventually led her to return to Detroit.

The fact that these and other historical narratives about Black people are hardly incorporated in mainstream Canadian histories exposes the fallibility of existing processes of curating the past. Ndlovu-Gatsheni asserts that dominant histories are "versions of the past" that unmask "dominant power configurations" at particular moments. Ndlovu-Gatsheni (2) argues that "there is no such thing as unmediated, unconstructed, and non-perspectival account of the past."

Recognizing the constructed nature of histories is an important point of departure in "uncovering the voices of those usually silenced by the mainstream" (Klein 22). Part of retrieving overlooked voices requires an openness to broadening what have traditionally counted as sources of historical data. It demands thinking outside of and without the box. One way of breaking ranks with business as usual is by taking seriously artifacts and stories found in unlikely places, like ordinary Black people's homes. Artist Deanna Bowen, for example, aims to do some of this work. Bowen's work focuses on the "'dark matter' in our midst: figures and events that have remained below the threshold of visibility not because they are impossible to find but because their existence reveals a systematized racism difficult for the majority culture to acknowledge" (McMaster Museum of Art).

The histories of Black Canadians featured during Black History Month were told from the perspectives of those who have been written out of dominant accounts. Displaying their agency, the narrators selected which stories they told and how they told them. They had the opportunity for their voices to be heard and a chance to offer alternative viewpoints on the past. While the allocation of space to the telling of Black histories is important, it is crucial to critically examine whose histories—among the diverse group of Black people living in Canada—emerge as master narratives during Black History Month in content by media industries. Neglecting to do this will result in replicating similar challenges that exist with dominant Canadian historical accounts. It is critical to include Black experiences in all their diversity precisely because the history of Blacks in Canada is by no means homogeneous. There were free Blacks, those who were enslaved, refugees and immigrants, Black children and Black adults. Black people worked in a range of occupations and owned all kinds of businesses.

Naming and Honouring Achievers in the Black Community

In dominant discourses, there is a downplaying of contributions of Black Canadians. Gaye argues that "for too long, the achievements of our community were rarely listed in textbooks, showcased in film, or shared with a wide audience. Black Canadians have come to expect their stories to be ignored in Canadian history." In response, a sizeable number of the articles on Black History Month named Black Canadians—living and dead, eminent and little-known—who have contributed to Canada in sport, education, art, business, media, and so on.

In the CBC News post "Canadian Olympic Hero Sam Richardson Honoured by His Former High School" (Ross), the focus was on how young Sam Richardson qualified to participate in the Commonwealth Games, formerly the British Empire

Games, in the 1930s. Richardson went on to secure gold and silver medals in the games. The article "Willie O'Ree, NHL's First Black Player, on Breaking Barriers and Challenging Racism in Hockey" (CBC News) discussed how O'Ree triumphed over racism in his chosen sport. Another CBC News article, "Black History Month without Iconic Local Musician Gerry Atwell Bittersweet, Say Family and Friends" (Carreiro), celebrated the late musician Gerry Atwell as well as his mother, Frances Atwell. Frances was among Winnipeg's first Black pharmacists. In a post on the death of Jackie Shane, the article presented the career of the Black soul singer (*Globe and Mail*, "Jackie Shane, a Pioneering Soul Singer, Dies at 78"). In "'High Time' to Honour Pair Chosen for Black History Month Stamps, Says Winnipeg-Based Creator" (CBC News) the spotlight was on two Black Canadians, Lincoln Alexander and Kathleen "Kay" Livingstone. Alexander was the first Black member of Parliament in Canada and Livingstone was an activist and former actress.

While many Black people were celebrated posthumously, there were others who were honoured while still living. To celebrate Black History Month (CBC News, "Faces of Local Heroes 'Give Us Hope'"), Sandwich Towne developed a wall of fame that featured "famous" Black people across the Windsor-Essex region. This wall highlighted the achievements of Black artists, educators, and business persons.

Naming Black Canadians and acknowledging their contributions achieves several goals. It expands the repertoire of Canadians who are celebrated in conventional historical accounts. This facilitates opportunities for all Canadians to learn about Black achievers. Featuring Black Canadians in the aforementioned ways also serves to instill a sense of confidence, worth, and belonging in Black people by deflating erroneous assumptions that their ancestors did not contribute anything to the country. Acknowledging the achievements of Black Canadians also works to inspire younger Black people to achieve in their own spheres. Writing about the importance of Black students seeing themselves represented in texts, Canadian educator and historian Natasha Henry explains that "students really feel a sense of pride when they see themselves reflected in the curriculum. It helps them identify as Canadian.… When you learn more about your ancestors, those [who have] gone before you, and what [they have] accomplished, it's empowering!" (Beckford).

Ideally, the achievements of all Black Canadians in their diversity should be recognized and celebrated in posts during Black History Month. In reality, however, the media make selections regarding the people they feature. As Neary and Ringrow argue, there are various factors that make offering of a complete picture in reports by the media unattainable. In that regard, beyond Black History Month, the CBC launched an expanded version of the website "Being Black in Canada," "featuring the stories and experiences of Black Canadians, highlighting narratives that matter to Black communities including relevant news pieces, individual successes, and historical content" (Koivusalo). Outside of mainstream media industries, furthermore, platforms like byblacks.com have curated a space through which stories of Black people are told. Another example is the Black History Canada Portal, which contains materials for teaching Black history in the country. The emergence of such online spaces creates more openings for stories of contributions—large and small—of ordinary Black people without fame or fortune to also be heard and immortalized.

Experiences of Anti-Black Prejudice in Canada

In conventional Canadian narratives, there is a denial and sometimes a minimizing of anti-Black racism in the country. The premier of Ontario, Doug Ford, for example, denied that Canada possessed "systemic deep roots of racism" similar to the United States (Canadian Press). Foster refers to this denial as the "made-in-Canada myth," elaborating that "the mainstream view is that everyone is treated justly, fairly and equitably in Canada. The dominant cultural narrative defines Canada as a raceless or post-racial society." Many Canadians are devoted to the idea that racism is a problem peculiar to the United States (Khan)—despite the fact that "disparities continue to exist unabated in education, child services, criminal justice and the workplace" (Foster).

Transcending the egalitarianism-in-Canada illusion, several Black History Month posts highlighted Black Canadians' experiences of prejudice. Speaking about what they had gone through in "Breaking the Black Stereotype: CBC Manitoba Chat Tackles Myths" (Carreiro), a panel discussed the stereotypes they contend with as Black people living in Manitoba. Black entrepreneurs discussed the systemic discrimination they faced, which made it difficult for them to access capital (CBC News, "Forum Bring Together Montreal's Black Business Leaders, Up-and-Coming Entrepreneurs"). In another CBC News post, "International Student Says Racial Stereotypes Still Abundant in New Brunswick" (Sturgeon), Jamaican student Husoni Raymond spoke about how some people treated him in accordance with the stereotypes about Black people that they hold.

Speaking about studies she had conducted on youth and racism over two decades, researcher Manju Varma, quoted in the post "Racism in Province's Schools Just Drives Immigrants to 'Bigger World,' Researcher Says" (Blanch), highlighted the problem of the racist name-calling that pervades schools. Varma argued that most schools conflate this type of racism with bullying. In the *Toronto Star* post "'I've Never Had a Black Teacher': Halifax Panel Tackles Inequality in the Classroom" (Cooke) one panellist—Sophia Wedderburn—discussed how she had not had any Black teachers in her school career. Furthermore, Wedderburn argued that the curriculum was Eurocentric. The moderator of the panel, DeRico Symonds, agreed that African Canadian history was being marginalized in classrooms. Also in the context of education, in the post "Black History Should Be Required Learning in School Curriculum, BC Mom Says" (Peng), Karina Reid from British Columbia campaigned for schools in the province to celebrate Black History Month. This was after she had not seen activities planned to commemorate the month on websites of school boards. In policing, Sergeant Deb Gladding recounted how a man had once closed his door in her face, preferring to deal with "someone like himself" (Grimaldi, "'Send Me Someone Else.' Officer Recalls Racism as York Police Celebrate Black History Month").

Beyond Black Canadians narrating their experiences with bigotry, Canadian prime minister Justin Trudeau admitted that involuntary bias and anti-Black racism does exist in Canada (CBC News, "Trudeau Says It's Time to Recognize"). This story was also carried by the *Globe and Mail* as well as the *Toronto Star*. In different posts, Trudeau reiterated that Canadians needed to critically reflect on the ways systemic racism manifests for Black Canadians (Bryden, "Trudeau Revisits Blackface Embarrassment"). Posting experiences of racism in these ways contributes to puncturing the aforementioned myth that there is no racism in Canada. The posts give voice to experiences that would otherwise remain unheard.

When reporting on anti-Black racism in Canada, it would be useful for the media to take an intersectional approach, which allows these outlets to provide audiences with granular, richer, and diverse accounts of racism. Black peoples' race often intersects with their other identities like gender, ability, ethnicity, age, class, and so on to exacerbate their experiences of prejudice and discrimination.

Despite anti-Black racism being a problem in Canada, Estrada contends that discussions on the topic remain one-sided because of the prevalence of denialism regarding the existence of racism in the country. Estrada elaborates that "some people will not hear you regardless of how truthfully you speak. They will not hear you regardless of how loudly or lovingly or profoundly you speak because they do not want to." Additionally, Morgan argues that speaking about racism for Black people is challenging and that there is an "exhausting burden of having to convince others of the truth of your lived experience." This can also partly be attributed to the fact that dominant discourses refute and diminish the existence of bigotry.

The police killing of George Floyd and several other deaths of African Americans triggered several organizations and groups in Canada to issue statements condemning the gruesome events in the United States. Most declarations also spoke boldly against anti-Black racism in Canada (African-Caribbean Faculty Association of McMaster University). In addition to statements, Canadian brands like Tim Hortons and BMO–Bank of Montreal had social media posts denouncing racism (@TimHortons; @BMO). Beyond issuing communications in the moment, Black entrepreneurs in Canada interviewed by the CBC also called for companies to take action to demonstrate the seriousness of their statements and hashtags (Dunne).

Commemorating Black History Month

All websites examined carried, to varying degrees, posts highlighting activities that took place around the country to mark Black History Month. Activities were often convened by Black Canadians and associations representing them. Other activities were hosted by schools, universities, galleries, provincial governments, Parliament, and so on.

At the centre of the festivities was a celebration of the diversity that characterizes Black Canadians. At some events, Black Canadians originally from West Africa were photographed donning clothes specific to their cultures. In addition, food was integral to these events (see CBC News, "8th Annual Black History Month Dinner"; Coppolino, "How to Eat Your Way through Black History Month in K-W").

Black History Month activities included movie nights, workshops, presentations, sports events, dinners, and galas (see CBC News, "More Than a Dozen Events to Mark Black History Month in Thunder Bay"; DePatie, "Winnipeg Celebrates Black History Month"; Ignatenko, "A Photo Exhibit Curated by Colin Kaepernick Is on Display"). Other activities for the month included showcasing Black art at galleries as well as musical and spoken word performances (CBC News, "'Love Thy Neighbour': St. Albert Art Gallery Celebrates Its First Black History Month Exhibition"). The CBC News post "200 Toronto Students Head to Parliament Hill as Part of Black History Month" reported how schools organized a trip to Ottawa to learn about contributions of Black Canadians in relation to the struggle for civil rights in the country. The *Toronto Star*'s "How Black Canadians Can Make Their Ancestors Proud" (Gooch) connected Black leaders from different generations and professions from across the country. Other Black History Month posts suggested reading their lists of books, written by Black authors, as a way to celebrate the month (Murdoch, "New Books to Explore during Black History Month").

While Black History Month was formally established in Canada in 1995, there have been calls (Eidinger; Beckford; Quigley; Kazia) for the celebration of contributions by Black Canadians to be mainstreamed. Confining conversations about Black histories to February ensures that they remain on the discursive margins in Canada. Henry explains that "Dr. Woodson [regarded as the pioneer of Black History Month (BHM)] intended that BHM would be a time when people would share what they learned throughout the other eleven months, not cram Black history into the month of February." Also commenting on Black History Month, Thompson called for a renaming of Black History Month to Black Literacy Month. Thompson elaborates that a Black Literacy Month would facilitate much more textured conversations about Black experiences in Canada. Thompson writes that "A Black Literacy Month would shift the focus from racism and struggle to a depth of understanding about the black experience, our socioeconomic contributions, and the similarities between blacks and other racialized communities."

There have also been calls for a complete abrogation of Black History Month. Writing in the context of the United States, Owens argues that "Black history is history. Period. To treat it as anything separate is reductive and racist. We can rectify this disparity by cancelling Black History Month. Instead, institutions must be held more accountable when it comes to consistently embracing black culture." Despite the varied suggestions, what emerges is the need to rethink the current way of doing Black History Month.

Less Prominent Narratives during Black History Month

While snippets of Canada's history with the enslavement of Black people is referenced in some posts (e.g., CTV News, "Black History Month in Canada"), this part of the country's past is not prominently featured in those that were examined. This deprioritizing of slavery histories in Canada contributes to the reason this past is not well known by many Canadians. The Government of Canada, in "About Black History Month," states that "few Canadians are aware of the fact that African people were once enslaved in the territory that is now Canada, or of how those who fought enslavement helped to lay the foundation of Canada's diverse and inclusive society." When the topic of slavery comes up, some Canadians often think about the sordid history of the United States in ways that neglect what happened in their own backyards.

Canadian academics Rinaldo Walcott and Afua Cooper contend that the tendency to tone down the aforementioned histories is not fortuitous (Miller).

They argue that it is "part of an orchestrated coverup and institutional denial by the country that slavery and systemic racism existed by minimizing the Canadian experience and leaving it to be drowned out by a flood of American narratives in media and literature" (Miller). Cooper asserts that a large portion of toning down Canadian experiences of slavery is as a result of "white guilt." Cooper explains that there is a realization in Canada that slavery pillaged from the lives of Black people, hence the feelings of culpability (Miller). The lack of concentrated attention on controversial Canadian histories with slavery works to augment mainstream accounts that frame Canada as historically better than the United States in its treatment of Black people.

Another neglected topic in the Black History Month posts relates to the difficulties that new Black migrants from Africa deal within Canada. Neglecting to publish experiences of marginality of this group serves to propagate the idea that Canada unconditionally embraces everyone.

While Black migrants from Africa encounter racism in Canada like other Black people in the country, Naidoo argues that the former group must face additional challenges. Notwithstanding that some migrants from Africa manage to secure suitable employment, a number of them note that they are "excluded from the Canadian labour market" (Baffoe 169). While not exclusive to African migrants, their foreign educational qualifications are discounted in Canada in ways that can make it difficult for them to find jobs (Creese). Yssaad and Fields (4) observe that "African-born immigrants had the lowest employment rate and highest unemployment rate of all immigrant groups, and these rates' differentials with the Canadian-born were particularly high for the African-born who had been in Canada for 5 years or less."

In addition, the "linguistic capital" of African migrants from Commonwealth countries is often obliterated in Canada (Creese). African migrants are usually encouraged to sign up for English as a Second Language (ESL) classes despite the fact that they are eloquent in the English language and trained in institutions modelled on the British system (Creese). Creese further observes that "pressure to take ESL classes signalled the perceived inadequacy of participants' command of English and the superiority of the local variant of 'standard English'" (Creese 301).

Furthermore, Creese argues that the migrants' "African English accents" were often considered subservient to the local variation. African migrants in a study in Vancouver (Creese) stated that they experienced discrimination based on their accents when they had searched for work and accommodations. Creese (305) argues that "in the Canadian context … African accents are embodied markers of individual incompetence, regardless of the individual's actual accomplishments." Viewing African migrants in these ways works to keep the new migrants on the fringes of Canadian society and reinforces the idea that they do not belong in the country.

CONCLUSION

Looking at the posts on Black History Month by the media in the case study, it was interesting that the overwhelming majority of them were posted on the CBC website. Even combined, there were fewer posts on Black History Month on the websites of CTV, the *Globe and Mail,* and the *Toronto Star.* This aligns with observations by Thompson, who argues that "the national media has scarcely even noticed that it's Black History Month. Outside of the *CBC* Newsworld program 'Being Black in Canada,' produced and hosted by Asha Tomlinson, and a few articles here and there in nationally circulated newspapers, if you don't live in central Canada, it could be very easy to forget that it's Black History Month." The abundance of Black History Month posts on the CBC website is hardly surprising. The national broadcaster's mandate compels it to cover topics like Black History Month in ways commercial media do not. Additionally, the differences in funding models between the CBC and the other media have implications for content. The CBC is partly funded by the government; therefore, its content is inclined to promote diversity and inclusion in the nation. Commercial media, on the other hand, largely rely on advertising revenue; thus, they are likely to prioritize content that will attract potential consumers for their advertisers. Rowland argues that while public broadcasters are speaking to citizens, commercial broadcasters are speaking to consumers. Commenting on the mainstream media in general, Fleras and Kunz (53) contend that they do not "exist to inform or entertain or even to persuade.... Mainstream media are first and foremost business ventures whose devotion to the bottom line is geared towards bolstering advertising revenues by attracting audiences and securing ratings." It would be interesting to conduct further research to understand why commercial media sources do not cover Black History Month as much as the CBC.

Circling back to the question about what the media prioritized given its pedagogical role, many Black History Month stories fell into the category of counterstories. Many posts provided histories and experiences of Black Canadians that were absent from dominant accounts in Canada. They named and acknowledged several Black Canadians for their contributions in the country and recounted histories of Black Canadian families that first settled in Canada, among other histories. This chapter argued that these narratives served to inculcate a sense of worth and belonging, especially for Black audiences. These accounts also provided Canadians in general with opportunities to learn and expand their knowledge about the histories of the country. Other posts on Black History Month highlighted experiences of racism that Black people face in contemporary Canada. These stories worked to debunk the dominant myth that anti-Black prejudice only occurs in the United States. These narratives have the potential to provide Canadians with the chance for introspection.

While the media in the case study prioritized specific content during Black History Month, detailed histories of slave ownership in Canada as well as the experiences of new immigrants from Africa did not receive much attention in the posts. Neglecting to focus on such topics in comprehensive ways works to fuel the illusion that Canada is better than the United States in terms of its past and present treatment of Black people. Precisely because Black Canadians are diverse, it is critical to ensure that their overlapping and intersectional experiences are highlighted.

In Canada, since the media participate in moulding the public's knowledge about Black History Month, it is important for them to be conscious of how they represent Black histories and experiences. It is critical for them to be mindful that they might be the only source of information on the topic for many Canadians; hence, they must be aware of what they are prioritizing and deprioritizing as well as whose stories are told and whose voices silenced. The challenge media industries have is ensuring that everyone is heard in the diverse group of Black Canadians.

CORE CONCEPTS

anti-Black racism: Racial discrimination specifically directed at Black people.

intersectionality: A term coined by legal scholar Kimberlé Crenshaw that refers to the ways people's multiple identities—like class, race, gender, ethnicity, ability, and so on—coalesce, overlap, and contribute to specific experiences of prejudice.

pedagogical tools: Teaching devices that are intended to communicate crucial lessons to people, resulting in enhanced comprehension of a subject.

SUGGESTED ACTIVITIES

1. Analyze the recent coverage and/or lack of coverage of Black History Month in a Canadian newspaper.

2.   Pick a group within the broader diverse group of Black Canadians and examine how a Canadian media industry recently covered or did not cover them during Black History Month.

REFERENCES

African-Caribbean Faculty Association of McMaster University. "Statement on the Killing of George Floyd and Racial Justice." *McMaster University Daily News*, 3 June 2020, dailynews.mcmaster.ca/articles/statement-on-the-killing-of-george-floyd-and-racial-justice/. Accessed 4 November 2020.

Alemán, Sonya M. "A Critical Race Counter-Story Chicana/o Subjectivities vs. Journalism Objectivity." *Journal of Culture and Education*, vol. 16, no. 1, 2017, pp. 73–91.

Ansell, Amy E. "Critical Race Theory." *Encyclopedia of Race, Ethnicity, and Society Vol. 1*, edited by Richard T. Schaefer, Sage Publications, 2008, pp. 345–347.

Baffoe, Michael. "The Social Reconstruction of 'Home' Among African Immigrants in Canada." *Canadian Ethnic Studies*, vol. 41–42, no. 3–1, 2009–2010, pp. 157–173.

Beckford, Lauren. "Beyond Black History Month." *etfoVoice*, Spring 2016, etfovoice.ca/feature/beyond-black-history-month. Accessed 31 July 2020.

Black History Canada Portal. "Black History Canada." *Canada's History Society*, 24 August 2011, canadashistory.ca/education/classroom-resources/black-history-canada. Accessed 26 March 2021.

Blanch, Vanessa. "Racism in Province's Schools Just Drives Immigrants to 'Bigger World,' Researcher Says." CBC, 3 February 2018, cbc.ca/news/canada/new-brunswick/racism-manju-varma-marcus-marcial-1.4516303. Accessed 31 July 2020.

@BMO. "At BMO we will always stand up for a society that is more just, where all people are valued, equally. That includes raising our voice to denounce racism whenever and wherever we see it." *Twitter*, 1 June 2020, twitter.com/BMO/status/1267593612667355139. Accessed 4 November 2020.

Bodenheimer, Rebecca. "What Is Critical Race Theory? Definition, Principles, and Applications." *ThoughtCo.*, 6 May 2019, thoughtco.com/critical-race-theory-4685094. Accessed 31 July 2020.

British Broadcasting Corporation. "What Is Representation?" *Bitesize*, 2020, bbc.co.uk/bitesize/guides/z9fx39q/revision/1. Accessed 22 September 2020.

Bryden, Joan. "Trudeau Revisits Blackface Embarrassment during Black History Month." CBC, 25 February 2020, cbc.ca/news/politics/justin-trudeau-blackface-1.5475399. Accessed 31 July 2021.

————. "Trudeau Revisits Blackface Embarrassment during Black History Month." CTV News, 24 February 2020, ctvnews.ca/politics/trudeau-revisits-blackface-embarrassment-during-black-history-month-1.4826184?cache=qpcupizl. Accessed 31 July 2021.

————. "Trudeau Revisits Blackface Embarrassment during Black History Month." *Toronto Star*, 24 February 2020, thestar.com/news/canada/2020/02/24/trudeau-revisits-blackface-embarrassment-during-black-history-month.html. Accessed 31 July 2021.

Buckingham, David. *Media Education: Literacy, Learning and Contemporary Culture.* Polity, 2003.

Byblacks.com "Home." 2020. Accessed 30 October 2020.

Canadian Association of Black Journalists (CABJ) and Canadian Journalists of Colour (CJOC). "Canadian Media Diversity: Calls to Action." *COJC.net*, 28 January 2020, j-source.ca/canadian-media-diversity-calls-to-action/. Accessed 7 April 2021.

Canadian Internet Registration Authority. "Canada's Internet Factbook." 2019, www.cira.ca/resources/corporate/factbook/canadas-internet-factbook-2019. Accessed 31 July 2020.

Canadian Journalism Foundation. "News Consumption Survey." April 2019, cjf-fjc.ca/sites/default/files/CJF%20News%20Consumption%20Survey.pdf. Accessed 31 July 2020.

Canadian Press. "Canada Doesn't Have Same 'Systemic, Deep Roots' of Racism as United States: Premier Doug Ford." *Global News*, 2 June 2020, globalnews.ca/news/7017967/doug-ford-george-floyd-racism/. Accessed 8 April 2021.

Carreiro, Donna. "Black History Month without Iconic Local Musician Gerry Atwell Bittersweet, Say Family and Friends." CBC, 2 February 2020, cbc.ca/news/canada/manitoba/gerry-atwell-black-history-month-1.5446838. Accessed 31 July 2020.

————. "Breaking the Black Stereotype: CBC Manitoba Chat Tackles Myths." CBC, 26 February 2020, cbc.ca/news/canada/manitoba/breaking-the-black-stereotype-cbc-manitoba-live-chat-to-tackle-myths-1.5475748. Accessed 31 July 2020.

Carter, Adam. "The Untold Story of How Hamilton's Black Community Was Built." CBC, 20 February 2018, cbc.ca/news/canada/hamilton/black-history-1.4543788. Accessed 31 July 2020.

CBC News. "8th Annual Black History Month Dinner & Gala to Celebrate Growing Community in Thunder Bay." CBC, 21 February 2019, cbc.ca/news/canada/thunder-bay/black-history-month-gala-1.5026948. Accessed 31 July 2020.

————. "200 Toronto Students Head to Parliament Hill as Part of Black History Month." CBC, 21 February 2018, cbc.ca/news/canada/toronto/black-history-month-students-ottawa-trip-via-rail-1.4544800. Accessed 31 July 2020.

CBC News. "Artistic Director Andrew Craig and Actors Laurence Dean Ifill and Allison Basha on the Play Fish and Rum." CBC, 15 February 2020, cbc.ca/player/play/1698507331936. Accessed 31 July 2020.

————. "Faces of Local Heroes 'Give Us Hope' Say Students Celebrating Black History Month." CBC, 5 February 2020, cbc.ca/news/canada/windsor/black-history-month-hall-of-fame-unveiled-1.5452253. Accessed 31 July 2020.

————. "Forum Brings Together Montreal's Black Business Leaders, Up-and-Coming Entrepreneurs." CBC, 4 February 2018, cbc.ca/news/canada/montreal/second-international-black-economic-forum-1.4519144. Accessed 31 July 2020.

————. "'High Time' to Honour Pair Chosen for Black History Month Stamps, Says Winnipeg-Based Creator." CBC, 1 February 2018, cbc.ca/news/canada/manitoba/winnipeg-black-history-month-stamps-1.4515777. Accessed 31 July 2020.

————. "More Than a Dozen Events to Mark Black History Month in Thunder Bay." CBC, 3 February 2020, cbc.ca/news/canada/thunder-bay/thunder-bay-black-history-months-1.5449481. Accessed 31 July 2020.

————. "Trudeau Says It's Time to Recognize Anti-Black Racism Exists in Canada." CBC, 13 February 2018, cbc.ca/news/politics/trudeau-black-history-month-1.4533194. Accessed 31 July 2020.

————. "'We Are the Roots': New Documentary Chronicles Triumphs of Alberta's Black Pioneering Families." CBC, 24 February 2018, cbc.ca/news/canada/edmonton/we-are-the-roots-new-documentary-chronicles-life-and-times-of-alberta-s-first-black-electrician-1.4548727. Accessed 31 July 2020.

————. "Willie O'Ree, NHL's First Black Player, on Breaking Barriers and Challenging Racism in Hockey." CBC, 4 February 2020, cbc.ca/player/play/1693465667807. Accessed 31 July 2020.

Colley, Sherri B. "One of Nova Scotia's First Black Nurses Recalls Struggles and Triumphs." CBC, 1 February 2018, cbc.ca/news/canada/nova-scotia/black-nurse-education-discrimination-graduate-whitney-pier-1.4512933. Accessed 31 July 2020.

Columbia Law School. "Kimberlé Crenshaw on Intersectionality, More than Two Decades Later." 8 June 2017, law.columbia.edu/news/archive/kimberle-crenshaw-intersectionality-more-two-decades-later. Accessed 31 July 2020.

Cooke, Alex. "'I've Never Had a Black Teacher:' Halifax Panel Tackles Inequality in the Classroom." *Toronto Star*, 12 February 2019, thestar.com/halifax/2019/02/12/ive-never-had-a-black-teacher-halifax-panel-on-tackling-inequality-in-the-classroom.html. Accessed 31 July 2020.

Coppolino, Andrew. "How to Eat Your Way through Black History Month in K-W." CBC, 9 February 2019, cbc.ca/news/canada/kitchener-waterloo/andrew-coppolino-black-history-month-food-2019-1.5009317. Accessed 31 July 2020.

Creese, Gillian. "Erasing English Language Competency: African Migrants in Vancouver, Canada." *Journal of International Migration and Integration*, vol. 11, no. 3, 2010, pp. 295–313.

CTV. "About CTV." 2020, ctv.ca/Corporate-Information/About-CTV. Accessed 31 July 2020.

CTV News. "Black History Month in Canada." CTV News, 21 February 2020, ctvnews.ca/search-results/search-ctv-news-7.137?page=2&sortOrder=date&q=Black+History+Month+Canada&fdate=&ftype=&fpage=. Accessed 31 July 2020.

———. "Sask. Family Has Deep Roots in Province's Black History." CTV News, 20 February 2019, regina.ctvnews.ca/sask-family-has-deep-roots-in-province-s-black-history-1.4305441. Accessed 31 July 2020.

Cukier, Wendy, Samantha Jackson, and Suzanne Gagnon. "The Representation of Women and Racialized Minorities as Expert Sources On-Air in Canadian Public Affairs Television." *Canadian Journal of Communication*, vol. 44, 2019, pp. 25–47.

Delgado, Richard, and Jean Stefancic. *Critical Race Theory: An Introduction.* New York University Press, 2001.

DePatie, Mason. "Winnipeg Celebrates Black History Month." CTV News, 1 February 2020, winnipeg.ctvnews.ca/winnipeg-celebrates-black-history-month-1.4793471. Accessed 31 July 2020.

Dunne, James. "Black Entrepreneurs Want Canadian Firms to 'Put Their Money Where Their Mouth Is' to Fight Racism." *CBC News*, 4 June 2020, cbc.ca/news/business/canadian-companies-black-entrepreneurs-fight-racism-1.5597323. Accessed 4 November 2020.

Eidinger, Andrea. "A Guide to Online Resources for Teaching and Learning about Black History in Canada." *Unwritten Histories*, 21 February 2017, unwrittenhistories.com/a-guide-to-online-resources-for-teaching-and-learning-about-black-history-in-canada/. Accessed 31 July 2020.

Entman, Robert M. "Framing: Towards Clarification of a Fractured Paradigm." *Journal of Communication*, vol. 43, no. 4, 1993, pp. 51–58.

Estrada, Meera. "Yes, There Is Systemic Racism in Canada—Our History Is Filled with It." *Global News*, 7 June 2020, globalnews.ca/news/7029694/canada-systemic-racism/. Accessed 16 October 2020.

Fleras, Augie. *The Media Gaze: Representations of Diversities in Canada.* University of British Columbia Press, 2011.

Fleras, Augie, and Jean Kunz. *Media and Minorities: Diversity in Multicultural Canada.* Thomson, 2001.

Foster, Lorne. "What Is the Black Canadian Experience?" *Toronto Star*, 2 February 2020, thestar.com/opinion/contributors/2020/02/26/what-is-the-black-canadian-experience.html. Accessed 31 July 2020.

Fürsich, Elfriede. "Media and the Representation of Others." *International Social Science Journal*, vol. 61, no. 199, 2010, pp. 113–130.

Fusch, Patricia I., and Lawrence R. Ness. "Are We There Yet? Data Saturation in Qualitative Research." *The Qualitative Report*, vol. 20, no. 9, 2015, pp. 1408–1416.

Gaye, Maimuna. "Recognize that Black History Is Canadian History." *Huffington Post*, 1 February 2019, huffpost.com/archive/ca/entry/black-history-is-canadian_b_14991340. Accessed 31 July 2020.

Gidengil, Elisabeth, André Blais, Neil Nevitte, and Richard Nadeau. *Citizens.* University of British Columbia Press, 2004.

Globe and Mail. "About Us." 2020, theglobeandmail.com/about/. Accessed 31 July 2020.

Globe and Mail. "Jackie Shane, a Pioneering Sour Singer, Dies at 78." 23 February 2019, theglobeandmail.com/arts/music/article-jackie-shane-a-pioneering-soul-singer-dies-at-78/. Accessed 31 July 2020.

Gooch, Tiffany. "How Black Canadians Can Make Their Ancestors Proud." *Toronto Star*, 9 February 2019, thestar.com/opinion/star-columnists/2019/02/09/how-black-canadians-can-make-their-ancestors-proud.html. Accessed 31 July 2020.

Government of Canada. "About Black History Month." *Canada.ca*, 21 February 2020, canada.ca/en/canadian-heritage/campaigns/black-history-month/about.html. Accessed 8 October 2020.

Government of Canada. "February is Black History Month." *Canada.ca*, 24 January 2020, canada.ca/en/canadian-heritage/campaigns/black-history-month.html. Accessed 8 October 2020.

Government of Canada. "Canadian Broadcasting Corporation (CBC)." *Canada.ca*, 10 August 2017, canada.ca/en/canadian-heritage/corporate/portfolio-organizations/canadian-broadcasting-corporation.html. Accessed 31 July 2020.

Grimaldi, Jeremy. "'Send Me Someone Else.' Officer Recalls Racism as York Police Celebrate Black History Month." *Toronto Star*, 5 February 2019, thestar.com/news/gta/2019/02/04/send-me-someone-else-black-officer-recalls-racism-as-york-police-celebrate-black-history-month.html. Accessed 31 July 2020.

Hackett, Robert A. "News Media and Civic Equality: Watch Dogs, Mad Dogs, or Lap Dogs?" *Democratic Equality: What Went Wrong?* edited by Edward Broadbent. University of Toronto Press, 2001, pp. 197–212.

Henry, Natasha. "Black History Month 2021: Black Canadian Counternarratives." *Teaching African Canadian History*, 29 January 2021, teachingafricancanadianhistory.weebly.com/blog. Accessed 27 March 2021.

Hermes, Joke. "The 'Ethnographic Turn': The Histories and Politics of the New Audience Research." *University of Leicester*, 9 February 2010, www2.le.ac.uk/projects/oer/oers/media-and-communication/oers/ms7500/mod1unit6/mod1unit6cg.pdf. Accessed 8 October 2020.

Hiraldo, Payne. "The Role of Critical Race Theory in Higher Education." *The Vermont Connection*, vol. 31, 2010, pp. 53–59.

Ignatenko, Margaryta. "A Photo Exhibit Curated by Colin Kaepernick Is on Display at Toronto Black History Month Festival." *Toronto Star*, 2 February 2020, thestar. com/news/gta/2020/02/02/photo-exhibit-from-nfler-colin-kaepernick-among-installations-at-toronto-black-history-month-festival.html. Accessed 31 July 2020.

Ishimwe, Leslie. "The Importance of Black History Month." *The Chronicle*, 28 February 2019, chronicle.durhamcollege.ca/2019/02/the-importance-of-black-history-month/. Accessed 27 March 2021.

Kazia, Alexandra. "Black History Month Should Be About More Than the Past." CBC News, 27 February 2014, cbc.ca/news/canada/black-history-month-should-be-about-more-than-the-past-1.2552753. Accessed 31 July 2020.

Khan, Janaya. "Don't Kid Yourself, White Nationalism Is on the Rise in Canada Too." *Flare*, 15 August 2017, flare.com/news/janaya-khan-white-nationalism-on-rise-in-canada/. Accessed 31 July 2020.

Klein, Rachel C. "The Teller's Tale: The Role of the Storyteller in the Life of the Story." PhD dissertation, University of San Francisco, 2009, repository.usfca.edu/diss/168.

Koivusalo, Tanya. "CBC Launches Expanded Website Being Black in Canada, Featuring the Stories and Experiences of Black Canadians." CBC/Radio Canada, 27 July 2020. cbc.radio-canada.ca/en/media-centre/being-black-in-canada-website-expanded. Accessed 30 October 2020.

Konguavi, Thandiwe. "'Love Thy Neighbour': St. Albert Art Gallery Celebrates its First Black History Month Exhibition." CBC, 1 February 2020, https://www.cbc.ca/news/canada/edmonton/art-gallery-of-st-albert-black-history-month-1.5449169. Accessed 30 May 2022.

Lule, Jack. *Understanding Media and Culture: An Introduction to Mass Communication.* Flatworld, 2017.

Malik, Asmaa, and Sonya Fatah. "Newsrooms Not Keeping Up with Changing Demographics, Study Suggests." *The Conversation*, 28 January 2020, theconversation.com/newsrooms-not-keeping-up-with-changing-demographics-study-suggests-125368. Accessed 27 March 2021.

Manitoba Education. "Black History and Anti-Racism in Canada." Government of Manitoba, 2021, edu.gov.mb.ca/k12/cur/multic/docs/black-history-anti-racism-canada.pdf. Accessed 26 March 2021.

Martinez, Aja Y. "A Plea for Critical Race Theory Counter-Story: Stock Story vs. Counter-Story Dialogues Concerning Alejandra's 'Fit' in the Academy." *Composition Studies*, vol. 42, no. 2, 2014, pp. 33–55.

McLeod, Susanna. "Jean Augustine." *The Canadian Encyclopedia*, 23 February, 2016, thecanadianencyclopedia.ca/en/article/jean-augustine. Accessed 14 July, 2022.

McMaster Museum of Art. "Deanna Bowen: A Harlem Nocturne." *McMaster Museum of Art,* 16 December 2019, museum.mcmaster.ca/tag/harlem-nocturne/. Accessed 3 November 2020.

Miller, Jason. "Why the Black Struggle in Canada Has All but Been Erased. Two Historians Explain Our Blind Spot." *Toronto Star,* 5 June 2020, thestar.com/news/gta/2020/06/04/why-the-black-struggle-in-canada-has-all-but-been-erased-two-historians-explain-our-blind-spot.html. Accessed 31 July 2020.

Morgan, Anthony. "The Suffocating Experience of Being Black in Canada." *Toronto Star,* 31 July 2015, thestar.com/opinion/commentary/2015/07/31/the-suffocating-experience-of-being-black-in-canada.html. Accessed 31 July 2020.

Moser, Gabrielle. "Every Family, Every Community Needs an Archivist—Deanna Bowen's Art Does This with Warmth and Care." CBC News, 18 October 2019, cbc.ca/arts/inthemaking/every-family-every-community-needs-an-archivist-deanna-bowen-s-art-does-this-with-warmth-and-care-1.5323540. Accessed 31 July 2020.

Muñoz, Frank M. "Critical Race Theory and the Landscapes of Higher Education." *The Vermont Connection*, vol. 30, 2009, pp. 53–62.

Murdoch, Sarah. "New Books to Explore during Black History Month." *Toronto Star,* 16 February 2018, thestar.com/entertainment/books/2018/02/16/new-books-to-explore-during-black-history-month.html. Accessed 31 July 2020.

Naidoo, Josephine C. "African Canadians." *The Canadian Encyclopedia*, 24 January 2020, thecanadianencyclopedia.ca/en/article/africans. Accessed 31 July 2020.

Nair, Roshini. "'Honey with the Medicine': Singer-Songwriter Khari McClelland on How Music Can Help Tell Difficult Truths." CBC, 9 February 2020, cbc.ca/news/canada/british-columbia/honey-with-the-medicine-singer-songwriter-khari-mcclelland-on-how-music-can-help-tell-difficult-truths-1.5010965. Accessed 31 July 2020.

Ndlovu-Gatsheni, Sabelo J. "Can Women's Voices Be Recovered from the Past? Grappling with the Absence of Women Voices in Pre-Colonial History of Zimbabwe." *Wagadu*, Summer 2005, colfax.cortland.edu/wagadu/Volume%202/Printable/ndlovu.pdf. Accessed 31 July 2020.

Neary, Clara, and Helen Ringrow. "Media, Power and Representation." *The Routledge Handbook of English Language Studies,* edited by Philip Seargeant, Ann Hewings, and Stephen Pihlaja, Routledge, 2018, pp. 294–309.

News Media Canada. *Circulation Report: Daily Newspapers.* 2015, nmc-mic.ca/wp-content/uploads/2016/06/2015-Daily-Newspaper-Circulation-Report-REPORT_FINAL.pdf. Accessed 7 October 2021.

Nowell, Lorelli S., Jill M. Norris, Deborah E. White, and Nancy J. Moules. "Thematic Analysis: Striving to Meet the Trustworthiness Criteria." *International Journal of Qualitative Methods*, vol. 16, 2017, pp. 1–13.

Ojo, Tomilola. "Black History Month in Canada: Microaggressions, Injustice and Solidarity with Indigenous People." *The Sheaf*, 8 February 2020, thesheaf.com/2020/02/08/black-history-month-in-canada-microaggressions-injustice-and-solidarity-with-indigenous-people/. Accessed 8 October 2020.

Owens, Ernest. "Cancel Black History Month." *The Philadelphia Inquirer*, 1 February 2019, inquirer.com/opinion/commentary/black-history-month--20190201.html. Accessed 31 July 2020.

Peng, Jenny. "Black History Should Be Required Learning in School Curriculum, BC Mom Says." *Toronto Star*, 6 February 2019, thestar.com/vancouver/2019/02/05/its-not-enough-to-encourage-black-history-month-in-schools-bc-mom-says.html. Accessed 8 October 2020.

Quigley, Joseph. "Is Black History Month Limiting the Teaching of Black History?" CBC News, 8 February 2016, cbc.ca/news/canada/black-history-month-debate-1.3423493. Accessed 31 July 2020.

Ross, Greg. "Canadian Olympic Hero Sam Richardson Honoured by His Former High School." CBC, 15 February 2018, cbc.ca/news/canada/toronto/canadian-olympic-hero-sam-richardson-honoured-by-his-former-high-school-1.4537615. Accessed 31 July 2020.

Rowland, Wade. *Saving the CBC: Balancing Profit and Public Service.* Linda Leith Publishing Inc., 2013.

Sturgeon, Nathalie. "International Student Says Racial Stereotypes Still Abundant in New Brunswick." CBC, 8 February 2018, cbc.ca/news/canada/new-brunswick/racism-students-new-brunswick-1.4526951. Accessed 31 July 2020.

Tawil, Yasmina. "What Exactly Is Media Representation Anyway?" *Arab Film and Media Institute*, arabfilminstitute.org/what-exactly-is-media-representation-anyway/. Accessed 17 September 2020.

Thompson, Cheryl. "Why We Need to Rethink Black History Month." *Rabble.ca*, 21 February 2014, rabble.ca/news/2014/02/why-we-need-to-rethink-black-history-month. Accessed 31 July 2020.

@TimHortons. "There is no place for racism, hatred and violence in our communities. We need to take accountability for calling out racism and hatred by name and stopping it. We are listening, so we can recognize racial and social injustice and commit to change." *Twitter*, 2 June 2020, twitter.com/TimHortons/status/1267888958375178243. Accessed 4 November 2020.

Tolley, Erin. *Framed: Media and the Coverage of Race in Canadian Politics.* University of British Columbia Press, 2015.

Toronto Star. "About the Star." *Toronto Star*, 2020, thestar.com/about/aboutus.html. Accessed 31 July 2020.

Yang, Jennifer. "Demeaned, Overworked and All Called George: How Black Train Porters Transformed Canada." *Toronto Star*, 1 February 2019, thestar.com/news/gta/2019/02/01/the-madness-of-being-george-how-black-train-porters-demeaned-overworked-and-called-by-the-same-name-helped-transform-canada.html. Accessed 31 July 2020.

Yosso, Tara J. *Critical Race Counter-Stories along the Chicana/Chicano Educational Pipeline*. Routledge, 2006.

Yssaad, Lahouaria, and Andrew Fields. "The Canadian Immigrant Labour Market: Recent Trends from 2006 to 2017." Statistics Canada, 24 December 2018, www150.statcan.gc.ca/n1/en/pub/71-606-x/71-606-x2018001-eng.pdf?st=ydfJ0n8G. Accessed 31 July 2020.

CHAPTER 10

Applying Critical Creativity: Navigating Tensions between Art and Business in the Creative City

Brandon McFarlane

INTRODUCTION

Artists, arts administrators, creative professionals, and policymakers (henceforth referred to as creatives) require the ability to critically evaluate how the emergence of the creative economy has impacted artistic and cultural production in Canada so that they make sound, strategic decisions. In the decades bracketing the millennium, there was a shift in government policy in which art and cultural funding was mobilized to produce economic outcomes. Explaining how an idea stimulates economic growth within a region and building partnerships with civic stakeholders can provide creatives with strategic advantages in highly competitive sectors with relatively scarce funding and resources. However, leveraging such opportunities can sometimes result in creatives unwittingly becoming complicit in the negative consequences of culture-based economic development and can present risks to artistic integrity and autonomy.

Critical creativity is a skill creatives can apply to navigate the tensions between art and business. Critical creativity was first theorized by Alexander Hollenberg, who argued that creativity involves critically engaging with creative outputs of the past and imagining how a new idea will impact a culture. In contrast to popular narratives that perpetuate myths that exclusively associate creativity with right-brain thinking, Hollenberg shows creativity is fundamentally constituted through criticality. One cannot determine if an idea is novel without an in-depth knowledge of past creative outputs, and failing to critically speculate upon an innovation's consequences risks producing disastrous change and second-order consequences—outcomes that are contrary to or undermine intended goals.

This chapter is organized into three sections that move from the macro-scale of sociocultural context to the micro-scale of everyday practice. The first delineates the creative turn in Canada, in which policymakers instrumentalized art and culture to advance economic imperatives. It identifies the key themes of creative city policy as well as a number of unintended consequences that produced new forms of inequity and exclusivity. It provides emerging creative leaders with pertinent knowledge about the sociocultural context of the creative city and models how critical creativity can be applied to strategically analyze complex intersections between policy, city building, and the creative industries. The second section argues that creative problem solving (CPS) provides a meaningful place to intervene. It briefly critiques the evolution of CPS to demonstrate the need to integrate critical creativity into existing models. Indeed, further developing CPS models provides efficient, high-impact pathways for transformative change because they are accessible and commonly applied by relevant stakeholders. The third section introduces thinking tools inspired by works of radical art and critical theory that can facilitate critical creativity. It provides practical, step-by-step processes that can be applied to enhance everyday problem solving with an emphasis on producing positive outcomes from the perspective of equity, diversity, and inclusion.

CRITICAL CONTEXT: KEY THEMES AND SECOND-ORDER CONSEQUENCES OF CREATIVE CITY DEVELOPMENT

Paul Makeham's analysis of urban planning discourse illuminates how contemporary civic stakeholders increasingly draw upon theatrical metaphors to conceptualize the design of spaces, experiences, and the built environment. Such strategies enable practitioners to conceptualize how architecture, art, culture, and design animate a space in both intentional (scripted) and unintentional (improvised) ways. Building upon Makeham, Laura Levin and Kim Solga delineated the emergence of the "creative city script" in cultural and urban planning discourse, in which cultural investments are rationalized via their ability to brand a region as creative to global audiences (38). For example, a municipality might build a new art gallery. In urban planning and cultural policy discourse, the art displayed in the gallery is often of secondary importance to how building the gallery expresses a city's commitment to art and culture. One might never visit the new Remai Modern in Saskatoon, but the building's construction can be leveraged by a host of civic stakeholders to promote the city's newfound creativity. Being able to critically interpret the creative city script is an essential skill for navigating the new uses and abuses of art and culture.

Theme #1: Investing in Culture Enhances Economic Competitiveness

Contemporary policy applies Richard Florida's research on the creative class and creative city to justify investment in art and culture. An economic geographer, Florida conducted a statistical analysis of American metropolitan regions to identify factors that drove economic growth in *Cities and the Creative Class*. He found that regions that attracted a critical mass of creative talent were top performers and, he theorized, would continue to drive growth in the 21st century. He labelled these regions creative cities because their economic success originated from the labour force's ability to reliably produce novel products, designs, and services and to apply their ingenuity to solve problems. He labelled this segment of the workforce the creative class, and he found they are attracted to regions with vibrant cultural scenes and populations that are tolerant of diversity. Hence, investing in culture is one way to attract members of the creative class to a region and, correspondingly, spur economic growth, a form of city building commonly referred to as culture-based development.

Creatives can leverage the creative city script to gain resources by articulating how their idea advances policy goals and achieves economic outcomes. Levin and Solga unpack how a host of civic stakeholders in Toronto—including politicians, bureaucrats, arts leaders, and businesses—mobilized the creative city script to facilitate an unprecedented wave of investment, dubbed "Toronto's Cultural Renaissance," in the first decade of the 21st century. The campaign attracted $257 million in investment for marquee institutions such as the Royal Ontario Museum, Art Gallery of Ontario, and Four Seasons Centre for the Performing Arts. The massive investment in civic infrastructure transformed the cultural offerings and architecture of downtown Toronto (Jenkins 170). Similarly, Janet Price, the CEO of Luminato, launched a successful fundraising and partnership campaign that involved "unabashedly deploying Florida's creative city vocabulary" to attract private and public investment, a strategy that secured $22.5 million in the contemporary art festival's first year (Levin and Solga 41). Savvy creative leaders are skilled at critically interpreting policy and cultural discourse, which enables them to strategically situate their creative practice or organization within the broader ecosystem.

Theme #2: Blurred Distinctions between Publicly Funded "Art" and Commercial "Entertainment"

Historically, Canadian cultural policy distinguished between areas of practice that were artistic—like literature, dance, and fine art—and commercial—such as film and television. The Massey-Lévesque Commission report (1951) was instrumental in establishing Canada's cultural infrastructure and institutions. It argued that Canada's vast geography and American imperialism were two factors discouraging the emergence of world-class cultural institutions. Market-oriented approaches would result in American cultural and economic hegemony because American industries were well established and had access to a massive domestic market. Canadian artists and creative industries could not compete either at home or abroad. Thinkers were also skeptical that American companies would support Canadian artists or tell Canadian stories. As such, the Massey report recommended protectionist and cultural-nationalist solutions, which created strategic but problematic binaries that associated the arts with public funding and advancing social goals, while entertainment was tied with commercial pursuits.

These binaries continued into the era of official multiculturalism via the Royal Commission on Bilingualism and Biculturalism (1963–69), the multiculturalism policy (1971), and the *Multiculturalism Act* (1988). These policies identified the need to move away from a singular Canadian identity associated with whiteness, Britishness, and the romance of the North, turning instead toward more inclusive formulations that recognized and celebrated diversity— including French Canadians and newcomers. Multicultural policies perpetuated cultural-nationalist and protectionist rubrics that continued to distinguish between government-funded "art" and commercially produced "entertainment," reimagining art and culture as tools to advance progressive social goals, such as attracting and settling newcomers and fostering inclusion within a diverse cultural mosaic.

Brendan Kredell delineated a significant shift in Canadian cultural policy and artistic production that began in the mid-1990s. Diverse disciplines such as dance, literature, film, photography, theatre, game design, interaction design, tourism and hospitality, casinos and gaming, interior design, and many others were amalgamated within the rubric of the creative industries. Policy—at all three levels of Canadian government—changed to prioritize areas that had the ability to generate profit and stimulate growth in other sectors. The policy shift addressed problematic binaries between art and commerce, as many films and video games are artistic and explore complicated social themes. Similarly, historically artistic areas of practice, such as literature and theatre, can be commercially viable, and not every work upholds radical or progressive politics.

Theme #3: Blurred Distinctions between Artistic and Entrepreneurial Labour

Florida's theorization of the creative class contributed to what Anne Harris labelled the "democratisation of creativity" in which Western society moved away from Romantic but elitist conceptualizations and embraced new theories emerging from psychological research that suggested everyone has the potential to be creative (2). Indeed, after centuries of primarily being associated with arts and crafts, creativity is now a top skill sought by employers. Florida coined the term *creative class* to describe labour in the creative industries, which he subdivided into two categories (*Cities and the Creative Class*). The super-creative core (such as artists, filmmakers, educators) apply their creativity to make new designs, products, and services. Creative professionals (such as urban planners, CEOs, lawyers, bankers, accountants) apply specialized knowledge to creatively solve problems. Through the 1950s to late 1980s, creativity was primarily associated with eccentrics—artists, beatniks, bohemians, hippies, and hipsters—but now it is common to describe historically "square" roles such as a CEO, accountant, or lawyer as creative.

Just as business roles were increasingly being conceptualized as creative, artists and art workers were increasingly described as entrepreneurs. This trend is, perhaps, best epitomized by Daniel Pink's proclamation that the "MFA is the new MBA" (21) in the *Harvard Business Review*. Pink was commenting upon how businesses were recruiting artists due to their creativity, resilience, and resourcefulness. Pink suggested that artistic training would become more valuable in the job market than an education in business. Such a statement, though, suggests a misunderstanding of and little appreciation for artistic creativity: an artist typically pursues an MFA to make art, not to transfer those skills to a day job that may have little to no connection to their artistic practice. *Artrepreneur* is a more appropriate term, as it acknowledges that many artists are in fact entrepreneurs operating sole proprietorships, and entrepreneurial thinking is an essential skill in the creative industries. Indeed, many funding streams in Canada require creatives to outline how their activities will generate profit either directly through sales or by securing benefits for other businesses or sectors (such as property development, tourism, and hospitality).

Second-Order Consequence #1: Increased Inequity

Creative policy is designed to facilitate culture-based development: civic stakeholders invest in art and culture with the aim of increasing property value and gaining other benefits for street-level commerce. Canadian municipalities are highly motivated to increase property value as property tax is one of the few reliable sources of revenue available to cities due to the division of powers between municipal, provincial, and federal governments. Increasing density, particularly through condo development, opens up other sources of revenue. For example, Section 37 of the *Ontario Planning Act* enables property developers to negotiate density accommodations in exchange for community benefits. Indeed, the Cultural Renaissance may have been a little too successful as it played a starring role in the gentrification of downtown Toronto.

Cultural investment concentrated in Toronto's downtown core, particularly along neighbourhoods bracketing the city's subway system. Sara Diamond et al. criticized governments and private industry for creating "public art deserts" in the city's geographically and economically marginalized neighbourhoods (4). Public art is concentrated in tourist districts and neighbourhoods experiencing rapid gentrification, which can be attributed to the city's reliance on Section 37 funding for the public art program. The vast majority of public art is technically owned by developers (or, rather, condo corporations), but they are required to guarantee public accessibility and maintain the work through its life cycle. Acknowledging the exclusivity of past practices, the top priority in the *Toronto Public Art Strategy 2020/2030* is "Creativity and Community Everywhere."

Ute Lehrer and Thorben Wieditz documented the condo boom in the downtown core that further disadvantaged equity-seeking communities by rapidly increasing the cost of living. They describe how Toronto transformed into three different cities, characterized by class and geography. There were dramatic increases in high-income neighbourhoods in the downtown core, with rich access to civic infrastructure and cultural opportunities, and in low-income neighbourhoods in the inner suburbs ("Condominium" 141). Middle-class neighbourhoods were rapidly disappearing as the city stratified. Culture-based gentrification was not only displacing people but also businesses: "disposable income of the new condominium residents contributes to making it difficult for low-income groups, as well as the stores and services that serve them, to remain in their places" ("Gentrification" 140). Rent for office and commercial space increased, thereby displacing long-term neighbourhood businesses and presenting grassroots arts organizations with dramatically increased expenditures. Indeed, Florida belatedly acknowledged these critiques, and many others, in *The New Urban Crisis*, which unpacks the inequities caused by culture-based redevelopment.

Second-Order Consequence #2: Superficial Creative Experiences

One artrepreneurial strategy regards the festivalization of culture: designing a carnival atmosphere to attract massive, broad audiences that, in many circumstances, have little interest in art. They create environments in which attendees can superficially consume contemporary art without necessarily participating in the rigorous intellectual and political engagement many performances command. Brian Batchelor's critical analysis of the Edmonton Fringe Festival's branding materials and public-facing communications unpacks how the design of festivals evidence their instrumentalization by global capitalism. A Fringe is a radically open festival that uses a lottery system—rather than curation—to select works; all ticket sales go directly to performers; and festivals primarily generate revenue through grants, on-site donations, amenity sales, and, more recently, corporate sponsorships. Batchelor playfully alludes to the tensions between commercialization and supporting grassroots theatre by quipping, "This beer festival has a theatre problem," a reference to a new trend in which more people attend (and party) at the beer tent than those who actually patronize theatre shows. He notes:

> In expanding to outdoor spaces and folding those secondary elements—
> the street performers, artisans and vendors, and KidsFringe—into the
> total festival, the Fringe evolved from a theatre event into a larger muni-
> cipal, family-friendly party ultimately defined by the production, selling,
> and therefore objectification of spatial and experiential difference within
> Edmonton's urban imaginary. (39)

Whereas grassroots theatre has, historically, been the main attraction, systemic pressures compel arts leaders to prioritize the beer tent to maximize advertising and sponsorship revenue. It also provides the opportunity to collect data that can enhance success on future grant applications by demonstrating impact in terms of hospitality and tourism.

These broadscale shifts appear to be impacting the aesthetics of contemporary art by rewarding works that create playful, interactive, and, often, family-friendly experiences. Fringes market their diversity as a key attractor: seasoned veterans perform alongside amateurs and emerging talent. The lottery system often brings together disparate themes and aesthetics in a single festival. Fringes offer low-risk opportunities to pilot new works and, indeed, have an admirable track record of incubating productions from equity-seeking communities (such as trey anthony's *da Kink my hair* and Ins Choi's *Kim's Convenience*). However, Batchelor contends that the shift away from artistic production to artrepreneurship has discouraged risk-taking, experimentation, and themes of social justice. Commercially successful Fringe producers create franchise-style shows: "they have remounted past successes and staged sequels to previously well-received and economically successful work (often with a same or similar cast)," and, as such, "difference is but a marker for cultural capital since the individual shows themselves are not inherently different from each other" (44). Feel-good comedies and ridiculous clown shows prevail due to a new, risk-adverse, and commercial culture within the Fringe community. Batchelor evidences the neoliberalization of Fringe festivals, which has produced a new scene that values spectacular aesthetics and apolitical works that echo the commercial goals of administrators, funding institutions, and corporate partners. His prescriptions, though, are problematic, as they recover Massey-era binaries that associate "serious" art with themes of social justice and "superficial" entertainment with commercial success.

Second-Order Consequence #3: New Forms of Exploitation

Intentionally producing a party atmosphere, though, does have its second-order consequences. Thea Fitz-James's research responds to the culture of sexual assault and harassment created by the carnivalesque atmosphere of Fringes by contemplating strategies for restorative justice. The beer tent provides an opportunity to interact with artistic talent with few barriers—one of the joys of a Fringe festival regards the chance to meet and talk with artists as well as the spontaneous networking, mentorship, and artistic exchanges that occur at the beer tent. However, the party atmosphere presents sex and alcohol as essential aspects of a Fringe festival's bohemian experience, which creates opportunities for predators, both within and outside of the scene, to sexually exploit artists and attendees. Indeed, the Edinburgh Fringe Festival—the world's largest—was called out in 2019 for failing to acknowledge and address its unfortunate history of sexual harassment and assault.

Artrepreneurial strategies can also sometimes result in organizations becoming complicit in "woke-washing," token gestures meant to enhance their brands from the perspective of social justice. Take, for example, *Streetscape*, a multifaceted series of workshops, talks, and interventions featuring collaborations between international artists and local youths. It was part of the 2008 Luminato Festival and staged in Regent Park, a community-housing neighbourhood that was in the middle of an ambitious private-public redevelopment. Heather McLean interviewed community art practitioners and found that locals were troubled by the ways in which powerful civic actors participated: "As one critic noted, wealthy philanthropists and corporate donors—especially white philanthropists—find programming cultural activities in Regent Park appealing because they are interactions that spur convivial civic engagement, but veer away from uncomfortable conversations about structural inequality" (2165). In other words, some wealthy patrons seem primarily motivated by a desire to brand themselves as woke social justice warriors who help BIPOC and low-income communities, but they are reluctant to participate in the difficult conversations pertaining to equity and inclusion—such as Luminato's complicity with culture-based gentrification. Similarly, another participant noted: "journalists, Luminato staff and corporate sponsors were excited to hobnob with big-name graffiti and mural artists. He laughed when he described the awkward interactions that took place: 'when journalists approached us and the youths we worked with, they were like, "And who are you?"'" (2165). The comments, and McLean's broader analysis, suggest some stakeholders are more interested in exploiting the neighbourhood's ethnic diversity and perpetuating propagandistic narratives about the culture-driven transformation of Regent Park rather than seriously engaging with urban art forms made for and by marginalized communities and the critical issues they raise about race, class, and geography.

CREATIVE PROBLEM SOLVING AND THE NEED FOR EFFECTIVE DYNAMIC BALANCE

Training in creative problem solving (CPS) has the potential to provide emerging creatives and seasoned professionals with the foresight they need to critically navigate the second-order consequences of the creative city. CPS is a methodology for the reliable generation of novel and useful ideas. It breaks down the creative process into tangible steps and provides thinking tools that activate targeted modes of cognition at the appropriate time (such as the ubiquitous brainstorming). CPS is an attractive option for facilitating critical creativity because it is highly accessible and is already broadly practised in the creative industries. In short, it provides a high-potential, high-impact means to enhance commonly applied practices and find common ground between a variety of stakeholders who are committed to equity, diversity, and inclusion but who may need some specialized thinking and leadership tools to guide systemic change.

CPS draws upon psychological research to systematize and demystify the creative process. Its origin dates back to the post–World War II marketing industry. Alex Osborn, a second-generation marketing executive, wanted to develop reliable processes for creativity that would provide a competitive advantage. He authored

Applied Imagination: Principles and Procedures of Creative Writing (1953), which explored the importance of creativity, how to effectively ideate, and how environmental factors affect creativity. The book drew upon scholarly research and his business experience, and in doing so, *Applied Imagination* introduced many influential strategies to mass audiences, such as brainstorming and facilitation principles that can be applied to enhance individual and group creativity. Osborn's *Applied Imagination* inspired a number of iterations of CPS, including the Osborn-Parnes Model (1966), Creative Problem Solving (VanGundy 1987), the Buffalo Creative Process Inventory or the FourSight Model (Puccio 2001; Puccio et al. 2011), and the Thinking Skills Model (Puccio et al. 2011). Each iteration further explored and refined processes through scholarly research by adding additional process stages, facilitation guidelines, and thinking tools. There are many creative processes; for a thorough review of creative processes and models, see R. Keith Sawyer's *Explaining Creativity: The Science of Human Innovation*.

CPS advocates cycling back and forth between phases of divergence and convergence—what Puccio et al. call "dynamic balance" (*Creative Leadership* 64). Divergence involves applying creative thinking to generate as many novel ideas as possible. Convergence involves applying critical and evaluative thinking to move toward a comprehensive solution. Guidelines stipulate that divergence and convergence should be done in isolation—hence, Osborn's guidelines for divergent thinking emphasize generating as many novel ideas as possible, deliberately seeking novel or highly unusual ideas, building upon ideas or those shared by others, and deferring judgment. Indeed, there is an emerging body of research demonstrating the efficacy of CPS in both educational (see Puccio et al., "Creative Problem Solving"; Ritter et al., "Fostering Students' Creative Thinking") and industry settings (see Puccio et al., "A Review"; Vernon et al., "An Evidence-Based Review"), especially in terms of how CPS strategies enhance divergent thinking. However, the efficacy of convergent or critical practices has received little scholarly attention until recently.

Arthur Cropley's "In Praise of Convergent Thinking" criticized creativity researchers for over privileging divergent thinking. In *The Dark Side of Creativity*, Cropley and others cautioned that long-standing biases risked nurturing the "dark side of creativity," the misapplication or blinkering of criticality that produces disastrous change and incubates malignant innovations. Creativity scholars were responding to international crisis instigated by malignant creativity, such as the innovative aspects of the September 11 terrorist attacks or the housing crisis in the United States. While the examples are admittedly extreme, they challenged the American idealism that had historically informed creativity studies: scholars had not yet thought deeply about the ethics and social consequences of creativity and innovation or how people might apply creativity studies insights to exploit or harm others (both intentionally and unintentionally). Cropley theorized that embracing convergent thinking would lead to a deep questioning of disciplinary practices and a renewed interest in how criticality enhances creativity.

Subsequent research has emphasized the importance of criticality and convergence in the creative process. Carter Gibson and Michael D. Mumford found that deep criticisms of novel ideas positively impacted the creativity of both the creator and criticizer: "it was found that the production of criticisms evidencing depth, specificity, and utility were consistently and strongly related to the production of higher quality, more original, and more elegant problem solutions" (328). In their discussion, they speculate that criticism enhances the creative process by identifying the "deep" and "fundamental issues" that demand creative attention (329). Their findings contest long-standing CPS guidelines that, since Osborn's *Applied Imagination*, have assumed that criticality negatively impacts divergent thinking and, as such, evaluation, critique, and similar constraints should be repressed. They build upon other studies (see Baer; Basadur et al.; Brophy; Runco; Runco and Acar) to further evidence that "idea evaluation may be as, if not more, important to creative problem solving than idea generation per se" (314).

The scholarly debate about the overvaluing of divergent thinking was confirmed by my own experiences as an educator and community researcher. At Sheridan College, I design and instruct undergraduate courses that introduce CPS strategies that empower creative leaders. The goal is not only to enhance students' employment prospects but also provide them with the knowledge and skills they need to facilitate positive, transformative change. In these courses, creative leaders often bring industry challenges to the classroom that we try to overcome through collaborative CPS sessions. Similarly, I have led a number of research collaborations with arts festivals that sought to resolve (or, at least, mitigate) the second-order consequences of the creative city through critical research and the application of CPS. When applying existing CPS strategies, we often encountered challenges in convergent phases. When students lacked a critical knowledge of the creative city, some would suggest highly novel but inappropriate ideas that exacerbated rather than resolved problems. Similarly, when ideas were evaluated during convergent phases, teams would sometimes advance novel but problematic ideas without meaningfully anticipating second-order consequences. Common examples are proposing that artists engage in sex work to generate revenue to underwrite their artistic practice or pitching well-intentioned diversity and inclusion initiatives that reproduced harmful stereotypes. We needed new CPS tools to facilitate the critical creativity necessary to overcome highly complicated challenges in the creative industries.

THINKING TOOLS FOR FACILITATING CRITICAL CREATIVITY

This section introduces tools for critical creativity that were developed for an audience of emerging creative leaders and established professionals. The tools are inspired by critical theory and works of art, and they seek to transform insights into accessible yet powerful tools for guiding critical conversations and the formulation of holistic innovations. It is important to note that the tools are prototypes that emerged in response to the issues outlined in the previous sections. Their efficacy has yet to be investigated via peer-reviewed research, but they have been productively applied in classroom and industry settings. They mark a pertinent starting point for integrating critical creativity into CPS models. For each, I briefly introduce the inspirational source, intended outcomes, and step-by-step process.

The Tetrad

In *The Global Village*, Marshall McLuhan and Bruce Powers introduced the tetrad as a tool for speculating upon and critically evaluating how an innovation might (or already has) changed society. Their analysis of technologies revealed that each innovation provides intended services but also unintentional disservices (6). Indeed, they present the tetrad as "a means of focusing awareness of hidden or unobserved qualities in our culture and its technologies" to "afford the user predictive power" so that they may anticipate and critique the second-order consequences of an innovation. They identified four archetypal consequences. First, an innovation enhances or improves something (e.g., commercialization enhances a not-for-profit art organization's bottom line). Second, an innovation replaces something else or renders it obsolete (e.g., commercialization reduces an art organization's reliance on government funding). Third, an innovation retrieves something that has been previously displaced or obsolesced (e.g., commercialization recovers the patronage system). And fourth, when taken to its logical extreme, an innovation reverses into its opposite (e.g., commercialization transforms a not-for-profit art organization into a business).

Process

1. State and clarify the proposed idea. Then generate as many answers as possible to the following prompts:
   A. What does the idea improve or enhance?
   B. What does the idea obsolesce or replace?
   C. What does it recover from older, obsolesced ideas?
   D. How might the idea reverse into its opposite?

Dada

The second critical creativity tool is inspired by Dionne Brand's *What We All Long For* (2005), a novel about diasporic twentysomethings in Toronto's Kensington Market. It represents an ideological conflict between neoliberalism and bohemianism that is mapped onto spaces and places in the city. The protagonist is Tuyen, an avant-garde artist who attempts to transform the traumatic experiences of her refugee family into art installations. Tuyen's foil is Binh, her older brother who holds an MBA from the University of Toronto and who invests in organized crime. Both are highly creative, but Tuyen attempts to use her creativity to advance the public good whereas Binh applies his creativity for crass, personal profit.

The narrator and the characters expose the many ways that neoliberalism finds value in what society generally deems useless. Binh applies an extreme form of neoliberal logic to justify human trafficking and forced prostitution as legitimate and desirable. He imposes a market-oriented worldview on all human activity to justify his malignant intentions. In contrast, Tuyen applies her artistic creativity to transform what neoliberal society values—private property, materialism, hard work, free markets, deregulation, exploitation—into the useless. The materialistic characters are all miserable and depressed—they surround themselves with possessions but lack community and meaningful friendships. Tuyen and other guerrilla artists appropriate private property to make art installations that recover histories and experiences blinkered by institutional racism. For example, Tuyen slowly transforms her bachelor apartment into a work that records the longings of Torontonians. The creative process slowly destroys the apartment. In short, Tuyen's Dadaism challenges neoliberalism by appropriating and reversing its logic.

Dada is a tool that helps one anticipate how an idea might be instrumentalized and, conversely, how an idea might reverse neoliberal co-option. If the "MFA is the new MBA," what happens when we flip the formula: the "MBA is the new MFA"? Such questioning may help creative leaders exploit creative economy discourse to gain access to resources and opportunities while nevertheless creating outputs that are grounded in social justice and the public good.

Process

1. State and clarify the idea that is being proposed. Generate as many responses as possible to the following prompts:
   A. How might we transform this useless idea into something useful?
   B. How might we transform this useful idea into something useless?

Thalia and Melpomene

This tool finds inspiration in the masks for comedy and tragedy. One is named after Thalia, the Greek Muse of Comedy, and the other is named after Melpomene, the Muse of Tragedy. Inspired by Edward De Bono's *Six Thinking Hats* (1985), which associates different styles of lateral thinking with colour-coded hats, this tool asks participants to put on "thinking masks" to critically evaluate an idea by applying the archetypes of comedy and tragedy.

The purpose of this thinking tool is to facilitate critical discussions about inclusion and exclusion. Art and culture contribute to the social good by building and supporting communities. As creative policies have shifted resources away from grassroots organizations to marquee cultural institutions, there is a pertinent need to critically evaluate how ideas include some communities while excluding others. One might apply Thalia and Melpomene thinking masks to evaluate how a festival's carnivalesque atmosphere impacts a variety of stakeholders. For example, consider a particular stakeholder: a parent with a young child who wants to attend some theatre shows at the local Fringe festival. Wearing the Melpomene masks, one might realize the parent may feel excluded from a Fringe festival due to long-standing theatre conventions discouraging audience-generated noise (a baby crying or cooing), the beer tent's party atmosphere, or the high cost of childcare in Canada. When wearing the Thalia mask, one might suggest institutionalizing relaxed performances, instituting "dry" or family-friendly hours at the beer tent, and setting up a childcare co-op program during the festival.

Process

1. Identify and research a stakeholder audience.
2. Put on the Thalia mask and ask: how might this idea integrate or include the stakeholder?
3. Put on the Melpomene mask and ask: how might the idea isolate or exclude the stakeholder?

Making Metaphors

CPS models often incorporate thinking tools that use metaphors to guide divergent thinking. The "Forced Connections" tool relates a random object to the challenge to generate novel ideas. For example, if we were thinking about how might we boost attendance at the local art festival, a facilitator might take a balloon and ask: What ideas does this balloon give you? And participants might respond: Rent a bouncy castle! Have a water balloon fight! Host an improv show on a hot air balloon ride! Hire buskers to perform and make balloon animals! Host a helium party where everyone is given a helium balloon at admission and they can breathe in the helium to change the pitch of their voice! Metaphoric thinking can also enhance concept coherence and criticality, especially when solving problems involving interdisciplinary collaboration and high levels of abstract thinking.

Victor P. Seidel and Siobhán O'Mahony have shown how interdisciplinary teams can struggle to communicate effectively when innovating due to their highly specialized knowledge. People may use the same words to describe radically different ideas, or one party may lack the technical knowledge to understand the information being shared by collaborators. Their research suggests using metaphors as conceptual prototypes can overcome communication challenges. For example, creative economy discourse is saturated with metaphors that combine ideas from the arts, architecture, cognitive science, economics, and urban planning to make new policy directions and related ideas understandable to everyday people. Indeed, much of the scholarship introduced in the first section critically analyzes common metaphors such as right-brain thinking, creative class, staging, "the MFA is the new MBA," artrepreneur, and so on to describe new intersections between business, art, and city building. Savvy creatives excel at making metaphors to clearly communicate and pitch ideas as well as interpreting metaphors to generate strategic insights.

Making Metaphors is also inspired by Matt Ratto's theorization of critical making. It applies artistic practices to research a topic and synthesize insights. Ratto's model involves three process steps that can be applied individually or as a team. First, participants research a topic using traditional means. Second, participants build a prototype on which they map insights. The prototype is not intended to be functional; rather, it is the metaphoric representation of the group's ideas and research. Third, the group reflects upon the research and prototype to generate insights and then edits the prototype accordingly. This phase involves exploring "alternative possibilities, and using them to express, critique, and extend relevant concepts, theories, and models" (253). To be as clear as possible, the prototype can take any form: use readily available materials like plasticine, building bricks, pipe cleaners, popsicle sticks, and so on to build conceptual prototypes.

Making Metaphors synthesizes Seidel and O'Mahony's research on metaphoric prototyping and Ratto's process for critical making. It is especially impactful during the early phases of the creative process, which involve problem identification and formulation. It helps the team identify the most pertinent challenges. It is also effective during later, convergent phases in which promising solutions are identified and evaluated. Novel and innovative ideas are notoriously difficult to communicate, hence Making Metaphors is one way of achieving concept coherence prior to rigorously evaluating ideas.

Process

1. Conduct primary and secondary research through traditional means.
2. Identify a new problem or idea that requires further clarification or development.
3. Make as many metaphors as possible to communicate or express the new idea.
4. Select the most compelling metaphor and make a physical representation of the metaphor (i.e., conceptual prototype) using readily available materials such as plasticine, building bricks, or illustrations.
5. Critically discuss the concept, metaphor, and prototype, and revise each to reflect new insights.

CONCLUSION

The emergence of the creative economy has produced tensions between art and business for artists, administrators, and other creative professionals. Creatives obviously need to make a living, and there is nothing inherently wrong or corrupt with applying artrepreneurial strategies to reach new audiences, increase revenue, provide audiences with novel experiences, or create radically new works. However, creatives can benefit from adopting critical and holistic perspectives so that they are aware of the insidious, second-order consequences of the creative city agenda and can resist becoming an unwitting agent of culture-based gentrification. This chapter introduced some novel strategies that can be applied to fight back against the "dark side" of the creative economy. The provided critical creativity tools are by no means encyclopedic and are admittedly idiosyncratic. But I hope readers will be inspired to further engage with the inspirational sources and contemplate how critical insights inspired by other works might be applied in their everyday lives.

CORE CONCEPTS

creative city script: The instrumentalization of theatre and performance tropes by urban planners and other stakeholders to brand a region as a global, creative city.

creative problem solving: A methodology for the deliberate and reliable generation of novel ideas that systematizes the creative process into broadly applicable phases.

critical creativity: The ability to critically engage with the creativity of the past and speculate upon how an innovation may transform society.

democratization of creativity: A broadscale shift in which Romantic conceptualizations of creativity emerging from artistic culture were replaced with democratic conceptualizations of creativity emerging from American psychological research, which contended that everyone is creative and creativity is a skill like any other that can be fostered through deliberate practice and training.

SUGGESTED ACTIVITIES

1. Apply the tetrad to critically analyze the creative city script in a representative policy or strategic document. Select a policy recommendation or strategic initiative, and critically evaluate the idea's consequences by applying the tetrad.
2. Select an art festival or cultural institution that you recently interacted with. Apply Melpomene to assess how a current practice excludes an underrepresented community and apply Thalia to imagine new, inclusive practices.
3. Apply Making Metaphors to synthesize some of the ideas introduced in this chapter. Consider making a visual metaphor or work of art that expresses key themes.

REFERENCES

anthony, trey. *da Kink in my hair*. Playwrights Canada Press, 2005.

Baer, John. "Evaluative Thinking, Creativity, and Task Specificity: Separating Wheat from Chaff Is Not the Same as Finding Needles in Haystacks." *Critical Creative Processes*, edited by M. A. Runco, Hampton Press, 2003, pp. 129–152.

Basadur, Min, et al. "Understanding How Creative Thinking Skills, Attitudes, and Behaviors Work Together: A Causal Process Model." *Journal of Creative Behavior*, vol. 34, 2000, pp. 77–100.

Batchelor, Brian. "'This Beer Festival Has a Theatre Problem!': The Evolution and Rebranding of the Edmonton International Fringe Theatre Festival." *Theatre Research in Canada*, vol. 36, no. 1, 2015, pp. 33–51.

Brand, Dionne. *What We All Long For*. Vintage, 2005.

Brophy, Dennis R. "Comparing the Attitudes, Activities, and Performance of Divergent, Convergent, and Combination Thinkers." *Creativity Research Journal*, vol. 13, 2000–2001, pp. 439–455.

Choi, Ins. *Kim's Convenience*. House of Anansi Press, 2016.

Cropley, Arthur. "In Praise of Convergent Thinking." *Creativity Research Journal*, vol. 18, 2006, pp. 391–404.

Cropley, Arthur, et al. *The Dark Side of Creativity*. Cambridge University Press, 2010.

De Bono, Edward. *Six Thinking Hats*. Key Porter Books, 1985.

Diamond, Sara, et al. *Redefining Public Art in Toronto*. OCAD University and University of Toronto, 2017.

Fitz-James, Thea. "Consent on the Fringe: Restorative Justice and Accountable Communities." *Canadian Theatre Review*, vol. 180, 2019, pp. 14–19.

Florida, Richard. *Cities and the Creative Class*. Routledge, 2005.

———. *The New Urban Crisis*. Basic Books, 2017.

Gibson, Carter, and Michael D. Mumford. "Evaluation, Criticism, and Creativity: Criticism Content and Effects on Creative Problem Solving." *Psychology of Aesthetics, Creativity, and the Arts*, vol. 7, no. 4, 2013, pp. 314–331.

Harris, Anne M. *The Creative Turn: Toward a New Aesthetic Imaginary*. Sense Pub, 2014.

Hollenberg, Alexander. "Challenging Creativity: A Critical Pedagogy of Narrative Interpretation." *English Studies in Canada*, vol. 43, no. 1, 2017, pp. 45–66.

Jenkins, Barbara. "Toronto's Cultural Renaissance." *Canadian Journal of Communication*, vol. 30, 2005, pp. 169–186.

Kredell, Brendan. "T.O. Live with Film: The Toronto International Film Festival and Municipal Cultural Policy in Contemporary Toronto." *Canadian Journal of Film Studies*, vol. 21, no. 1, 2012, pp. 21–37.

Lehrer, Ute, and Thorben Wieditz. "Condominium Development and Gentrification: The Relationship Between Policies, Building Activities and Socio-Economic Development in Toronto." *Canadian Journal of Urban Research*, vol. 18, no. 1, 2009, pp. 140–161.

———. "Gentrification and the Loss of Employment Lands: Toronto's Studio District." *Critical Planning*, Summer 2009, pp. 138–160.

Levin, Laura, and Kim Solga. "Building Utopia: Performance and the Fantasy of Urban Renewal in Contemporary Toronto." *The Drama Review*, vol. 53, no. 3, 2009, pp. 37–53.

Makeham, Paul. "Performing the City." *Theatre Research International*, vol. 30, no. 2, 2005, pp. 150–160.

McLean, Heather E. "Cracks in the Creative City: The Contradictions of Community Arts Practice." *International Journal of Urban and Regional Research*, vol. 38, no. 6, 2014, pp. 2156–2173.

McLuhan, Marshall, and Bruce R. Powers. *The Global Village: Transformations in World Life and Media in the 21st Century*. Oxford University Press, 1992.

Osborn, Alex. *Applied Imagination: Principles and Procedures of Creative Writing*. Creative Education Foundation Press, 1953.

Parnes, Sid J. *Manual for Institutes and Programs*. Creative Education Foundation, 1966.

Pink, Daniel H. "9. The MFA Is the New MBA," in "Breakthrough Ideas for 2004." *Harvard Business Review*, vol. 82, no. 2, 2004, pp. 13–37.

Puccio, Gerard J. *Buffalo Creative Process Inventory: Technical Manual*. FourSight, 2001.

Puccio, Gerard J., et al. "A Review of the Effectiveness of CPS Training: A Focus on Workplace Issues." *Creativity and Innovation Management*, vol. 15, no. 1, 2006, pp. 19–33.

————. "Creative Problem Solving in Small Groups: The Effects of Creativity Training on Idea Generation, Solution Creativity, and Leadership Effectiveness." *Journal of Creative Behavior*, vol. 54, no. 2, 2018, pp. 453–471.

————. *Creative Leadership: Skills that Drive Change*. 2nd ed., Sage, 2011.

Ratto, Matt. "Critical Making: Conceptual and Material Studies in Technology and Social Life." *The Information Society*, vol. 27, 2011, pp. 252–260.

Ritter, Simone M., et al. "Fostering Students' Creative Thinking Skills by Means of a One-Year Creativity Training Program." *PLoS One*, vol. 15, no. 3, 2020, pp. 1–18.

Runco, Mark A. "Idea Evaluation, Divergent Thinking, and Creativity." *Critical Creative Processes*, edited by M. A. Runco, Hampton Press, 2003, pp. 69–94.

Runco, Mark A., and Selcuk Acar. "Divergent Thinking as an Indicator of Creative Potential." *Creativity Research Journal*, vol. 24, 2012, pp. 66–75.

Sawyer, R. Keith. *Explaining Creativity: The Science of Human Innovation*. 2nd ed., Oxford University Press, 2012.

Seidel, Victor P., and Siobhán O'Mahony. "Managing the Repertoire: Stories, Metaphors, Prototypes, and Concept Coherence in Product Innovation." *Organization Science*, vol. 25, no. 3, 2014, pp. 691–712.

VanGundy, Arthur B. *Creative Problem Solving: A Guide for Trainers and Management*. Quorom Books, 1987.

Vernon, David, et al. "An Evidence-Based Review of Creative Problem Solving Tools: A Practitioner's Resource." *Human Resource Development Review*, vol. 15, no. 2, 2016, pp. 230–259.

CHAPTER 11

Transforming Industry Standards: Tensions between Social Change and Media Production Education

Ki Wight

INTRODUCTION

A persistent tension exists around the concept of *industry standards*, which is frequently used in post-secondary media production programs that educate the next generation of filmmakers, content creators, and digital media artists. The focus on industry standards in these programs results in a tendency to prioritize technological, craft, and economic aspects of media education over critical, social, and ethics-oriented studies (Ashton and Noonan; Banks; Giroux; Nam). Exploring the tension between critical and industrial functions of any creative industries education is important because institutions of higher learning influence how industry ethics are established and eventually practised by graduates (Saha). In other words, how educators define industry standards has the potential to limit the ways students come to understand industry responsibilities. Given the lack of common creative or media industries ethical codes, and given social justice movements urging media industry change, it is important for educators to consider the social implications of how they teach industry practices. To explore the persistent tensions of *industry standardness*, this chapter will draw on creative industries and higher education research, as well as my own experiences as an instructor and media industry professional. This chapter concludes with a summary of theories and practices that offer possibilities for educators, practitioners, and students to better critically examine, resist, or transform our notions of industry standards. These considerations are important because social change might happen in media classroom spaces by educating with a focus on how industry work processes may be harmful and how social movements influence change in creative industries practices.

Under the broad umbrella of the creative industries, the media industries, also referred to as mass media or the entertainment industries, comprise companies that produce, distribute, or provide services to commercial films, series, news, games, and animations. Media production education refers to post-secondary programs offering media industry–related training. Media production education programs commonly include theoretical, historical, and/or critical courses, but their primary focus is to educate students in hands-on project-based learning for the purpose of gaining work. This chapter focuses on public institutions that offer media industry education because the question of what is public about public education might come into conflict with industry-specific practices. In an era of widespread social change movements, particularly movements within the media industries them-selves, this chapter explores tensions that exist between critical and social func-tions of public higher education, along with more industrial conceptions or uses of it. In writing this chapter, I am also reminded of a student who came to class with an urgent question fuelled by social movement conversations: *Is the film industry too racist to accept me?* After presenting this question to my colleagues to ensure that our department would address this student's concerns at the program level, one responded: *Well, we don't do social justice education.* These conflicting comments bring to life my concerns about how to integrate critical, social, and career-focused educational content.

Using creative and media industries conceptual and empirical research, the following tensions will be explored in this chapter:

1. What is the purpose of public media production education?
2. How are the media industries engaging with current social change movements?
3. How do media production education programs engage with current social change movements?

While this chapter reviews arguments that question industrial logics in media edu-cation, it is written with the understanding that it is very important for students to find meaningful employment after graduation. That said, I aim to illustrate ways that critically informed media production education can enhance the capacity of graduates to thrive and transform the media industries in socially just ways.

TENSION #1: WHAT IS THE PURPOSE OF PUBLIC MEDIA PRODUCTION EDUCATION?

I have often heard my educator colleagues talk about training students in a vigorous way as a means to show them that industry work is *hard*. But what does it mean for industry work to be hard? The choice to characterize work in this way indicates that teacher-practitioners might accept and endorse the challenging aspects of media industry work. Challenges include long hours, toxic work environments, normalized precarity, and top-down power structures. If the industries do not follow any broad ethical codes, and if media production educators accept damaging aspects of industry work, then teaching to industry standards might normalize, rather than challenge, harmful work practices. This section explores research about unjust or dangerous workplace norms in the creative industries and links these to contemporary higher education practices. Themes exploring hard work, precarity, the myths of good work, gender- and race-based industry barriers, and institutional inaction will be addressed.

Hard Work and Good Work

The academic field of the creative industries, including production studies, has researched the ways that difficult, discriminatory, or unattainable working conditions are normalized and played against moral discourses of perseverance, passion, merit, and talent (Banks; Harvey; Saha). While these challenging aspects of work culture are well established, what is not as well known is how creative industries instructors understand their role in relation to these cultural critiques. There is a competing discourse to normalized notions of hard work: that studying creative production offers students the chance to do *good work* by preparing them for dream jobs in the creative industries. Hesmondhalgh and Baker define *good work* as work with self-affirming qualities such as autonomy, meaning, intellectual appeal, and security. A defining feature of media education marketing, in particular, is the promise of a career with creative passion and fulfillment. As summarized below, the depiction of living a creative dream is in stark contrast to the realities of hard work that both is precarious and operates with technical and social duress.

Long Hours and Difficult Conditions

Hard work in the context of the media industries usually implies exceptionally long working hours in physically and psychologically harsh environments (Allen).

Media production days typically span twelve- to sixteen-hour shifts with constantly changing physical working conditions. For many jobs, the industry requires keeping up with rapidly changing technologies, whether employed or not (Ashton, "Upgrading the Self"). While many of these traits are certainly not limited to the media industries, they combine to toxic and dangerous effect with the industry's rigid hierarchies that tend to reward conformity and complicity (Banks; Campbell; Gill; McRobbie; Saha). Given these working conditions, there is an established value in the industry of dogged perseverance at any cost. The working conditions alone likely pose barriers for those who cannot work the unpredictable and long hours due to family or cultural obligations or bodily limitations. Mental health challenges, injuries, and substance abuse are all well-documented issues faced by industry workers as they struggle to keep up (Serebrin). Furthermore, the top-down hierarchies and precarious nature of contract-based work creates an environment where workers avoid complaining or expressing concern about working conditions, what Frechette calls "go along to get along" (194). The pressures of media industry work are certainly in stark contrast to a happy pursuit of creative passions, and it is uncertain how media educators accept or refute these conditions. As explored in the next sections, the illusions of inspiring and collaborative *good work* are often used to normalize precarity and hide practices of exclusion.

Precarity and the Myth of Good Work

In McRobbie's book *Be Creative*, she discusses various contradictions in the notion of *good creative jobs*. She explains how social systems enact power through human internalization and, then, performance of social rules. Her research shows that creative work is often done uncritically, tirelessly, and without financial or social reward under the guise of passion or creative fulfillment. Work in these contexts is also precarious, as is it mostly contract-based and for others' economic benefit. Even unpaid work is normalized through discourses of building portfolios and gaining experience. Day jobs or side gigs, particularly in restaurant or other service industries, are seen as normal mechanisms for getting ahead in a creative career (McRobbie). The idea that one must constantly work, and always be productive and ready to upgrade current skill sets, gives the impression that being industry-ready is an all-encompassing lifestyle (Ashton, "Upgrading the Self"; McRobbie). Given the potential for workplace harm, it is critical that educators actively address the critiques of the myths of good work without valorizing unjust hard work. A closer look at gender and race in the cultural industries reveals that inequitable workplace practices impact some people more than others.

Industry Barriers: Gender and Race

Feminist and critical race scholars have noted that the pressures of mythical good creative work are more intensely experienced by women and racialized cultural workers. In studying working conditions of women in gaming, de Castell and Skardzius (844) detail how production companies focus on employees' personal love of gaming in order to exploit workers' skill sets and avoid changing hostile work conditions for women. Gill's study of new digital media work spaces points to emerging gender-based inequities; the seemingly cool and informal nature of newer media work actually leads to misperceptions of egalitarian work practices. In fact, Gill notes that the freelance and unstructured nature of this work leads to an "individualization of risk" (86) that hides vastly different rates of access to technology, pay, and career advancement. Campbell's work echoes these observations, noting significant differences in opportunities based on the "old boys' club" (11) sensibility that leads to the disproportionate advancement of white male-identified artists and a lack of opportunities for racialized artists in traditional venues. This research signals that gender- and race-based discrimination is endemic to creative work. And if it is endemic, it is likely embedded in media education, too. Following is a closer look at how racism is embedded in cultural industries practices.

It is important to explore how racialized creative workers are constrained in or denied access to creative industries work. Saha explains that it is important to avoid addressing racial inequity by simply changing racial representations. Instead, he urges us to focus on how race and racism is produced in media workplace contexts. Through explorations of production practices, including common workplace myths he calls "industry lore" (129), Saha looks at how core elements of production pipelines[1] contribute to the limiting, objectifying, and derisive treatment of racialized bodies. From media genres to the way content is marketed, Saha shows how industry pipelines consistently and uncritically place white workers and representations as necessary for business success. This is evident, for example, in the historical prevalence of white heroes and racialized villains in action genre content, or in recent media industry studies evidencing exceptionally low rates of racialized or Indigenous women working in key production roles (Brinton and McGowan). Saha's work speaks directly to my concerns about how industry standards might normalize practices of exclusion in industry-oriented educational programs.

Discrimination, Diversity Initiatives, and Meritocracy

Industry discourses of talent and meritocracy can translate to inequitable educational practices. Allen et al.'s study of creative industries work placements evidences two ways that discrimination arises in higher education: they found barriers to obtaining work placements based on gender, race, and dis/ability, and they revealed that instructors managing work placements believe that their process offers students equal access. One way to read this research is that there is a problem with how media production instructors understand equality and equity, as formally granting people equality does not mean that all people access opportunities equally. Therefore, instructors might not be able to see how their classroom practices are creating unjust student outcomes. The concept of equity is crucial, as it takes into consideration the different pathways, deficiencies, and barriers that might exist in being able to access common social systems. In wider discourses of diversity and equity, there is the critique that when formal processes, policies, and other workplace structures like committees are established, their presence in organizations is often seen as standing in for the actual act of creating equity (Ahmed). Saha's work on race in the media industries echoes this theory, as it shows that simply hiring diverse workforces does not yield structural and functional changes in business activities. Thus, if we are concerned with making media employment socially just, it is important to look closer at the ways our educational systems uncritically accept and solidify unjust social practices.

Banks's research details how the belief in "natural talent" is a myth and is not based on objective factors (69–70). His work explains that while the creative industries are supposedly open to anyone with the will or talent to participate, expensive creative industries educational programs are now positioned as gatekeepers to industry entrance, with evidence of bias based on applicants' race, gender, and class (Banks). Similarly, in a 2013 study, Gaztambide-Fernández et al. reviewed the admissions practices of a specialized public arts high school in Canada and determined that talent-based admissions criteria were synonymous with racial and class-based social advantage. These examples evidence the potential harms of creative industries education practices and call into question the purpose of industry-oriented education in the post-secondary landscape.

Critical Thinking in Media Production Training

Media content is generally produced through the cooperative labour of craft-based production crews. Historically, many of these positions have educated their ranks through on-the-job apprenticeship-style training. Thus, media production as a field is different than media or communication studies, which exist within universities and colleges as a means to critically study media representations and effects. In recent years, with the trend toward enhancing the economic and professional functions of university, media production programs have emerged and become popular on the premise that they feed trained students to hungry industry pipelines (Ashton and Noonan; McRobbie). The tension in these newer industry-based production programs is between the critical traditions associated with media and communication studies and rote craft practices. If these production programs are focused on industry job contexts, why do they exist in higher education when apprenticeship models of industry jobs are still practised? What are these industry programs educating for, and why are these programs in universities?

Over the past few decades, public post-secondary institutions have grappled with decreasing government funding and increasing global and domestic competition for students. In response to this, government and institutional policies have tended to mandate, develop, and support programs that offer students more overtly career-ready education (Ashton and Noonan 8). While it is clearly important for students to graduate with job prospects, questions have been raised about the impacts of this career-ready framing of higher education. This market-readiness is usually critiqued as a manifestation of neoliberalism, an ideology based on the principles of fierce individualism and market-based decision-making. Giroux has highlighted the impact of neoliberalism on higher education, noting the reduction of program focus on critical competencies. According to Giroux, removing critical, social, and political literacies from public education has the potential to reduce students' capacity for democratic participation due to its emphasis on individualism. Coté and Allahar describe this shift as one away from education, and its critical and democratic functions, to one of vocationalism and training. They recommend educators avoid seeing industrial versus critical education as a dichotomy and instead find ways to embed values of criticality in technical and rote learning. These theorists offer a warning to instructors: without critical function, normalized industry workplace harms will continue.

Ashton notes that industry professionals are seen by students as legitimate sources of information, so it makes sense that teacher-practitioners critically consider how they teach ("Making It Professionally"). An important question arises: *what are the critical skill sets of media production instructors who are both teachers and industry professionals?* It seems prudent for media production programs to consider deeply how to prioritize criticality throughout program engagement with students and to offer opportunities for meaningful instructor professional development. Given that professional growth and change are core traits of media industry work, the following section considers how both the media industries and media production education programs are responding to current social change movements that are significantly impacting media landscapes. The scholarship explored aims to tease apart and challenge the ways hard work and good work are engaged in media production education.

TENSION #2: HOW ARE THE MEDIA INDUSTRIES ENGAGING WITH CURRENT SOCIAL CHANGE MOVEMENTS?

This section is about how social movements are influencing discourse and material change in the media industries. It will offer a quick survey of social movements like #MeToo, #BlackLivesMatter, #TimesUp, and #IdleNoMore, along with examples of changing policies and practices in the media industries. It will also look at statistical data on media industries inequities. These points will be used to interrogate the ways that industry standards might be changing to include principles of equity and social justice.

Social Media and Social Change

Social media has amplified various social change movements to the point of being nearly omnipresent in broader society (Mendes et al.). As social media movements amplify critical voices, increase awareness of social injustice, and build communities that loudly resist discrimination, media workplaces are increasingly called upon to take action where misrepresentations and abuses occur. Frechette outlines the impact that the feminist #MeToo[2] and #TimesUp[3] movements have had on the media industries, particularly how they have shown that sexual assault, harassment, and abuse of power are endemic. Revelations and social pressures have occurred in a variety of ways: social media campaigns widely name offences and the people committing them; public petitions circulate regularly; racial justice movements like #BlackLivesMatter and women's rights organizers keep researching and initiating campaigns; legal action is taking place for workplace offences; and investigative journalism has shed light on wrongdoings. The media industries have responded by firing prominent abusers; changing workplace conduct and safety regulations; initiating gender and racial parity programs; and overhauling auditioning and other hiring practices where abuses have been revealed (Frechette). High-profile criminal cases, notably the conviction of US studio mogul Harvey Weinstein and the prominent case against Canadian broadcaster Jian Ghomeshi, have set the stage for change in media workplace practices. In the case of Ghomeshi, even though he was acquitted due to a lack of evidence, his case launched the widespread social media campaign #BeenRapedNeverReported

(Mendes et al.). This hashtag has helped raise public awareness about the reasons women often feel pressured to keep rape private. These examples show that social movements have spurred some direct change within the media industries, leading me to believe that it is critical to build awareness of social movements when educating for media work.

Journalism is a media practice within the creative industries that has grappled with social media and social movements in their business and education operations. Journalism scholars Callison and Young review impacts of social media movements on journalism practice and look closely at the legacy of unjust journalism coverage about Indigenous Peoples.[4] Their work explores the resistant and reframing practices of feminist, decolonial, and Indigenous journalism in order to challenge how traditional reporting relates to dominating social orders, settler colonialism, and environmental justice. Their study of social media activism describes these movements as a newer kind of journalistic action that observes and critically comments on real-time events, particularly how these events are misrepresented or omitted by conventional media outlets. Social media reporting, then, is capable of calling journalism to account for its legacy of "representational harms" (Callison and Young 4). Their research uncovers that change is slow due to journalism's false claims to objectivity, or what they call its "view from nowhere" (4), which does not value stories from specific positionalities or lived experiences. They note that supposed objectivity, combined with a disciplinary self-conception of liberal open-mindedness, hides bias in the framing of news stories. Callison and Young's review of resistant and reframing journalism practices are useful examples for how other media industries can change. Their work offers guidance for media educators to teach industry practices with overt understandings of histories of representational violence, including teaching students the critical skill of accounting for their media practice choices. This has broad implications for media education as their work shows how necessary it is to centre awareness of bias and just practices throughout media-making production processes. In other words, it is important to teach students to think deeply about the social elements of their content creation.

Industry Introspection and Responses

There are clear examples of efforts and constraints in realizing more just media cultures. These efforts are about both representation and workplace practice. One industry strategy to address equity has been to diversify actors and storylines beyond patriarchal and mostly white male gazes. But changing the race or gender of a character does not necessarily create more just representation. Saha cautions that because creative work is happening within commodified contexts, we should be aware that the social impacts of supposedly diversified content might be what he calls either "enabling" or "constraining" (141). In other words, more diversity does not enable more just media production. For example, when racialized or non-normative content is produced, it has a tendency to be called "niche" and distributed on smaller channels or streams (Harvey 159). Another example of a constraining function of diversity endeavours is how social inequities are often portrayed as isolated instances from the past. The plethora of representations of North American Black culture in historical stories about slavery might be constraining, as these representations are stuck in an unjust and horrifying past. These stories are in contrast to enabling representations in films such as the blockbuster *Black Panther*, which engages Afrofuturism to inspire agency in beyond-colonial visions of Black lives (Strong and Chaplin). Black feminist media scholarship has also developed many enabling strategies for asserting Black subjectivities and counter-subjectivities in media representations (Patterson et al.). Filmmaker Joey Soloway's concept of the "female gaze" follows Black feminist media scholars by asking both audiences and filmmakers to play with the idea that characters on screen are not objects but instead in complex relationship to pressures of patriarchal culture. These examples show that problems of representation are deeply connected to workplace cultures. If we care about equitable treatment in creative industries processes, then we must consider who is working, what they are working on, and the conditions of their work.

The activism that is fuelling changes in representation are also gaining traction in the larger commercial entertainment sector. While gender- and race-based activism and advocacy have been around for many decades in Canada, the tenor and broad awareness of social justice movements have ignited long overdue industry responses.[5] For example, the Racial Equity Media Collective launched the widely supported Producer's Pledge: Reclaim/Reframe in order to rectify the poor representation of BIPOC in cultural institutions. The pledge asks Canadian producers to make "purposeful and substantive commitments to reclaim representation, reframe hiring practices, and ongoing learning as they pertain to anti-black racist, anti-indigenous racist and all anti-racist practices and policies" (Kay). Further to the producer's pledge, the BIPOC TV & FILM advocacy group recently launched an industry-supported online roster called hirebipoc.ca as a means of resisting systemic racism in the Canadian media industries' hiring practices (Ramachandran). These two actions offer the chance for producers, media companies, and production crews to work in more equitable ways and with more public accountability. These are initiatives that enable direct changes to media practice, and these changes have been informed by longer-standing statistical analysis of who actually gets to make media content in front of, or behind, the cameras.

Diversity and Equity by the Numbers

Many research, policy, and workplace hiring initiatives in the media industries have focused on gender parity and, more recently, racial parity. The concept of *parity* is based on the principle of equality, and it maintains that if gender and race are more equally populated or balanced in the media industries, then more socially just industry outcomes will occur. Equality has been challenged as a concept by social justice scholars as it does not account for people's unequal social conditions that might prevent access to institutions like schools, work, and other places of power (Henry et al.). Gender parity, in particular, became popularized in 2018 after the actor Frances McDormand promoted Stacy L. Smith's idea of an "inclusion rider" at the Academy Awards as a means for high-ranking actors to use their star power to require productions to obtain parity in production hiring and payment practices (Harvey 167). Racial parity has also been a long-standing focus of statistical research by US-based news associations such as the American Society of News Editors (ASNE) and the Radio Television Digital News Association (RTDNA). In 2020, the Canadian Association of Journalists (CAJ) also began the practice of collecting race- and gender-based data. While parity measures do not account for the entire problem of creating a more just workplace culture, numbers do matter because they evidence irrefutable problems of who gets access to media work and representation. The quantitative media research has shown the wide gender-based and racial gaps in the Canadian and US media systems, with comparable inequities existing outside of these two countries (Brinton and McGowan; Brannon Donoghue). In recent years, this research has uncovered that earlier feminist activism benefited mostly white women and did not substantially include women of colour and Indigenous women (Brinton and McGowan). These studies clearly establish that inequitable cultures still thrive in the media industries and contribute to an understanding of industry standards.

Brinton and McGowan are long-time media industry professionals, scholars, educators, and activists in Canada. Their experience and research notes the severe underrepresentation of women in most media industry job categories in Canada despite women graduating at nearly equal rates from public media production university programs. They highlight the significant challenges faced by racialized women in a 2019 Women in View study that saw white women's production roles increase to 28 percent, but only 1.8 percent of these production contracts went to "women of colour and none to Indigenous women" (254). Brinton and McGowan's long-standing activism contributed to a significant change in 2019 wherein the Canadian Radio-Television and Telecommunications Commission (CRTC) implemented several changes, including requirements for all private broadcasters (who collectively fund Canadian series and feature film content) to collect and publish data on gender in lead roles and to submit plans for addressing gender gaps in the year ahead. While initiatives like this are mandating industry change, these actions are notably missing processes to address racial inequity. Brinton and McGowan comment that there is also consistent fear and pushback from companies and unions alike about the potential for gender parity measures to negatively impact business, particularly international business, that seeks the financial stability of Canadian government support for their productions. These concerns are reminiscent of meritocracy discourses discussed in the first section, wherein institutions mask discrimination by focusing on hiring those they arbitrarily deem as the best talent. Despite these concerns, it is clear that when tangible action is required and recorded, change is likely to follow. Looking beyond Canadian borders, these kinds of industry actions are also taking place.

The Canadian and Hollywood media economies are deeply connected because of our language and cultural similarities, as well as geographic proximity, and so it is important to consider how Canada's media industries are aligned with movements in the Hollywood system. Researchers such as Brannon Donoghue and organizations such as the Geena Davis Institute on Gender in Media, echo similar data and industry changes as their Canadian counterparts. Brannon Donoghue's work focuses on where disjunctures exist between industry awareness and decisive action—for example, the difference between knowing about gender parity and the action of transformed hiring policies. She notes that the burden of change often falls back on feminist lobbying efforts over private company initiatives. While by-the-numbers approaches to social change issues do not necessarily instigate change on their own, this work certainly connects to the core concerns of this chapter by seeking avenues where change can happen, such as in the space of media production education classrooms. Certainly, this work starts with ensuring that media professionals who teach in media education programs are aware of, and integrate, the critiques of statistical realities and organized social lobbying into their curriculum and teaching.

These examples of media industry engagement evidence that social change within the media industries is occurring due to different kinds of media activism. The volumes of voices in digital social movements, activist communities, and industry lobbying groups are influencing changes in government policy and private industry practice. This indicates that *industry standards* are beginning to shift to more equitable orientations, but it is unclear if media production education is working in tandem with changing industry cultures and practices. The next section explores what the primary philosophical, social, and political orientations are of media production education programs in relation to their positionings of industry standards.

TENSION #3: HOW IS MEDIA PRODUCTION EDUCATION ENGAGING WITH CURRENT SOCIAL CHANGE MOVEMENTS?

This section explores how social justice and critical thinking is framed within media production education and higher education. It will review some contradictions in practice and in instructional and institutional responsibilities to social change. Media production education typically engages in competing discourses of technology, craft, aesthetics, and economics. What might the challenges be to adding social justice to this mix? Technology and craft skills development are often a priority in these programs, and these topics tend to assume a social and political neutrality. However, if technological or craft-based skill sets are emphasized as core program learning outcomes, it is likely that social and critical content, including ethics, are treated as a specialized topic instead of being essential to media practice. This section explores the tensions and interactions between principles of critical studies and craft skills instruction through the following questions: What responsibility do media education instructors have to keep up with social movements? And how do instructors see themselves with respect to social movements and social responsibilities inherent to public education?

Media Production Instructors' Knowledge of Social Justice

There is minimal research, particularly in Canada, on how media production instructors or programs engage with social justice movements and the concepts of equity and ethics. The exception to this might be in the field of journalism that addresses journalism's various codes of ethics and, to some extent, its representational harms. What has been established is that production programs do indeed train for what Hjort calls "how filmmakers become filmmakers" (1), and she connects the social values embedded in education to students' sense of agency navigating professional work. In studying how industry professionals who become teachers impact students' learning, Ashton notes that teacher-practitioners have "buy-in" from students to bridge critical and social issues in the media industry but that there is not a clear sense of the teacher-practitioners' confidence in doing so ("Industry Practitioners" 185–89). Hjort's and Ashton's research share the concern that more needs to be understood about how media educators engage social and critical concepts in curricula.

In 2019, Lindsey Richardson, a journalist with the Aboriginal People's Television Network, broke a story about Inuk filmmaker Stephen Puskas' human rights complaint against the National Film Board of Canada (NFB). Puskas was hired in 2017 as an associate producer through a NFB training and mentorship production program. Puskas claimed that he was given no training, not integrated into the workflow of the production, and culturally marginalized and demeaned in the process (Richardson). This story points to the ways Indigenous people might be marginalized in media industry production and industry training settings. It also shows the dire need to educate media professionals on Indigenous history and rights, per the 86th Call to Action of the Truth and Reconciliation Commission of Canada (*Honouring the Truth, Reconciling for the Future*). Finally, Puskas' case against the NFB indicates that industry training programs' focus on diversity might only be disingenuous "performance" of diversity (Ahmed 116–17), as the educators responsible for Puskas' mentorship did not bring critical or cultural awareness to their responsibilities. Allen et al.'s review of creative industries workplaces evidences a dimension of these problems, as they found that institutional conceptions of meritocracy and liberalism mask or outright deny inequities and leave many students feeling "out of place" (197). While there is a gap in research on media education relationships to equity and social justice, we can infer from these examples that this is an area that Canadian education systems need to address in order to contribute to equity in media industries practices through the training of the next generations of practitioners.

In general higher education theory and research, there are significant data on the ways that inequities manifest and are perpetuated in institutions. In particular, the work of Henry et al. has made comprehensive contributions to understanding how Canadian post-secondary institutions have avoided equitable institutional transformation. Their work tackles many barriers to equity, and their broad recommendations could be taken up at program levels. These include looking at policies to see how they might mask discrimination; including concepts of diversity throughout every institutional action (from hiring policies to teaching and learning support to curriculum design); enhancing the potential for success of racialized and Indigenous faculty and students through specialized and resourced programs; recognizing and rewarding cultural and community-based research and action; tracking and reporting on equity data in detail; initiating mentorship programs for racialized faculty and students; requiring programs to evaluate and challenge everyday racism; and supporting institutional equity offices to proactively address ongoing institutional barriers. If these principles were applied to media education, they could yield more diverse ideas and representations in media practices. Such a transformation would impact who gets to participate in media education and how students and workplace cultures are shaped through this education. An area of focus that might offer some insight on how to bridge ethics and equity in media education is the exploration of the tensions between theory and practice in these programs.

Separating or Integrating Theory and Practice

The theory-practice divide stems from both public and educational discourses. Connolly's 2019 study of vocational film schools finds that public discourses assign greater economic value to media production programs over theoretically based media studies programs, as the former supposedly offer greater access to work. His study indicates that this bias toward hands-on training is unfounded, as students from both programs travel post-graduate career opportunities in different but successful ways. Connolly's work seems particularly critical as a means to respond to broad trends in education that place too much value on market-ready discourses, even if it is important for students to find meaningful work. Ashton's study of an industry-focused video game design program in the United Kingdom affirms Connolly's findings, as industry employers actually define well-educated students as ones who have both technical and critical thinking skill sets. Ashton's study is useful for instructors who are looking for ways to embed critical thinking within production coursework through what he calls "everyday pedagogies" ("Making It Professionally" 49) that ask students to evaluate their own lives in relationship to industry demands. In considering how to structure critical traditions in media production education, Nam suggests that education beyond media effects is required in order for students to be able to see outside the status quo. Nam suggests that media production program design and curricula should be reorganized using critical media literacy principles throughout, including building agency, contesting harmful cultural norms, and using media for social action. The principles of critical media literacy offer a chance to bridge theory and practice, but this also requires instructor and institutional will to orient curricula in this manner.

Institutional Responsibilities and Educational Actions

There is, again, a shortage of research on how media education institutions relate to industry calls for social change. In light of this, this section will address critical commentary about media education's responsibilities to social justice. Callison and Young note that there is minimal journalism education in Canada on the impact of the field of journalism on public conceptions of Indigenous Peoples. This evidences that institutions need to better address legacies of representational harm in their curricula. As noted earlier in the chapter, the field of journalism studies has an overt contradiction between its supposed objectivity and their industry codes of ethics,[6] alongside the industry's significant barriers to equity and just representation (Callison and Young). While many film, animation, and visual effects companies or broadcasters have their own workplace standards and practices, there are no overarching ethical codes that inform practitioner conduct, or their relationship to publics, as in the field of journalism. What this means, then, is that there are no guiding principles on equity outside of the kinds of advocacy and social justice initiatives undertaken by social movements within or outside the industry. This might explain the tendency in media production education to avoid prioritizing critical and socially conscious curricula; the lack of centralized ethical codes might signal to media professionals that issues of equity are less important than other craft skills. Petrie and Stoneman's account of film schools in Europe and the United States establishes critical theory and equity-oriented media practice as essential training for creative innovation and for navigating career precarity in the decreased political economy of newer smaller-scale digital media production opportunities (Petrie and Stoneman). This research is compelling, as it shows how critical thinking and social awareness in education is actually a core industry skill set.

Beyond looking at the kinds of workers who are produced by media education, there is also the issue of how media education responds to the prevalent revelations of sexual assault, harassment, and other abuses. In their manuscript on digital feminist activism, Mendes et al. urge higher education programs to engage social movements, as the more students can learn about social media discourses and technologies in critical ways, the more they will be able to address gender, sexuality, or racialized inequities throughout their production pursuits. The authors also point out that both schools and workplaces are geographies where sexual assault is endemic and, therefore, both institutions have the responsibility of taking action to create physical safety. Centring principles of equity in media education programs enables training on media ethics and just representation, but it also contributes to physical safety in media workspaces. Recognizing that more research is needed on the specific relationships between social justice and media production education, I hope this chapter sparks critical investigations into how industry standards might come to be recognized as centring community-mindedness, reciprocity, and social good.

Possibilities and Actions for Educators, Practitioners, and Students

If media production educators and students work to centre social justice, their actions could make media workplace cultures and representations more socially just. This section offers brief summaries of ideas and actions to transform notions of *industry standards* in post-secondary media production education:

1. Critical media literacy: Apply principles of critical media literacy to production assignments. This includes critically evaluating and contesting dominating narratives and media ownership structures, along with enhancing notions of agency, social change, and social responsibility. To raise fluency between production practices and social media movements, consider engaging critical media commentary in social media spheres.

2. Anticolonial and de/colonizing media education: Support students in "recognizing and deconstructing dehumanizing colonial logics in media and generat[ing] anticolonial alternatives" (Cordes and Sabzalian 184). This approach grapples with the ongoing material impact of colonial representational structures as well as the "incommensurability" (Tuck and Yang 30) of these structures with sovereign Indigenous and de/colonized futures. The path forward for anticolonial and de/colonizing media education might also include unsettling dominant media tropes, particularly of Indigenous Peoples and colonial dispossession of land and languages, rethinking dominating production methods and classroom hierarchies toward relationality and community responsibility and representing Othered populations from their perspectives. In this approach, representation would focus on resilience, resistance, resurgence, fluidity, agency, and sovereignty (Bhattacharya; Callison and Young; Cordes and Sabzalian; Cote-Meek; hooks).

3. Public sphere production opportunities: Redvall describes how the collaboration of Danish public broadcasting with film schools serves the function of practical and professional technical training along with refined storytelling capacity by engaging students in the broadcaster's requirement for "double storytelling"—storytelling that serves the fictional plot but always contains "ethical and social layers" (Redvall 81). Engaging with non-profit, social justice, or advocacy organizations in production-based learning, or bringing students to witness and record real-time social actions or injustices,[7] is a way to directly bridge media training to social action and revise media framing and futures.

4. Practising "nothing about us without us": Avoid telling stories about groups or histories beyond your own lived experiences unless key creatives like writers, directors, and actors with that lived experience can be fully party to the production creation. Ensure the lived experience is represented within the realm of production crew, too (Cizek et al.).

5. Technology as a "diagnostic" (Callison and Young 43–44): Engage technologies, particularly new technologies, by requiring content producers to explain and account for what kind of a professional and social ethic will be engaged by the technology. For example, have creators answer questions like: what does it mean to portray a specific story in virtual reality rather than by more traditional film means?

6. Community support structures: Several creative industries researchers have indicated that creative collectives and care communities assist practitioners in navigating and responding to marketplace precarity, building community alliances, often with respect to navigating other social challenges like sexism or racism, in their professional engagements (Campbell; McRobbie).

7. Hiring for diversity and critical literacies: When hiring instructors, media education staff, and production crews, hire with diversity in mind, but also hire in a way that prioritizes critical and social justice literacies as a core competency (Sensoy and DiAngelo). If a person is to be hired that is lacking in these competencies, state that equity and social justice are core principles of the job, and professional development on these topics will be a requirement for employment.

CONCLUSION: INDUSTRY STANDARDS ARE SOCIAL STANDARDS

> Because we believe our culture and society can be better, and we can play an active role in transforming them. (Mary Celeste Kearney, cited in Harvey 176)

The statement above from Kearney's manifesta for feminist media criticism is a meaningful mantra for media industries students, educators, and industry professionals. This sentiment implicates the theories and practices that inform our educational and production choices, and it squarely situates media culture within the realm of social change. The research presented in this chapter reveals that media production education is well situated to grapple with public discourses and social movements that are pitting economic concerns against those of social justice. It is useful to consider how students envision the future of the media or creative industries and how educators can teach to these transformations. According to Viczko et al., skills-gap discourses in higher education emerge from marketplace rhetoric about industrial needs and limit the ways students are educated for democratic agency by overly determining how students see the potential impacts of their education on society (128). In other words, how we frame industry discourses and industry-specific skill sets has the potential to limit how students understand the function and reach of their education in society. It seems prudent in this era of widespread social injustice, and even the fake news and disinformation phenomena, to equip students to see their education as a way to contribute to bettering social outcomes. As creative industries cultures are firmly part of our contemporary social lives, it is essential that teaching to media industry standards prioritizes social concerns throughout media production education.

CORE CONCEPTS

critical media literacy: An instructional approach that combines critical pedagogy, media literacy, and critical theory to explore how media representations contain bias, control political and social agendas, and can resist or create counter-narratives to dominating messages.

equity: A concept that addresses that even in situations where formal procedural or legal equality exists, that the rights afforded by equality are not evenly distributed in society due to resource and opportunity barriers that inhibit access to social institutions.

industry standard: A term used to indicate a best practice or overriding standard that guides all work done within a specific workplace field or broad context.

social justice: A concept used to describe how equality or equity is realized in society.

social movement: A social grouping or campaign organized to effect social, cultural, or political change.

SUGGESTED ACTIVITIES

1. Writing our own industry standards: Thinking about the social role of media in public life, write a list of socially oriented industry standards. This might be similar to ethical considerations in a journalistic code of conduct. Consider this from the position of media workers, and think beyond behavioural

conduct. How would you describe best practices for the social and ethical aspects of how work is produced, marketed, and distributed?

2. Media counter-futures: Thinking into the future, envision a media landscape that is much different than the one we have now. What are the core themes and representations in mass media stories, who is creating them, and by what means?

NOTES

1. *Pipeline* is a media industry term that summarizes the entire production process from start to finish.

2. The influential hashtag coined by activist Tarana Burke to bring attention to the epidemic of rape and sexual harassment.

3. A hashtag movement working to end workplace harassment, assault, and discrimination.

4. In addition to a reckoning about Indigenous misrepresentations in news media, the murder of George Floyd by a US police officer and the ongoing activism of #BlackLivesMatter have led to journalists and news outlets being called to account for debasing racial framing. These calls focus on more accurate reporting of police violence, notably by focusing on the dignity of people impacted by this violence (Emmanuel).

5. It is worth noting that Indigenous media activism has been occurring for decades in the careers of filmmakers like Alanis Obomsawin, whose work has consistently exposed Indigenous Peoples' experiences of racism, dispossession, and state violence by Canadian authorities. Gender-based advocacy and activism is long-standing, particularly in the Women in Film organizations nationally and globally (Brinton and McGowan).

6. The Society of Professional Journalists code of ethics is widely used, and some principle tenets are to avoid stereotyping and consider potential harm in media news framing.

7. My thanks to Doreen Manuel (Secwepemc/Ktunaxa), the director for the Bosa Centre for Film and Animation at Capilano University, for her leadership in connecting students directly to social justice movements and actively witnessing, recording, and engaging with active injustice. Manuel's work led to training prominent Indigenous media professionals such as Rose Stiffarm (Siksika, Cowichan, Tsartlip, Aaniiih, and Nakoda), who was on the front line of Indigenous media reporting in the Indigenous resistance to the Dakota Access Pipeline at the Standing Rock Reservation. Without this kind of reporting, much of the state violence perpetrated against the protestors would not have been covered.

REFERENCES

Ahmed, Sara. *On Being Included: Racism and Diversity in Institutional Life*. Duke University Press, 2012.

Allen, Kim. "'What Do You Need to Make It as a Woman in This Industry? Balls!':
Work Placements, Gender and the Cultural Industries." *Cultural Work and Higher
Education*, edited by Daniel Ashton and Caitriona Noonan, Palgrave Macmillan,
2013, pp. 232–253.

Allen, Kimberly, et al. "Doing Diversity and Evading Equality: The Case of Student
Work Placements in the Creative Sector." *Educational Diversity*, edited by Yvette
Taylor, Palgrave Macmillan UK, 2012, pp. 180–200.

American Society of News Editors. Newsroom Diversity Survey, members.newsleaders.org/
newsroom_diversitysurvey. Accessed 19 October 2021.

Ashton, Daniel. "Industry Practitioners in Higher Education: Values, Identities and
Cultural Work." *Cultural Work and Higher Education*, edited by Daniel Ashton and
Caitriona Noonan, Palgrave Macmillan, 2013, pp. 172–194.

———. "Making It Professionally: Student Identity and Industry Professionals
in Higher Education." *Journal of Education and Work*, vol. 22, no. 4, 2009,
pp. 283–300.

———. "Upgrading the Self: Technology and the Self in the Digital Games Perpetual
Innovation Economy." *Convergence: The International Journal of Research into New
Media Technologies*, vol. 17, no. 3, 2011, pp. 307–321.

Ashton, Daniel, and Caitriona Noonan, editors. *Cultural Work and Higher Education*.
Palgrave Macmillan, 2013.

Banks, Mark. *Creative Justice: Cultural Industries, Work and Inequality*. Rowman &
Littlefield, 2017.

Bhattacharya, Kakali. "De/colonizing Educational Research." *Oxford Research
Encyclopedia of Education*, Oxford University Press, 2021.

Brannon Donoghue, Courtney. "Hollywood and Gender Equity Debates in the #metoo
Time's Up Era." *Women in the International Film Industry*, edited by Susan Liddy,
Springer International Publishing, 2020, pp. 235–252.

Brinton, Susan, and Sharon McGowan. "Gender Advocacy in Canadian Film and
Television: Are Women Finally Breaking Through?" *Women in the International
Film Industry*, edited by Susan Liddy, Springer International Publishing, 2020,
pp. 253–268.

Callison, Candis, and Mary Lynn Young. *Reckoning: Journalism's Limits and Possibilities*.
Oxford University Press, 2020.

Campbell, Miranda. "'Shit Is Hard, Yo': Young People Making a Living in the Creative
Industries." *International Journal of Cultural Policy*, vol. 26, no. 4, 2018, pp. 1–20.

Canadian Association of Journalists. 2020 Canadian Newsroom Diversity Survey, caj.ca/
diversitysurvey. Accessed 19 October 2021.

Cizek, Katerina, et al. *Collective Wisdom*. PubPub, 2019.

Connolly, Steve. "Student and Teacher Perceptions of the Differences between 'Academic' and 'Vocational' Post-16 Media Courses." *Media Practice and Education*, vol. 21, no. 1, 2020, pp. 5–17.

Cordes, Ashley, and Leilani Sabzalian. "The Urgent Need for Anticolonial Media Literacy." *International Journal of Multicultural Education*, vol. 22, no. 2, 2020, pp. 182–201.

Coté, James E., and Anton L. Allahar. *Lowering Higher Education: The Rise of Corporate Universities and the Fall of Liberal Education*. University of Toronto Press, 2011.

Cote-Meek, Sheila. *Colonized Classrooms: Racism, Trauma and Resistance in Post-Secondary Education*. Fernwood Publishing, 2014.

de Castell, Suzanne, and Karen Skardzius. "Speaking in Public: What Women Say About Working in the Video Game Industry." *Television & New Media*, vol. 20, no. 8, 2019, pp. 836–847.

Emmanuel, Adeshina. "How Coverage of the Police Is Changing." *Nieman Reports*, vol. 75, no. 2, 2021, pp. 18–25.

Frechette, Julie. "#timesup: Breaking the Barriers of Sexual Harassment in Corporate Media for You and #metoo." *Censored 2019: Fighting the Fake News Invasion*, edited by Mickey Huff and Andy Lee Roth, Seven Stories Press, 2019, pp. 185–208.

Gaztambide-Fernández, Rubén A., et al. "'Talent' and the Misrecognition of Social Advantage in Specialized Arts Education." *Roeper Review*, vol. 35, no. 2, 2013, pp. 124–135.

Gill, Rosalind. "Cool, Creative and Egalitarian? Exploring Gender in Project-Based New Media Work in Euro." *Information, Communication & Society*, vol. 5, no. 1, 2002, pp. 70–89.

Giroux, Henry A. *Neoliberalism's War on Higher Education*. Haymarket Books, 2014.

Harvey, Alison. *Feminist Media Studies*. Polity Press, 2020.

Henry, Frances, et al. *The Equity Myth: Racialization and Indigeneity at Canadian Universities*. UBC Press, 2017.

Hesmondhalgh, David, and Sarah Baker. *Creative Labour: Media Work in Three Cultural Industries*. Routledge, 2011.

Hjort, M. *The Education of the Filmmaker in Europe, Australia and Asia*. Palgrave Macmillan, 2013.

Honouring the Truth, Reconciling for the Future: Summary of the Final Report of the Truth and Reconciliation Commission of Canada. The Truth and Reconciliation Commission of Canada, 2015, http://www.trc.ca. Accessed 25 March 2021.

hooks, bell. *Teaching Critical Thinking: Practical Wisdom*. Routledge, 2010.

Kay, Jeremy. "Canadian Indie Producers Launch Pledge to Tackle Systemic Racism." *Screen Daily*, June 2020, https://www.screendaily.com/news/canadian-indie-producers-launch-pledge-to-tackle-systemic-racism-exclusive/5151121.article.

McRobbie, Angela. *Be Creative*. Polity Press, 2016.

Mendes, Kaitlynn, et al. *Digital Feminist Activism: Girls and Women Fight Back against Rape Culture*. Oxford University Press, 2019.

Nam, Siho. "Critical Media Literacy as Curricular Praxis: Remapping the Pedagogical Borderlands of Media Literacy in US Mass Communication Programmes." *Javnost—The Public*, vol. 17, no. 4, 2010, pp. 5–23.

Patterson, Ashley N., et al. "Black Feminism and Critical Media Literacy: Moving from the Margin to the Center." *Meridians*, vol. 15, no. 1, 2016, pp. 40–64.

Petrie, Duncan, and Rod Stoneman. *Educating Film-Makers Past, Present and Future*. Intellect, 2014, http://site.ebrary.com/id/10902218.

Radio Television Digital News Association. Local Broadcast Newsroom Survey, https://www.rtdna.org/research.

Ramachandran, Naman. "Canadian Broadcasters Must Hire BIPOC Crew to Get Greenlight." *Variety*, July 2020, p. 3.

Redvall, Eva Novrup. "Craft, Creativity, Collaboration, and Connections: Educating Talent for Danish Television Drama Series." *Production Studies, The Sequel!: Cultural Studies of Global Media Industries*, edited by Miranda Banks, Bridget Conor and Vicki Mayer, Routledge, 2016, pp. 75–88.

Richardson, Lindsey. "Inuk Filmmaker's Experience with NFB Prompts Human Rights Complaint." *APTN News*, July 2019, p. 7.

Saha, Anamik. *Race and the Cultural Industries*. Polity Press, 2018.

Sensoy, Özlem, and Robin J. DiAngelo. "'We Are All for Diversity, but …': How Faculty Hiring Committees Reproduce Whiteness and Practical Suggestions for How They Can Change." *Harvard Educational Review*, vol. 87, no. 4, 2017, pp. 557–580.

Serebrin, Jacob. "Dying for Movies: Suicide Highlights Labour Issues in Canada's Visual Effects Sector." *CityNews*, Nov. 2020, https://toronto.citynews.ca/2020/11/04/dying-for-movies-suicide-highlights-labour-issues-in-canadas-visual-effects-sector/.

Soloway, Joey. *The Female Gaze*. TIFF Talks, 2016, https://www.youtube.com/watch?v=pnBvppooD9I. Accessed 8 November 2020.

Strong, Myron T., and K. Sean Chaplin. "Afrofuturism and *Black Panther*." *Contexts*, vol. 18, no. 2, May 2019, pp. 58–59.

Tuck, Eve, and K. Wayne Yang. "Decolonization Is Not a Metaphor." *Decolonization: Indigeneity, Education & Society*, vol. 1, no. 1, 2012, pp. 1–40.

Viczko, Melody, et al. "The Problem of the Skills Gap Agenda in Canadian Post-Secondary Education." *Canadian Journal of Educational Administration and Policy*, no. 191, 2019, pp. 118–130.

Glossary

anti-Black racism: Racial discrimination specifically directed at Black people.

audience commodity theory: The understanding that, in consumer capitalist-based media systems, the attention and buying power of audiences are the primary market commodities being produced and consumed. According to this theory, media content is provided to audiences as a "free lunch" in order to attract their attention, commodify their buying power, and teach audiences what to buy.

civic audiences: An alternative to both corporate nationalism and audience commodities that conceptualizes audiences as democratic citizens of a given geopolitical place.

corporate nationalism: The phenomena in which either (1) private corporations appropriate and commodify national symbols for profit or (2) governments partner with private corporations in a symbiotic relationship. In either case, the drive for increased corporate profits is prioritized over any appeals to national pride, unity, or hope.

creative citizenship: Creative citizenship (Luka) involves (1) stakeholders and participants who embody a set of narrowcast audiences to develop shared objectives together, (2) to cultivate a series of networked and sometimes innovative creative production practices (creation), and (3) to find new, often collaborative, ways to share content and knowledge (distribution) that (4) are inclusive and thereby reflect embedded and explicit policy commitments to equity and diversity.

creative city: A city that aims to foster and promote a favourable environment for various forms of creativity. It is characterized by a concentration of cultural industries and related structures (economic, political, and built environment).

creative city script: The instrumentalization of theatre and performance tropes by urban planners and other stakeholders to brand a region as a global, creative city.

creative problem solving: A methodology for the deliberate and reliable generation of novel ideas that systematizes the creative process into broadly applicable phases.

critical creativity: The ability to critically engage with the creativity of the past and speculate upon how an innovation may transform society.

critical media literacy: An instructional approach that combines critical pedagogy, media literacy, and critical theory to explore how media representations contain bias, control political and social agendas, and can resist or create counter-narratives to dominating messages.

critical race theory (CRT): A critical way of interrogating the systemic manifestations, effects, and legacies of racism in society. Rather than focusing on individual instances of racism or racist behaviours, CRT addresses structural and institutionalized racism—particularly in colonial and imperialist societies.

cultural citizenship: The notion that citizenship ought to be, at least in part, culturally based and also that citizens have a right to access cultural forms of production relevant to their geopolitical and national affiliations.

cultural and creative districts: Geographically defined areas in a city with a concentration of buildings and spaces dedicated to artistic, cultural, and/or creative activities.

cultural policy: Government measures to encourage or protect activities in various areas of culture. In Canada, it includes all artistic expressions along with communication sectors and mass culture (and creative) industries.

democratization of creativity: A broadscale shift in which Romantic conceptualizations of creativity emerging from artistic culture were replaced with democratic conceptualizations of creativity emerging from American psychological research, which contended that everyone is creative and creativity is a skill like any other that can be fostered through deliberate practice and training.

digital film technology: The process of recording moving images using digital image sensors instead of film.

digital storytelling: The practice of communicating lived experiences and histories through personal narration online using the technological affordances of available digital media like the computer, the Internet, the smartphone, and software programs.

diversity management: Emerging from the private sector, diversity management sees all forms of diversity—not just gender—as something individuals can leverage to their benefit. Diversity management argues that a diverse workforce is more creative and thus more profitable than a non-diverse workforce.

documentary film: A non-fictional film intended to present reality for the purposes of instruction or to create an historical record.

e-diaspora: A collective that is not necessarily bound by identity but shares a common goal or movement as an imagined community. These goals or movements can change with the addition of new members and new interactions.

equity: A concept that addresses that even in situations where formal procedural or legal equality exists, that the rights afforded by equality are not evenly distributed in society due to resource and opportunity barriers that inhibit access to social institutions.

experimental film: A mode of filmmaking that re-evaluates cinematic conventions and explores non-narrative forms or alternatives to traditional forms.

feature film: A fictional narrative film with a running time long enough to allow it to stand alone in a program.

freelance artists: Artists who work contract to contract or gig to gig rather than have stable and long-term employment.

gender mainstreaming: Emerging from international development agencies and public administration in the 1990s, gender mainstreaming recognizes that policies and interventions are not neutral and may impact women and men differently. To address this inequality, gender mainstreaming takes the form of policy interventions and bureaucratic measures to reduce the workforce inequality of women in various industries.

the grind: Taking on of as many jobs and opportunities as possible, no matter how bad, with the belief that this will eventually lead to financial and artistic success.

heritage: Tangible and intangible aspects of the past that hold meaning for us and that we choose to pass on to future generations.

impact measures: Flexible impact measures for organizational activities in the creative industries (the work undertaken by creative hubs, for example) incorporate four broad categories of assessment: aesthetic/artistic and cultural; business and economic; social and physical; and knowledge sharing and sense-making elements.

industry standard: A term used to indicate a best practice or overriding standard that guides all work done within a specific workplace field or broad context.

intersectionality: A term coined by legal scholar Kimberlé Crenshaw that refers to the ways people's multiple identities—like class, race, gender, ethnicity, ability, and so on—coalesce, overlap, and contribute to specific experiences of prejudice.

marginalized communities: Groups excluded from mainstream economic, political, social, and cultural participation because of identity markers like race, ethnicity, gender, sexuality, and class. Groups become marginalized based on their subordinate relationship to dominant groups who hold power in, and control over, society.

meritocracy: A system of norms that argues that innate skill, talent, or achievement are the defining standards to evaluate the worth of individuals. Meritocracy does not account for structural differences and inequalities that may impact ability or access for all individuals.

multiculturalism: The presence of, and support for the presence of, several distinct cultural or ethnic groups within a society.

pedagogical tools: Teaching devices that are intended to communicate crucial lessons to people, resulting in enhanced comprehension of a subject.

pipeline: A metaphor largely used in science, technology, engineering, and math (STEM) for conceptualizing the pathway individuals pass through, from early childhood interest in a certain field, through education, to a sustained career in these fields. The pipeline metaphor argues that increasing the number of individuals (gender and sexual minorities, BIPOC, etc.) at the start of the pipeline, and addressing leaks and blockages along the way, increases participation and presence in the downstream workforce.

podcasting: The practice of audio recording speech for digital distribution that listeners can interact with on a webpage or through an application at any time. Its affordances include audience subscriptions, unrestricted episode lengths, low-cost production, and lack of fixed scheduling; it is also unregulated and targeted at niche audiences.

political economy: The study of the social relations that determine the allocation of resources from production to distribution.

precarity: The increasing social and financial insecurity and flexibilization of work and labour.

public broadcasting: The provision of news, education, and entertainment to (and supported by) the public; a democratic alternative to both private/corporate broadcasting and state broadcasting. While public broadcasting is publicly funded, it remains operationally independent from government influence.

screendance: A hybrid, movement-based art form, defined not by the moving subject alone but also by the movement of the camera, frames, and editing process, which exists only as it is rendered in film, video, or digital technologies.

social justice: A concept used to describe how equality or equity is realized in society.

social movement: A social grouping or campaign organized to effect social, cultural, or political change.

tokenism: The expectation of an individual to represent a whole identity category, such as race, gender, or sexuality.

triple bottom line: A term coined by John Elkington to draw attention to the social, environmental, and economic costs of capitalism. Rather than simply focusing on profit models, the TBL asks us to consider a more wholistic approach to the impact of business activity. This is made more complex by Hawkes and others' assertion that the idea of *social* includes the cultural and civic impacts of the culture sector and creative industries.

value: The importance, worth, or usefulness of something. The capacity of art, culture, and aspects of the past to have effects or impacts on those who experience them, and the marking or raising of those activities or aspects as important to human lives.

Contributor Biographies

Susan L. T. Ashley is an associate professor in the Creative and Cultural Industries Management master's program at Northumbria University, Newcastle-upon-Tyne, United Kingdom. Her research studies what, how, and why heritage knowledge is created, shaped, communicated, and consumed in the public sphere. She is a UK Arts and Humanities Research Council fellow "(Multi)Cultural Heritage" and a recent visiting professor at York University in Toronto. She has published widely, including *A Museum in Public: Revisioning Canada's Royal Ontario Museum* (2019) with Routledge, *Diverse Spaces: Identity, Heritage and Community in Canadian Public Culture* (2013), and the forthcoming *Whose Heritage? Challenging Race and Identity in Stuart Hall's Post-nation Britain* with Routledge. She holds a PhD in Communication and Culture from York University.

Anouk Bélanger is a professor in the Department of Social and Public Communication at University of Quebec in Montréal—UQAM. Her interests include critical cultural theory, popular culture, urban culture, and popular media. Her research has come to focus on the emergence of creativity as a key trend in the cultural transformations of post-industrial cities such as Montreal. She is currently co-directing a research lab on Montreal's popular culture (Atelier de chronotopies urbaines : scènes et cultures populaires). She is a regular member of CRICIS-UQAM (Centre of Research on Information, Communication and Society) and of CRIEM-McGill (Centre for Interdisciplinary Research on Montréal).

Miranda Campbell is an associate professor in Creative Industries at The Creative School, Toronto Metropolitan University. Her research focuses on creative employment, youth culture, and small-scale and emerging forms of creative practice. She is the author of *Reimagining the Creative Industries: Youth Creative Work, Communities of Care* (Routledge, 2022) and *How to Care More: Seven Skills for Personal and Social Change* (Rowman & Littlefield, 2022). Her book *Out of the Basement: Youth Cultural Production in Practice and in Policy* (McGill-Queen's University Press, 2013) was shortlisted for the Donner Prize for the best public policy book by a Canadian. Her involvement with creative communities includes coordination and board of director roles with Rock Camp for Girls Montreal, a summer camp dedicated to empowerment for girls through music education, and with Whippersnapper Gallery, an artist-run centre focusing on emerging artists in Toronto.

Jeff Donison is a PhD candidate in the Communication and Culture program at York University in Toronto. He holds a MA from the University of Western Ontario in popular music and culture. He has previously written reviews on podcast production and voice for *Digital Journalism* and the *Journal of Radio & Audio Media*, and his original work has been published in *Radio Journal, Participations*, and *Stream*. His current research focuses on participatory cultures and digital technology, specifically dealing with race, identity, and representation in Canadian podcasting and the use of sound as a primary epistemological tool for decolonizing historical narratives.

Joëlle Gélinas is a PhD candidate in communication at the University of Quebec in Montréal. She is a member of the Research Group on Information and Surveillance (GRISQ) and of the Center of Research on Information, Communication and Society (CRICIS) as well as an associate researcher at the Institute for Research and Socioeconomic Information (IRIS). Her work mainly focuses on culture, digital technologies, and urban space. These interests have led her to work on research projects on creative districts and policies, smart city strategies, big data and AI industries, as well as intimacy and social media.

Mary Elizabeth (M. E.) Luka is an assistant professor, arts and media management at the University of Toronto, where she examines modes and meanings of co-creative production, distribution, and dissemination in the digital age for the arts, culture, media, and civic sectors. Dr. Luka holds a Connaught New Researcher Fellowship, examining creative networks and partnerships in Canada, the United Kingdom, and Australia. Dr. Luka is a founding member of the Critical Digital Methods Institute at the University of Toronto Scarborough, of Narratives in Space + Time Society, a research-creation group in Halifax, Nova Scotia, and of the Fourchettes, a technoculture research group. She is the policy co-lead on *Archive/ Counter-Archive: Activating Canada's Moving Image Heritage* at York University, Canada, and an advisory member of Aarhus University Future Making Research Consortium, Digital Living Research Commons (DLRC), Denmark. Previous research is found in *Topia*; *Canadian Journal of Communication*; *Public*; *Canadian Theatre Review*; *Information, Communication & Society*; *Social Media & Society*; chapters in *Energy Culture: Arts and Theory on Oil and Beyond*; *Internet Research Ethics for the Social Age*; *Diverse Spaces: Examining Identity, Heritage and Community within Canadian Public Culture*, other anthologies about transitions in creative industries, and commissioned research for the Department of Canadian Heritage.

Brandon McFarlane is a professor of creativity and leadership at Sheridan College. He is an award-winning teacher who synthesizes creativity studies and humanities insights to prepare art, business, and design students to thrive in the creative industries. He founded the Creative Humanities research hub, which collaborates with cultural not-for-profits to solve pertinent social challenges, and he facilitates experimental approaches to humanities research and pedagogy. He edits www.creativehumanities.ca, which features undergraduate research and collaborations with the Toronto Fringe Festival and Breakthroughs Film Festival. His scholarship explores how the emergence of the creative economy is modifying Canadian culture with an emphasis on cultural policy and aesthetic responses in Canadian fiction. A prolific reviewer, he authors the annual omnibus "Review of Emergent Fiction" for the *University of Toronto Quarterly*.

Selina Linda Mudavanhu is an assistant professor in the Department of Communication Studies and Media Arts at McMaster University. She holds a PhD in media studies. Selina's research interests include critical media studies, critical race studies, media and social media texts, and the politics of representation and media audiences. Her current research focuses on understanding the ways meanings are constituted in texts as well as the likely implications of these constructions. Selina is also interested in the manner in which ordinary people speak back to power and create alternative meanings on social media platforms and through methodologies such as digital storytelling.

Matthew E. Perks is a PhD candidate at the University of Waterloo in the Department of Sociology and Legal Studies. His research focuses on the socio-economics of the video game industry and how these inform and alter the design decisions and identities of video game developers. His interests surround community management and moderation, platform capitalism, and labour within the video game industry. In his doctoral work, he focuses on the increasingly embedded nature of community management in game development and how this impacts media creation and developer identity. He has published on the role of journalism in the game industry in *Games and Culture* and the work of cultural intermediaries in independent games development in *Media Industries*. You can find more on his work at IndieInterfaces.com and matthewperks.me.

Ryan J. Phillips is a sessional instructor in Toronto Metropolitan University's Department of Politics and Public Administration. He completed his PhD in Toronto Metropolitan University's Communication and Culture program. His research is situated within the field of Critical Advertising Studies, where he studies the promotional cultures of food and sports media. Some of his other works have interrogated the political economy of *Hockey Night in Canada* as well as the potential benefits of adopting free-to-air broadcasting rights for culturally significant events in Canada.

Cheryl Thompson is an assistant professor in the School of Performance at The Creative School, Toronto Metropolitan University. She is author of two books, *Uncle: Race, Nostalgia, and the Politics of Loyalty* (Coach House Books, 2021) and *Beauty in a Box: Detangling the Roots of Canada's Black Beauty Culture* (Wilfrid Laurier University Press, 2019). She specializes in the intersectional study of race, visual culture, and representation. With the assistance of multiple SSHRC grants, she is writing a third book on Canada's history of blackface; building a research website that includes artifacts, playbills, images, and newspaper clippings; and co-producing a feature-length documentary in collaboration with Toronto-based Pink Moon Studio. In addition to writing for the *New York Times*, she is a frequent contributor to the *Zoomer Magazine, Spacing, Herizons, The Conversation*, and multiple other news sites. Thompson has a PhD in Communication Studies from McGill University and is a former Banting Postdoctoral Fellow (2016–2018) at the University of Toronto.

Madison Trusolino (she/her) is a PhD candidate at the University of Toronto in the Faculty of Information. Madison researches the cultural industries, gender and sexuality, and feminist political economy. She has worked as a researcher for the Canadian Live Music Association as well as for Cultural Workers Organize, an ongoing research project that examines labour movements in the cultural industries. Her work can be found in *Maisonneuve Magazine* and the *International Journal of Cultural Policy*. She is currently completing her SSHRC-funded dissertation on women and LGBTQ+ comedians' experiences of work and resistance in the North American comedy industry.

George Turnbull is an award-winning stage and screen scholar and practitioner. Nominated for the prestigious Vanier Canada Graduate Scholarship, he is a PhD Candidate (ABD) in the Cinema and Media Studies program at York University where he is undertaking his research in screendance with support from the Joseph-Armand Bombardier Canada Graduate Scholarship from the Social Sciences and Humanities Research Council of Canada. Turnbull served a one-year term as the elected Graduate Student Representative of the Film Studies Association of Canada (FSAC-ACÉC) from 2019 to 2020, and he currently sits on the Editorial Board of Canada's leading dance publication, *The Dance Current*. Turnbull has previous affiliations with film and dance departments at: Queen's University; the University of California, Los Angeles; the California Institute of the Arts; and Toronto Metropolitan University.

Jennifer R. Whitson is an associate professor in the Department of Sociology and Legal Studies and at the Stratford School of Interaction Design and Business, both at the University of Waterloo. She studies the secret life of software, mostly at the nexus of digital games and surveillance studies. She has been conducting ethnographic fieldwork with game developers since 2012. Past projects included work on digital media surveillance, social influences on software development processes, and gamification. She has published in edited collections such as *The Gameful World*, published by MIT Press, as well as the journals *First Monday*, *Games and Culture*, *FibreCulture*, and *New Media & Society*. You can find more of her work at IndieInterfaces.com and jenniferwhitson.com.

Ki Wight is a critical media studies scholar whose work looks at the relationship between media education, media culture, and systems of oppression. She is a full-time lecturer at Capilano University in North Vancouver, Canada, in the Communication Studies, Women's and Gender Studies, Interdisciplinary Studies, and Motion Picture Arts programs, and she holds a PhD in Equity Studies in Education from Simon Fraser University. Before teaching at Capilano University, Ki was a film and television producer and executive for Canadian and international productions. Her work engages critical and de/colonial pedagogy, critical race and critical whiteness studies, feminist and queer theory, and cultural studies.